Teaching
the Representation
of the Holocaust

Modern Language Association of America
Options for Teaching
Joseph Gibaldi, Series Editor

Teaching the Representation of the Holocaust. Ed. Marianne Hirsch and Irene Kacandes. 2004.

Teaching Tudor and Stuart Women Writers. Ed. Susanne Woods and Margaret P. Hannay. 2000.

Teaching Shakespeare through Performance. Ed. Milla Cozart Riggio. 1999.

Teaching the Literatures of Early America. Ed. Carla Mulford. 1999.

Teaching Literature and Medicine. Ed. Anne Hunsaker Hawkins and Marilyn Chandler McEntyre. 1999.

Teaching Oral Traditions. Ed. John Miles Foley. 1998.

Teaching Contemporary Theory to Undergraduates. Ed. Dianne F. Sadoff and William E. Cain. 1994.

Teaching Children's Literature: Issues, Pedagogy, Resources. Ed. Glenn Edward Sadler. 1992.

Teaching Literature and Other Arts. Ed. Jean-Pierre Barricelli, Joseph Gibaldi, and Estella Lauter. 1990.

School-College Collaborative Programs in English. Ed. Ron Fortune. 1986.

New Methods in College Writing Programs: Theories in Practice. Ed. Paul Connolly and Teresa Vilardi. 1986.

Teaching Environmental Literature: Materials, Methods, Resources. Ed. Frederick O. Waage. 1985.

Part-Time Academic Employment in the Humanities: A Sourcebook for Just Policy. Ed. Elizabeth M. Wallace. 1984.

Film Study in the Undergraduate Curriculum. Ed. Barry K. Grant. 1983.

The Teaching Apprentice Program in Language and Literature. Ed. Joseph Gibaldi and James V. Mirollo. 1981.

Options for Undergraduate Language Programs: Four-Year and Two-Year Colleges. Ed. Renate A. Schulz. 1979.

Options for the Teaching of English: Freshman Composition. Ed. Jasper P. Neel. 1978.

Options for the Teaching of English: The Undergraduate Curriculum. Ed. Elizabeth Wooten Cowan. 1975.

Teaching the Representation of the Holocaust

Edited by
**Marianne Hirsch and
Irene Kacandes**

The Modern Language Association of America
New York   2004

For information about obtaining permission to reprint material from MLA
book publications, send your request by mail (see address below), e-mail
(permissions@mla.org), or fax (646-458-0030).

Library of Congress Cataloging-in-Publication Data
Teaching the representation of the Holocaust / edited by Marianne Hirsch
and Irene Kacandes.
        p. cm. — (Options for teaching, ISSN 1079-2562 ; 18)
    Includes bibliographical references and index.
    ISBN 0-87352-348-2 (hardcover : alk. paper) — ISBN 0-87352-349-0
(pbk. : alk. paper)
  1. Holocaust, Jewish (1939–1945), in literature—Study and teaching.
2. Holocaust, Jewish (1939–1945)—Study and teaching. I. Hirsch,
Marianne. II. Kacandes, Irene, 1958– III. Series.
    PN56.H55T44 2004
    809'.93358—dc22   2004019450

Cover illustration of the paperback edition: *Past Lives (for the Children of
Izieu)*. © Lorie Novak 1987. Novak writes: "*Past Lives* was made during
the trial of Klaus Barbie. The image of children hidden in a boarding
school in Izieu, France, before being deported and murdered, was
publicized as evidence of Barbie's crimes against humanity. In my
projected collage of the children, of Ethel Rosenberg, and of me clutching
my mother, I see my generation as bearing the weight of this past."

Published by the Modern Language Association of America
26 Broadway, New York, New York 10004-1789
www.mla.org

Contents

Part II: Genres

Part IV: Classroom Contexts

Marianne Hirsch
and Irene Kacandes

Introduction

"Can the Story Be Told?": Generations of Memory

In his remarkable memoir *Literature or Life*, Jorge Semprun describes the days between his liberation in Buchenwald and his repatriation. "Can the story be told? Can anyone tell it?" he wonders, assuring his reader that he is not doubting the capacities of language to "contain everything." "But can people hear everything, imagine everything? Will they be able to understand? Will they have the necessary patience, passion, compassion, and fortitude?" (13–14). Semprun's misgivings are a topos of Holocaust memoirs. One might think of Primo Levi's famous recurrent dream in Auschwitz of trying to tell his story at his sister's dinner table, only to have it fall on deaf ears (60); of Charlotte Delbo's sense that what she experienced in Auschwitz is "useless knowledge" (115–231); or of Paul Celan's image of the poem as a "message in a bottle" searching for an "addressable you" (396). Even before they return from the camp, Semprun and his fellow prisoners heatedly debate the most effective genre for their narration and the amount of artifice necessary to make people understand. Would cinema be the best? they ask. No, because "the most significant events of camp life have surely never been filmed" (126). Would eyewitness accounts, reportage, be better, or fiction, because fiction lets you imagine?

This discussion in Buchenwald movingly anticipates many of the questions about representation that have preoccupied the teaching and writing about the Holocaust in the last half century, questions that have become more pointed as the generation of witnesses and survivors is leaving our midst. The second, the third, and subsequent generations — the generations of current college faculty members and students, and of *their* future students — have come to accept as a given that our access to the events of the Holocaust is multiply mediated. But this does not mean that the questions of how to tell and how to be heard are not still as vital as they were for the survivors of Buchenwald in 1945.

Nevertheless, there have been radical generational shifts in transmission concerning what aspects of the story are told, what questions persist, what layers remain unexplored. That the Holocaust has appeared intermittently as front-page news for over a half century has been due to controversies over its history, its memory, and its representation. Every generation, every decade since the end of World War II has confronted new controversies that test the ethical limits of memory and memorialization. And each generation has required ever more sophisticated conceptual tools with which to evaluate these controversies. Paradoxical though it may sound, one could say that since the conclusion of World War II, the Holocaust has remained poignantly present in very different areas of social and cultural life. Should a monastery be built on the grounds of Auschwitz? Should there be a monument to the murdered Jews of Europe in Berlin, the capital of the perpetrator nation? What should that monument look like? What stories should and should not be told in popular media? Is it legitimate for Steven Spielberg to tell the story of one good German, Oskar Schindler, when there were very few such rescuers? Can the Holocaust be funny, the subject of imaginative play, as it is for Roberto Benigni in *Life Is Beautiful*? What is the status of historical truth versus interpretation? Should Holocaust deniers be allowed to advertise in college newspapers? Is Deborah Lipstadt committing libel when she calls David Irving a denier? These debates and other recent ones — over the historical interpretation in Daniel Goldhagen's *Hitler's Willing Executioners*, over the truth of Binjamin Wilkomirski's *Fragments*, over how to deal with the fact that some of the works in our most prized museums may have been stolen from Jewish homes, over the holdings of Swiss banks, over the accuracy of the exhibition *The German Army and Genocide*, or over the good or bad taste of the exhibition *Mirroring Evil: Nazi Imagery / Recent Art* — are carried out in the public media. For teachers and students in the humanities, the Holocaust has become a limit case, a prime site for testing aesthetic and ethical theories about mediation and representability. (For what remains the single most important volume on issues of representation and the Holocaust, see S. Friedländer, *Probing*.)

Art Spiegelman's *Maus* is often read and taught as a text that illustrates our multiply mediated access to the private and public history of the Holocaust. It tells the story of the parents' survival in Auschwitz, even while performing the son's efforts at understanding and representing that story. The original three-page "Maus," published in *Funny Animals* in 1972, already inscribes the problematics of representation. Its first panel is a cartoon redrawing of the famous Margaret Bourke-White photograph of liberated prisoners in Buchenwald. There are photo corners at the edges, showing us that this is a drawing of a photograph and that this is a photo in an album, a family album. The small arrow marked "Poppa" pointing to one of the prisoners in the back row shows the son's inability to imagine his father's past other than by way of repeatedly circulated and already iconic public images, images that have become part of his consciousness and his family album. But in Spiegelman's animal fable the Jewish prisoners are represented as mice, and the Nazis will be drawn as cats, introducing further layers of mediation that acknowledge yet again the artifices that have always been necessary to make people understand.

If *Maus* addresses the conflicts of the second generation, as

Illustration in the original "Maus." © Art Spiegelman 1972. Published in the comic book *Funny Animals*.

played out in public debates of the 1980s and 1990s, further chronological distance only increases the problem of conceptualization and communicability. "There was a certain impossibility of communicating evil, just as it is impossible to communicate its opposite," the Polish artist Piotr Uklanski said in an interview about the controversial exhibition *Mirroring Evil* held at the Jewish Museum in New York City in 2002. "How can you communicate to anyone the experience of a concentration camp? It no longer has anything to do with reality" ("Mirroring"). His installation *The Nazis*—a series of 166 photographs of famous movie stars dressed for the roles in which they portray Nazis in film—is less about evil or about Nazis than about the ways in which, in the postwar culture of stardom, even Nazism has been commodified (see Rothberg on commodification as a category of Holocaust representation). This distance from reality makes it all the more necessary to focus on the conventions of representation in our teaching of the Holocaust. The questioning of conventions suggests the need to debunk "the simple notion that we can get beyond representation or outside of history," as David Bathrick puts it in his essay in this volume.

Thus, while this volume contains analyses of many different types of representations of the Holocaust, at its heart is the question of representation itself. It is our conviction that the Holocaust, like any other historical period, cannot be taught separately from the question of how it is represented. At the same time, we need to emphasize that any teaching of representation must be grounded in a historical understanding of what we have come to call the Holocaust. As teachers of literature and culture we are particularly attuned to this complex relation between history and representation and its many possible permutations in our current study of the humanities.

Representation, and the special place it holds in the humanities curriculum, is also the subject of our introduction. We propose that the study of the Holocaust has the potential for bringing into sharper relief a number of current preoccupations in the humanities. Thus our aim here is to introduce several different pedagogical and theoretical issues that anyone teaching Holocaust representation is likely to encounter. We also point our readers to other texts that will allow them to explore these issues in greater depth.

Why Do We Teach This Difficult Subject?

Despite the magnitude of the historical events we call the Holocaust, its study developed slowly. The first academic books did not appear until the early 1960s. (Raul Hilberg's pathbreaking *The Destruction of the European Jews* was initially published in 1961.) College courses lagged even further. Among the first were Destruction of European Jewry, taught by Erich Goldhagen at Brandeis University starting in 1965; Contemporary Jewry, taught by Raul Hilberg at the University of Vermont, first offered in 1968; and The Holocaust in Literature and Culture, taught by Sander L. Gilman at Cornell

University, beginning in 1973. Not until the late 1970s and early 1980s did a remarkable number of universities institute courses on Holocaust history and literature (e.g., James Young taught Literature of the Holocaust at the University of California, Santa Cruz, and Sidra DeKoven Ezrahi offered a course with the same title at Hebrew University in Jerusalem in 1979). This time frame coincides with a shift in Holocaust consciousness that commentators date around 1978, with the airing of the NBC series *Holocaust*, watched by 120 million people; Jimmy Carter's commission on the Holocaust (which eventually resulted in the establishment of the United States Holocaust Memorial Museum in Washington, DC); and the public outcry over the Nazi march in Skokie, Illinois (on the significance of 1978, see Greenspan 45). Since the 1990s, college courses on the Holocaust have become so firmly established in most university curricula that we barely ask ourselves anymore why we teach this difficult subject.

In the last decade, a number of universities have initiated teaching and research centers on the Holocaust and genocide. More than twenty institutions of higher education offer some type of program related to the Holocaust, including undergraduate concentrations and minors, and several now offer advanced degrees. These pedagogical and research efforts at the high school and university level are supported by pedagogy and research centers that offer teacher workshops and classroom materials — most notably, among numerous other institutions, at the United States Holocaust Memorial Museum; the Museum of Tolerance in Los Angeles; and the Holocaust Educational Foundation based in Skokie, Illinois.

We have heard students say that a course on the Holocaust is as essential a part of their liberal arts education as a course on Shakespeare. Why? What do they hope to learn? For virtually every discipline in the humanities, the Holocaust has provided some of the greatest intellectual challenges in recent decades. For the historian Michael Marrus, for example, "Holocaust history [is] one of the most sophisticated and methodologically self-conscious fields of historical study" (6). By teaching the Holocaust one can introduce students to philosophical debates about good and evil; to sociological theories of violence, authority, obedience, conformity, resistance, and rescue; and to psychological theories of tolerance and prejudice, of trauma, memory, and survival. The Holocaust can focus a study of the history of racism and antisemitism, of assimilation and marginality, of exclusion and genocide. In courses on literature and representation, the Holocaust can provide some of the most sophisticated interrogations of representability, of the limits of art, of speech in the face of unspeakability, and of the intersection of ethics and aesthetics. Where is the line between fiction and truth? How can trauma be told; how can it be heard? What will enable us to imagine the extent of the atrocity even as we acknowledge our own distance from the event, evading exploitation, appropriation, trivialization? What literary genres—fiction, poetry, drama, film and video, diaries, oral testimonies, memoirs, memorials, museums—can enable students to receive the story in ways that do justice to its scope? What are acceptable forms of identification, empathy, active listening? And, most specific to the goals of this volume: what are the pedagogical approaches that will most effectively open up these questions?

Certainly, teaching the Holocaust, in our experience, has provided some of the most intense, challenging, exhilarating, and painful classroom encounters. This college subject may require more probing than any other, more pedagogical thinking, careful planning, self-scrutiny, and more open exploration of the stakes involved by the teacher. Teachers will need to question not only in what discipline to offer the course, what to include in the syllabus, and what assignments to design but also how to initiate a diverse group of students, two and soon three generations removed from a chapter of history that has come down to them as the most traumatic and unassimilable of the twentieth century. We have to find strategies that will enable students to learn and respond without being utterly devastated or traumatized; to balance affect and analysis, feeling and thinking; to empower them to speak even while teaching them when to be silent. We have to be open to learning from them, because, clearly, their generation will have different needs and different thresholds from ours. And we have to be ready to call into question the very possibility of teaching and learning in the face of extremity.

Teaching Terminology

"Please excuse me, I use the term 'Holocaust' reluctantly because I do not like it," Primo Levi writes. "But I use it to be understood. Philologically it is a mistake. . . ." Like Levi, we use the term in this volume "to be understood," though we also want to contextualize it. Levi believes that Elie Wiesel coined the term and then "wanted to take it back" (qtd. in Agamben 28). Although the term enables us, too, to be understood, it requires etymological explanation and interrogation. *Holocaust* from the Greek *holocauston* originally meant a sacrifice completely burned by fire. In 1 Samuel 7.9 of the Septuagint, the Greek translation of the Hebrew scriptures, the word was used to mean a "burnt offering to God." Its use to describe the destruction of the European Jews by the National Socialists can be traced back to the 1950s. Because its religious origin implies a form of explanation, or justification, or at least sacralization, many object to its use. Can one say that Jews were sacrificed? But what are the linguistic alternatives?

The term *shoah* is used in Israel, as well as in many European countries. It enters some courses on the subject by way of the title of Claude Lanzmann's film. *Shoah* in Hebrew means "catastrophe," and some find that it, too, has unfortunate connotations. Does not the term "catastrophe" erase the agency of the crime? Still, the term was used as early as 1940 in a publication in Jerusalem entitled *Sho'at Yehudei Polim* (The Shoah of the Jews of Poland). Perhaps it would be more appropriate to employ a term that was used by many of the victims themselves at the time. That word would be the Yiddish *hurban* (or *churban*), also meaning "catastrophe" but with specific reference to the destruction of the Temple. *Hurban* thus also suffers from the connotative problems of *shoah*. Not only does it erase agency, it also makes the mass murder of European Jews the last in a series of catastrophes befalling world Jewry. The only term in current use that does refer to the agency of the crime is the word *genocide*, a term used in France to refer to the destruction of European Jews but used in a number of wider contexts as well. Regrettably, *genocide* elides the specificity of the Nazi crimes, inscribing this event into a broader history of systematic exterminations on the basis of nationality, ethnicity, or religion. Teachers can use the dilemma of terminology and agency to introduce the perpetrators' ominous and yet euphemistic term "final solution" (*Endlösung*; on euphemistic labeling and dehumanization, see Bandura 378–79).

The difficulty of terminology introduces students not just to notions of inexpressibility and the limits of language, and to the multilingualism of this event, but also to the problem of precisely defining what we have come to call for convenience's sake the Holocaust. For example, when one uses the term, is one trying to reference (only) the attempted annihilation of European Jewry? Even if yes, we must clarify that this attempt involved vastly more than intentional killing in extermination camps. (The term "Auschwitz," too, misleads when used as shorthand, since it obscures the number of locations involved in the killing operations.) Boycotts, emigration, hiding, assumed identities, ghettoization, resistance, pogroms, slaughters carried out by the *Einsatzgruppen* are equally important elements of the full picture of Nazi persecution and extermination of European Jewry. Furthermore, examining terminology can lead us to other groups targeted by the Nazis, especially to the Roma-Sinti (Gypsies), who were the only other racial category slated for complete destruction in the Nazi program for domination of Europe. In fact, with regard to percentage of their respective world populations, the Roma-Sinti were slaughtered to an even greater extent than the Jews. Our terminological discussion with our students should therefore include *Porrajmos*, the word by which the Roma-Sinti designate the destruction of their people (Hancock; Milton). For similar reasons, we need to introduce the phrase "life unworthy of life" (*lebensunwertes Leben*), by which the Nazis justified their first genocidal campaign against people with disabilities, a campaign that historian Henry Friedlander considers the true beginning of the Holocaust.

Defining precisely what we mean when we say "Holocaust" will necessarily involve debates about this event's uniqueness, its incommensurability as opposed to its comparability. As with so many of the issues related to representation we are raising here, there are numerous ways to convey this debate to students. One might begin by foregrounding the particular context in which we study and teach the Holocaust in the United States: as a people with its own troubled history of suffering, persecution, and genocide. An acknowledgment of the relation of Holocaust representation and memorialization to the representation and memorialization of slavery and the Native American genocide is fundamental to any Holocaust course taught in the United States. (See Rothberg's essay in this volume for useful suggestions on how to foreground the United States context in our teaching.) An approach students are likely to have encountered in middle or high school can help in this regard: secondary school curricula like *Facing History and Ourselves* (www.facing.org) are founded on the belief that learning about the Holocaust is to learn about the workings of racism and prejudice that we can find in our own culture and in many others; therefore to educate ourselves about them is one way to prevent them in the future. A text like Gordon Allport's *The ABC's of Scapegoating* (published by the Anti-Defamation League of B'nai B'rith in 1959 and not copyrighted, to facilitate wide distribution) takes a similar approach and is well suited to the college classroom even today. One can take up the issue of uniqueness versus comparability more explicitly by considering the German *Historikerstreit* ("historians' debate"; consult Maier or LaCapra, "Representing" and *History*) or the controversial reactions to Christopher Browning's *Ordinary Men* (1992) or Goldhagen's *Hitler's Willing Executioners* (1996). (See Zeitlin's essay in this volume.) In our own experience, we have observed that while arguments of the Holocaust's incommensurability still hold a certain validity in psychoanalytic frameworks like that of trauma, our current students may be skeptical of them, from what they know of genocidal killing in Cambodia, Rwanda, and the former Yugoslavia. This knowledge sharpens the need to learn the terms that will allow students to appreciate both the uniqueness of each of these events and the shared histories of violence, oppression, and survival. Some, like Eric D. Weitz in this volume, argue that "on the larger canvas of school and university curricula and of research, the singular focus on the Holocaust no longer suffices" and that, in the future, the Holocaust will increasingly be taught in a comparative framework that will sharpen these questions. (See the essays in this volume by Hill and by Weitz for suggestions on teaching the Holocaust in the framework of comparative genocide.)

In considering terminology with our students, we also clarify the variations that they will see of the term meaning "hatred of Jews"—that is, *antisemitism* and *anti-Semitism*. Regardless of typography, the term is problematic because of the way it embeds the concept of race in the element "Semitism." The adjective *semitic* traditionally refers to descendants of Noah's son Shem and has been applied to languages and ethnic groups that include Arabs and Jews. The concept of antisemitism has been used (originally as a euphemism) for hatred of Jews only. In this book, we have chosen antisemitism, one word with no hyphen, because we feel that this spelling downplays the chimeric element of "Semitism." We also point out that related words like *philo-Semitism* are troublesome for similar reasons.

Who Has the Right to Speak about the Holocaust?

The question of my own subject position was a blind spot I was forced to confront by someone else's intrusive behavior. This issue was raised for me, however, not by teaching colleagues or students but rather by fellow Holocaust scholars: I had been puzzled by the physical inspection I often receive at meetings of the Association of Jewish Studies and the Holocaust Educational Foundation (participants inspecting my name tag, peering at my necklaces, and scrutinizing my face) until I surmised that the inquisitors were trying to ascertain if I was Jewish. Of course I don't mean that everyone looks at me in this way, but it had never occurred to me when I first started to work and teach in Holocaust studies that who I was could or should have anything to do with my interest in the subject, until I noticed these curiosity seekers inspecting me. I have since discovered that there seems to be particular concern about pedigree when it comes to Holocaust studies. More tragically for my father than for me, I have that pedigree. But is that something I should share with my students? Is it something I am right to share here? Usually I raise the issue of subject

positions as a topic in my class. And I have revealed occasionally but not consistently my own identity as the child of
a survivor when it feels that it would be dishonest of me not
to. Still, I feel vulnerable when I do—vulnerable personally
but also intellectually. Does my admission make a difference
in how readers of my work and students in my class value
my comments or my syllabus? Does it undermine my argument that every citizen of our times should study the Holocaust? Is it possible that my compulsion to work and teach
in this area is derived from family history—even if I did not
begin to study the Holocaust for this reason, even if I did
not consciously know that I was the child of a survivor at
the time I began my Holocaust studies? If I further reveal
myself and tell you that I am not Jewish and that my father
was mistaken for a Jew because he was circumcised and that
that was why he ended up in a Nazi deportation camp in
northern Greece during the war, that I didn't know this
until I was in my late twenties, and that my father refuses to
talk to his children about it, will it change one's evaluation
of my right to speak? to teach? to coedit this book?

—Irene Kacandes

Of the many wonderful students I have had in courses on
the Holocaust, two stand out for the failure I felt in teaching them. One, a young man, sat in the back of the room
and never spoke during class. I thought he was uninter-
ested, bored. It was not until I read his final journal, after
the end of the course, that I found out that he was the
grandchild of a German woman who was a teenager during
the 1930s and an enthusiastic member of the Nazi youth
organization Bund Deutscher Mädchen. During the entire
course, he was struggling with his love for his grandmother
and his knowledge of her beliefs as a young girl, her collu-
sion in a system that produced the atrocities he was studying. Could I have been helpful to him if I had known? My
experience with another student makes me wonder. This
young woman was taking the course without the knowledge of her mother, who had raised her with the belief that
everything she was learning in school about the Holocaust
was vastly exaggerated. Her mother had even refused to allow
her to go on a field trip to a Holocaust museum. In her

journals, this student vacillated: should she write on behalf
of her mother's beliefs and argue against the course readings, or should she write on behalf of those readings, trying
implicitly to convince her mother that her mother was
wrong? In my conversations with this student I had to go
beyond the intellectual and conceptual to another level, a
level on which, because of my own subject position as Jewish and as a child of survivors, we had difficulty meeting.
—Marianne Hirsch

Classroom dynamics, such as the ones we expose from each of
our own perspectives above, can themselves be used to teach issues
of representation. As the question is sometimes, quite problemati-
cally, framed, Who "owns" the Holocaust? Who has the right to speak
for its victims? Nations? Individuals? Survivors? Descendants of victims or survivors? Competing over the ownership of any world calamity may seem inappropriate, even obscene. And yet the question of
to whom the Holocaust belongs comes up repeatedly in the public
debates we have listed above. Who has the authority to decide what
happens on the grounds of Auschwitz? to decide whether the United
States should have a Holocaust museum on the Washington Mall?
to build a Holocaust memorial in the center of Berlin?

Who has the right to speak is a question Holocaust classroom
teachers must be prepared to deal with. Colleagues and students
may explicitly or implicitly challenge one's authority to study or to
teach this material. Must those who teach the Holocaust be themselves survivors or — more likely for our time and the future — children and grandchildren of survivors? Who counts as a survivor —
only those who were interned in concentration or extermination
camps? Or must we include those who survived in hiding, who
changed their names and identities, who were forced to escape or
emigrate? Does one need to have been a member of a group targeted for extermination, like Jews or Roma-Sinti? What about political prisoners? Some members of our classes may even challenge the
authority of certain fellow students. Others may feel that they themselves have no right to speak—if they are not Jewish, for example, or

otherwise personally touched by this history. Do Jews have a special knowledge; are all Jews more deeply affected? Such preconceptions may have to be addressed and demystified from the start.

It is our conviction that the historical phenomena designated by the term *Holocaust* and the representational issues raised by these phenomena should be as widely studied as possible, for themselves, of course, but also for the limit case they present and the discussions they can provoke. It is important that these discussions be as inclusive as a classroom and teaching situation, with its built-in power differentials, will allow. Our students can benefit from the realization that "biology as destiny" was an ideology that the Nazis embraced fully and that led to the Holocaust. Humanists often think of literature as humanizing and individualizing. In our view, it is perhaps the medium that also best enables a transcendence of the biographical and identitarian.

Marianne Hirsch's notion of postmemory identifies an intersubjective transgenerational space of remembrance, linked to a cultural or collective trauma that is not strictly based on identity or familial connection. It is defined through an identification with the victim or witness, modulated and carefully delimited by the unbridgeable distance that separates the participant from the one born after (*Family Frames* and "Surviving Images"). Geoffrey Hartman's notion of "witnesses by adoption" similarly enlarges the familial framework to encompass broader spaces of empathy and identification. (For a discussion in this volume of the problem of authenticity, see the essay by Ezrahi; for a discussion in this volume of the literature of the second generation, see the essay by Sicher.)

Identification, Empathy, Responsibility: Victims, Perpetrators, Bystanders, Rescuers

Where do we position ourselves when we teach the Holocaust, and where do students position themselves when they study it? More than we might expect, our students come to our classes because of earlier experiences with reading texts like Anne Frank's diary or Elie Wiesel's *Night* or because of encounters with popular films like *Schindler's*

List. (For suggestions on teaching these texts, see the essay in this volume by Bos on Anne Frank, by Weissman on *Night*, and by Zeitlin on *Schindler's List*.) The strong reactions our students had to those texts as adolescents can be harnessed not just to get them into our classrooms but, more important, to help them think through critical and complex moral and representational issues. Any kind of discussion of subject positions can lead into the more specific question of identification. Identification with the victims, however, is only one of a number of possible points of entry and perhaps one of the more problematic. The distinction among and the invitation to explore the positions of victim, perpetrator, bystander, and rescuer have provided an important paradigm for the study of the Holocaust. Hilberg's *Perpetrators, Victims, Bystanders* (1992) is based on this paradigm, as is an older volume, *Survivors, Victims, and Perpetrators*, edited by Joel Dimsdale (1980); both could be of help in teaching issues related to position and identification.

Identification with victims is the strategy most often used in contemporary popular genres and in museums and memorials. The United States Holocaust Memorial Museum's Identity Card Project, for example, invites visitors to engage in an act of straightforward identification: each visitor receives an ID card at the entrance and is invited to walk through the museum "as" that person. In the project's initial design, visitors were meant to choose an ID card that corresponded to their own gender and age to facilitate identification even more. Inserting the card into machines on each floor would gradually reveal the course of the person's fate during the war, whether he or she survived or not. As a pedagogical strategy, identification with victims is both powerful and dangerous: it risks being appropriative and projective. As Dominick LaCapra cautions:

> Empathy itself, as an imaginative component not only of the historian's craft but of any responsive approach to the past or the other, raises knotty perplexities, for it is difficult to see how one may be empathetic without intrusively arrogating to oneself the victim's experience or undergoing (whether consciously or unconsciously) surrogate victimage. (*History* 182)

The psychoanalyst Dori Laub warns similarly about secondary trauma: whether professional or amateur, listeners must "not become the victim," lest they risk their own traumatization (58).

In our discussions with our students, we might want to question the ethics of identification or to explore some of the alternative forms of identification suggested by the works we are studying with them. What kind of identification might allow us to say, "It could have been me; it was me, also," and, at the same time, to assert categorically, "But it was not me!"? Eve Kosofsky Sedgwick's distinction between "identification with" and "identification as" can be useful in this regard (59–63), as can be LaCapra's notion of "empathic unsettlement" ("Trauma" 722). The distancing devices in texts like *Maus*, Philip Roth's *The Ghost Writer* (discussed in this volume by Hungerford), Sebald's *The Emigrants,* and Yehoshua's *Mr. Mani* (discussed in this volume by Newton), as well as in much poetry (see the essays in this volume by Omer-Sherman and by Baer, and especially the discussion of post-Holocaust poetry by Gubar) can provide models of nonappropriative identification and empathy.

Limiting their identification to victims, however, may prevent students from considering the agency of the crimes that they are studying. Students are in fact drawn to consider the position of perpetrators, bystanders, and rescuers, wondering whether they would have been capable of resisting had they been alive in Nazi Germany or whether they would have collaborated. An exercise used in many diversity-training workshops to illustrate the difference between prejudice and racism can be valuably incorporated into the beginning of the term. Students are asked to divide themselves into smaller discussion groups by birth order: those who are oldest, middle, youngest, or only children speak among themselves about what that position in the family was like. Then the larger group reconvenes, and those in a certain group are asked to keep silent while all the others tell them what ideas they have about that particular role. The group on the hot seat is then asked what it feels like to hear the comments of the others. The exercise can be used to demonstrate that human beings easily develop prejudices — for example, the stereotypical judgments that oldest children are bossy or youngest children spoiled. Is it "human nature" that leads us to such categorization? Students can be made to realize that if they act on those ideas, no matter how commonly held, without taking the specifics of the individual or context into account, they are acting on stereotypes that are akin to racism. This exercise can effectively segue into a unit on antisemitism and the controversies about the extent to which it played a role in the popularity of the Nazis and their ensuing genocidal policies.

Another effective way to consider the role of perpetrators and bystanders in the classroom is to show Leni Riefenstahl's film *Triumph of the Will*. In our experience, it can elicit strong—and uncomfortable—reactions in students, who often are impressed by the aesthetic dimension of the film and by the solidarity and euphoria of the rally participants seemingly documented in it. A short response essay, in which students describe their reactions to the film, can provide a forum for processing uncomfortable feelings. Follow-up discussion in class can offer further contextualization for the idea of collaboration and for the power of totalitarian aesthetics. Lanzmann's *Shoah* is another good choice for exploring the multifaceted problematic of the bystander position. (On teaching about perpetrators and antisemitism, see the essays in this volume by Zeitlin and by Heschel and Gilman. On *Shoah*, see the essays in this volume by Bathrick and by Spitzer.)

An interrogation of the role of the United States government or of the Roman Catholic Church during the Holocaust (and in other, more recent world conflicts) can also provide opportunities to foreground the question of identification and responsibility. We have shown the film *America and the Holocaust* to facilitate such discussion about the role of our own country, and we have assigned Rolf Hochhuth's play *The Deputy* (*Der Stellvertreter*) to launch discussions about the role of the Roman Catholic Church.

Even while discussing these different positions explicitly, it is important to explore with students what it means to witness the Holocaust from their own, retrospective vantage point, from the point of view of their present. Since memoirs as well as oral and written testimonies have become privileged genres in teaching the

Holocaust, students come into contact with individual witnesses who seem to be addressing them, directly, as listeners. As Laub has written:

> Testimony is the narrative's address to hearing; for only when the survivor knows he is being heard, will he stop to hear—and listen to—himself. . . . Insofar as they remind us of a horrible, traumatic past, insofar as they bear witness to our own historical disfiguration, survivors frighten us. (71–74)

Laub's reflections on listening to trauma are helpful companion pieces to the teaching of testimony, as is James Young's notion of "received history": "the combined study of both what happened and how it is passed down to us" that captures the effects of the past on the present and of the "telling" on the witness and the listener (41). (On oral testimony and listening to trauma, see the essays in this volume by Hartman and by Brodzki; on reading diaries and memoirs, see the essay in this volume by Stark.)

In the terms of Kacandes's recent work, students can be invited to become "co-witnesses" to the traumas they encounter through reading and listening, whether in testimony; memoir; or other, more distant narrative, artistic, or poetic forms. She has proposed that when reading fiction of or fiction as trauma, one must "consider the levels of the story and discourse, *and* the levels of the production and reception of the text." Most important for our purposes here is her concept of "transhistorical-transcultural witnessing," in which readers at a historical or cultural remove co-witness the stories in the text by acknowledging and explicating those stories as uncompleted attempts at recounting individual or collective traumas (*Talk Fiction* 95, 96). Heeding specialists' warnings about the deformation involved in translating traumatic memory into narrative memory, she cautions that would-be readers–co-witnesses must be as self-conscious as possible about the stories *they* construct about trauma narratives (140; see also Kacandes, "You" 201–04). This self-consciousness is something we can model for our students in class and urge them to develop in their analyses.

For many of us who teach in North America, this self-consciousness will partly involve considerations of what has been termed the Americanization of the Holocaust. Teachers will at least want to raise the issue of the interest in the Holocaust in the United States and the cultural work that courses on the subject are doing in the United States curriculum. For example, is student interest in the Holocaust displacing the opportunity to consider calamities that have been perpetrated on our continent or by our governments and fellow citizens elsewhere? Why is there a Holocaust museum on the Mall in Washington when we don't have a museum of slavery—and didn't have until 2004 a museum of Native American culture? (For demonstrating the range of subjects related to the idea of the Americanization of the Holocaust, we can recommend Flanzbaum; Novick.)

Finally, analyzing the roles of perpetrators, rescuers, bystanders, victims, and co-witnesses in memoir, film, and fiction will lead to a confrontation with other identity markers, such as gender. Does gender matter when an entire people is targeted for extermination and when the first step in that process is a form of dehumanization that removes subjectivity, agency, and thus also gender from the victims? Does gender matter in an exclusively male hierarchy of leadership such as that of the Nazis? Thinking about these questions—and also about who is telling the story, about how that story is told, and about who is listening—necessitates that we raise, and probe deeply, our own and our students' assumptions about the functioning of gender. (See the essays in this volume by Horowitz, by Zeitlin, by Miller, by Greenberg, and by Spitzer for considerations of gender.)

Balancing Affect and Analysis: Trauma and the Holocaust Classroom

If one of the greatest challenges for the teacher is enabling students to be self-conscious about their subject positions and their acts of co-witnessing, another is the disturbing tension between affect and analysis. Saul Friedländer acknowledges this tension as constitutive:

> The numbing or distancing effect of intellectual work on the *Shoah* is unavoidable and necessary; the recurrence of strong emotional impact is also often unforeseeable and necessary. . . . But neither the protective numbing nor the disruptive emotion is entirely accessible to consciousness. ("Trauma" 51)

The tension between affect and analysis is fundamental to the study of trauma, and thus it returns us to the fundamental question of this book and this introduction: the question of representation. The distinction in trauma studies, based on Pierre Janet's work on traumatic dissociation, between narrative memory and traumatic reenactment has led some scholars to qualify the very notion of representation to make space for what the art historian Jill Bennett has termed a "poetics of sense memory [that] involve[s] not so much *speaking of* but *speaking out of* a particular memory or experience" (87). Such texts produce affect in the reader, listener, or spectator, evoking rather than representing bodily memories. (Brodzki's essay in this volume provides a review of issues in trauma studies, and Greenberg's essay in this volume on Charlotte Delbo considers the notion of deep memory or sense memory.)

The classroom, as a space of analysis, does not easily lend itself to dealing with the emotional work of co-witnessing the Holocaust. Indeed, Shoshana Felman has suggested that strong emotions can threaten to "break the very framework of the class" (47, 48). Felman's account of her experiences teaching video testimony and Sondra Perl's essay in this volume can help prepare the teacher for the possible magnitude of both the numbing and the disruption of which Friedländer warns. Being forewarned about such "crises," to borrow Felman's term, can not only help in the moment when the teacher has to improvise a response in the classroom but also help build space for the expression of affect into the syllabus, precisely so that students, in the face of their strong emotional reactions, can still analyze issues such as representation. Felman and Perl address the crises through a writing assignment, and we too have found that students benefit from being allowed to confront their individual responses in their own writing, thus both supplementing and enhancing class lectures and discussions. As Perl shows, the regularity of a journal also enables students to trace the progression of their responses over the course of the term. There are obviously many possible journal assignments. In addition to Perl's account on "writing the Holocaust," we offer two that we have used in our teaching.

1. A reading journal, kept on an ongoing basis, responding to and reflecting on the readings, films, and lectures. This journal should not consist of reading notes and should not simply record unsubstantiated, vague impressions (I like / I don't like); it should display your responses to the materials—both personal and intellectual—with sufficient clarity and detail so they make sense on later reading and review. Your journal entries should serve you as points of entry into our scheduled class discussions—reflections of your questions, critiques, emotions, and analyses. As we move along in the syllabus, you will find yourselves able to bring comparative elements into your journal entries and to revise assessments and earlier reactions on the basis of additional information.

We expect you to include entries (1–2 pp.) for each scheduled class, film, and lecture. At the conclusion of part 1 and part 2 of the course, we ask you to write longer journal entries, reflecting in a more summary way on the readings and films. Please choose one or two issues that have emerged in that course unit and analyze it or them in greater depth (3–4 pp.).

2. A media folder and course diary. Each week you should select at least one item from a newspaper, magazine, radio, or television report or Internet posting that in your judgment relates to the course. Cut or print out the article if possible and physically add it to the notebook you'll be turning in at midterm and at the end of class. Summarize the content briefly in any case. Mention any observations you might have about the relation of the writer or commentator to the material. In several sentences describe the connection you make to our course. Try to include what drew your attention to this particular item. Please add additional entries about any reading or class discussion where, because of lack of time or personal reasons, you did not feel free to express your opinion.

These types of exercises obviously provide ways for students to begin to synthesize the large amounts of material that inevitably get assigned in courses on the Holocaust as well as facilitate the creation of connections between the mid-twentieth-century catastrophe and our current world. Furthermore, they can provide a forum for individual students to express feelings of discomfort about identifications they might be making with certain groups, such as victims or perpetrators, or about the dynamics of identification or intellectualization that take place in the classroom.

In addition to journals, we have found that group assignments can be helpful in enabling students to work together outside class, since the classroom cannot contain all their responses and concerns. In group projects, students aid one another in processing some of the material. One model is to use a group research assignment to explore an area that has not received sufficient coverage in class. Video testimonies lend themselves to group assignments: each group can study one testimony, researching the witness's hometown and the ghettos or camps mentioned in the testimony and commenting on the form that the narrative takes, the kinds of memory that appear, the forms of address that are invoked. Groups can study different recent controversies about Holocaust memorialization or different recent exhibitions or films. Group assignments can culminate in a forum in which the groups present their work to one another. (On possible group assignments, see the essays in this volume by Rogowski and by Rothberg.)

Approaches to Teaching: Interdisciplinarity, Multilingualism, and the Holocaust

Just as students benefit from collaborative work in courses on the Holocaust, so do faculty members. As a subject of representation the Holocaust stretches the limits of representability; as a subject of study it stretches the limits of disciplinarity. What preparation do teachers need for this undertaking? Those teaching any aspect of the Holocaust in any field, no matter what their background, will encounter areas outside or adjacent to their expertise. Historians will want to teach film or memoir or ethical, religious, or philosophical writings; scholars of literature will want to teach history; film scholars will want to consider issues of trauma and memory. Germanists or Americanists will need some training in Jewish studies. That Holocaust studies has been burgeoning as an interdisciplinary, multilingual, and theoretically informed scholarly field is acknowledged in our volume by essays from the fields of history (Bergen, Spitzer, Weitz), religion (Heschel), and political philosophy (Hill), in addition to the many different specializations represented in the modern languages, film, and visual culture.

First-time teachers have had a number of resources available to them, from excellent anthologies to the summer workshops organized by the Holocaust Educational Foundation and the United States Holocaust Memorial Museum. These organizations have assumed that the Holocaust cannot be taught in strictly disciplinary fashion and that every teacher will need some additional training. There are also extremely helpful resources on the World Wide Web. We particularly recommend two sites that offer excellent guidance and primary and secondary materials in numerous disciplines: the list of links by Dan Graf and the list of links by David Dickerson (other Web resources are discussed in Zeitlin's and in Hartman's essay in this volume).

As for helping our students with the range of materials any course is likely to include, we note that useful handouts on basic specific disciplinary practices designed for undergraduates are available in *A User's Guide to German Cultural Studies* (ed. Denham, Kacandes, and Petropoulos). Topics such as "How to View a Film," "How to Read History," "How to Read Statistics," and "How to Use an Archive" may be particularly helpful to literature majors. These pages are not copyrighted and thus can be distributed directly to students or used as a model for a teacher's own handout. In terms of orientation to the fundamental scope of the Holocaust, we recommend Martin Gilbert's *Atlas of the Holocaust*, available in paperback. (For suggestions on suitable historical overviews, consult

Bergen's essay in this volume. For an account of creating an inter-disciplinary course at a small liberal arts college, see Horn's essay in this volume.)

For this volume, we have assembled a number of disciplinary and generic approaches with the aim of enabling teachers (and students) to consider the possibilities and the limitations of each. Thus even the ground on which most Holocaust curricula are built—that of history—can, and perhaps should, become a subject of discussion and interrogation, as it does in the essay in this volume by Doris Bergen. In the late 1940s, Theodor W. Adorno famously questioned whether one could write poetry after Auschwitz ("Cultural Criticism"); in the 1950s, he changed his mind, affirming poetry and other literary forms as the only appropriate forms of representation ("Commitment"). Even Hilberg, the most exacting of political scientists, and the most suspicious of nondocumentary forms, later in his career sent us to the poets for help in seeking to understand ("I Was Not There"). In other words, teachers should be prepared for and perhaps even comforted by the idea not only that there is no one discipline or genre adequate to the task but also that even the experts change their mind on how best to work toward a pedagogy of the Holocaust. (See Suleiman's essay in this volume for the questioning of such basic topics as generations and autobiography versus fiction.)

In addition to disciplinary and generic categories, teachers have to confront issues of language, translation, and translatability. Surely internment in Nazi concentration camps counts as one of the most multilingual experiences of the twentieth century. Nazi policy was to have each camp house prisoners of as many different nationalities and language groups as possible: minimizing the inmates' ability to communicate could only strengthen the power of the jailors. Survivors have described their isolation as they were separated from their compatriots, relocated from one camp to another, and placed in yet a different population, so that relationships would remain transient, communication minimal, and resistance nearly impossible. Knowledge of different languages, especially German, could prolong a person's life. The most important factor in Primo Levi's initiation into the world of the camp is his limited ability to understand German and the insane logic of that place, which he can call only by its German name, *Lager*. "The confusion of languages is a fundamental component of the manner of living here," he writes (38). But Levi and other witnesses go further, stressing the incapacity of any language to contain the experience:

> Just as our hunger is not that feeling of missing a meal, so our way of being cold has need of a new word. We say "hunger," we say "tiredness," "fear," "pain," we say "winter," and they are different things. They are free words, created and used by free men who lived in comfort and suffering in their homes. (123)

Teachers and students will thus not only have to deal with the factor of translation as they consider works originally written in German, Yiddish, French, Hebrew, Italian, Russian, Polish, or Hungarian but also have to think about the issue of translatability itself. (Rosen's essay in this volume examines the implications of teaching the Holocaust in English.)

This Volume

A computer search for help on teaching the Holocaust will turn up more books and articles than any college teacher likely has time to read. Similarly, in literary and cultural studies, the representation of the Holocaust has seen the publication of innumerable books, articles, special issues, books series, dictionaries and encyclopedias, atlases and chronologies, the organization of conferences and special sessions, and the multiplication of helpful sites on the World Wide Web. Why then did we urge the MLA to do a volume on Holocaust pedagogy? Paradoxically perhaps, this very burgeoning of scholarly interest, the fundamental interdisciplinarity of the field, as well as the increasing theoretical sophistication of such work have revealed the relative dearth of reflections on teaching representation.

Little of the pedagogy materials available is directed to university teachers and even less to university humanities teachers, under whose auspices—at least according to our casual observations—more and more college courses on the Holocaust are being taught. Furthermore, despite their titles, many of these materials have greater informative and theoretical than specifically pedagogical value. Series of volumes like those from the Holocaust Educational Foundation's Lessons and Legacies conferences or the single volume published by the Center for Holocaust Studies at the University of Vermont (Scrase and Mieder), for instance, offer excellent compilations of chronologies, terminology, or the latest historical research, but not many concrete tips on teaching. Not much thought is given to make sophisticated scholarly work accessible to undergraduates. The same lack obtains in the numerous resources available on the World Wide Web. We therefore welcome the recently published volumes *Teaching Holocaust Literature* (Totten), *The Curriculum and the Holocaust: Competing Sites of Memory and Representation* (Morris), and *The Holocaust: Theoretical Readings* (Levi and Rothberg). Here college teachers can find many practical suggestions: "Analyzing Stories about the Holocaust via a Multiple Intelligences and Reader-Response Approach" (Totten 125–42); "Representation and the Effects of Anti-Semitism" (Morris 57–85); excerpts from "Nazi Culture, Fascism, and Antisemitism" and "Uniqueness, Comparison, and the Politics of Memory" (Levi and Rothberg 103–44, 441–79). New dictionaries on Holocaust writers offer useful biographical and bibliographic materials (Kremer). Our anthology is in a kindred spirit, but its emphasis on issues of representation and its consideration of a wider range of genres will make it a good complement to these important efforts. The essays in our volume are designed to be useful in a number of different pedagogical settings, ranging from courses on literature to those on history, memory, and representation. These essays should also be adaptable to different levels of background and expertise.

Our volume offers helpful definitions, specific readings and interpretations, and accounts of the critical and pedagogical controversies surrounding certain issues. We encouraged all contributors to share practical tips when appropriate. Even as they treat their individual subjects, they also describe the courses they are teaching, the approaches they have used, the problems they have encountered, the challenges they have faced, the discoveries they have made. Inevitably, some essays offer more in the way of background information, others more pedagogical suggestions.

The authors in the volume's first section, "Critical Paradigms," take up pedagogical challenges that are sure to be encountered when one teaches the representation of the Holocaust, even while offering useful approaches and interpretations of individual texts. Doris L. Bergen provides suggestions on how to teach key historiographical issues—When did the Holocaust begin? Who were its victims?—and some controversial historical texts, like Goldhagen's *Hitler's Willing Executioners* and Jan Gross's *Neighbors*. At the same time, she shows the importance of interrogating the very status of history with our students. Sidra DeKoven Ezrahi traces the ubiquity of the rubric "authenticity" in our thinking about the Holocaust and insists on the importance of teaching students to question it. Her texts (and authors) range from the poetry of Miklós Radnóti to novels like Jurek Becker's *Jacob the Liar* or Jaroslaw Rymkiewicz's *The Final Station: Umschlagplatz*, from plays like Peter Weiss's *The Investigation* to the feigned memoir of Binjamin Wilkomirski, *Fragments*. Froma I. Zeitlin's description of her course unit on perpetrators focuses on texts such as Gitta Serenyi's *Into That Darkness*, Bernhard Schlink's *The Reader*, and Steven Spielberg's *Schindler's List*. In their reflections on the long history of antisemitism, a topic crucial to any attempt to teach Holocaust representation, Susannah Heschel and Sander Gilman offer examples from the New Testament to *The Merchant of Venice* and nineteenth-century scientific texts. Sara R. Horowitz convincingly argues for the importance of highlighting gender in our teaching and accounts for the skepticism with which many have approached this question. She presents readings of gender in relation to victims and perpetrators in specific texts, such as Spiegelman's *Maus*, Ilona Karmel's *An Estate of Memory*, short stories by Ida Fink and Marcie Hershman, and films like Sanders-Brahms's *Germany, Pale Mother*, and Riefenstahl's *Triumph of the Will*.

Each of the last three essays in this section helps make dimensions of the Holocaust intelligible in a specific way: Bella Brodzki gives an overview of the critical field of trauma studies, Eric D. Weitz takes on the challenge of teaching comparative genocide, and Alan Rosen explains the multilingualism of both the historical events of the Holocaust and its representations. Brodzki elucidates how an examination of trauma is relevant to literary analyses of Holocaust texts, including how knowledge of trauma transforms our notions of language and textuality. In the process, she takes up texts like Primo Levi's *The Drowned and the Saved* and *Moments of Reprieve*, Charlotte Delbo's *Days and Memory*, and Claude Morhange-Bégué's *Chamberet: Recollection of an Ordinary Childhood*. Weitz explicates the particularities of the Holocaust related to Germany's bureaucratic and military culture and territorial ambitions, while also explaining that there was nothing exceptional in the Nazi drive to create homogeneity by deploying the ideology of race to murder groups of people. He offers suggestions on books with an explicitly comparative approach and on texts for teaching other genocides of the twentieth century, like those in Cambodia and Rwanda. Discussing the Holocaust as a multilingual event, Rosen makes us aware of a central paradox in United States classrooms as well as in his own at Bar Ilan University in Israel: English is central to our teaching of the Holocaust and yet marginal to the actual events and their agents. He suggests using texts like Peretz Opoczinski's semiautobiographical "The Jewish Letter Carrier," Cynthia Ozick's *The Shawl*, and John Hersey's *The Wall* to make this paradox salient for our students.

The writers in the volume's second section approach the Holocaust through genre, considering poetry (Gubar), fiction (Hungerford), diaries and memoirs (Stark), audio and video testimony (Hartman), film (Lubin), drama (Rogowski), children's literature (Kertzer), second-generation Holocaust fiction (Sicher), monuments (Young), and visual culture (Bathrick). These essays discuss a specific genre not so much to suggest which texts to use as to elucidate some of the challenges of teaching works of that genre. Given space, we would certainly have liked to include essays on philosophy, ethics, religion, music, and painting and sculpture. Still, in the essays of this section readers can find allusions to national contexts: Germany (Young, Rogowski), Israel and the United States (Hartman, Sicher, Lubin), Eastern Europe (Stark). There are also detailed discussions of textual examples: Lanzmann's *Shoah* (Bathrick), *Schind-*

ler's List and Europa, Europa (Lubin), Levi's Survival in Auschwitz (Stark), Philip Roth's The Ghost Writer and D. M. Thomas's The White Hotel (Hungerford), Grossman's See Under: Love (Sicher). Readings are offered: of Jane Yolen's Briar Rose and Carol Matei's Daniel's Story (Kertzer); of lesser-known poems by Nellie Sachs, Paul Celan, and Dan Pagis (Gubar); of Max Frisch's play Andorra (Rogowski); of Gilo Pontecorvo's Kapo (Bathrick); and of Michael Verhoeven's The Nasty Girl (Lubin).

The volume's third section, "Selected Texts," narrows the focus by looking at key works. While a certain canon of literary and filmic texts has already emerged in college courses on Holocaust literature and representation, only some of these can be covered here. The most well known are Anne Frank's diary (Bos), Wiesel's Night (Weissman), Levi's Survival in Auschwitz (Druker), Paul Celan's poem "Death Fugue" (Baer), and Lanzmann's film Shoah (Spitzer). Texts that have received more recent attention by Holocaust scholars are Pagis's poem "Written in Pencil in the Sealed Railway-Car" (Omer-Sherman), Ozick's The Shawl (Levine), Delbo's Auschwitz and After (Greenberg), Georges Perec's W or the Memory of Childhood (Suleiman), and A. B. Yehoshua's Mr. Mani and W. G. Sebald's The Emigrants (Newton). Under selected texts we include an essay by Nancy K. Miller on a runaway best seller in Europe that has recently been published in an English version: Ruth Klüger's memoir Still Alive: A Holocaust Girlhood Remembered. Spiegelman's Maus, perhaps the most widely taught text in recent years, is discussed by no fewer than seven of our authors (Bathrick, Brodzki, Charlson, Ezrahi, Horowitz, Rosen, and Sicher) to illustrate the paradigms of their essays, even as it appears at the beginning of this introduction. For this reason it does not appear in this section. Each individual text is inscribed in one or more specific pedagogical frames that are applicable to other texts as well. For example, one might turn to Susan Rubin Suleiman's essay for a discussion of the position of the child survivor or the 1.5 generation; to Miller's essay for generic reflections on the memoir and a discussion of mother-daughter dynamics in Holocaust literature; to Adam Zachary Newton's essay for a generic definition of "not quite Holocaust fiction"; to Leo Spitzer's essay for reflections on the relationship of the documentary to history; to Judith Greenberg's essay for an analysis of trauma and language.

The essays in the fourth section, "Classroom Contexts," are more practical in nature. Together, they present a variety of institutions and courses in which the representation of the Holocaust is taught. Individually, they contain specific accounts of institutional and classroom struggles, as well as suggestions about a number of important issues: how to win support for a multidisciplinary Holocaust course at a small liberal arts college (Horn), how to create a program on the Holocaust that serves both the campus and the local community (Scrase), or how to design a unit on the Holocaust in a Jewish American literature course (Charlson). Renée A. Hill describes her course The Holocaust and Comparative Genocide in a historically black university and concludes that this context offers the same challenges that any other academic institution might. In describing a culminating project that involves memorialization and writing, Michael Rothberg foregrounds the context in which his students are learning: that of the United States. Sondra Perl's writing assignments are sensitive to the environment of the large urban university her students attend.

The rich and suggestive essays of this volume will provide important resources to teachers of the Holocaust. We are grateful to their authors for the care they have given to these reflections on pedagogy, and we are grateful to the many colleagues who have read and commented on individual essays and on the book as a whole. We also thank the staff members of the MLA publications department for their support and encouragement. And we thank, especially, Gail Vernazza for her brilliant administrative help during every stage of this project.

We dedicate this book to Susanne Zantop and Half Zantop, in loving memory of their friendship and their dedication to teaching.

Works Cited

Adorno, Theodor W. "Commitment." *Notes to Literature*. Vol. 2. Ed. Rolf Tiedemann. Trans. Shierry Weber Nicholson. New York: Columbia UP, 1992. 76–94.

———. "Cultural Criticism and Society." *Prisms*. Trans. Samuel Weber and Shierry Weber. Cambridge: MIT P, 1967. 17–34.

Agamben, Giorgio. *Remnants of Auschwitz: The Witness and the Archive*. Trans. Daniel Heller-Roazen. Cambridge: Zone, 1999.

Allport, Gordon. *The ABC's of Scapegoating*. New York: Anti-Defamation League of B'nai B'rith, 1959.

America and the Holocaust. The American Experience. Dir. Martin Ostrow. Narr. Hal Linden. Fine Cut Productions. WGBH Educ. Foundation, 1994.

Bandura, Albert. "Selective Activation and Disengagement of Internal Control." *Social Foundations of Thought and Action: A Social Cognitive Theory*. Englewood Cliffs: Prentice, 1986. 375–89.

Bennett, Jill. "The Aesthetics of Sense-Memory: Theorising Trauma through the Visual Arts." *Trauma und Erinnerung / Trauma and Memory: Cross-Cultural Perspectives*. Ed. Franz Kaltenbeck and Peter Weibel. Vienna: Passagen, 2000. 81–95.

Browning, Christopher R. *Ordinary Men: Reserve Police Battalion 101 and the Final Solution in Poland*. New York: Harper, 1992.

Celan, Paul. "Speech on the Occasion of Receiving the Literature Prize of the Free Hanseatic City of Bremen." *Selected Poems and Prose*. Trans. John Felstiner. New York: Norton, 2001. 395–96.

Delbo, Charlotte. *Auschwitz and After*. Trans. Rosette C. Lamont. New Haven: Yale UP, 1995.

Denham, Scott, Irene Kacandes, and Jonathan Petropoulos, eds. *A User's Guide to German Cultural Studies*. Ann Arbor: U of Michigan P, 1997.

Dickerson, David M. *Educational Projects and Resources*. IGC Networks. 10 Dec. 1999 <http://ddickerson.igc.org/education.html>.

Dimsdale, Joel. *Survivors, Victims, and Perpetrators: Essays on the Nazi Holocaust*. Washington: Hemisphere, 1980.

Felman, Shoshana. "Education and Crisis; or, The Vicissitudes of Teaching." Felman and Laub 1–56.

Felman, Shoshana, and Dori Laub. *Testimony: Crises of Witnessing in Literature, Psychoanalysis, and History*. New York: Routledge, 1992.

Flanzbaum, Hilene, ed. *The Americanization of the Holocaust*. Baltimore: Johns Hopkins UP, 1991.

Friedlander, Henry. *The Origins of Nazi Genocide from Euthanasia to the Final Solution*. Chapel Hill: U of North Carolina P, 1995.

Friedländer, Saul, ed. *Probing the Limits of Representation: Nazism and the "Final Solution."* Cambridge: Harvard UP, 1992.

———. "Trauma, Transference and 'Working Through' in Writing the History of the *Shoah*." *History and Memory* 4 (1992): 39–59.

Gilbert, Martin. *Atlas of the Holocaust*. Oxford: Pergamon, 1988.

Goldhagen, Daniel Jonah. *Hitler's Willing Executioners: Ordinary Germans and the Holocaust*. New York: Knopf, 1996.

Graf, Dan. *Holocaust and Jewish Studies Sites*. Virginia Wesleyan Coll. 24 Feb. 2004 <http://facultystaff.vwc.edu/~dgraf/holocaus.htm>.

Greenspan, Henry. "Imagining Survivors: Testimony and the Rise of Holocaust Consciousness." Flanzbaum 45–67.

Hancock, Ian. "Gypsy History in Germany and Neighboring Lands: A Chronology Leading to the Holocaust and Beyond." *The Gypsies in Eastern Europe.* Ed. David Crowe and John Kolsti. New York, 1991. 11–30.

Hartman, Geoffrey H. *The Longest Shadow: In the Aftermath of the Holocaust.* Bloomington: Indiana UP, 1996.

Hilberg, Raul. *The Destruction of the European Jews.* Rev. ed. 3 vols. New York: Holmes, 1985.

———. "I Was Not There." *Writing and the Holocaust.* Ed. Berel Lang. New York: Holmes, 1988. 17–25.

———. *Perpetrators, Victims, Bystanders: The Jewish Catastrophe, 1933–1945.* New York: Asher, 1992.

Hirsch, Marianne. *Family Frames: Photography, Narrative and Postmemory.* Cambridge: Harvard UP, 1997.

———. "Surviving Images: Holocaust Photographs and the Work of Postmemory." *The Holocaust and Visual Culture.* Ed. Barbie Zelizer. New Brunswick: Rutgers UP, 2001. 214–46.

Hochhuth, Rolf. *The Deputy.* Trans. Richard Winston and Clara Winston. New York: Grove, 1964.

Kacandes, Irene. *Talk Fiction: Literature and the Talk Explosion.* Lincoln: U of Nebraska P, 2001.

———. "'You Who Live Safe in Your Warm Houses': Your Role in the Production of Holocaust Video Testimony." *Insiders and Outsiders: Jewish and Gentile Culture in Germany and Austria.* Ed. Dagmar Lorenz and Gabriele Weinberger. Detroit: Wayne State UP, 1994. 189–213.

Kremer, S. Lilian. *Holocaust Literature: An Encyclopedia of Writers and Their Work.* New York: Routledge, 2002.

LaCapra, Dominick. *History and Memory after Auschwitz.* Ithaca: Cornell UP, 1998.

———. "Representing the Holocaust: Reflections on the Historians' Debate." S. Friedlander, *Probing* 108–27.

———. "Trauma, Absence, Loss." *Critical Inquiry* 25 (1999): 696–727.

Laub, Dori. "Bearing Witness; or, The Vicissitudes of Listening." Felman and Laub 57–74.

Levi, Neil, and Michael Rothberg, eds. *The Holocaust: Theoretical Readings.* New Brunswick: Rutgers UP, 2003.

Levi, Primo. *Survival in Auschwitz: The Nazi Assault on Humanity.* Trans. Stuart Woolf. New York: Touchstone, 1996.

Maier, Charles S. *The Unmasterable Past: History, Holocaust, and German National Identity.* Cambridge: Harvard UP, 1988.

Marrus, Michael R. "'Good History' and Teaching the Holocaust." *Perspectives: American Historical Association Newsletter* 31.5 (1993): 1, 6–12.

Milton, Sybil. "Nazi Policies towards Roma and Sinti, 1933–1945." *Journal of the Gypsy Lore Society* 5th ser. 2.1 (1992): 1–18.

"Mirroring Evil." Interview with Piotr Uklanski. Prod. Sara Fishko. *Golems, Memory, Evil.* Studio 360. WNYC. 6 Apr. 2002.

Morris, Marla. *The Curriculum and the Holocaust: Competing Sites of Memory and Representation.* Mahwah: Erlbaum, 2001.

Novick, Peter. *The Holocaust in American Life.* Boston: Houghton, 1999.

Rothberg, Michael. *Traumatic Realism: The Demands of Holocaust Representation.* Minneapolis: U of Minnesota P, 2000.

Scrase, David, and Wolfgang Mieder, eds. *The Holocaust: Introductory Essays.* Burlington: Center for Holocaust Studies, 1996.

Sedgwick, Eve Kosofsky. *Epistemology of the Closet.* Berkeley: U of California P, 1990.

Semprun, Jorge. *Literature or Life.* Trans. Linda Coverdale. New York: Penguin, 1997.

Spiegelman, Art. "The First Maus." *The Complete Maus.* CD-ROM. New York: Voyager, 1994.

Totten, Samuel, ed. *Teaching Holocaust Literature.* Boston: Allyn, 2001.

Young, James E. "Toward a Received History of the Holocaust." *History and Theory* 36.4 (1997): 21–43.

Part I

Critical Paradigms

Doris L. Bergen

The Barbarity of Footnotes: History and the Holocaust

The Holocaust scholar Raul Hilberg was once asked to comment on Adorno's famous line about poetry after Auschwitz. If poetry after Auschwitz was barbarism, Hilberg replied, what on earth could be said about footnotes? Hilberg's remark draws our attention to the inadequacy of history—and of scholarship in general—in the face of the horror and suffering of the Holocaust. At the same time, with the metonymic device of the footnote, Hilberg acknowledges the particular tools that historians and political scientists (like him), whose work is archivally based, bring to the study of the Holocaust and its representations. What can history, with its footnotes, archives, facts, and dates, offer those who teach literature?

Historians of the Holocaust often find themselves in the difficult and rather awkward position of the answer person. In a sense my contribution to this volume reproduces that dynamic. I have given many talks to nonhistorians and observed one thing that every audience shares: an interest in "the facts." A visit by a historian becomes an opportunity to ask specific questions: Was Hitler "part Jewish"? How many Jews left Germany after the Nazis came to power? What is a Gypsy? Could German protest, or the pope, or the American bombing of Auschwitz have stopped the killing? No matter who they are, people want answers, guidelines, something firm to hold on to in the swirl of disorientation and nausea that is a common reaction to study of the Holocaust. Almost never can history fulfill that desire; the who, what, and how questions that historians can resolve unequivocally turn out to be only the tip of the iceberg of why. Many people leave a historical presentation resolved to turn elsewhere with their big questions—to philosophy, religion, psychology, or literature. The tension between the necessity of history and its inadequacy, between the expectations placed on it and the impossibility of meeting them, is present in every class that engages the Holocaust and its representations.

My goals in this essay are modest: I outline some key historical findings and suggest useful texts for literature teachers and their students who want to familiarize themselves with the Holocaust as history. At the same time, I reflect on the nature of historical knowledge: historians, too, deal in representations that are constructed and interpretations that are contested and provide no direct access to the truth. Nevertheless, or perhaps precisely therefore, history can help set up frameworks to think about the Holocaust and provide insights into its context, scope, definition, and nature. Moreover, the textuality of history is limited in particular ways by the concrete realities of human life and death. The following discussion is organized around five points that anyone who teaches the Holocaust might want to consider: chronology matters; the Holocaust was part of a war; the Holocaust was an event of global dimensions; not all those targeted for murder and annihilation were Jews, although Nazi programs of persecution and mass killing put Jews at the center; sometimes lines between the categories of perpetrators and victims, or perpetrators and bystanders were, and remain, blurred to the point of nonexistence.

Chronology, Confusion, and Order: Creating a Framework

Although an obvious point, it bears repeating: the Holocaust occurred in time. Nonhistorians sometimes mock historians' obsession with dates, but familiarity with the timing and order of events is essential if we are to understand anything about causality or perceive the implications of particular actions and decisions. Students in courses on the Holocaust are often alarmingly eager to get to the gas chambers, to bypass the processes of persecution, isolation, expropriation, and experimentation that led up to and made possible Nazi efforts to annihilate the Jews of Europe. That rush to plunge straight into the deepest circle of hell maximizes the shock value and emphasizes the mystery and unknowability of the Holocaust, but playing up the unimaginable horror detracts from what is perhaps a more important goal of teaching in this area: helping students and ourselves recognize the familiarity of genocidal situations and behaviors. What could be more banal and everyday than the passage of time? Anyone can imagine from personal experience how long six years is: from 1933, when Hitler became chancellor of Germany, to 1939, the beginning of World War II, or from 1939 to 1945, when the war finally ended. Locating the Holocaust in time is a powerful way to communicate its life-and-death reality.

The best overview of the chronology is still Hilberg's monumental work *The Destruction of the European Jews* (in three volumes or the one-volume student edition). Leni Yahil's book *The Holocaust* is a fascinating complement and challenge: whereas Hilberg focuses on decision making and bureaucratic processes, Yahil includes the perspective of those targeted for expropriation, ghettoization, and annihilation. Léon Poliakov, Yehuda Bauer, Michael R. Marrus, Rita Steinhardt Botwinick, and Robert S. Wistrich have all written short accounts that are helpful for professors and students alike. Saul Friedländer's *Nazi Germany and the Jews*, so far available only as volume one, dealing with 1933 to 1939, is a nuanced, insightful treatment of those crucial years between Hitler's rise to power and the invasion of Poland. Friedländer's sophisticated book is also accessible for undergraduate students.

It is ironic but no coincidence that some of the most heated debates among historians of the Holocaust involve chronology. In the 1970s and early 1980s, the so-called intentionalists and functionalists almost came to blows over whether the total eradication of European Jewry was the intention of Adolf Hitler and other top Nazis from early on or whether the mass slaughter evolved in response to developments and pressures related to war and occupation. By the 1990s, most historians had accepted a sort of compromise position that paid attention to long-term ideological motivations while recognizing the power of initiatives and contingencies on the ground. A good example is Christopher R. Browning's *Ordinary Men*, a book well suited for undergraduate reading.

In classic Hegelian style, however, that synthesis generated a new round of disagreements, this time about the precise timing of Hitler's decision for total destruction of Europe's Jews. When did the Holocaust begin? Scholars like Gerhard L. Weinberg ("Comments") and Richard Breitman argue against the notion of a single moment of decision and emphasize instead a process that by the summer of 1941 was under way in full force. Since late 1939, people deemed handicapped, beginning with handicapped children, had been subject to programs of systematic murder. The German attack on Yugoslavia, which began in spring 1941, included mass killings of civilians, many of them Jews. And German efforts to stir up pogroms in newly conquered territories after the invasion of the Soviet Union in June 1941 counted on slaughter not only of Jewish men of an age to fight back but also of women, children, and old people.

Browning developed a different interpretation that pushed Hitler's decision back to the fall of 1941, when Germans, flushed with victories over the Soviet Union, began implementing programs of mass killing on a previously inconceivable scale (*Nazi Policy*). Subsequent scholars, like Christian Gerlach, have posited even later dates for the decision, arguing, for example, that only in late 1941 did territorial solutions of what Nazis called the Jewish problem cross the line to become the "final solution" of total annihilation. Nonhistorians often get impatient with what can seem like ridiculous and cold-blooded wrangling over details. Nevertheless, these debates about timing have revealed much about causal connections, individual motivations, and the nature of planning and coordination in the Holocaust. Even if a new synthesis emerges, however, disagreements about chronology are likely to continue, because dates can serve as a kind of screen for historians struggling with the endless task of understanding how the Holocaust happened. At the same time, dates represent in a concrete manner one way that history, although representational, differs from literature: German troops crossed the border to Poland on 1 September 1939, not 1 September 1938; Adolf Hitler killed himself on 30 April 1945, not 30 May.

War and Genocide: Establishing the Context

The history of the Holocaust is inextricably linked to World War II. The war gave Nazi Germany a framework for systematic killing; it also supplied most of the Nazis' victims. Without the war, millions of Jews from all over Europe would not have come into German hands; nor could peacetime have supported the training of units solely for the purpose of killing or provided rationalizations acceptable to members of the public who perhaps shared prejudices against target populations but might have balked at wholesale butchery. In war, killing is considered normal.

Weinberg coined a phrase that captures the links between Nazi war and genocide: "race and space" ("World"). As Eberhard Jäckel shows, those intertwined concepts — the struggle for so-called racial purity and the quest for lebensraum (living space) for the purportedly superior Aryans — drove the Nazi project from the time Hitler penned *Mein Kampf* in 1924 to the collapse of the "thousand-year Reich" in 1945. For Hitler and Nazi true believers, the Holocaust was the war. The sense of urgency that compelled them, the conviction that the clock stood at five to midnight for the Aryan race, reflected their belief that eradication of those deemed racially destructive — Jews above all, but also Roma-Sinti (Gypsies) and people considered handicapped — was imperative wherever the Reich imposed its rule. Hitler could no more wait until victory to launch his genocidal programs than he could delay attacking the Soviet Union until the war had been won. Those offensives were precisely what the war was all about.

Professors and students interested in exploring links between the Holocaust and the war might begin with Weinberg's essay "The 'Final Solution' and the War in 1943." More detail is available in his massive *A World at Arms*. Omer Bartov's works on the German army are useful (*Eastern Front* and *Hitler's Army*), as are Michael Geyer's discussion of "mass death" (9) and the essays collected by Ulrich Herbert. The collection of documents edited by Jeremy Noakes and Geoffrey Pridham allows students (and professors) to see the connections for themselves. My survey *War and Genocide: A Concise History of the Holocaust* presents the basic points in a straightforward way.

As with chronology, the connections between the Holocaust and the war remain the site of intense debate, much of it focused on the role of the Wehrmacht, the German military, in the murder of civilians, especially Jews. In the mid-1990s, the Hamburg Institute for Social Research opened an exhibit on the Wehrmacht and the crimes of the Third Reich (*Vernichtungskrieg*). Centered on photographs, many of them graphic depictions of men in uniform engaged in horrific acts of brutality, the exhibit rekindled familiar defenses about the supposedly clean and honorable German soldier. It also sparked dissension among scholars, some of whom noted mistakes in the exhibit, such as photographs that had been wrongly attributed. This dispute highlights the paradoxical relation between history and representation. Photographs—undeniably representations rather than facts in themselves—cannot be used as historical sources without regard to something one might call their truth content. A historian who offers as evidence of German atrocities a photograph of a man in a Soviet NKVD uniform shooting someone into a mass grave can—and should—be called to task for misrepresenting, or at least misunderstanding, the past.

The Wehrmacht exhibit inspired a great deal of important research at every stage of its existence: preparation, criticism, revision. Access to sources closed until the collapse of Communism and new methodologies and tendencies in the field of history, such as interest in issues of gender, ethnicity, and everyday life, combined to raise new questions and offer new places to look for answers (e.g., Heer and Naumann). The opening of the iron curtain through Europe created the possibility of exploring Nazism and Stalinism together—where they belong chronologically—without the dead end of cold-war recriminations. It is no surprise that some of the most challenging responses to the Wehrmacht exhibit came from scholars in Poland like Bogdan Musial, who recognize links between the Holocaust and the war but show us a very different and much more complex war in east-central Europe than Americans expect. Much remains unclear about the precise roles played by individuals and organizations in acts of killing that often occurred on the periphery of German power. Nevertheless, the simple fact of the inseparability of the Holocaust and World War II complicates and enriches teaching of the Holocaust and its representations in myriad ways.

The Holocaust as World History: The Scope of Destruction

Any effort to engage the war in discussions of the Holocaust automatically leads to a related insight: the Holocaust was a global event. Not only did Nazis draw their targets from all over Europe; they sought world domination. Every part of the world played some role in the drama of the Holocaust: as potential and actual sites of refuge for Jews and others; as postwar havens for the perpetrators; as beneficiaries of stolen properties; as places occupied by, allied with or against, or neutral toward the war's aggressors. Anyone who teaches the representations of the Holocaust has already encountered this reality: by the time you have considered even a handful of standard works—by Elie Wiesel, Cynthia Ozick, Primo Levi, Claude Lanzmann, and Aharon Appelfeld, for example—you have crossed almost every border in Europe, and many beyond.

Historical scholarship, which still tends to be organized around national (and linguistic) categories, offers rich and bewildering possibilities for those who want to educate themselves about related developments in a specific country: in Romania, for example, or Belarus or the Soviet Union as a whole (resp., Ioanid; Dean; Dobroszycki and Gurock). Two very different studies that examine the global scope of Nazism and the Holocaust are Norman Goda's examination of Nazi plans for North Africa and America, *Tomorrow the World*, and Judith Miller's comparative look at Holocaust commemoration, *One by One by One*. At least portions of both could be read productively by undergraduates.

What could be controversial about something as obvious as the international scope of the Holocaust? Perversely, perhaps, one of the most heated controversies of the 1990s focused on precisely this issue. In his best-selling book *Hitler's Willing Executioners*, Daniel Jonah Goldhagen, a political scientist by training, argued that the Holocaust was the direct result of uniquely German, eliminationist anti-semitism. There is no denying that Germans played the central—and decisive—role in organizing and perpetrating the Holocaust as a program of killing that went far beyond local pogroms or national schemes of expropriation. Nevertheless, to accept Goldhagen's position is to shrink the scope of the Holocaust to its German components, German perpetrators driven by uniquely German hatreds and cured after 1945 by the democratization—and Americanization—of Germany, at least Germany's western side. Anyone who takes seriously even a small part of the vast literature on the Holocaust, however, will see the horrific scale of destruction that spilled far over the borders of German culture and conquest.

The public nature of history and its political and legal uses (and abuses) constitute another kind of limit to pure representationality. People in positions of power make decisions—about justice, restitution, punishment, and the need for reconciliation or commemoration—on the basis of history. Accordingly, historians have a responsibility to reveal their sources and present them with integrity so that others can make the critical judgments necessary to challenge or accept those findings and their implications. History—and historians—can be called to bear witness to the Holocaust not only in an abstract sense but also in a court of law.

Not Just Jews: Defining the Holocaust

One of the thorniest issues for anyone teaching the Holocaust and its representations must be the matter of definition. Who belongs inside the category "victims of the Holocaust" and who does not? Historians — like museum planners, journalists, filmmakers, and just about everyone else — do not agree among themselves on this question. Some, like both Sybil Milton and Henry Friedlander, insist on a definition that encompasses the three groups targeted most systematically for destruction: people deemed handicapped, Jews, and Gypsies (Roma-Sinti). Guenter Lewy, in contrast, holds to the uniqueness of the Jewish experience, even while studying the fate of Gypsies under Nazism. Other scholars, such as Michael Zimmermann or Donald Kenrick and Grattan Puxon, take a broadly inclusive approach that sometimes avoids labeling non-Jews as victims of the Holocaust but that nevertheless demonstrates unmistakable parallels. Additional examples include Christian Streit's work on Soviet POWs; Richard C. Lukas on Poland (*Forgotten Holocaust* and *Out of the Inferno*); Burkhard Jellonnek, Günter Grau, and Geoffrey J. Giles on homosexuals; materials from the Watchtower Society on Jehovah's Witnesses; the special issue of the *Journal of the History of Sexuality* edited by Dagmar Herzog; and chapters in the collections edited by Michael Berenbaum and Abraham Peck and by Robert Gellately and Nathan Stoltzfus. On this issue, too, disagreement among scholars has been productive, because it has generated detailed studies of groups of people often neglected and forgotten by almost everyone outside their own circles.

Only a few works go beyond the "mosaic of victims" or "forgotten victims" approach (resp., Berenbaum; Steininger) to demonstrate direct links — ideological and practical — between Nazi attacks on Jews and Nazi treatment of non-Jewish target groups (e.g., Burleigh and Wippermann; Müller-Hill). Likewise, only a small number of serious histories sidestep claims of uniqueness to reflect on parallels between the Holocaust and other historical genocides (Naimark; Weitz; and the collections edited by Bartov and Mack and by Gellately and Kiernan).

Gitta Sereny's *Into That Darkness* is a powerful example of a study that both reveals connections among Nazi programs of killing and makes superb undergraduate reading. Sereny interviewed Franz Stangl, most famously commandant of Treblinka but also onetime commandant of Sobibor and earlier an operative in the euphemistically named Euthanasia Program. She demonstrates how not only ideology and methods but also personnel linked Nazi murder of the handicapped with genocide of Jews. By showing how these programs were connected, Sereny broadens the definition of the Holocaust without setting up destructive hierarchies of suffering. As a journalist, she proves that historians have no monopoly on the skills needed to explore ties among victim groups: detailed archival research, collection and analysis of oral testimonies, precise argumentation. Deployed well, those historical tools may not produce the final definition of the Holocaust, but they will complicate easy categories that all too often restrict rather than promote understanding.

Blurred Lines and Taboos: Confronting the Nature of the Holocaust

With the title of his book, *Perpetrators, Victims, Bystanders*, Hilberg popularized a schema for categorizing people involved in the Holocaust. Others have added further classifications such as "rescuers" and "beneficiaries." These groupings are useful both in organizing information and in focusing challenges to conceptual rigidity. Indeed, some of the most exciting work in Holocaust studies considers the ways that lines among the categories of perpetrator, victim, and bystander are blurred in all directions. Here historians might learn from their counterparts in literature and other disciplines, who have often shown more willingness to venture into the "gray zones," to use Primo Levi's phrase. Whatever one might think of books like Leslie Epstein's *King of the Jews* and movies like *The Night Porter* and *Schindler's List*, there is no doubt that they open up possibilities to discuss victims who were also somehow complicit in perpetrators' acts, to examine perpetrators who sometimes sympathized with their victims, and to consider rescuers who were also beneficiaries of genocide. Perhaps it is precisely the reluctance of historians to engage such possibilities — and to take the kind of heat that accompanies violations of taboos — that has drawn so much popular attention to these borderline cases.

Two intense controversies in the field of Holocaust history involve such blurring of the boundaries. One deals with Pius XII and more generally the role of the Vatican and the Catholic Church in the Holocaust. Many people—Catholics and non-Catholics—include Catholics on their mental list of victims of the Holocaust. Catholics, however, cut across the familiar classifications: there were Catholic perpetrators, from the nominally Catholic Hitler to the Croatian priest who crossed himself after he killed Serbs and Jews; Catholic bystanders, beneficiaries, and rescuers all over Poland and elsewhere in Europe; and Catholic victims, including some, like Edith Stein, who had converted from Judaism and were targeted as Jews despite their religious affiliation. Historians like Saul Friedländer (*Pius XII*), Klaus Scholder, John Conway, and Michael Phayer have presented some of these nuances, regarding not only Catholics but Protestants as well. A good introduction to this issue for students is Robert P. Ericksen and Susannah Heschel's collection, *Betrayal: The German Churches and the Holocaust.* More influential among the general public than any of these studies, however, has probably been one single (often misquoted) line: "First they came for the trade unionists . . . then they came for the Catholics. . . ." The comfort of a closed category of victim is hard to surrender.

A second controversy, sparked by Jan Gross's book *Neighbors,* involves the role of (non-Jewish) Poles in the Holocaust. Gross describes how in July 1941, the gentile Poles of a town called Jedwabne murdered their Jewish neighbors. According to Gross's account, there was little urging from the Germans and no coercion; the Poles took the initiative. In a dramatic way, Gross, a professor of politics and European studies at New York University, challenges the division between perpetrator and victim by showing that it was possible for many Poles to be both. Indeed, one of the innovative—and generally neglected—aspects of Gross's analysis has to do with the somewhat paradoxical connection he suggests between those categories. In many cases, he indicates, it was precisely those Poles who had cooperated most enthusiastically with the Soviets between 1939 and 1941 who were most eager to attack Jews once the Germans arrived. Fearful that they would be the new victims, they rushed to demonstrate their support for the German cause—and to deflect charges of collaboration with Communism—by hurling accusations, and much more, at the Jews. In this vicious cycle, it is not primarily victims who become perpetrators but people fearful that they might reap what they have sown, who cover their tracks when the wind changes direction by seizing the initiative for new crimes. Categories like victim, perpetrator, bystander, rescuer, and beneficiary belong at the beginning of an analytic process, not at the end.

———

I would like to be able to say that the five ideas I have addressed represent some kind of consensus among historians of the Holocaust. Indeed, few would argue with the claims that chronology matters; that the Holocaust was part of the war and an event of international scope; that attacks on Jews were one component—albeit a central one—of an interlocking system of prejudice, violence, and genocide; and that lines among perpetrators, victims, and bystanders were often blurred. It is all the more astonishing, then, to see that each of these topics is in fact a site of contestation. The debates themselves attest to the importance of the issues involved. They also serve to remind us that the most significant contribution of the discipline of history to the study of the Holocaust may not be firm answers to all those questions but the insight that the answers, when they come, are surrounded with complexity and ambiguity.

Works Cited

Bartov, Omer. *The Eastern Front, 1941–45: German Troops and the Barbarisation of Warfare.* London: St. Martin's, 1985.

———. *Hitler's Army: Soldiers, Nazis, and War in the Third Reich.* New York, 1991.

Bartov, Omer, and Phyllis Mack, eds. *In God's Name: Genocide and Religion in the Twentieth Century.* New York: Berghahn, 2001.

Bauer, Yehuda. *A History of the Holocaust.* New York: Franklin Watts, 1982.

Berenbaum, Michael, ed. *A Mosaic of Victims: Non-Jews Persecuted and Murdered by the Nazis.* New York: New York UP, 1990.

Berenbaum, Michael, and Abraham Peck, eds. *The Holocaust and History: The Known, the Unknown, the Disputed, and the Reexamined.* Bloomington: Indiana UP, 1998.

Bergen, Doris L. *War and Genocide: A Concise History of the Holocaust.* Lanham: Rowman, 2003.

Botwinick, Rita Steinhardt. *A History of the Holocaust: From Ideology to Annihilation.* Upper Saddle River: Prentice, 1995.

Breitman, Richard. *Official Secrets: What the Nazis Planned, What the British and Americans Knew.* New York: Hill, 1998.

Browning, Christopher R. *Nazi Policy, Jewish Labor, German Killers.* Cambridge: Cambridge UP, 2000.

———. *Ordinary Men: Reserve Police Battalion 101 and the Final Solution in Poland.* New York: Harper, 1997.

Burleigh, Michael, and Wolfgang Wippermann. *The Racial State: Germany, 1933–1945.* New York: Cambridge UP, 1991.

Conway, John S. *The Nazi Persecution of the Churches.* New York: Basic, 1968.

Dean, Martin. *Collaboration in the Holocaust: Crimes of the Local Police in Belorussia and Ukraine, 1941–44.* New York: St. Martin's, 2000.

Dobroszycki, Lucjan, and Jeffrey S. Gurock, eds. *The Holocaust in the Soviet Union.* Armonk: Sharpe, 1993.

Ericksen, Robert P., and Susannah Heschel, eds. *Betrayal: The German Churches and the Holocaust.* Minneapolis: Augsburg Fortress, 1999.

Friedlander, Henry. *The Origins of Nazi Genocide: From Euthanasia to the Final Solution.* Chapel Hill: U of North Carolina P, 1995.

Friedländer, Saul. *Nazi Germany and the Jews.* New York: Harper, 1997. Vol. 1 of *The Years of Persecution.*

———. *Pius XII and the Third Reich.* New York: Knopf, 1966.

Gellately, Robert, and Ben Kiernan, eds. *The Spector of Genocide: Mass Murder in Historical Perspective.* Cambridge: Cambridge UP, 2003.

Gellately, Robert, and Nathan Stoltzfus, eds. *Social Outsiders in Nazi Germany.* Princeton: Princeton UP, 2001.

Gerlach, Christian. *Kalkulierte Morde: Die deutsche Wirtschafts- und Vernichtungspolitik in Weissrussland 1941 bis 1944.* Hamburg: Hamburger, 1999.

Geyer, Michael. "The Place of the Second World War in German Memory and History." *New German Critique* 71 (1997): 5–40.

Giles, Geoffrey. "The Institutionalization of Homosexual Panic in the Third Reich." Gellately and Stoltzfus 233–55.

Goda, Norman J. W. *Tomorrow the World: Hitler, Northwest Africa, and the Path toward America.* College Station: Texas A&M UP, 1998.

Goldhagen, Daniel Jonah. *Hitler's Willing Executioners: Ordinary Germans and the Holocaust.* New York: Knopf, 1996.

Grau, Günter, ed. *Hidden Holocaust? Gay and Lesbian Persecution in Germany, 1933–1945.* Trans. Patrick Camiller. London: Cassell, 1995.

Gross, Jan. *Neighbors: The Destruction of the Jewish Community in Jedwabne, Poland.* Princeton: Princeton UP, 2001.

Heer, Hannes, and Klaus Naumann, eds. *Vernichtungskrieg: Verbrechen der Wehrmacht, 1941–1944.* Hamburg: Hamburger, 1995.

Herbert, Ulrich. *National Socialist Extermination Policies: Contemporary German Perspectives and Controversies.* New York: Berghahn, 2000.

Herzog, Dagmar, ed. *Sexuality and German Fascism.* Spec. issue of *Journal of the History of Sexuality* 11.1–2 (2002): 1–356.

Hilberg, Raul. *The Destruction of the European Jews.* Chicago: Quadrangle, 1961. Rev. ed. 3 vols. New York: Holmes, 1985.

———. *Perpetrators, Victims, Bystanders: The Jewish Catastrophe, 1933–1945.* New York: Harper, 1992.

Ioanid, Radu. *The Holocaust in Romania: The Destruction of Jews and Gypsies under the Antonescu Regime, 1940–1944.* Chicago: Dee, 2000.

Jäckel, Eberhard. *Hitler's World View: A Blueprint for Power.* Trans. Herbert Arnold. Cambridge: Harvard UP, 1981.

Jellonnek, Burkhard. *Homosexuelle unter dem Hakenkreuz: Die Verfolgung von Homosexuellen im Dritten Reich.* Paderborn: Schöningh, 1990.

Kenrick, Donald, and Grattan Puxon. *Gypsies under the Swastika.* Hatfield, Eng.: U of Hertfordshire P, 1995.

Levi, Primo. "The Gray Zone." *The Drowned and the Saved.* Trans. Raymond Rosenthal. New York: Vintage, 1988. 36–69.

Lewy, Guenter. *The Nazi Persecution of the Gypsies.* Oxford: Oxford UP, 2000.

Lukas, Richard C. *The Forgotten Holocaust: The Poles under German Occupation, 1939–1944.* Lexington: UP of Kentucky, 1986. New York: Hippocrene, 1990.

———. *Out of the Inferno: Poles Remember the Holocaust.* Lexington: UP of Kentucky, 1989.

Marrus, Michael R. *The Holocaust in History.* Hanover: UP of New England, 1987.

Miller, Judith. *One by One by One: Facing the Holocaust.* New York: Simon, 1990.

Milton, Sybil. "The Context of the Holocaust." *German Studies Review* 13 (1990): 269–83.

Müller-Hill, Benno. *Murderous Science: Elimination by Scientific Selection of Jews, Gypsies, and Others in Germany, 1933–1945.* Trans. George R. Fraser. Plainview: Cold Spring Harbor Laboratory, 1998.

Musial, Bogdan. *Kontorrevolutionäre Elemente sind zu erschiessen.* Berlin: Propyläen, 2000.

Naimark, Norman. *Fires of Hatred: Ethnic Cleansing in Twentieth-Century Europe.* Cambridge: Harvard UP, 2001.

Noakes, Jeremy, and Geoffrey Pridham, eds. *Foreign Policy, War and Racial Extermination.* Exeter, Eng.: U of Exeter P, 1988. Vol. 3 of *Nazism 1919–1945: A Documentary Reader.*

Phayer, Michael. *The Catholic Church and the Holocaust, 1930–1965.* Bloomington: Indiana UP, 2000.

Poliakov, Léon. *Harvest of Hate: The Nazi Program for the Destruction of the Jews of Europe.* New York: Holocaust Lib., 1979.

Scholder, Klaus. *The Churches and the Third Reich.* Vol. 1. Trans. John Bowden. Philadelphia: Fortress, 1988.

Sereny, Gitta. *Into That Darkness: An Examination of Conscience.* New York: Vintage, 1983.

Steininger, Rolf, ed. *Vergessene Opfer des Nationalsozialismus.* Innsbruck: Studien, 2000.

Streit, Christian. *Keine Kameraden: Die Wehrmacht und die sowjetischen Kriegsgefangenen, 1941–1945.* Stuttgart: Deutsche, 1978.

Vernichtungskrieg: Verbrechen der Wehrmacht, 1941–1944. Ed. Hannes Heer and Klaus Naumann. Hamburg: Hamburger Institut für Sozialforschung, 1995. Catalog published in conjunction with the exhibition *Vernichtungskrieg: Verbrechen der Wehrmacht 1941 bis 1944.*

Watchtower Society. *Jehovah's Witnesses Stand Firm against Nazi Assault.* 1995.

Weinberg, Gerhard L. "Comments on the Papers by Friedlander, Breitman, and Browning." *German Studies Review* 18 (1994): 509–12.

———. "The 'Final Solution' and the War in 1943." Weinberg, *Germany* 217–44.

———. *Germany, Hitler, and World War II: Essays in Modern German and World History.* New York: Cambridge UP, 1995.

———. *A World at Arms: A Global History of World War II.* New York: Cambridge UP, 1994.

———. "The World through Hitler's Eyes." Weinberg, *Germany* 32–35.

Weitz, Eric D. *A Century of Genocide: Utopias of Race and Nation.* Princeton: Princeton UP, 2003.

Wistrich, Robert S. *Hitler and the Holocaust.* New York: Modern Lib., 2001.

Yahil, Leni. *The Holocaust: The Fate of European Jewry.* Trans. Ina Friedman and Haya Galai. New York: Oxford UP, 1990.

Zimmermann, Michael. *Rassenutopie und Genozid: Die nationalsozialistische "Lösung der Zigeunerfrage."* Hamburg: Christians, 1996.

Sidra DeKoven Ezrahi

Questions of Authenticity

The vast imaginative literature that has emerged after and in the shadow of the Holocaust can be surveyed through different lenses, yielding mutually exclusive clusters of meaning and languages of representation. Each of these lenses profoundly reflects and affects the way we come to understand the interaction of history and the imagination. When we review this literature more than fifty years after the liberation of the camps, we are inevitably, then, endorsing or challenging critical and theoretical positions that should be elucidated along with the texts under consideration. This essay attempts to present the major approaches or typologies that have evolved in studies of Holocaust literature, each based on a different epistemology, aesthetics, and ethics and each promoting, in turn, a different cultural canon based on claims of authenticity.

The fading chorus of witnesses and survivors of the Holocaust produces a sense of the urgency of the testimonial mission in those who remain, along with a persistent ambivalence about the role of the imagination. The magnitude of the devastation and the dissemination of modern culture through the mass media have contributed to the widespread fear of simulation, of the appropriation of what is perceived as unique and unduplicatable, and have generated a kind of proprietary attitude on the part of those who assume the role of guardians of collective memory. This posture, designating the boundaries and venues of *le droit de parole*, challenges the usual freedoms attached to artistic representation. Literary texts, like sculptures or monuments, once introduced into ritual, consensual space, alter significantly to conform to the dimensions of that space. Paul Celan's "Todesfuge," written at the war's end in Romania, was eventually co-opted into the commemorative calendar and pedagogical agenda in West Germany and became perhaps the most widely recited and performed poem in postwar Europe. Dan Pagis's six-line Hebrew poem "Written in Pencil in the Sealed Railway-Car," which poses as the artifact of a desperate act of communication at the edge of oblivion, was in fact written in Israel some twenty years after the liberation of the camps. This instance of a mercifully dynamic relation between history's inexorability and poetry's freedom was frozen when the poem was recruited into memorial space—as words chiseled in stone beside the actual artifact of a boxcar at Yad Vashem, the Holocaust Martyrs' and Heroes' Remembrance Authority in Jerusalem. Such poems serve all rememberers by relinquishing their subversive potential and participating in the ritual of assent that sustains the social order after a major upheaval. The close but adversarial proximity between commemorative occasions and artistic productions, or between artifacts and art, with the performing arts, monuments, and museums forming a bridge between them, reveals some of the tensions between consensual protectionism of the past and the marketplace of free exchange between past and present.

A persistent claim in representations of the Holocaust is that since those who died in the gas chambers cannot speak, every voice is a presumption, an approximation, of the speech that could not issue from that ultimate place. The voices that have been heard are measured, then, by degrees of access, by the privileged status of the witness or the act of witnessing and by relative claims to authenticity and artistic license. Such a presumption is most explicitly endorsed in Claude Lanzmann's nine-hour film *Shoah*: the Holocaust or Shoah was enacted (and thus can only be reenacted) in its ultimate form in the crematorium. Every aspect of the persecution of the Jews during World War II is located as a station along a track heading straight for the center of what French writer David Rousset called, in the immediate postwar period, "l'univers concentrationnaire."

The positions explored below are determined by the perception that the concentrationary universe indeed consists of concentric circles, of which the gas chamber was the center or black hole, that to be in Drancy was to be on the way to Auschwitz. Conversely, to have spent the war years as a fugitive in the forests or among peasants, as did Aharon Appelfeld or Ida Fink, was to have inhabited the outer circles of that universe. By this logic, multiple points of reference or departure are not equally valid but rather mark degrees of separation from the "Event" itself (Ezrahi, "Representing"). Although understandable as an immediate reflex, over time the seductions of this position take on the weight of an ethical imperative, with serious consequences for the future of the imaginative enterprise. All challenges to this imperative involve boundary crossing and the risk of being judged inauthentic or mendacious. While mapping out the parameters of authenticity, this essay argues, finally, that it is precisely in the dangerous territory beyond those parameters where an alternative ethical discourse is evolving that responds more adequately and democratically to the challenges of our time and place.

Illo tempore: Authentic Times and Places

What might be described as the most fundamentalist or absolutist approach to Holocaust representation validates only writing produced in the ghettos and camps themselves, claiming that their testimonial value adheres exclusively to that time and place; anything written after the war, even by the same author, who is now no longer a victim but a survivor, is but a shadow of the authentic object. Such an approach, which eliminates the distance between the "man who suffers and the mind which creates" (Eliot 54) and elevates art produced in ghettos and camps to a kind of artifactual status, grants more validity to Yiddish poems written by Avraham Sutzkever in the

Vilna Ghetto than to the same poems revised or to other poems written on the same subject by the same poet but after the war (see Sheintuch, esp. the introduction). Itzhak Katzenelson—who wrote the Yiddish poem cycle known as the "Song of the Murdered Jewish People" out of his sufferings and observations in the Warsaw Ghetto, then buried the manuscript in the transit camp at Vittel and perished in Auschwitz—was regarded throughout war-torn Europe as the one who immortalized the agony and the struggle of his fellow Jews. "All that we thought, felt, or imagined, he wrote about," the resistance leader Mordecai Tenenbaum admitted in a letter from the Bialystok Ghetto to his sister in Palestine after Katzenelson's death. "We furnished him with the debris of our misery, and he made it eternal, sang of it, it was our common property" (qtd. in Poliakov 232–33). Shortly before he disappeared into the oblivion of the death camp, David Fogel, the restless Hebrew poet who had traversed much of Eastern and Central Europe, stopped time to write, "The winds of devastation will blow through the world / And I was here for one more moment" (261; trans. mine).

The most authentic text of all, by this strictest of measures, would be the last poems of the Hungarian Jewish poet Miklós Radnóti, who died at the age of thirty-three in a long forced march at the war's end. Ten poems were discovered in his trench-coat pocket when his body was exhumed from its mass grave more than a year after the liberation of Hungary; their claim to credibility is as both an articulation and an artifact of a culture's demise.[1] Worth noting and often overlooked is that everything in the last blood-stained verses, including their classical form, is a protest against the poet's absurd fate:

> Crazy. He stumbles, flops, gets up,   and trudges on again.
> He moves his ankles and his knees   like one wandering pain,
> Then sallies forth, as if a wing   lifted him where he went,
> And when the ditch invites him in   he dare not give consent;
> And if you were to ask why not?   Perhaps his answer is
> A woman waits, a death more wise, more beautiful than this . . .[2]

The cultural activities—poetry and drawing contests in such places as the ghettos of Vilna, Lodz, and Theresienstadt and literary publications in occupied Warsaw and elsewhere—provided the unlikely laboratory for many of the manuscripts and drawings that have survived. So highly valued were such activities that, in a daring and nearly unprecedented rescue mission, Sutzkever, who won the Vilna Ghetto Prize for his poem "The Grave Child," was airlifted to safety in the Soviet Union from the forests to which he had escaped with the partisans.

Tadeusz Borowski, a Polish survivor of both Auschwitz and Dachau, who wrote his stories in a DP camp in Munich immediately after liberation (and who took his own life six years later), exhibits the kind of proximity in both the circumstances and the substance of his writing that would qualify him as the closest postwar reflection of "that" place.

Ad Hominem: Authentic Selves

Parallel to the hierarchy of authority ascribed to temporal and physical proximity is the hierarchy of persons: this logic dictates that the literature written after the war by survivors themselves, or even by their children, carries an authority not shared by those who were not there. Primo Levi's Italian memoir *Survival in Auschwitz* and Jorge Semprun's French novel *The Long Voyage*, the first written immediately and the second sixteen years after the writer's liberation, bear the mark of personal authenticity, like the tattooed numbers on the arm of an aging survivor. Although there is an implicit distinction made by many readers between Jewish and non-Jewish victims, non-Jewish writers like Borowski or Semprun speak from the authority conferred on them by their years of incarceration in the camps and also, strangely, by the freedom conferred on them by their having in some sense chosen their fate as political prisoners instead of having been chosen by fate, as the Jews were.

Such ad hominem authority determines the degree of poetic license granted to or withheld from certain writers. The credibility Levi gained with his memoir of Auschwitz extended to such subsequent flights of fiction as *The Periodic Table*. The autobiographical quality of Semprun's *The Long Voyage* camouflaged its experimental form as a Proustian narrative unfolding in the confines of a boxcar hurtling toward the concentration camp but suspended in a kind of memory time and space. The postwar expressionist Hebrew poetry of Abba Kovner was treated in Israel with the reverence, if not widespread comprehension, that accrued to him as a leader of the partisans, as one who not only had been incarcerated in but also had fought his way out of the Vilna Ghetto.

Art Spiegelman, with the authority of his status as a son of survivors, challenged consensual boundaries of both language and subject. The daring representation of the Jewish victims and survivors as mice and the Nazis as cats in his cartoon narratives *Maus I* and *Maus II* and his violation of certain ethical proprieties in speaking boldly of pathological behavior in families of survivors—proprieties that had remained largely inviolable outside the professional therapeutic community—were liberties (grudgingly) granted him as a member of the family.

Such credibility may extend even to the most audacious counternarratives: Jurek Becker, a child survivor of the Lodz Ghetto who came of age in postwar East Germany, wrote a novel and film, *Jacob the Liar* (*Jakob der Lügner* [1969]), based on the invention of a reality more palatable than the one engulfing the Jews under the sign of the swastika. The outside world is filtered into the ghetto through the imaginary radio of Jacob Heym, who counters the growing despair among his fellow inmates by inventing good news. The entire narrative is premised on the epistemological as well as the aesthetic and moral assumption that the deeds of the Nazis, in the universe of the ghettos and camps, are not really "indexible"—and that they can therefore be effaced by an act of will. Based on his overhearing an actual news report on the position of a division of Russian troops, Jacob weaves a fantasy of military progress that brings the Allied forces to within a few kilometers of the ghetto. At the moment in the story when such developments should have brought about the liberation of the ghetto, the order appears in real time for the liquidation of the ghetto and the deportation of all its Jews. One of the first in a series of counternarratives of the Holocaust, this novel, like any survivor narrative, must nevertheless yield to the inexorable historical force that finally defeated all its victims. The enabling fiction is ultimately rescinded, and the Jews are consigned to their actual fate. The last scene takes place in a cattle car.

By contrast, a writer like D. M. Thomas, who as a Welsh poet and novelist is ethnically, culturally, and experientially far removed from the events that he represents, takes liberties even with this last historical imperative. In the final chapter of his English novel *The White Hotel*, he resurrects his heroine, who has died in the mass pit at Babi Yar, exercising a divine prerogative that no survivor has invoked. The critical controversy over this novel focused on Thomas's questionable use of documentary sources, but at the heart of such controversies is a public withholding of poetic license for radically revisionist modes of representation from those writers not perceived as being authentically connected to the events represented.

Thomas's novel became one of the test cases of the limits of poetic license—or what Saul Friedländer called the "limits of representation." Where an artistic representation is explicitly counter-historical, as in the final section of Thomas's novel or the entire of Becker's narrative, it presents an opportunity for fruitful discussion about the ethical and aesthetic dimensions of the literary imagination as repository of a world that might (should) have been. This subjunctive role of the imagination became a focus of popular and critical debate in the 1990s in response to such films as Roberto Benigni's *Life Is Beautiful* (*La vita è bella* [1998]; see the screenplay by Benigni and Cerami)—defined with the opening credits as a "fable" (*favola*)—and Radu Mihaileanu's *Train of Life* (*Train de vie* [1998]; see Ezrahi, "After Such Knowledge").

Where falsification is not an explicit premise of the text but rather an act of deception, critical debate centers on forgery, denial, and arrogation of the dubious privilege of having been there. An enthusiastic readership at first conferred on and then rescinded validation from Binjamin Wilkomirski's narrative *Fragments*.[3] When it was assumed, as advertised, that Wilkomirski had survived the most horrendous atrocities as an infant and preverbal toddler in Maidenek and Auschwitz-Birkenau, his disjunctive narrative was hailed as a breakthrough in representation of the fragmented nature of recovered memory. After it was discovered that his identity was forged—or, to put a more generous spin on it, that his pathology had found an objective correlative in the life of an incarcerated Jew — many readers remained at a loss as to how to evaluate the nature of the enterprise. Some of those who wanted to rescue the text as an innovation in the language of representation attempted to redefine the memoir as a novel, as if the novel form were a trash can of failed historical records or fabricated autobiographical accounts. The discussions around this issue are especially instructive, since they define the different stages and shifting boundaries of the search for a language adequate to cataclysmic experience.

Textual Authority

This brings us to that realm of putative authenticity that inheres not in time, place, or persons but in genres and in generic claims for access to or distance from the "Event" itself. Documentary or pseudo-documentary literature has the appeal of authenticity, even when it takes significant liberties with the facts. The German playwright Peter Weiss, in his documentary drama *The Investigation*, constructed a patchwork of quotations from the protocols of the trials of the perpetrators of Auschwitz held in Frankfurt from 1963 to 1965. The credibility of this play, based on its documentary evidence and on the structure of the courtroom procedure itself, may have shielded Weiss in certain quarters from criticism for his Marxist approach to the concentrationary system. The documentary guise allowed him to launch a major assault on every concept of chosenness or uniqueness. "I see Auschwitz as a scientific instrument that could have been used by anyone to exterminate anyone," said Weiss, who was himself half German and half Jewish. "For that matter, given a different deal, the Jews could have been on the side of the Nazis. They could have been the exterminators. *The Investigation* is a universal human problem" (qtd. in Clausen). In the 1980s, the Israeli playwright Yehoshua Sobol explored that avenue even further; through a re-creation of life in the Vilna Ghetto, he combined the validating languages of memory and document in a performative context that addressed moral challenges of power and chosenness in contemporary Israel.[4]

The fictional language that most closely approximates the object represented is a kind of "concentrationary realism" (Ezrahi, *By Words* 49). The short fictions of Borowski, written directly after the war, are enacted in a suspended present tense that allows no egress into past or future, into the realm of dream, memory, or metaphor. Borowski's suicide in 1951 is often read back into his work as a kind of inexorable closure to a life formed in and defined by Auschwitz. Although the "hermeneutics of suicide" is commonly and indiscriminately performed on survivor-writers who take their own lives, including Celan and Levi, it may be more justified in the case of Borowski: the world of his (re)invention is so hermetically sealed under the sign of the swastika, so deterministic, that memory becomes a mythical force that precludes the possibility of any life beyond, before, or after. The fictions of the Hebrew novelist Aharon Appelfeld, written at great distance in time and place from the events that shaped them, remain trapped in the same eternal present; even the act of writing itself does not provide an alternative center of gravity (see Bernstein 58).

Interpretive Communities: Beyond Authenticity

The critical approach that insists on confining authenticity to any one space — physical, temporal, personal, generic — and withholds validation from all nonauthentic supplicants can be expanded *ad absurdum*. Its rigid application as criterion for judging fictitious texts exposes the eccentricities and dangers of such an exclusive principle. In the first part of David Grossman's Hebrew novel *See Under: Love*, Momik, the nine-year-old protagonist and center of consciousness, claims an authority as the child of survivors that his Israeli author cannot. Momik's notebook, a desperate attempt to construct the story of his parents' untold lives "Over There" (50), becomes a kind of document to which the novel itself is a commentary. The remaining three sections of the novel are flights of fancy that can derive their authority only from Momik's obsessive efforts at documentation. Some of the absolutists who embraced the novel embraced Momik, others embraced Grossman himself, as putatively a child of survivors; still others condemned Grossman for defying the limits of representation, because he was *not* a child of survivors.

To understand fully the nature and impact of Grossman's transgressive writing, we must go beyond authenticity and proximity as touchstones of representation. What is astounding, and ultimately liberating, is that where it is not authenticity but a different kind of truth claim that structures the imagination, more traditional forms of storytelling and more conventional literary tropes become available again. In different interpretive communities, the search for a unique language adequate to unprecedented experience has yielded to a search for recovery of artistic conventions as a way to restore social order in the wake of cataclysm and to reclaim a purchase on the future that is continuous with the pretraumatic past. The survivability of the self, based on the simple narrative principle of chronology, or of the group, based on Jewish theodicy or romantic reflex, provides a safe haven for deep memory and an alternative point of departure and return for specific memories. The primary reference in such texts is to an Edenic, inviolable past, personal or collective. Much of the literature of survivors—from Ilona Karmel in English to Ida Fink in Polish to Ladislav Fuks in Czech—and much of the literature informed by what has been loosely associated with the midrashic imagination—from Elie Wiesel in French to Isaac Bashevis Singer in Yiddish—can be explored under the rubric of some grand narrative of survival. In such a narrative, there is even room for the comic, if by comic we understand the world as it should be; "when the world is a world again," in Karmel's phrase (350), the world as seen from that always elusive star of redemption.

A refamiliarization with or reversion to cultural languages and local landscapes is one sign of a struggle that is no longer based in or resolved by questions of authenticity and exclusivity. Ironically, an imaginative approach to the historical material that takes account of our increasing distance from it and becomes less focused on the representation of the events themselves and more on the work of memory, mourning, and reconstruction in different interpretive communities is, though culturally more local, also more amenable to universal ethical legacies.

The passage of time is a dimension of this enterprise. In the early years after the war, the survivors constituted a remnant scattered over the globe, whether writing in their native tongue in exile or in the language of their adoptive country: Celan writing in German in Paris; Sutzkever writing in Yiddish, Fink in Polish, Pagis and Appelfeld in Hebrew in Israel; Wiesel writing in French and Karmel in English in the United States. (The egregious exception was Primo Levi, who returned to his native Turin after the war to reconnect with Italian, his mother tongue — and with his mother — a privilege hardly any of his fellow survivors enjoyed.)

In one generation, however, specific cultural agendas began to define the representation of the past in each of the communities most affected. Israel, Germany (before and after unification), and the countries of the former Soviet Union provide the most dramatic examples of the shift from a concern for authenticity to an explicit encounter with the past in terms of the present. In the process, the Holocaust leaves the realm of inexplicable historical event that can only be witnessed to to become a paradigm or ultimate reference for postwar aesthetics and ethics.

It is striking that in both Israel and Germany and for very different reasons, what replaced authenticity as the touchstone of Holocaust representation was its very antithesis: empathetic projection. In Israel, the enterprise of collective rehabilitation and recovery of repressed memories gave way during the last decades of the twentieth century to a multivalent, often brutally honest, examination of the unhealed trauma of mass victimization for an embattled society. In its most radical form, memory was projected onto the Palestinian-Israeli battlefield through empathic acts of impersonation and self-indictment (Ezrahi, "Representing" and "Acts of Impersonation").[5] In Germany, the *Vergangenheitsbewältigung* ("coming to terms with the past") involved layers and generations of encounter with the Nazi legacy and a reparational revisiting of the past on the part of the children and grandchildren of perpetrators (see Santner).

Much has been written on the reflections of the Holocaust in Israeli and German societies. It is in countries of the former Soviet Union, that area of the postwar world that had been hidden from the Western gaze, where we can now get a glimpse of the dynamic nature of an "unfettered" relation with the past. Under the thaw of the 1990s, Eastern European writers, poets, and filmmakers undertook to reclaim their landscape from the ruins of a thousand-year-old Jewish civilization, the scars of a twelve-year German Reich and the erasures of postwar Communist regimes.

This development is the more remarkable given the sense of apocalyptic despair and abject suffering expressed by writers in the late 1940s and 1950s in the Eastern European countries most directly affected by the ravages of the Holocaust. The survivor-writer Adolf Rudnicki came to the West from Poland less than a decade after the war and described himself as "l'homme des ruines" ("man of ruins") living in an "époque des fours" ("era of crematoria") (307, 326, 734; see Rawicz). His non-Jewish compatriot Tadeusz Różewicz expressed disbelief that "poetry had survived the end of the world as though nothing had happened" and identified his own writing as a poetry of "salvaged words . . . uninteresting words . . . from the great rubbish dump, the great cemetery" (qtd. in Hamburger 247).

Some thirty years later, the Hungarian Jewish novelist Imre Kertész and the Romanian Jewish writer Norman Manea, who had spent their childhood in the ghettos, camps, and forests and their young adulthood under Communist regimes that camouflaged those places under the rubric of "the war," began to revisit the same sites through the lens of a hard-won personal and political freedom. Through that lens the Holocaust becomes, in Kertész's words, a "global experience" and the Jews living in its aftermath the bearers of "an ethical task": "consciousness based on the ethics of cognition" (176).

One of the most striking examples of empathetic revisitation as an act of revisionism is found in the Polish writer Jaroslaw Rymkiewicz's *The Final Station: Umschlagplatz*. Rymkiewicz places the Umschlagplatz—that area of the Warsaw Ghetto where the Jews were gathered for deportation to the concentration and death camps—at the center of a search for an alternative geography on which to build a Polish future. Weaving fiction and documentary into a novel-memoir, this writer interrogates the lives of those who lived through that awful time as well as those who live after—and might have lived differently:

It is on *Umschlagplatz* that the history of Polish Jews came to an end, was arrested and seemingly terminated. There are few such places on this planet. . . . We who live in its immediate vicinity, in the very heart of Warsaw, ought to reflect on what it means for us, not in terms of the past, but in terms of our own reaction to what once happened there. . . . I am chiefly interested in the future. What does *Umschlagplatz* signify in Polish life and Polish spirituality, and what does it portend for posterity? We live within the orbit of their death. That is why I needed a plan of *Umschlagplatz*. (3, 7–8)

The generation that came of age in the 1980s began to re-create new-old languages and ethics of representation; in each of these cultures, artists working in the visual, literary, and performative media began to localize memory in sites that form alternatives to Auschwitz and to the notion of a predetermined universe of concentric circles with a black hole at its center.

———

Those who view the receding past on an inexorable track leading back to the crematorium; who travel into the future with their stony faces turned toward Auschwitz; who insist on preserving the unique memory of that place as a moment frozen in time, space, and persons have created a culture of the unsayable, the elusive, the inscrutable, and the immutable. Authenticity and authority are strictly safeguarded, and Auschwitz is the sole determinant and ultimate extinguisher of meaning. For those who seek alternative sites, alternative histories, and alternative moral discourses in local landscapes, Auschwitz becomes dynamically and diversely representable and authorizes the infinite horizons of a post-Holocaust universe.

Notes

1. For a perfect simulation of the artifact and its authenticating power, see Pagis. For a consideration of the revived interest in the place of things or objects and the material world as antidote to a theory-laden perspective on culture, see Brown.
2. "Forced March" is translated and discussed by Ozsvath (211–12).

3. For early overviews of the book, its author, and its reception, see Gourevitch; Lappin. Probably the most extensive work has been done by Stefan Maechler. In "Wilkomirski the Victim," he probes the implications of this controversy for memory and its social conventions. He updates his findings in *The Wilkomirski Affair*. On the subject of authenticity and narrative avenues of memory, see also Suleiman. The line between impersonation and imposture remains a thin one; multiple acts of impersonation and self-invention characterize the writing and personae of Jerzy Kosinski and Jakov Lind and have also generated heated controversy. See Ezrahi, *By Words Alone* 152–61; Sloan; Hammel et al. On the related subject of camouflage and its impact on the work and self-representation of hidden children, see Ezrahi, "See under: 'Memory.'"

4. Sobol's trilogy, *Ghetto, Adam, and Ba-martef* (In the Cellar), was produced between 1984 and 1990. For a parallel meditation on the banality of evil in the American context, see Arthur Miller's *Incident at Vichy*.

5. Yehoshua Sobol and David Grossman are in the vanguard of two generations of writers, poets, playwrights, and filmmakers who are invoking the Holocaust as a platform for an ongoing struggle with memory and conscience in contemporary Israel. Pagis can be said to have been one of the first and most daring articulators of a poetics of empathy.

Works Cited

Becker, Jurek. *Jacob the Liar*. Trans. Leila Vennewitz. New York: Plume, 1999.

Benigni, Roberto. *Life Is Beautiful* [*La vita è bella*]. 1998. DVD. Miramax, 2002.

Benigni, Roberto, and Vincenzo Cerami. Life Is Beautiful: *A Screenplay*. Trans. Lisa Taruschio. New York: Hyperion, 1998.

Bernstein, Michael André. *Foregone Conclusions: Against Apocalyptic History*. Berkeley: U of California P, 1994.

Borowski, Tadeusz. *This Way for the Gas, Ladies and Gentlemen*. Trans. Barbara Vedder. New York: Viking, 1967.

Brown, Bill. "Thing Theory." *Critical Inquiry* 28 (2001): 1–22.

Celan, Paul. "Todesfuge." 1952. Trans. John Felstiner. *Paul Celan: Poet, Survivor, Jew*. By Felstiner. New Haven: Yale UP, 1995. 31–32. *"Die Todesfuge." Eine multimediale Annäherung*. 18 Mar. 2004 <http://www.celan-projekt.de/>.

Clausen, Oliver. "Weiss/Propagandist and Weiss/Playwright." *New York Times Magazine* 2 Oct. 1966: 132.

Eliot, T. S. "Tradition and the Individual Talent." *The Sacred Wood: Essays on Poetry and Criticism*. 1920. Bartleby.com Great Books Online. 16 Aug. 2004 <http://www.bartleby.com/200/>.

Ezrahi, Sidra DeKoven. "Acts of Impersonation: Barbaric Space as Theatre."

Mirroring Evil: Nazi Imagery / Recent Art. Ed. Norman Kleeblatt. Exhibition catalog. New Brunswick: Rutgers UP; Jewish Museum, 2001. 17–38.

———. "After Such Knowledge, What Laughter?" *Yale Journal of Criticism* 14.1 (2001): 287–313.

———. *By Words Alone: The Holocaust in Literature.* Chicago: U of Chicago P, 1980.

———. "Representing Auschwitz." *History and Memory* 7.2 (1996–97): 120–53.

———. "See under: 'Memory': Reflections on Saul Friedlander's *When Memory Comes.*" *History and Memory* 9.1–2 (1996): 364–75.

Fink, Ida. *"A Scrap of Time" and Other Stories.* Trans. Madeline Levine and Francine Prose. New York: Schocken, 1987.

Fogel, David. *Kol ha-shirim* [Collected Poems]. Ed. Dan Pagis. Ha-kibbutz ha-me'uhad, 1975.

Friedländer, Saul, ed. *Probing the Limits of Representation: Nazism and the "Final Solution."* Cambridge: Harvard UP, 1992.

Fuks, Ladislav. *Mr Theodore Mundstock.* Trans. Iris Urwin. London: Cape, 1969.

Gourevitch, Philip. "The Memory Thief." *New Yorker* 14 June 1999: 48–68.

Grossman, David. *See Under: Love.* Trans. Betsy Rosenberg. New York: Farrar, 1989.

Hamburger, Michael. *The Truth of Poetry: Tensions in Modern Poetry from Baudelaire to the 1960s.* New York: Harcourt, 1969.

Hammel, Andrea, Silke Hassler, and Edmond Timms, eds. *Writing after Hitler: The Work of Jakov Lind.* Cardiff: U of Wales P, 2001.

Karmel, Ilona. *An Estate of Memory.* Boston: Houghton, 1969.

Kertész, Imre, "Long, Dark Shadow." *Contemporary Jewish Writing in Hungary: An Anthology.* Ed. Susan Rubin Suleiman and Éva Forgácz. Lincoln: U of Nebraska P, 2003. 171–80.

Kovner, Abba. *A Canopy in the Desert: Selected Poems.* Trans. Shirley Kaufman. Pittsburgh: U of Pittsburgh P, 1973.

———. *"My Little Sister" and Selected Poems.* Trans. Shirley Kaufman. Oberlin: Oberlin Coll. P, 1986.

Lanzmann, Claude. *Shoah: An Oral History of the Holocaust: Complete Text of the Film.* Pref. Simone de Beauvoir. New York: Pantheon, 1985.

Lappin, Elena. "The Man with Two Heads," *Granta* 66 (1999): 9–65.

Levi, Primo. *The Periodic Table.* Trans. Raymond Rosenthal. New York: Schocken, 1984.

———. *Survival in Auschwitz.* Trans. Stuart Woolf. New York: Collier, 1959.

Maechler, Stefan. *The Wilkomirski Affair: A Study in Biographical Truth.* Trans. John E. Woods. New York: Random, 2001.

———. "Wilkomirski the Victim: Individual Remembering as Social Interaction and Public Event." *History and Memory* 13.2 (2001): 59–95.

Mihaileaunu, Radu. *Train of Life*. Paramount Classics, 1999.

Miller, Arthur. *Incident at Vichy*. New York: Viking, 1965.

Ozsvath, Zsuzsanna. *In the Footsteps of Orpheus: The Life and Times of Miklós Radnóti*. Bloomington: Indiana UP, 2000.

Pagis, Dan. "Katuv be-iparon ba-karon he-hatum" [Written in Pencil in the Sealed Railway-Car]. *Points of Departure*. Trans. Stephen Mitchell. Philadelphia: Jewish Publication Soc., 1981. 23.

Poliakov, Léon. *Harvest of Hate*. London: Elek, 1956.

Rawicz, Piotr. "Adolf Rudnicki et 'Les Fenêtres d'or.'" *Le Monde* 18 June 1966: 11.

Rousset, David. *L'univers concentrationnaire*. 1945. Paris: Minuit, 1981. Trans. as *The Other Kingdom*. Trans. Ramon Guthrie. New York: Reynal, 1947.

Rudnicki, Adolf. "Voyage en Occident." *Les temps modernes* 14.150–51 (1985): 307+.

Rymkiewicz, Jaroslaw M. *The Final Station: Umschlagplatz*. Trans. Nina Taylor. New York: Farrar, 1994.

Santner, Eric. *Stranded Objects: Mourning, Memory, and Film in Postwar Germany*. Ithaca: Cornell UP, 1990.

Semprun, Jorge. *The Long Voyage*. Trans. Richard Seaver. New York: Grove, 1964.

Sheintuch, Yehiel. *Yeshayahu Spiegel: Proza sifrutit mi-getto lodj* [Isaiah Spiegel: Literary Prose from the Lodz Ghetto]. Jerusalem: Magnes, 1995.

Shoah. Dir. Claude Lanzmann. Aleph-Historia, 1985. Videocassette. New Yorker Films, 2004.

Sloan, James Park. *Jerzy Kosinski: A Biography*. New York: Dutton, 1996.

Sobol, Yehoshua, *The Trilogy* Ghetto, Adam *and* Ba-martef [Ghetto, Adam, *and* In the Cellar], produced between 1984 and 1990.

Spiegelman, Art. *And Here My Troubles Began*. New York: Pantheon, 1991. Vol. 2 of *Maus: A Survivor's Tale*.

———. *My Father Bleeds History*. New York: Pantheon, 1986. Vol. 1 of *Maus: A Survivor's Tale*.

Suleiman, Susan. "Problems of Memory in Recent Holocaust Memoirs." *Poetics Today* 21 (2000): 543–59.

Sutzkever, Avraham. "The Grave Child." Fragment. *Abraham Sutzkever*. Trans. Joseph Leftwich. New York: Yoseloff, 1971. 73–80.

Thomas, D. M. *The White Hotel*. Harmondsworth: Penguin, 1993.

Weiss, Peter. *The Investigation*. Trans. Jon Swan and Ulu Grosbard. New York: Atheneum, 1966.

Wilkomirski, Binjamin. *Fragments: Memories of a Childhood, 1939–1948*. Trans. Carol Brown Janeway. New York: Schocken, 1996.

Froma I. Zeitlin

Teaching about Perpetrators

Nonchalantly the officer approached me, beating a swagger stick against the seam of his freshly pressed breeches. The instant I saw him I could not tear my gaze from him. His entire person seemed to have something utterly super-human about it. Against the background of bland colors he projected an unfadable blackness. In a world of men with harrowed faces, with smashed eyes, bloody, bruised and disfigured limbs, among the fetid, broken human bodies, he seemed an example of neat perfection that could not be sullied: the smooth, polished skin of his face, the bright golden hair showing under his peaked cap, his pure metal eyes. Every movement of his body seemed propelled by some tremendous internal force. The granite sound of his language was ideally suited to order the death of inferior, forlorn creatures. I was stung by a twinge of envy I had never experienced before, and I admired the glittering death's head and crossbones that embellished his tall cap. I thought how good it would be to have such a gleaming and hairless skull instead of my Gypsy face which was feared and disliked by decent people. (Kosinski 113–14)

Thus does the child narrator of Jerzy Kosinski's *Painted Bird* describe his first glimpse of an SS officer in a remote area of southeastern Poland. In a few sentences, Kosinski manages to sum up the essence of both terror and, yes, glamour of Nazi ideology as embodied in this all too familiar image, bequeathed to us by the propaganda of the Third Reich and perpetuated in the storehouse of our collective memory. In the eyes of this already brutalized dark-haired child, struggling to make sense of the inhospitable world that threatens him at every turn, this towering figure of seemingly superhuman strength, made of metal and granite, whose appearance spells mastery and death, is living proof of the existence of a "master race" and its right to dominate and destroy those others who by definition as radical others are deemed unworthy of life. For us, this figure evokes a panoply of familiar stereotypes: black-and-red Nazi banners flaunting the sinister swastika, goose-stepping soldiers in precise formation, torchlight parades with a multitude of arms raised in stiff salute and thousands of voices crying, "Sieg Heil." As emblems of evil incarnate, these images and symbols have lost none of their terrifying efficacy to remind us of the enormous cataclysm that followed in the wake of an apocalyptic dedication to policies of annihilation. Directed by a fanatic will to power in the grip of a national delusion of racial superiority, these policies unleashed a war of destruction that cost millions of lives and called into question the very notion of humanity, as we once knew it.

The most indelible achievement of the Third Reich was the virtual destruction of European Jewry. Nazi methods combined age-old antisemitic tactics (such as ghettos and badges with a yellow star), more conventional massacres raised to an unprecedented scale (e.g., by mass shootings), and technological inventiveness that industrialized death (gas chambers) and reduced the remains of human beings (hair, teeth, bone) to utilitarian products. Above all was the systematic dehumanization of the victims with terrible cruelty, long before they reached the killing fields or the gates of the death camps.

How then can any course that focuses on the Holocaust, whatever the context or field of study, not confront the issue of the perpetrators? They are the core, after all, of the entire catastrophe. Who invented the system of extermination of an entire group of people, labeled and defined only in terms of race? Who carried out such unspeakable atrocities? What were their motivations? What sustained them? To address this problem at any level is to walk a tightrope between two unsatisfactory extremes: demonizing the perpetrators as the embodiment of absolute evil, on the one hand, and, on the other, insisting on the existence of "the little Nazi" in all of us. Were these monsters, or were they normal human beings capable, as we know, of being loving spouses and parents, writing tender letters home, while at the same time torturing, gassing, shooting, and more generally creating a world of such inverted values that even those who endured it often recall it in disbelief? Could indoctrination into Nazi ideology account for the abdication of moral responsibility in the mobilization and execution of such acts of savagery by apparently ordinary people?

The first time I taught a Holocaust course more than fifteen years ago in a department of comparative literature — one that included diaries, memoirs, oral testimony, fiction, poetry, visual images, and film — I instinctively made a place for the perpetrators. To my mind it was essential at some point to confront them face-to-face, as it were, and even to examine their point of view. It was not enough merely to label them evil and depraved, or even insane, as some have insisted. This effort to mystify genocidal desire, thus situating these extremes of evildoing outside the boundaries of our mental universe, would be too easy. Nor was I willing to step outside history to claim that anyone, including ourselves, could have followed such a path. Like Inga Clendinnen, writing so many years after the Holocaust, I felt it essential to try and "dispel the 'Gorgon effect' — the sickening of imagination and curiosity . . . which afflicts so many of us when we try to look squarely at the persons and processes implicated in the Holocaust." Like her, I wanted my students to try and "arrive at a clearer understanding [or experience] of at least some of those persons and processes" (4), even if our approach was not historical as such but focused broadly on issues of representation. At the same time, it would be impossible to overlook the power of the Nazi image, as Kosinski describes it, in the popular consciousness and the uses and abuses of that image over time.

My strategies for looking at the perpetrators are discussed in greater detail below. I consider significant Nazi documents; important individual perpetrators, one (Adolf Eichmann) in a documentary film of his 1961 trial, the other (Franz Stangl) in a written account; groups of perpetrators, such as the Nazi doctors particularly at Auschwitz; members of a reserve police battalion that participated in mass killings of Jews; and cinematic representations—Agnieszka Holland's *Europa, Europa* and Steven Spielberg's *Schindler's List*.

By now, one might say that a certain canon of essential texts, documents, documentary and feature films, and repertoires of images has developed, along with excellent resources on the Web. Anthologies of documents and excerpts from secondary sources are especially useful (Berenbaum; Dawidowicz; Niewyk). Recommended too is the extended discussion of the perpetrators in Clendinnen's *Reading the Holocaust*, which treats some of the same material to which I refer.

Official Nazi Documents

Heinrich Himmler's speech to the SS-Gruppenführer (major generals) at Posen, Poland, 4 October 1943, is an extraordinary document. The original speech was over three hours long. A recording as well as notes in Himmler's own hand exist. His brief comments on the extermination of the Jewish race (as well as on other undesirables) are worth reams of pages devoted to the perverse ambitions and justifications of Nazi ideology. This crime is a matter, Himmler declares, that can never be spoken of publicly. One statement in particular says it all:

> Most of you must know what it means when 100 corpses are lying side by side or 500 or 1,000. To have stuck it out and at the same time . . . to have remained decent fellows, that is what has made us hard. This is a page of glory in our history which has never been written and is never to be written. . . .[1]

The Wannsee Conference was held in a villa outside Berlin on 20 January 1942. This conference, chaired by Reinhard Heydrich,

Himmler's second in command, brought together fourteen heads of the most important government ministries, to present plans for the formal organization and implementation of "the final solution," that is, the systematic deportation of all the Jews of Europe, estimated at eleven million, to the east for extermination. It also included discussions of how to treat "persons of mixed blood" in different degrees (as first defined in the Nuremberg Laws of 1935). The minutes were recorded by Adolf Eichmann; a copy was found in the files of the German Foreign Office after the war and presented in evidence at the Nuremberg trials. Aside from the obvious documentary value of these protocols (augmented by Eichmann's later testimony), the casual enthusiasm of these cheerful bureaucrats in discussing the logistics of the SS plans, amid convivial drinking, surprised even Heydrich (see *"Final Solution"*).

A docudrama, *The Wannsee Conference* (1984), re-creates the conference in real time (87 minutes), using an ensemble of actors as the participants and the precise words of the minutes of the meeting (in German, with subtitles). Many have found this film (or excerpts thereof) an excellent classroom tool, although I have never used it.[2] The protocols themselves are available in several collections of Holocaust documents (Berenbaum 65–71). The text can also easily be found on the Web (but beware of Holocaust-denial sites).[3]

Individual Perpetrators

Far more compelling are the various documentary films based on the Eichmann trial. This was the first trial to be videotaped in its entirety, and excerpts from each day's proceedings were televised at the time. It is fair to say that a turning point in the postwar history and understanding of the Holocaust came in 1961, with the capture of Eichmann from Argentina by agents of Israel's Mossad. Brought to Israel to stand trial, by his consent, Eichmann faced judgment as the tireless bureaucrat, who orchestrated the "final solution" of European Jewry, from his first feat as organizer of the Central Office for Jewish Emigration in Vienna in August 1938 to the very end of the war, when, as chief of the Jewish Office of the Gestapo (from 1942 on), he succeeded in deporting 450,000 Hungarian Jews after his negotiations to exchange Jews for trucks (and for money) broke down. The man, described by other Nazi officials as fanatic in his compulsive obsession with the "Jewish question" and ruthlessly efficient in the organization of mass murder over which he presided, presents a very different picture at his trial. Sharp-nosed, tight-lipped, and emotionless, the "man in the glass booth" stares down the parade of witnesses and exhibitions of evidence, often with an indifferent smirk, to proclaim his innocence of "crimes against humanity" and "crimes against the Jewish people." He was a mere functionary; he was only obeying orders; he never killed anyone with his own hands. In fact, he was the victim of those higher-ups who made the policies that he was compelled to implement. His pathetic bureaucratic demeanor persuaded at least one important observer, Hannah Arendt, of the "banality of evil" in her famous book about the trial. The firestorm that followed her assessment, along with her indictment of the Jewish councils (*Judenräte*) as facilitating Nazi plans, brought to light her numerous factual errors and lack of knowledge. But the book has important merits and challenges any facile notion that the most heinous of malefactors must look and act the part. What students find most compelling when they view one or another of the documentaries is actually looking at the face of Eichmann. Motivated by a combination of curiosity and horror, students do not necessarily agree in their assessment of his performance (and hence of his character). For some, he is merely a figure of colorless mediocrity; for others, he looks like the embodiment of radical evil. The Eichmann trial, designed by Israel to instruct the world of what happened, also gives an overview of the Holocaust in all its ramifications. While the trial itself may raise further questions about the nature of justice and the legitimacy, in the eyes of some, of such proceedings, the fact that once again trials for war crimes are being held makes the Eichmann case especially relevant today.

Three major documentaries are available. These are *Witness to the Holocaust: The Trial of Adolf Eichmann* (1981); *The Specialist*, a recent and more experimental film (2000); and *The Trial of Adolf*

Eichmann, a documentary produced for PBS (1997). I recommend the PBS documentary for several reasons. An excellent Web site accompanies the film, with a wealth of supporting material (*Trial*). The film gives a historical overview of the entire genocidal enterprise from its origins to its end. Like the others, it uses footage from the original videotapes to show Eichmann, the nature of the indictments against him, and the legal issues involved. But it also gains in perspective by looking back at the trial through the eyes of some of the participants (lawyers, judges, witnesses), more than thirty-five years later. We see them in their roles at the time and see them now in their reminiscences and reflections on what transpired.

Adolf Eichmann may have been the chief official responsible for the coordination and implementation of mass extermination. He may have visited Auschwitz a few times as well as other killing sites. Indeed, he claimed in his defense that he could not be considered guilty on the ground that he was not directly involved in the day-to-day operations. Franz Stangl is an altogether different case. Starting out as a policeman from Linz in Austria, he was transferred to T4, the euthanasia project in Germany, and subsequently became commandant of two extermination camps, first of Sobibor (March–Sept. 1942) and then of Treblinka (Sept. 1942–Aug. 1943). All told, approximately 250,000 Jews died in Sobibor. For Treblinka the figures range from 750,000 to 900,000.[4] Always dressed in white riding clothes, Stangl gained a reputation as an efficient administrator and received an official commendation as the "best camp commander in Poland." Like Eichmann, he initially escaped, eventually finding refuge in South America with his family (he worked for Volkswagen in Brazil under his own name). Tracked down in 1967, he was brought back to Germany to stand trial.

If there is any single work that deserves to be read in any Holocaust course, it is Gitta Sereny's *Into That Darkness*, subtitled *An Examination of Conscience*. An English journalist of Hungarian origins, she attended Stangl's trial, and afterward, in 1970, she went to the prison where he was incarcerated and conducted a number of interviews with him. Her book is an account of these interviews, expanded further by investigative research in which she evaluates what he told her against historical records and the memory of others who had known him: his wife and friends, other perpetrators, Jewish victims. Additionally, Sereny uses Stangl's life as the point of departure for a more complex exploration of Nazi Germany, ordinary Germans (and Austrians, like Stangl), the workings of the euthanasia program and then of the death camps.[5] Against this broader background, her aim is not only to probe the mind of a seemingly innocuous man, to hear his own account of who he was and how he judged what he had done. As the subtitle of her book suggests, she also wants to bring him finally to some acknowledgment, if not of guilt, then of remorse. In this she succeeds at the end — but only to some extent.[6] As Sereny puts it at the outset, the work was

> not intended to be primarily an account of horror, though horror is unavoidable, nor is it only an effort to understand one man who was uniquely implicated in the greatest tragedy of our time. It is a demonstration of the fatal interdependence of all human actions, and an affirmation of man's responsibility for his own acts and their consequences. (15)

What especially distinguishes Sereny's journalistic achievement is a penetrating intelligence and an innate moral poise in her ability to humanize her subject without in the least exonerating him.[7]

Groups of Perpetrators

In this category are Robert Jay Lifton's *The Nazi Doctors*, Christopher Browning's *Ordinary Men: Reserve Police Battalion 101 and the Final Solution in Poland*, and Daniel Goldhagen's *Hitler's Willing Executioners: Ordinary Germans and the Holocaust*. Excerpts are available in Donald Niewyk's *Holocaust* (resp., 152–68, 168–84, 184–97). Despite the considerable social and educational differences between doctors and policemen, Lifton and Browning investigate the motivations of these two types of Nazi killers in an attempt to understand and interpret the actions of men in their collective professional identities. Goldhagen insists more generally on a specifically German form of antisemitism and, in particular, challenges Browning's conclusions.

Lifton deals with the Nazi doctors, particularly those at Auschwitz, who in addition to their medical experiments supervised every aspect of the extermination procedures, from selecting prisoners on the ramp to certifying the effects on them of the lethal gas. Nazi antisemitism was founded on a combination of traditional prejudice against Jews and a modern, political, "scientific" variety based on new racial theories. Science and particularly the medical profession were instrumental from start to finish in the conception and execution of genocide, which was preceded first by forced sterilization and then by the euthanasia program of undesirables in Germany itself. Lifton suggests a number of psychological mechanisms to account for doctors' compliance and complicity, despite the substantial differences in their individual histories. But in querying the reasons killing became a "therapeutic imperative" in Nazi ideology and how doctors sworn to protect life turned to killing as a form of healing, Lifton looks to the medical imagery of Nazi racial ideology and its notions of disease and cure. "The unifying principle of the biomedical ideology was that of a deadly racial disease, the sickness of the Aryan race; the cure, the killing of all Jews" (qtd. in Niewyk 154). Extermination was therefore intended to purify the body politic of its defilement, of the parasites or vermin that infested it, for which the killing gas Zyklon B, originally meant for disinfection, became directly and terrifyingly appropriate. Translating metaphor into reality gives old prejudice and scapegoating a legitimate scientific function.

Browning's study investigates a single reserve police battalion of older, "ordinary" men (i.e., not in the SS) who were sent to keep order behind German lines in Poland and found themselves commanded to kill local Jews instead. He charts the gradual habituation of most of the group (with a few exceptions) to committing mass murder by shooting at close range, after the initial shock and revulsion of their first encounters had worn off.

> With a conservative estimate of 6,500 Jews shot during earlier actions like those at Jozefow and Lomazy and 1,000 shot during "Jew hunts," and a minimum estimate of 30,500 Jews shot at Majdanek [Maidanek] and Poniatowa, the battalion had participated in the direct shooting deaths of at least 38,000 Jews. . . . (qtd. in Niewyk 173)

While not dismissing the effects of Nazi indoctrination, Browning looks less to ideology as the main motivation than to group dynamics, which exercised peer pressure on the men, isolating the nonconformists and interpreting their moral disgust or refusal to participate as a failure of masculine toughness.

In Niewyk's collection, Browning's contribution is followed by excerpts from Goldhagen's controversial *Hitler's Willing Executioners* (184–97). Starting from a study of the same battalion but extending the examination to many other aspects of the Holocaust, such as the work camps and death marches, Goldhagen proposes a radical "exterminationist antisemitism," endemic in German culture and politics, that afflicted one and all. Nazi killers were not "ordinary men"; they were "ordinary Germans." They did not need to learn to endure the tasks imposed on them; otherwise, how to account for the widespread evidence that they positively reveled in fulfilling those tasks with such atrocious levels of gratuitous cruelty? Space does not permit a judicious discussion of Goldhagen's claims, which are not without merit, but the crudeness of his historical and sociological models and his hyperventilated rhetoric lay his claims open to skepticism and refutation. Nevertheless, the pairing of these excerpts from the work of Browning and Goldhagen will provoke stimulating debate among students.

Goldhagen's indictment includes all Germans, men and women alike. It is a known fact that most German women supported their Führer to a quite astonishing degree and were no less zealous than German men in their adherence to Nazi ideology, although they had little power or influence in the Third Reich. They were famously relegated, for the most part, to "Kinder, Kirche, Küche" ("children, church, kitchen"). Their main contribution, as in many militaristic states, was to ensure the reproduction of the body politic through extensive childbearing—all the more so in a regime that had turned to eugenics to produce a "master race." The BDM (Bund Deutscher Mädel [League of German Girls]), the counterpart of the Hitlerjugend, the obligatory youth movement for boys, was an effective means of indoctrinating girls into their future roles. Physical fitness for boys prepared them for military service; for girls, it was meant to ensure healthy motherhood.[8] To what extent, then, can we speak of female perpetrators in this harshly masculine society?

Leni Riefenstahl, Hitler's favorite filmmaker, responsible for the famed propaganda films *Triumph of the Will* and *Olympia*, protested that her only interest was in making art, but if she aided the regime in this way, she could hardly be considered either a pioneer in propaganda or a major malefactor. Claudia Koonz, in her study of Gertrud Scholtz-Klink (excerpted in Rittner and Roth 287–308), who was the top woman leader in the Nazi regime, indicts women more generally for providing a safe haven for their men in the name of family solidarity. She also draws on Sereny's interviews with Stangl's wife, who was horrified to discover her husband's activities but, despite her initial revulsion, did not ultimately abandon him. Sereny, it is true, at the end confronts Frau Stangl with the difficult question of Frau Stangl's own guilt in failing to deliver an ultimatum to her husband (excerpted in Rittner and Roth 270–76). But however reprehensible women's moral abdication may have been, I find it difficult to equate their behavior with the actions of their menfolk, who were so intimately involved in the extermination process and held such undisputed power.

To be sure, SS women were guards in the concentration camps and their annexes, and in considerable numbers—they constituted ten percent of the camp personnel. Even so, they were never employed in the death camps, which were designed solely for extermination (such as Belzec, Treblinka, Chelmno, and Sobibor). Their functions in Lublin-Maidanek and Auschwitz-Birkenau, where gassings also took place, were limited to the supervision of the activities in the women's camps, even though they could (and did) brutalize their prisoners and had the power to mark women for death. In all cases, however, even in Ravensbrück, an exclusively female camp, the SS commandant was a male. Elsewhere, highly placed women were invariably subordinate to men. A few of the SS guards, like Maria Mandel, Ilse Koch, and Irma Grese, have left vivid traces in the record of extreme, even flamboyant, cruelty to women prisoners in their charge.[9] Women too were capable of the most radical manifestations of evil, but a focus on them also has its danger in provoking titillating accounts of "the deadlier of the species."

Bernhard Schlink's controversial novel *The Reader* (1997) re-volves around the belated revelation that the young male narrator's older lover, Hanna, was once a concentration camp guard. When she faces trial, many years later, for atrocities committed against women prisoners during the death marches of winter 1945, the nar-rator deduces the secret that Hanna strove so hard to conceal all her life, to her terrible detriment, namely, that she is illiterate. While the book does not, cannot, exonerate Hanna's guilt on this ground, it never sufficiently clarifies her character to our satisfaction. She re-mains opaque to us, as she does to the narrator, who is torn between his initial love for her and the horror he feels at the revelation of her crimes.[10] This opacity is perhaps the most disturbing aspect of the novel, which also functions to some extent as an allegory of relations between the second generation and their elders. "We all condemned our parents to shame, even if the only charge we could bring was that after 1945 they had tolerated the perpetrators in their midst" (90). I have vastly oversimplified the moral issues posed by this provocative book, which I have taught now several times at the end of my course, with gratifying results. Yet I would still maintain that Nazi ideology necessarily excluded women from leadership roles and only rarely gave them "equal opportunities" as perpetrators.

Cinematic Representations

My above recommendations for confronting the perpetrators of the Holocaust rely on evidentiary material and historical inquiry. While these provide significant background material, they do not address the most pressing problems faced by many courses taught in lan-guage and literature departments that deal with representation and its increasingly prominent role in the transmission of knowledge about the Holocaust. A special concern is the impact of popular cul-ture in shaping public memory, and nowhere is that impact more powerful than in the cinema. Others in this volume discuss the teaching of film and visual culture in specific detail. In the matter of the perpetrators, however, it is essential to recall how much the cin-ema has contributed to the creation and perpetuation of their image, so well captured in the words of Kosinski's child narrator quoted above. One of the works in the controversial 2002 exhibition at the Jewish Museum in New York, entitled "Mirroring Evil: Nazi Imagery / Recent Art" (Kleeblatt), draws attention to this phenomenon. Entitled merely "The Nazis," the installation by the young Polish artist Piotr Uklanski displays a frieze of 166 photographs of glamorous movie stars, dressed as the sinister Nazis they portrayed in film (108–10 and plate 5).

My interest here lies elsewhere. I recommend two fairly recent films, directed by outstanding practitioners of their craft, that enjoyed substantial commercial success. Both work with and against popular stereotypes of the perpetrators. Both are based on true stories, whose plots, however, are quite extraordinary. In fact, if truth were not stranger than fiction, as the saying goes, their improbability in the light of the more general experiences of Holocaust victims would be cause for scandal. Even so, both have been criticized for offering a nonstandard and hence potentially misleading version of the catastrophe that might undercut or diminish its enormity.

The first film, *Europa, Europa*, directed by Holland (1991), is based on the memoir of Solomon Perel, a German Jewish adolescent who somehow finds himself as the mascot of a Wehrmacht division on the eastern front and later as a student in an elite school for the Hitlerjugend. Space does not permit full discussion of this picaresque film, which has its comic moments, but the problems of identity the film raises in Solly's masquerade (problems for himself as for others) and in the portrayals of the unknowing Germans he encounters give a more complex picture than usual of the "ordinary" perpetrator and, along the way, expose the absurdity of Nazi racial theories.

The second, *Schindler's List*, directed by Spielberg (1993), is a far more challenging case. Seen by millions all over the world, winner of numerous Academy Awards, this epic film was adapted from the "nonfiction novel" by Thomas Keneally, which itself won the prestigious British Booker award in 1982. The film was rapturously received by the press and ordinary viewers but was also soundly scolded by intellectual critics who scorned its Hollywood provenance and focused on its many faults, as they saw it, in style and substance.[11]

No other product of popular culture is perhaps as useful for raising questions of the proprieties and limits of mimetic realism in shaping the memory of the Shoah for current (and future) generations. By now there is a substantial body of criticism on the film, such as Yosefa Loshitsky's edited volume of essays (see too Gellately; Machel; and Mintz). I would argue strongly that the film is a worthwhile addition to any Holocaust course — as a powerful cinematic experience (for some, too powerful); as a locus of controversy; and, for the purposes of this discussion, in its portrayal of the perpetrators.

The story concerns the strange, enigmatic figure Oskar Schindler, who accomplished the improbable feat of saving 1,100 Jews from deportation and death. A small-time German profiteer who came to Kraków to make money in a wartime economy, he took over an enamelware factory and employed Jewish forced labor from the ghetto to make his fortune. When the ghetto was liquidated in April 1943 and its remaining inhabitants were sent to the nearby labor camp, Plaszow, Schindler began to protect "his" Jews from the murderous conditions in the camp under Amon Goeth. Later, in 1944, when the camp too was about to be liquidated and its prisoners deported to Auschwitz, Schindler managed to convince the authorities to allow him to take a group of Jews to a munitions factory he was constructing in Czechoslovakia.

Especially relevant to our topic is the portrayal of the two central Nazi figures. Schindler ultimately complicates any conventional stereotype in the ambiguity of his person and his actions. Goeth, the brutal and sadistic SS officer who oversaw the destruction of the Kraków ghetto and became the commandant of Plaszow, more than confirms the stereotype. How Schindler, a carelessly unscrupulous man, an adventurer and bon vivant who pursued a life of high living and compulsive womanizing, turned into a heroic rescuer remains an unanswerable question. Nothing in his background suggests the reasons for his moral conversion from a shrewd opportunist bent on personal gain. Goeth, however, even by SS standards, was a criminal, a psychopathic monster. (So was Kurt Franz, deputy to Stangl at Treblinka.) Goeth killed for pleasure and for sport; his random shootings were as common as his mass executions. His excesses of lust were notorious, including a level of black-market corruption that eventually led to his arrest by Nazi authorities.[12] The neat emplotment of this story, however, which is organized around the binary opposition between the figures of the reformed redeemer and the worst perpetrator (represented as the dark, even parodic, twin of the other), might suggest to the casual viewer a convenient bending of historical veracity about Goeth in the interest of cinematic legibility and popular expectation. Yet if, for some, Goeth evokes all the clichés of B-movie Nazis, it also seems to me somewhat quixotic to refuse such depictions as though such men did not exist or did not do what they did. For however we address the unfathomable depths of inhumanity that characterized the implementation of the Holocaust; however we may look for complexity of motive and circumstances in the perpetrators or come to realize how ordinary, how mediocre, they might actually have been; however we may become aware of the dangers of a morbid, even voyeuristic, fascination with the power of evil, there is no escaping the fact that what happened with such stunning efficiency in a few short years was just that.

Notes

1. Relevant excerpts of the speech may be found in Dawidowicz (132–39), in Berenbaum (91–95), and on the Web (e.g., Himmler, *Posen Speech* and *Speech*).
2. Another re-creation of the Wannsee Conference is a film entitled *Conspiracy* (2001), starring Kenneth Branagh, who won an Emmy for his portrayal of Heydrich.
3. A Teacher's Guide to the Holocaust offers the Wannsee protocols and many other primary documents (*Documents*). For the text alone, see *Wannsee Protocol*.
4. Stangl said at the Treblinka trial: "Regarding the question of the optimum amount of people gassed in one day, I can state: according to my estimation a transport of thirty freight cars with 3,000 people was liquidated in three hours. When the work lasted for about fourteen hours, 12,000 to 15,000 people were annihilated. There were many days that the work lasted from the early morning until the evening. . . . I have done nothing to anybody that was not my duty. My conscience is clear" (*Treblinka*).
5. Sereny also follows the escape and pursuit of Stangl after the war's end and the Catholic Church's complicity in aiding Nazi war criminals. Given the length of the book, this section may be omitted in a course.

6. Stangl died of a heart attack in prison the day after Sereny's last interview with him.

7. See too Clendinnen's sensitive reading of Sereny (107–13). It is worth noting that Sereny's work may have played a substantial role in Claude Lanzmann's treatment of Treblinka in *Shoah*, not just in method and focus, but also in the identity of some of the witnesses that through her interviews he tracked down.

8. The film *Europa, Europa*, discussed below, offers a useful depiction of both organizations.

9. After the war, these women and others like them were put on trial to face execution and imprisonment like their male peers.

10. There have been a number of studies of women perpetrators, mostly in the camps, but these are for the most part in German, with a few in French.

11. A story about the Holocaust with a "happy ending"? A story that shows the exception (the "good" German, the rescuer) rather than the rule? A film on this topic that includes sex scenes? A film that showed "too much," that didn't respect the implicit taboo on representing the unrepresentable, especially in the scenes at Auschwitz? At the same time, a film that could suggest only a small part of the violence that was daily inflicted on the victims, that underrepresented what really happened.

12. Goeth was tried in September 1946 by a Polish court and hanged near the site of Plaszow.

Works Cited

Arendt, Hannah. *Eichmann in Jerusalem: A Report on the Banality of Evil.* New York: Viking, 1963.

Berenbaum, Michael, ed. *Witness to the Holocaust.* New York: Harper, 1997.

Browning, Christopher. *Ordinary Men: Reserve Police Battalion 101 and the Final Solution in Poland.* New York: Harper, 1992.

Clendinnen, Inga. *Reading the Holocaust.* Cambridge: Cambridge UP, 1999.

Conspiracy. Dir. Frank Pierson. 2001. Videocassette. HBO Home Video, 2002. DVD. Warner Home Video, 2002.

Dawidowicz, Lucy, ed. *A Holocaust Reader.* New York. Behrman, 1976.

Documents. A Teacher's Guide to the Holocaust. Florida Center for Instructional Technology, U of South Florida. 2001. 31 May 2004 <http://fcit.coedu.usf.edu/holocaust/resource/document/document.htm>.

Europa, Europa. Dir. Agnieszka Holland. 1991. Videocassette. MGM/UA Studios, 1992, 1999. DVD. MGM/UA Studios, 2003.

"The Final Solution": Eichmann's Evidence on the Wannsee Conference. Australian Inst. for Holocaust and Genocide Studies. Shalom Coll. U of New South Wales, Kensington. Comps. Alexander Westwood and Darren O'Brien. 31 May 2004 <http://www.aihgs.com/doc22.htm>.

Gellately, Robert. "Between Exploitation, Rescue, and Annihilation: Reviewing *Schindler's List.*" *Central European History* 26 (1994): 475–89.

Goldhagen, Daniel Jonah. *Hitler's Willing Executioners: Ordinary Germans and the Holocaust.* New York: Knopf, 1996.

Himmler, Heinrich. *Himmler's October 4, 1943 Posen Speech.* Nizkor Project. Dir. Ken McVay. 31 May 2004 <http://www.nizkor.org/hweb/people/h/himmler-heinrich/posen/oct-04-43/>.

———. *Speech of the Reichsfuehrer-SS at the Meeting of SS Major-Generals at Posen, October 4th, 1943.* Ed. Stuart D. Stein. Web Genocide Documentation Centre, Resources on Genocide, War Crimes and Mass Killing. U of the West of Eng. 8 Jan. 1999. 31 May 2004 <http://www. ess.uwe.ac.uk/genocide/SS2.htm>.

Keneally, Thomas, *Schindler's List.* New York: Simon, 1982.

Kleeblatt, Norman, ed. *Mirroring Evil: Nazi Imagery / Recent Art.* New Brunswick: Rutgers UP; New York: Jewish Museum, 2001.

Kosinski, Jerzy. *The Painted Bird.* New York: Bantam, 1983.

Lifton, Robert Jay. *The Nazi Doctors: Medical Killing and the Psychology of Genocide.* New York: Basic, 1986.

Loshitsky, Yosefa, ed. *Spielberg's Holocaust: Critical Perspectives on* Schindler's List. Bloomington: Indiana UP, 1997.

Machel, Frank. "A Reel Witness: Steven Spielberg's Representation of the Holocaust in *Schindler's List.*" *Journal of Modern History* 67.1 (1995): 83–100.

Mintz, Alan. *Popular Culture and the Shaping of Holocaust Memory in America.* Seattle: U of Washington P, 2001.

Niewyk, Donald, ed. *The Holocaust: Problems and Perspectives of Interpretation.* Problems in European Civilization. Boston: Houghton, 1997.

Perel, Solomon. *Europa, Europa.* Trans. M. B. Dembo. New York: Wiley; Washington: US Holocaust Museum, 1997.

Rittner, Carol, and John K. Roth, eds. *Different Voices: Women and the Holocaust.* New York: Paragon, 1993.

Schindler's List. Dir. Steven Spielberg. Universal Studios, 1993. DVD. Universal Studios, 2004.

Schlink, Bernhard. *The Reader.* Trans. Carol Brown Janeway. New York: Pantheon, 1997.

Sereny, Gitta. *Into That Darkness: An Examination of Conscience.* New York: Random, 1983.

Shoah. Dir. Claude Lanzmann. 1985. DVD. New Yorker Films, 2003.

The Specialist. Dir. Eyal Sivan. Kino Intl., 1999. Videocassette. Kino Video, 2000. DVD. Public Media, 2002.

Treblinka: Deathcamp. The Holocaust: Crimes, Heroes and Villains. By Louis Bülow. 4 Jun. 2004 <http://auschwitz.dk/Treblinka.htm>.

The Trial of Adolf Eichmann. Prod. Daniel P. Polin. ABC News Productions. Public Broadcasting Service. 30 Apr. 1997. 31 May 2004 <http://www.pbs.org/eichmann>.

"Wannsee, Berlin, January 20, 1942." *Wannsee Conference*. Multimedia Learning Center, Museum of Tolerance Online. Simon Wiesenthal Center. 1997. 31 May 2004 <http://motlc.wiesenthal.com/text/x34/xm3417.html>.

Wannsee Conference. Dir. Heinz Schirk. 1984. Videocassette. Home Vision Entertainment, 1999.

Wannsee Protocol, January 20, 1942: Translation. Remember.org. Dir. Joseph Korn. 31 May 2004 <http://remember.org/wannsee.html>.

Witnesses to the Holocaust: Trial of Adolf Eichmann. Prod. Lori Perlow. 1987. Videocassette. Warner Home Video, 1988.

Susannah Heschel and Sander Gilman

Reflections on the Long History of European Antisemitism

Why do so many people hate the Jews? Why did the Nazis choose to target Jews for murder and not another minority—people with green eyes, or Methodists? Our students find the question deeply troubling, and since most find prejudice against Jews utterly foreign to their own experience, explaining antisemitism in the context of a course on the Holocaust becomes tantamount to reinterpretating Western civilization. Exploring a variety of analyses of the history of antisemitism teaches them the complexity of understanding human motivation and the limits to scholarly answers. We open our courses on the Holocaust with a brief survey of Judeophobia in the Greco-Roman world and follow a trajectory of Judeophobia through early and medieval Christianity (contrasting it with Islamic attitudes toward Jews), the economic tensions and expulsions of the early modern era, and the newer forms of racial antisemitism that emerged in the second half of the nineteenth century and were so significant in the Nazi movement.[1]

Scholarship on antisemitism exists in a variety of disciplines (psychology, sociology, social history, art history, theology, to name a few), and we draw from several media to illustrate ways in which antisemitic notions can be transmitted. We begin with the Christian Gospels of Matthew and John on the Crucifixion of Jesus, various paintings of the scene, and the Good Friday sermons by the church father John Chrysostom. The repetition of medieval motifs in modern garb is easy to demonstrate: for example, we discuss the blood libel that arose in the twelfth century, then look at images from the Nazi newspaper the *Stürmer*, in which Jews are depicted as economically and sexually predatory. In reading primary-source documents, we discuss whether the hostility toward Jews arose from economic competition, couched in religious language, or whether it was a theological rivalry making use of secular grievances. Are Jews the primary target or a displacement for hostility toward a king or government policy? Students are inevitably impressed by how easily latent antisemitic fantasies can be aroused and manipulated by political parties and regimes. But they have difficulty considering how Jewish communities through the centuries might have responded to antisemitic movements differently and how living an antisemitic environment affected Jewish self-perception, politics, and even religious thought. It is vital that we provide our students with the critical tools to examine racist and antisemitic texts from the past, because they need these tools to grapple with such texts in the contemporary world.

The initial distinction that we make is between attitudes toward Judaism in the pre-Christian, Greco-Roman world and Christian teachings about Judaism. Pagan hostility toward Jews was political and ethnic, expressed in mockery of elements of Jewish religious teachings and resentment at the special privileges accorded Jews in the Roman Empire, which permitted Jewish religious observance to take precedence over certain civic obligations (Schäfer). Ancient Egyptians, such as Manetho, ridiculed Old Testament accounts of Israelite origins and religious practices, and Greeks who admired Jewish monotheism still argued that there was nothing original or authentic in Judaism. In these cases Jews were never the litmus test of difference; they were only one of many groups (including Africans) used to define the positive aspects of Greco-Roman culture against the barbarians.

Whatever the mockery, pagan resentment was never central to the self-definition of Romans or Greeks. Moreover, Roman authorities were by and large tolerant of religious pluralism and sympathetic to Jewish ethnic interests. Even in the ancient Jewish world, far greater conflicts existed. The Jewish community at Qumran, for example, viewed itself as the sole true remnant of Israel, the only group that would merit redemption, and its rage at the Jewish establishment in Jerusalem, both the temple priests and Pharisees, produced vitriolic texts that rival later Christian diatribes against Judaism (Sanders).

By contrast, Christian theology introduced a new dimension: it colonized Judaism theologically, appropriating its Scriptures (now called the Old Testament) and drawing on its central religious ideas (a messiah, redemption, election, covenant) to explain and justify its own claims regarding Jesus as the Christ anticipated by the prophets. Judaism formed the basis for the Christian religion yet was also rejected: it was the old covenant, Israel in the flesh, which had no continuing validity now that Jesus had been sent to fulfill its promises.

In the context of a course on the history of the Holocaust, we introduce selected passages of the New Testament, to illustrate three motifs of anti-Judaism: defamation, supersession, and deicide. We situate the material both historically and rhetorically. Jesus's negative comments about the Pharisees, in Matthew 23, for example, are understood by most New Testament scholars as one of many first-century Jewish criticisms of the Pharisees (the rabbis of the first century) and the Sadducees (the priests of the Jerusalem Temple), such as the material in the Dead Sea Scrolls (Meier; Sanders; see Vermes). We note that Jesus himself is identified by most scholars as a Pharisee and that he uses the argumentation of a Pharisee when debating issues of Jewish law, such as those of the Sabbath. Indeed, we point out that Jesus himself never violated the Sabbath, though he defended his disciples against charges that they had. We also have the students look at the term *Pharisee* in the *Oxford English Dictionary*, to see how the word has become synonymous with "hypocrite," based on the passages in Matthew 23. Whatever the historical reality, the rhetorical reality has had a life of its own.

To illustrate the notion of supersession, we have students read the account of the transfiguration, Luke 9.28–36, in which Jesus, Moses, and Elijah appear in a vision but then Moses and Elijah disappear behind a cloud, leaving only Jesus. The failure to convert the Jews to the new Jesus movement became a theological problem: both Jews and Christians believed the Jews were descended from Abraham, in covenant with God, so why did the Jews fail to recognize Christ as the messiah and the fulfillment of scriptural promises? As Paul writes in Romans 9–11, Jews are fathers of election but enemies of the Gospel (Romans 11.28). Out of this failure, the church developed a doctrine of Israel according to the flesh (the Jews), who read the Bible literally and were therefore blind to its veiled teachings about the coming of Christ, in contrast to Israel according to the spirit (Christians). Jewish religious blindness, combined with stubbornness, kept Jews from realizing that Judaism was no longer valid, that it had been superseded by Jesus and the new covenant. While some Christian theologians understand Paul to be asserting that Israel must become Christian before the kingdom of God can arrive (Romans 11.25), most historians understand Paul to be reassuring gentile Christians that they are honorary Jews, grafted like a branch onto the olive tree of Judaism (Romans 11.17 and 11.24; see Sanders; Stendahl).

Finally, the prominence of the deicide charge against the Jews in Christian polemics makes it important to clarify for students that the Gospel authors deliberately deflect their readers' attention from Roman responsibility for Jesus's death to protect their religious movement from Caesar's wrath. Crucifixion was a punishment practiced only by Romans, although most scholars agree that a Jewish court turned Jesus over to Roman authorities, for reasons that remain debated (Sanders; Meier). The impact on the Western imagination of the persistent Christian belief that the Jews killed Christ, however false, has to be emphasized. Accounts of the Passion, particularly in the Gospel of John, were read aloud in churches each year on Good Friday, frequently inciting mob attacks on Jews, as Christians emerged from church filled with wrath that the Jews had murdered Christ. We share with students, too, that the collective responsibility of all Jews for deicide was not formally withdrawn by the Roman Catholic Church until the Second Vatican Council in the 1960s and that it is no longer part of most Christian religious instruction.

What we urge students to consider are the political implications of theological positions and the uniqueness of the Christian relationship with Judaism. The anxiety of the early church fathers over Jewish practices, for example, can be discussed as part of the difficulty in establishing a clear distinction between Judaism and Christianity. We also stress similarities between the early theological trajectories of the two religions, noting that, increasingly, contemporary historians are recognizing the influences of Christianity on Jewish self-understanding and liturgical practice, so that a unidirectional development from Judaism to Christianity can no longer be claimed (Becker and Reed).

Indeed, recent scholarship has concluded that no sharp or sudden break between Judaism and Christianity occurred in the late first or second century, as had been assumed (Becker and Reed). Instead, historians now believe that both Judaism (post-70 CE, the year the Jerusalem Temple was destroyed by the Romans) and Christianity emerged in the Mediterranean basin simultaneously and with mutually reinforcing theological approaches to Scripture. Only gradually, in the fourth century, with Constantine's conversion of the Roman Empire to Christianity, did the two communities take radically different paths.

The doctrine of supersession meant that the central theological pillars of Christianity depended on Judaism even as they rejected the possibility of a continuing covenant between God and the Jews who rejected Christ. That most Jews failed to recognize Jesus as the promised messiah led to accusations of their spiritual blindness, and such teachings made it easy for many to wrongly believe that the Jews, rather than the Romans, were responsible for Jesus's crucifixion. Augustine stated in his manual for new converts to Christianity: "The New Testament is concealed in the Old; the Old Testament is revealed in the New" (134). Supersession not only transformed the

Torah into Christianity's Old Testament but also brought about a linguistic transformation of Jesus from Jew to gentile. The hidden language of the Jews disappears from the tradition of the early church, even though it was preserved in what came to be called the New Testament as a sign of the difference of Christ's nature from that of the Jews. The linguistic shifts attributed to Jesus by the Gospel authors inaugurate what later became a modern antisemitic motif identified by Sander Gilman: the belief that Jews speak a secret language, *mauscheln*, undecipherable to gentiles, that provides the glue to their conspiratorial and destructive nature.

At the time of his death, Jesus is reported by two of the Gospels to have cited Psalm 22.1 not in Hebrew but in Aramaic, the Jewish vernacular of first-century Palestine. In the earliest Gospel, Mark, Jesus "at the ninth hour . . . [cries] with a loud voice, saying 'Eloi, Eloi, lama sabachthani?,' which means, My God, my God, why hast thou forsaken me?" (15.34–35). The onlookers, according to Mark, mistakenly hear Jesus calling for Elijah rather than for God. Matthew, written subsequently, alters Jesus's last words: "And about the ninth hour Jesus cried with a loud voice, saying, 'Eli, Eli, lema sabachthani?,'" which the bystanders again misunderstand as a call for Elijah (27.46–47). Jesus is here speaking the language of the Jews: his words are translated in the Gospel text for readers to understand what he is saying and to avoid the misunderstanding of the bystanders. Gospel readers perceive the foreignness of Jesus's language, which is eliminated by the later Gospels of Luke and John, written for a Greco-Roman audience. Aramaic encodes Jesus as Jewish; it is the hidden language of the Jews, a magical language of difference that is positive but still signifies him as a Jew, and the Gospels attempt a progressive de-Judaization of him.

In the later Gospel accounts of the passion, Christ speaks directly to the reader, and there is no misunderstanding of the onlookers. In Luke's Gospel, Jesus says, "Father, into your hands I commend my spirit: and having said thus, he gave up the ghost" (23.46). In John, the last Gospel, Christ is taken to Golgotha and says, "It is finished: and he bowed his head, and gave up the ghost" (19.30). Here, Jesus's language needs no translation; it is transparent, familiar not foreign. The two later Gospels provide a verbal sign of difference between the image of the Jews and that of the early Christians represented in the text—Jews who were at the time becoming Christians in a world where the valorized language was Greek. As Christians read through the Gospels in their canonical order, from Matthew to John, they lose the image of Christ as one who sounds Jewish and replace him with the image of one who sounds like themselves (whether they speak Greek, Latin, German, or English). Jesus becomes a Christian as he ceases to be understandable to Jews. Thus the hidden language of Aramaic, which marks Christ as a Jew, that is, as a non-Greek-speaking Jew, gradually disappears in the text of the New Testament.

After Christianity became the official religion of the Roman Empire, the cross was linked to the sword, and Jews entered an era in which they were politically subservient to a religion that sought their conversion both in order to save their souls and to bring about the second coming of Christ. On the basis of the Pauline formulation in Romans 11.28, Augustine crucially defined Christian-Jewish coexistence during the Middle Ages: Jews served as witnesses to the truth of Christianity, both through the testimony of their Scriptures predicting the advent of Christ and through their abject status as evidence of God's rejection of them for refusing to become Christians. Keep the Jews alive, Augustine suggests, for the good of Christian pedagogy, as visible signs of Christianity's truth and God's judgment against them. This theological schema probably saved Jews from extermination at the hands of the church (J. Cohen, *Living Letters*).

We can find buried in the admonishment of Augustine the pattern followed for centuries: periods of pogroms, murders, and expulsions of Jews alternated in the Middle Ages with periods of quiet coexistence, tolerance, and even mutual admiration. We balance information about marauding Christians with information about ways in which individual Jews and Christians peacefully coexisted. Jewish and Christian women, for example, likely had close personal contact, serving in one another's homes as midwives, wet nurses, and servants and sharing communal ovens. Often local bishops protected

Jews from riots, and the Vatican rejected the accusation that Jews were responsible for the plague. Recent DNA evidence suggests widespread marriage of Jewish men with Christian women, at least outside the Germanic areas. The teachings and practices of each religion were fructified by those of the other; each borrowed concepts as well as customs from the other. For instance, Jews began to light yahrzeit (memorial) candles under the influence of Catholic Church practices, aspects of the Passover seder were composed as a theological response to Christianity, and the Shechinah (feminine presence) of God was described by Jewish mystics in language drawn from Christian descriptions of the Virgin Mary. Ultimately, no other two religions have had such strong mutual bonds of aversion and fascination, repulsion and attraction (Wolfson). Although Christian theology introduced crucial anti-Jewish fantasies, it also provided a foundation to protect Jews, and the church never contemplated a genocide of the Jews. It is worth emphasizing that some historians argue that it was the end of church dominance and the introduction of secularism that led to the Holocaust (Yerushalmi).

By the High Middle Ages, Jews in Christian Europe were increasingly accused of dangerous, inhuman behavior (Trachtenberg). In the twelfth century, the blood libel first emerged in England; according to it, Jews kidnapped a Christian boy, tortured him to death, and then used his blood to bake matzo. Similar charges were brought against Jews in Europe and Russia as late as the early twentieth century. The Fourth Lateran Council of 1215 set forth special clothing for Jews as part of their social segregation, a ruling that was enforced or ignored at the will of local rulers but that contributed to a widespread feeling that Christians needed to be protected from contamination by Jews. During the plague in the fourteenth century, Jews were accused of poisoning wells. Stories were told in medieval Europe that Jews desecrated the eucharistic host, causing it to bleed (Rubin). These accusations can be presented to students as examples of the medieval demonization of Jews in the popular imagination, a demonization that did not receive sanction from the upper echelons of the church but was an easily manipulated political tool. That Jews desecrated the eucharistic host, for example, was claimed by priests who wanted to rouse the piety of their congregants. They suggested that the Jews attacked the wafer because even Jews believed it was the body of Christ—so how could a Christian deny transubstantiation (Hsia)? Throughout the discussion of medieval Christian attitudes toward Jews, we show slides of representations of Jews in medieval art—in the paintings, statues, stained glass windows, murals, woodcuts, sculptures, and manuscript illustrations that conveyed to the illiterate through visuality the denigrations argued by theologians in texts. For example, we show photographs of the famous wood carvings of Jews riding a pig (the *Judensau*), which are found in many German churches; paintings that depict Jewish ritual murder of Christian boys; sculptures that depict a blinded synagogue in contrast to a triumphant church; and murals that show Jews wearing the prescribed distinctive clothing and behaving in a vulgar fashion (Schreckenberg).

Since they occupied tenuous economic positions and were forbidden from owning land, Jews often became moneylenders, which made them further targets of popular resentment but also sources of needed capital—capital that rulers could confiscate by expelling the Jews. Indeed, Jews were expelled from numerous kingdoms, principalities, and towns throughout Europe, starting with the expulsion from England in 1290 and quickly extending to France and the German principalities. The most significant expulsion came in Spain in 1492, where a large and prosperous Jewish community had lived for centuries, producing a golden age of cultural vitality during the Muslim control of the country in the Middle Ages. With the conquest of Spain by Christians and the inauguration of a period of reactionary politics and religious authority in the thirteenth century, culminating in widespread riots against Jews in 1391, large numbers of Jews agreed to be baptized. Yet while their conversion supposedly fulfilled Christian wishes, the Jewish converts, called conversos, were treated with suspicion, and the Inquisition was established in Spain in 1483 to investigate the fidelity of their faith. Within twelve years, thirteen thousand conversos were condemned to death. In 1492, Spain expelled all its Jews, many of whom fled to Portugal, which expelled them a few years later, or to the Muslim Ottoman Empire, where they found refuge (Netanyahu). In Christian Europe, the crown used expulsions to confiscate Jewish wealth and property but also as a tool to win popular political support, appealing to both economic and religious resentment of Jews.

It is important to point out to our students that Jews came to be demonized in Christian culture in ways that were rare in the Muslim cultures where Jews lived (M. Cohen). Theology provides only a partial explanation for the difference. In the economies of northern Europe, Jews stood as unique figures involved in international commerce at a time when most Christians were engaged in agriculture and mistrustful of trade. Jews served the local rulers as moneylenders and later as bankers; they became symbols of hated rulers and their taxes. In the economies of the Islamic world, international commerce and systems of credit were common and respected, and Jews were seen as playing a helpful rather than an exploitative role in the society. The international Islamic empire was composed of numerous ethnic groups; the Jews, one group among many, were not perceived as strange and other. While some outbreaks of persecution occurred, they were insignificant compared with those in the Christian world, and Jews in Muslim lands were hardly ever subjected to expulsion or forced to convert to Islam.

During the early modern period in Europe, the image of the Jew was fraught. Italian Renaissance thinkers such as the Christian humanist Pico della Mirandola in the fifteenth century explored Jewish mystical texts to gain deeper understanding of the mysteries of the divine (Wirszubski). Pico's work stood in a Christian tradition that began in the thirteenth century and tried to prove to Jews that their own rabbinic texts confirmed the truth of Christianity (J. Cohen, *Friars*). At the same time, he stimulated a new interest by Christians in studying Hebrew and Jewish texts.

For Martin Luther a hundred years later, the failure of Jews to become Christians was one more example of the papal paganism of the Roman Catholic Church (Oberman). He writes, "If I had been a Jew and had seen such fools and blockheads teach the Christian faith, I should rather have turned into a pig than become a Christian" (qtd. in C. Wagner; "That Christ Was Born a Jew" [1523]). He expected that Jews would become his allies and convert to the new reformed Christianity. When they not only failed to do so but also saw little difference between the reformer and his Catholic brethren, he raged against them. Already in the 1520s, Luther complained about the stubbornness of the Jews, using the same vituperative language he heaped on all his enemies—princes, bishops, and especially the pope. By the 1540s, Luther endorsed a campaign of violence against the Jews, writing that their books should be burned, synagogues destroyed, and rabbis forbidden from teaching; the Jews should be expelled without any protection and their children taken from them. His proposals were not carried out, primarily because there were few Jews living in Protestant-controlled areas. Luther's legacy to antisemitism is not limited to his calls for violence against Jews; it runs deeper, to his differentiation between Judaism as a religion of law and Christianity as a religion of love, a distinction he claims to find in the writings of Saint Paul. The distinction became central to many modern antisemitic tracts that claimed Jews lacked morality because theirs was a heteronomous, legalistic religion without a conscience.

The Reformation thus found itself in continuity with the most egregious antisemitic writings of the Church. The wars of religions that occurred over the next century invariably placed the Jews in the camp of the enemy—no matter what their political or apolitical stance. With the rise of capitalism, theological motifs of Judeophobia were transformed into economic ones. Secret magical practices attributed to Jews, for example, were transmuted into myths of an international Jewish monetary conspiracy. Since their religion permitted Jews to charge interest on loans, they were damned as an exploitative people, taking advantage of Christians, able magically to animate the inanimate, bringing life (interest payments) forth from silver and gold. Jews had long been prevented from owning land and joining craft guilds, so they were forced to become moneylenders or merchants, occupations that aroused resentment among the Christian peasantry, who did not distinguish between the Jews' economic and religious roles. Given their occupations, most Jews lived in urban areas and moved easily into key roles in the newly emerging capitalist economy of early modern Europe. Joseph Oppenheimer, financial adviser to the duke of Württemberg in the eighteenth century, is a telling example: after the death of the duke in 1737, Oppenheimer was arrested and eventually murdered, blamed for establishing the rule of absolutism, the centralization of wealth and concentration of power in the hands of the duke (Stern). Given the derogatory appellation "Jud Suess," Oppenheimer was turned by antisemites into an evildoer who had exploited Christian wealth for his own power, most notoriously in the Nazi film *Jud Suess*, made in 1940.

Historians differ widely in their interpretations of modern antisemitism. Were Christian theological charges against Judaism transmuted into the language of race and biology (Tal), or is modern antisemitism an independent political phenomenon, a reaction to the crises of modernity (Pulzer; Rürup)? Is racism the product of religion or a repudiation of it? Social theorists have considered antisemitism as the product of authoritarian personalities or social structures, or as the result of the loss of traditionally defined status during periods of political upheaval. All sorts of events and situations can elicit antisemitic resentment: migrations, changes of regime, minority competitions, economic downturns, political conflicts. Historical overviews of Jewish experience reveal centuries of continuity of antisemitism, but when specific outbreaks are contextualized, the picture is different: Jews are revealed to be one of several local targets of discrimination. For example, the Jewish ghettos established in sixteenth-century Italy can be viewed either as part of a long tradition of Christian society's exclusion of Jews or as part of a broader effort in post-Tridentine Italy to isolate various groups—nuns were put into enclosures, prostitutes in special neighborhoods, and Jews in ghettos (Stow).

The period of the Enlightenment in England, France, and Germany led to expanded civil rights for Jews and eventually to their emancipation from legal strictures that prevented their full equality as citizens. Yet that emancipation came at a price. Jews were pressured to demonstrate their fidelity to the nation by abandoning religious and cultural practices that enhanced their difference from the surrounding Christian society. At the same time that Jews attempted to assimilate, a Romantic reaction to the Enlightenment advocated the concept of a *Volk*, which narrowed the definition of the nation. Herder, Fichte, Schlegel, and other German thinkers linked the identity and culture of a *Volk* with its language and defined Jews as foreign and unassimilable. Several academic fields—linguistics, anthropology, Oriental studies—as well as many intellectuals argued for a linguistic origin of nations that determined their immutable cultural essence (Olender). For example, Richard Wagner, in his notorious pamphlet, which we often assign to students, *Judaism in Music*, first published in 1850, argued that Jews possess a hidden language and speak European languages only as foreigners. As a result, they are incapable of creativity and cannot participate in European culture. Most important in Wagner's essay is its revolutionary tone, as Paul Lawrence Rose has pointed out. For Wagner, Jews are not simply marginal to Germany but an insidious danger through the hidden influence they exert. According to him, Jews are not assimilating into German society and shedding their Jewish otherness; rather, Germans are being Judaized, unwittingly infected by Jewishness, and thereby weakened.

Antisemitism's most important and dangerous function in the modern period was its support of nationalism. Just as Christianity took shape by defining its identity in contrast to Judaism, France's national identity was renegotiated around the Dreyfus affair (Bredin; Derfler). The French had been one of the first nations to grant full civil emancipation to the Jews during the French Revolution, yet the country was the site of the most explosive antisemitic political events of the late nineteenth century. Alfred Dreyfus, a Jewish captain in the French military, was accused of treason and sentenced to a life of hard labor on Devil's Island. The outcry over the case divided France between those who believed he had been falsely accused and those who believed Jews should play no prominent role in French culture. Dreyfus and the Jews were the focus of a national debate over the nature of the French nation, its political and cultural direction. The event also demonstrated that antisemitism often functions in a circular fashion, closed to falsifiability: when Dreyfus was eventually exonerated, French antisemites claimed his freedom proved not his innocence but the power of Jews to win freedom for a guilty Jew.

Such beliefs played into the view that the Jews formed a vast international conspiracy to dominate the world. This idea was certainly present in France before Dreyfus; it was present in the widely read work of Edouard Drumont. However, the international repercussions of this affair made it a commonplace. By the beginning of the twentieth century, agents of the Russian imperial secret police composed and published the notorious and widely disseminated *Protocols of the Elders of Zion*, which purports to be the minutes of meetings of a Jewish cabal and remains one of the primary texts for antisemites in the twentieth and twenty-first centuries (Segel). The text describes an international Jewish conspiracy to enslave the Christian world economically and politically. Though shown to have been a forgery, it won widespread appeal in the early decades of the twentieth century in Europe and the United States (where it was published by Henry Ford) and was quoted in Hitler's *Mein Kampf*.

The racism popularized by the French diplomat Arthur de Gobineau, in his *Essay on the Inequality of the Human Race* (1853–55), and the so-called race scientists of the nineteenth century classified Jews at a low level of human development. A common motif was that the alleged economic exploitation practiced by Jews resulted from their inherent vulgar nature. Wilhelm Marr, a writer and founder in 1879 of German's League of Anti-Semites, argued that a character flaw leads Jews to siphon the wealth and resources of non-Jews for themselves. That the Jews' character was shaped not by their religion but by their biological origins was central to the racist ideologies that arose in the nineteenth century. According to these ideologies, racial categories affected both the physical body and the spirit of a person, and they were immutable. Houston Stewart Chamberlain, in his best seller of 1901, *Foundations of the Nineteenth Century*, popularized the notion of an Aryan race characterized by its physical beauty and strength and by a superior spirit. Chamberlain and other racial theorists drew on earlier stereotypes of Jews in defining them as materialistic and legalistic.

Christianity itself came under scrutiny in racist literature: was it a Jewish religion, inimical to the German soul, or was it an Aryan religion? Chamberlain popularized the idea that Jesus was not a Jew but an Aryan. The idea was based on the claim, historically false, that Galilee was populated by Aryans and on the claim that the spirit of Christianity represented an Aryan religiosity. A Jew could not have founded a religion as extraordinary as Christianity—clearly Jesus must have been an Aryan, Chamberlain argued. Racists who had believed that Christianity was a Jewish religion inimical to Germany were reassured by this argument. It was popularized during the Third Reich by Protestant theologians to express their support for the Nazi regime. Led by the New Testament scholar Walter Grundmann, a number of theologians and pastors sought to de-Judaize Christianity by removing the Old Testament from the Bible, purging the New Testament of all positive references to Jews, and removing Hebrew words from the hymnal. The goal was to grant a religious sanction to Nazi policies. Writing in 1941, Grundmann declared, "If someone is upset about Germany's attitude toward the Jews, Germany has the historical justification and historical authorization for the fight against the Jews on its side!" (Heschel, "When Jesus" 69).

Just as the priests and secular authorities of the Middle Ages at times exploited popular fear of Jews for political purposes, antisemitism in the nineteenth century became a vehicle to attack modernity and its discontents. For reactionaries nostalgic for the past, Jews were associated with all the evils of the modern world. They were blamed for urbanization and its ills, for the stock market and its crashes, for modern culture and its rejection of classical motifs and representational art. Christian politicians, such as Adolf Stoecker, a late-nineteenth-century Berlin court preacher and political demagogue, used antisemitism to distract the working class from economic and class oppressions (Engelmann). Standing in the elevated chancel of an enormous, ornate Protestant cathedral, wearing the long robes of a pastor, he blamed the workers' financial difficulties on Jewish corruption, giving the workers a passionate cause while assuring them of the kaiser's sympathies. In most cases, hatred of Jews deflected attention from the corruption or oppression of a political regime or from the dislocations of cultural innovation. Both capitalism and socialism, modernity and the failure to modernize, were blamed on Jews, in a paranoid contradiction that ignored empirical evidence. Antisemitism became popular because it served, as Shulamit Volkov has written, as a "cultural code," a means of identifying oneself. The frustration for Jews was the shift from a demand that they assimilate into European Christian society to expressions of outrage by antisemites that Jews had assimilated so successfully that they were no longer easily recognizable and therefore constituted a hidden danger.

What do we need to tell our students about the critical concept of racial antisemitism? The categories "Aryan" and "Semitic" were initially introduced as linguistic families but transformed into categories of race by the mid–nineteenth century. Racial theory was generally less concerned with defining the nature of the Aryan than with exposing the degeneracy of the Semitic, which was quickly equated with the Jewish rather than with the Arab. Racial speculation was concerned less with physical attributes than with cultural and spiritual qualities, which were viewed as inherited and immutable. In the late nineteenth century, when nation was closely connected to language, Jews were said to lack a language (Hebrew was viewed as a dead language, Yiddish as a corrupt version of German) and thus the ability to participate in Western national culture and civilization. They also were said to lack a conscience, to be legalistic, to exploit non-Jews, and to be concerned with amassing wealth rather than developing culturally. As an example, we present our students with the discourse of Jewish degeneracy that was rampant in Europe at the end of the nineteenth century and that linked Jewishness and femininity in Otto Weininger's highly popular book *Sex and Character*, written in 1903. The range of influence of this discourse includes Zionist writers such as Max Nordau, who sought to overcome Jewish degeneracy by establishing a Jewish political state. Similar images were used in the emerging discipline of criminology, as both Nancy Harrowitz and Marilyn Reizbaum have shown, demonstrating that antisemitism can be divorced from Jews and made a rhetorical tradition that is applied to other others. Since students have usually read the novel *Dracula*, we draw on recent interpretations by Ken Gelder and by Judith Halberstam to discuss ways in which the figure of

Dracula, though not identified in the novel as a Jew, incorporates antisemitic motifs—such as blood sucking, unnatural lust, cultural and linguistic strangeness, and physical ugliness—to create monstrosity. In particular, we look at the contrast created in the novel between Dracula and Englishness as a metaphor for the anxieties expressed in antisemitic literature, of the (Jewish) monster infecting the innocent (European) victim. Rhetorical traditions that arose in antisemitic contexts, in other words, can be used in a range of settings, directed against a range of perceived enemies.

Analyzing the political uses of antisemitic ideas is crucial, and so is teaching some of the subtle—and not so subtle—visual images associated with Jews. We often show our students excerpts of the notorious Nazi propaganda film of 1940 *Der ewige Jude* (The Eternal Jew) or photographs from Nazi propaganda publications; and we ask students to analyze connections between these images and those of medieval Christian art. The juxtaposition in the film of rats, filth, and bacilli with Jewish prayer and the danger of assimilated, wealthy Jews provides an excellent template to analyze motifs of monstrosity associated with Jewishness. Visual constructions of Jews lead easily to discussions of the body, sexuality, and gender. We ask the students to consider how antisemites portray Jews as constituting a third gender or as possessing an abnormal body and sexuality. The distortions of the Jewish body in images of the nose, for example, usually evoke a strong response from students. The antisemitic charges of economic exploitation are linked in class discussions with vampirism, and the spiritual blindness of the Jews in failing to recognize Jesus as the messiah is linked to modern notions of Jewish degeneracy. Economic stereotypes regarding Jews are particularly important in modern antisemitism, and we encourage students to consider images of Shylock and the construction of Jewish wealth in antisemitic literature as unearned, exploitative, excessive, and abnormal. The link between those images and Karl Marx's critique of capitalism can be nicely established, opening for students the question of why the political left has been ambivalent toward Jewish political rights, since Marx's important essay "On the Jewish Question," published in

1844, created imaginary links between capitalist exploitation and Jewishness.

Before 1933 German Jews were not simply passive onlookers to the world of antisemitic discourse, nor did they feel threatened or hampered in their professional and personal lives. Rather, they made extraordinary contributions to German cultural and intellectual life. Indeed, they viewed Germany as their beloved homeland and believed optimistically that antisemitism could be overcome through political and social channels. The Jewish historian Abraham Geiger argued in the 1860s that Jesus was a Pharisee who simply preached the common, liberal Judaism of his day, whereas Christianity was a religion invented by Paul about Jesus (Heschel, *Abraham Geiger*). In that way, Geiger sought to reinvent Western civilization, including Christianity and Islam, as derived from Judaism. In contrast, another historian, Heinrich Graetz, produced an eleven-volume *History of the Jews*, published between the 1850s and 1870s, which opened nearly every chapter with a description of the persecution of Jews by Christians, resulting in a lachrymose narrative of Jewish history. His *History* was cited by antisemites such as Heinrich von Treitschke as evidence that Jews defamed Christianity. In the last decades of the nineteenth century, German Jews turned to other tactics: defamations of Jews were brought to the state attorney for prosecution; public declarations of opposition to antisemitism were issued by German gentiles; and Jews published numerous books about Judaism, in the hope of overcoming hostility through education. The integration of Jews into German society continued, despite antisemitism, but there were also Jews who experienced such sharp hostility that they had difficulty affirming a positive Jewish identity and internalized the contempt for Jews that was rampant around them; Theodor Lessing called the phenomenon "Jewish self-hatred" (Gilman).

The most important Jewish challenge to antisemitism was the Zionist movement, which argued that European antisemitism would never be overcome and that the only solution to Europe's so-called Jewish problem was the creation of a Jewish state. Such a state would normalize the political and cultural status of the Jews, recognizing their nationhood by reviving their own language, Hebrew, and giving them the political framework of statehood. The Zionist movement began to take shape in Russia following the widespread pogroms of 1881–82 and in Central Europe with the publication of Theodor Herzl's pamphlet *The Jewish State* in 1896. Yet Zionism, while it sought to undermine antisemitism by reviving Jewish national political identity, culture, language, and masculinity, failed to stop the progress of antisemitism; it was used as an additional example by antisemites for their conspiratorial fantasies regarding Jews (Penslar).

While Weimar democracy seemed to bring a promise of equality for Jews in German society, racist ideology continued to flourish, and the democratic state was not welcomed by everyone (Niewyk). Zionism, which never won much support from German Jews, who felt it undermined their promise of assimilation, was welcomed by some antisemites as a way to remove Jews from Germany. Some antisemites warned against Eastern European Jews entering Germany and built on the piety, Yiddish language, and poverty of Eastern European Jews to create an image of them as primitive and repugnant.

The development of racial antisemitism is central to the background of National Socialism. At the same time, historians agree that the Nazi Party did not win votes because of its antisemitism. Most political parties had some antisemitic rhetoric, so that Hitler's invective against the Jews did not appear particularly unusual. Once the Nazis were in power, their attacks on Jews worried Germans less on humanitarian or ethical grounds than out of concern for Germany's image abroad. The removal of Jews from the civil service seems to have struck most Germans as an act of fairness: Jews were thought to hold more power and wealth than they rightly deserved. By the time the 1935 Nuremberg laws disenfranchised Jews, most Germans approved, having come to accept the racialist doctrines of the Nazi state. At the same time, acts of violence directed against Jews, especially the pogrom of November 1938, evoked shock and disgust, but more at the street violence and property destruction than at the fact that Jews were the target. The increasing isolation of Jews from German society and its public places meant that once actual deportations began, few Germans retained social connections to Jews (Bankier).

Nazi antisemitism was successful because it appealed to well-established cultural traditions in Germany. While the images of Jews and the charges against them were far stronger than the images and charges before, they built on deep-seated sentiments that Jews were foreign, powerful, dangerous, and alien to the German nation. In the Nazi regime, antisemitism functioned to rally party activists with the promise of revolutionary action to rid Germany of its Jews. More cautious Nazis, concerned with rebuilding Germany's economy, as well as large sectors of the population were displeased with the violent tactics used against the Jews, because these tactics disturbed public law and order and created negative reactions abroad; but these people too approved the fundamental Nazi promise of eliminating Jews from German life. When *Der ewige Jude* was first shown in German cinemas in November 1940, the popular response was positive. As David Bankier has shown, Germans imagined the Allied bombings of their cities during the war as retribution for Kristallnacht. Although knowledge of the murder of Jews was widespread in the German civilian population by 1943, Germans tried to avoid awareness of the Holocaust in order to evade complicity in it.

Historians and theologians have long been disturbed by the failure of the Protestant and Catholic Churches to protest antisemitism during the Third Reich and to object to the abandonment of democracy and civil freedoms (Ericksen and Heschel). Indeed, the churches cooperated willingly with the Nazi racial laws, providing baptismal certificates that would "prove" Aryan identity. Some placed swastikas on the altar and introduced Nazi salutes and songs into the services. Of the few church leaders who openly opposed Hitler, almost none spoke out in support of the Jews. On the contrary, many theologians attempted to justify Hitler's actions toward the Jews on religious grounds. Like Grundmann, they argued that Jews persecuted Jesus and all Christians who followed him, so that Hitler was acting in defense of Christianity. Others, members of the Confessing Church, gave support only to those Jews who were baptized and saw no theological reason to support Jews and oppose the Nazi regime.

Yet even while Christian theological hostility toward Judaism remained intact, some individual Christians acted to protect Jews from deportation, explaining their motivation as rooted in their religious faith.

Antisemitism both clarifies and confuses the actions taken during the Holocaust. Studying the long and vicious history of antisemitism explains why the Nazis deemed the murder of the Jews an act of redemption for Germany. Moreover, the failure of the German Catholic Church, the Vatican, and the German Protestant Church to speak out in opposition to the Holocaust while it was ongoing, or to condemn it immediately after the defeat of the Nazis, is clarified by the context of their theological teachings regarding Judaism. At the same time, we have to recognize and explain what motivated the many Christians, often pious, who hid Jews, saving them from murder. Antisemitism, while deeply pervasive in European culture, could also be transcended in the name of higher moral values and even in the name of Christianity itself.

Note

1. We teach in different institutions—Heschel at Dartmouth, Gilman at the University of Illinois, Chicago—and offer our courses in different departments: Heschel teaches History of the Holocaust through the Jewish Studies Program and the History Department; Gilman teaches Holocaust literature and representation.

Works Cited

Augustine. *The First Catechetical Instruction*. Trans. Joseph P. Christopher. Westminster: Newman Bookshop, 1946.

Bankier, David. *The Germans and the Final Solution: Public Opinion under Nazism*. Oxford: Blackwell, 1992.

Becker, Adam H., and Annette Yoshiko Reed, eds. *The Ways That Never Parted: Jews and Christians in Late Antiquity and the Early Middle Ages*. Tübingen: Mohr Siebeck, 2003.

The Bible, King James Version: Old and New Testaments, with the Apocrypha. Electronic Text Center, U of Virginia Lib. 30 Aug. 2004 <http://etext.virginia.edu/kjv.browse.html>.

Bredin, Jean-Louis. *The Affair: The Case of Alfred Dreyfus*. Trans. Jeffrey Mehlman. New York: Braziller, 1986.

Chamberlain, Houston Stewart. *Foundations of the Nineteenth Century.* Trans. John Lees. London, New York: Lane, 1911.

Cohen, Jeremy. *The Friars and the Jews: The Evolution of Medieval Anti-Judaism.* Ithaca: Cornell UP, 1982.

———. *Living Letters of the Law: Ideas of the Jew in Medieval Christianity.* Berkeley: U of California P, 1999.

Cohen, Mark R. *Under Crescent and Cross: The Jews in the Middle Ages.* Princeton: Princeton UP, 1994.

Derfler, Leslie. *The Dreyfus Affair.* Westport: Greenwood, 2002.

Engelmann, Hans. *Kirche am Abgrund: Adolf Stoecker und seine antijüdische Bewegung.* Berlin: Institut Kirche und Judentum, 1984.

Ericksen, Robert P., and Susannah Heschel. *Betrayal: German Churches and the Holocaust.* Minneapolis: Augsburg-Fortress, 1999.

Gelder, Ken. *Reading the Vampire.* New York: Routledge, 1994.

Gilman, Sander. *Jewish Self-Hatred: Anti-Semitism and the Hidden Language of the Jews.* Baltimore: Johns Hopkins UP, 1986.

Gobineau, Arthur de. *The Inequality of Human Races.* Trans. Adrian Collins. London: Heineman, 1915.

Graetz, Heinrich. *A History of the Jews.* Trans. Henrietta Szold. 6 vols. Philadelphia: Jewish Pub. Soc. of Amer., 1891–98.

Halberstam, Judith. "Technologies of Monstrosity: Bram Stoker's *Dracula.*" *Cultural Politics at the Fin de Siècle.* Ed. Sally Ledger and Scott McCracken. New York: Cambridge UP, 1995. 248–66.

Harrowitz, Nancy A. *Antisemitism, Misogyny, and the Logic of Cultural Difference: Cesare Lombroso and Matilde Serao.* Lincoln: U of Nebraska P, 1994.

Herzl, Theodor. *The Jewish State.* New York, 1946.

Heschel, Susannah. *Abraham Geiger and the Jewish Jesus.* Chicago: U of Chicago P, 1998.

———. "When Jesus Was an Aryan: The Protestant Church and Antisemitic Propaganda." Ericksen and Heschel 68–89.

Hsia, R. Po-chia. *The Myth of Ritual Murder: Jews and Magic in Reformation Germany.* New Haven: Yale UP, 1988.

Marx, Karl. "On the Jewish Question." *Karl Marx: Selected Writings.* Oxford: Oxford UP, 2000. 46–70.

Meier, John P. *A Marginal Jew: Rethinking the Historical Jesus.* 3 vols. New York: Doubleday, 1991–2001.

Netanyahu, Benzion. *The Origins of the Inquisition in Fifteenth-Century Spain.* New York: Random, 1995.

Niewyk, Donald L. *The Jews in Weimar Germany.* New Brunswick: Transaction, 2001.

Oberman, Heiko. *The Roots of Anti-Semitism in the Age of Renaissance and Reformation.* Philadelphia: Fortress, 1983.

Olender, Maurice. *The Languages of Paradise: Aryans and Semites, a Match Made in Heaven.* Trans. Arthur Goldhammer. New York: Other, 2002.

Penslar, Derek. "Antisemites on Zionism: From Indifference to Obsession." *Convergence and Divergence: Antisemitism and Anti-Zionism in Historical Perspective.* 24–25 Mar. 2004. Sarnat Center for the Study of Anti-Jewishness. Brandeis U. 10 May 2004 <http://brandeis.edu/ centers/ sarnat/participants/penslar.pdf>.

"Pharisee." Def. 2. *The Oxford English Dictionary.* 2nd ed. 1989.

Pulzer, Peter G. J. *The Rise of Political Anti-Semitism in Germany and Austria.* Cambridge: Harvard UP, 1988.

Reizbaum, Marilyn. "Max Nordau and the Generation of Jewish Muscle." *The Image of the Jew in Europe, 1880–1914.* Ed. Bryan Cheyette and Nadia Valman. London: Vallentine Mitchell, forthcoming.

Rose, Paul Lawrence. *Revolutionary Antisemitism in Germany from Kant to Wagner.* Princeton: Princeton UP, 1990.

Rubin, Miri. *Gentile Tales: The Narrative Assault on Late Medieval Jews.* New Haven: Yale UP, 1999.

Rürup, Reinhard. *Emanzipation und Antisemitismus: Studien zur "Judenfrage" der bürgerlichen Gesellschaft.* Göttingen: Vandenhoeck, 1975.

Sanders, E. P. *Paul and Palestinian Judaism: A Comparison of Patterns of Religion.* Philadelphia: Fortress, 1977.

Schäfer, Peter. *Judeophobia: Attitudes toward the Jews in the Ancient World.* Cambridge: Harvard UP, 1997.

Schreckenberg, Heinz. *The Jews in Christian Art: An Illustrated History.* New York: Continuum, 1996.

Segel, Binjamin W. *A Lie and Libel: The History of the Protocols of the Elders of Zion.* Lincoln: U of Nebraska P, 1995.

Stendahl, Krister. *Paul among Jews and Gentiles.* Philadelphia: Fortress, 1976.

Stern, Selma. *The Court Jew: A Contribution to the History of Absolutism in Europe.* New Brunswick: Transaction, 1985.

Stow, Kenneth R. *Theater of Acculturation: The Roman Ghetto in the Sixteenth Century.* Seattle: U of Washington P, 2001.

Tal, Uriel. *Christians and Jews in Germany: Religion, Politics, and Ideology in the Second Reich, 1870–1914.* Trans. Noah Jonathan Jacobs. Ithaca: Cornell UP, 1975.

Trachtenberg, Joshua. *The Devil and the Jews: The Medieval Conception of the Jew and Its Relation to Modern Antisemitism.* New Haven: Yale UP, 1943.

Vermes, Geza, ed. and trans. *The Complete Dead Sea Scrolls in English.* New York: Penguin, 1997.

Volkov, Shulamit. *Antisemitismus als kultureller Code: Zehn Essays.* Munich: Beck, 2000.

Wagner, Clarence H., Jr. "Christian Anti-Semitism." 1992. *Anti-Semitism and Holocaust.* Christian Action for Israel. 1999–2003. 10 May 2004 <http://www.cdn-friends-icej.ca/antiholo/cantisem.html>.

Wagner, Richard. *"Judaism in Music" and Other Essays.* Trans. William Ashton Ellis. Lincoln: U of Nebraska P, 1995.

Weininger, Otto. *Sex and Character.* London: Heinemann, 1906.

Wirszubski, Chaim. *Pico della Mirandola's Encounter with Jewish Mysticism.* Cambridge: Harvard UP, 1989.

Wolfson, Elliot. *Circle in the Square: Studies in the Use of Gender in Kabbalistic Symbolism.* Albany: State U of New York P, 1995.

Yerushalmi, Yosef. "Response to Rosemary Ruether." *Auschwitz: Beginning of a New Era?* Ed. Eva Fleischner. New York: Cathedral Church of Saint John the Divine, 1977. 97–107.

Sara R. Horowitz

Gender and Holocaust Representation

In his comix *Maus*, Art Spiegelman depicts the experiences of his parents, Vladek and Anja, survivors of the Nazi genocide, and the effect of the Holocaust on his own life. Through a series of taped conversations over several years, Vladek rebuilds the past; by the time Art begins the project, Anja has been dead for several years. As Art searches for her diaries, Vladek reassures him of their superfluousness. "I can tell you . . . She went through the same what me: TERRIBLE!" (*My Father* 158). Indeed, Vladek's account, beginning in prewar Poland and ending in postwar New York, encompasses Anja. Only at the end of the first volume, *My Father Bleeds History*, does Vladek confess that, in an attempt to "make an order" with his memories after Anja's suicide, he burned her notebooks (159).

Contemplating Anja's missing diaries opens up a space for introducing gender analysis in teaching about the Holocaust. Coming on Vladek's belated confession, many students express dismay at the devaluing of Anja's experiences; the silencing of her voice; and the generally diminished, if beloved, image that emerges. In Vladek's stories, Anja appears sensitive, loving, and emotionally fragile, utterly dependent on her husband for survival. In Art's recollections, Anja's maternal love is both overbearing and inconstant, smothering him with emotional neediness and abandoning him through suicide. Responding to student observations, I note that Anja's absent journals can serve to exemplify the marginality of women's experience in constructing a master narrative of the Nazi genocide. In the absence of her words, Anja's story is recoverable only through the reconstruction of Vladek's and Art's memories, bearing their interpretation; anything she experienced while apart from them is utterly lost. Similarly, in many male Holocaust narratives, women figure as peripheral and helpless victims. These skewed depictions of women impel us to ask not only what is hidden but also what is transacted through the construction of gendered Holocaust narratives.

Exploring what underlies Anja's missing diaries, I might lead students to consider how Vladek's recollections evade moments of failure and loss. At the conclusion of the second volume of *Maus*, *And Here My Troubles Began*, Vladek's remembrance terminates with his reunion with Anja soon after liberation. "We were both very happy, and lived happy, happy ever after," he says, then demands that Art switch off the tape recorder (136). Vladek thus blocks everything that happens later. To maintain the happy, fairy-tale closure, Vladek must keep out any counternotes—including Anja's suicide; Vladek's recurrent nightmares; his anguish over their first son, Richieu, murdered in the Nazi genocide. While the reader cannot know how Anja's journals depicted the past, a number of revealing facets of her life slip through. Jarring details, powerfully at odds with Vladek's otherwise seamless portrayal of his fragile wife, indicate that her journals may have narrated not only a different perspective but also a past unknown to her husband and son.

Comparing Vladek's and Anja's versions of the past might help us understand what fuels Vladek's narrative construction of his wife. Early on, for example, Vladek learns that Anja has been involved in anti-Nazi "conspirations" (27), translating documents for Communist resisters. Pursued by the police, she has the presence of mind to hide incriminating material and evade capture. Vladek forbids this dangerous work, assuring Art that Anja "was a good girl, and of course she stopped all such things" (29). Notable in this episode is not only Anja's coolness in crisis but also her engagement, at great peril, in a cause broader than personal survival. While Vladek protects his family, Anja puts herself at risk for the welfare of strangers. Was she as "good" a girl as her husband believed, ceasing all such activity? In any event, Anja as activist, selfless, bold, contradicts the portrait drawn by Vladek and Art. What is at stake for Vladek in constructing this helpless version of his wife and opposing to it his own competence? Vladek casts himself as protector—a role denied him in actuality, at least with regard to Richieu. As though in compensation, his narrative accords him a hyperbolic version of husbandly heroism.

This discussion of *Maus* illustrates that gender analysis has a place in the teaching of any Holocaust representation, not only those by or about women. These approaches help us understand something about male and female experience and memory; they also deepen our understanding of the nature and aftermath of atrocity and the evolving cultural meanings of the Holocaust. Although gender does not mean only women, some of the earliest gender studies of the Holocaust focused on women. New attention to the writing, art, and oral history of women survivors has resulted in the discovery, rediscovery, or reinterpretation of their works. Reading these works alongside others by male survivors and measuring them against gendered generic conventions and stock figures (e.g., the heroic male fighter, the woman in distress, the safety of domestic space) have led to a reconsideration of women's and men's experiences, memories, coping strategies, and responses to trauma. Gendered readings have resulted in further thinking about sexuality and gender under Fascism. What roles were assigned men and women in the Third Reich? How did gender affect the perceptions and experiences of perpetrators, rescuers, and resisters?

The focus on gender is relatively recent, still considered controversial by many Holocaust scholars. Some researchers see the methodologies of women's and gender studies as inherently flawed when applied to the study of the Holocaust. Others fear that a focus on women or gender issues would eclipse the horror of genocide, either by domesticating it or by de-emphasizing its centrality to the Holocaust in favor of an emphasis on patriarchy. Cynthia Ozick has argued that, because the Nazi genocide targeted Jews as Jews and did not target women as such, focusing on women is inherently misguided (Ringelheim 144). Ozick and others suggest that such a focus would enfold the Holocaust into a history of women (rather than a history of the Jews or Roma in Europe), flattening crucial differences in experience, history, and ideology. Such an approach, some argue (e.g., Langer), would result only in competitive victimization. Some historians of the Holocaust (e.g., Bauer) see gender analysis as valid but of only secondary importance.

Some critics, particularly those outside academic discourse (e.g., Gabriel Schoenfeld), understand gender criticism as writing by and about women that would inevitably distort history to promote a feminist agenda. Many scholars fear that bringing sexuality into the discussion of victims or perpetrators and their respective cultures would be inappropriately titillating or voyeuristic. As students evaluate or criticize gender approaches, they become aware of differences among them and of ongoing debates in feminist and gender theory. Noticing issues of gender enables us not only to consider issues pertaining to women and men during the Holocaust but also to think through broader questions about the nature of Holocaust representation. As the above reading of *Maus* indicates, to ask questions about the portrayal of Anja is to ask questions about Vladek as well and, more generally, about how and why particular narrative constructions of masculinity and femininity mediated the Holocaust.

Since few students are familiar with the history of the Nazi era and fewer still have considered the perspective of gender, I find it useful to suggest outside readings and to summarize some of the findings of social historians and others regarding conditions and behavior of men and women during the Nazi era (some of which are noted in the bibliography that follows this essay). I frequently assign readings from works that integrate contemporary cultural and feminist theory and the complex issues of narrative, memory, and representation that have occupied Holocaust studies. (See, for example, the collection edited by Julia Epstein and Lori Lefkovitz, which brings theoretical perspectives to bear on issues of memory, trauma, and imagination; the collection by Renate Bridenthal, Atina Grossmann, and Marion Kaplan, on women in Nazi Germany. See also the work by Mary Felstiner; by Marianne Hirsch ["Gendered Translations," "Marked," and "Nazi Photographs"]; and my essay "Wounded Tongue," one of the few to address tropes of Jewish masculinity in connection with the Holocaust.) Because gender does not exist as an isolated category but must be studied in specific contexts, this background information helps students understand how nationality, ethnicity, religion, and class interact with questions of gender.

I apply gender analysis to all levels of teaching and in all contexts — whether a course on Holocaust literature or a seminar on life writing. This approach can open familiar texts in new ways. For example, Elie Wiesel's *Night*—perhaps the most widely read book about the Holocaust — narrates the writer's experiences in the men's barracks at Auschwitz. We know that women faced the same nightmarish conditions — filth; starvation; grueling, often pointless or toxic labor; omnipresent death. The Nazi genocide targeted Jewish men and Jewish women alike. At the same time, Eliezer's plunge into a world of men points to crucial differences. Because pregnant women and young mothers were sent immediately to gas chambers, Wiesel's mother and younger sister do not survive the first selection. Eliezer and his father, however, serve as slave labor, which provides a deferral of death that allows for the boy's survival. The book traces the father's rapid deterioration, disabling him from sustaining his son emotionally and physically in the harshness of the camp. In a reversal of the father-son relationship characteristic of Holocaust narratives, Eliezer looks out for his father, guiltily resenting the burden. The erosion of their relationship illustrates the dehumanizing, self-destroying capacity of Nazi atrocity. In addition, Eliezer's struggle with God takes place against the education and worldview of the Orthodox, Eastern European Jewish male — the study of sacred texts, the rhythms of thrice-daily prayer. The Holocaust challenges his identity as a Jewish man.

Looking at such works through the lens of gender challenges

students' constructs about masculinity and femininity, both generally and in extremis. A key hypothesis that has become central (although by no means uncontested) in the study of women and the Holocaust suggests that women supported one another in the struggle to survive while men competed aggressively for individual survival. To some extent, Holocaust memory narratives support this view. For example, in reading Charlotte Delbo's *Auschwitz and After*, my students are moved by the depiction of how other women help Delbo remain standing during a roll call or how they stand guard as she takes a forbidden drink or washes in a stream. Similarly, my students note that Sara Nomberg-Przytyk's *Auschwitz: True Tales from a Grotesque Land* depicts women risking their lives for one another, performing secret abortions to preserve the lives of pregnant women, or smuggling food. In oral testimony, many women credit their survival to a mother or sister who supported them, often at great sacrifice. In her novel about women in a labor camp, *An Estate of Memory*, Ilona Karmel describes "makeshift camp families"—camp "sisters," as some survivors have termed them—"women, young girls, whom loneliness unaccustomed and sudden had brought together" (7), who look out for one another. One such family shares food and distasteful work, taking risks for one another. Forced to choose among hideous actions to ensure survival, the women decide that fighting for group rather than individual survival is ethical. By contrast, in *Survival in Auschwitz*, for example, Primo Levi describes a world in which each man mostly looks out for himself.

At the same time, I point out to my students that Holocaust narratives also provide counterevidence for both women's and men's behavior in extremis. For example, while Karmel's surrogate families demonstrate women's altruism, one might argue that each such group competes against others instead of working for the survival of women generally. Karmel traces the way that the pressures of atrocity unravel group cohesion and the ethics of cooperation. One woman thinks, "What is it? Anything done for someone else is a sacrifice, a noble deed; but try to do the same thing for yourself and the sacrifice becomes a disgrace. Why? I too am someone" (342). In rare reflective moments, each woman senses inner discontinuities: kindness and cruelty, fear and courage, selfishness and altruism. In *Survival in Auschwitz*, Levi describes moments of communion and support among men amid fierce competition for resources. Memoirs by other men (e.g., Jorge Semprun [*Literature* and *Long Voyage*], David Weiss Halivni) describe gathering in the camps for intellectual exchange or religious study with the last remnants of strength. If differences in the behavior of men and women were less sharp than some scholars hypothesize, we might ask why bonding and nurturing play a greater role in women's memory writing. As in the portait of Anja Spiegelman, generating narratives that reflect conventionally gendered roles — aggressive men, nurturing emotional women — memory writing may serve to restore a sense of manhood or womanhood shattered by atrocity.

Gender analysis helps students examine different cultural interpretations of the Holocaust, considering not only the contexts in which it took place but also the contexts in which it is remembered. The portrayal of men, women, and gender-associated conventions is linked to particular kinds of narrative meanings. For example, some Holocaust representations construct narratives of heroics — a way of telling that focuses on the heroism and the triumph (physical or spiritual) over evil. Students see this type of narrative as upbeat, if not about the Holocaust then about human possibility, God, culture, the predominance of good. By contrast, other representations construct narratives of atrocity, emphasizing radical loss and the rupture of values. These contrasting narrative impulses figure importantly in representations of pregnancy.

Narratives of heroics depict women subverting the genocidal will of the Nazis to save a pregnant woman. These narratives stress the protective agency of women; pregnancy becomes a biological inner resistance that triumphs over external evil. Narratives of atrocity depict women especially vulnerable to Nazi brutality, with mothers too weak to sustain or survive pregnancy. Women may kill a newborn to keep the mother alive, or Nazis may murder both. In Karmel's novel, three women conceal the pregnancy of a fourth, then smuggle her baby to safety, an act given symbolic weight. "So the child, carried like a parcel out of the camp, kept growing, until it was big enough to take upon itself the burden of their longing for a proof, for the sign that out 'in the Freedom' they still mattered" (277). In Nomberg-Przytyk's "Esther's First Born," the namesake of the biblical heroine who saves her people from a genocidal decree insists on carrying to term, when a secret abortion could save her from death. Both writers juxtapose elements of atrocity and heroics. Karmel describes another infant born in the camp, discovered by the SS and left to starve. Women secretly feed the baby sugar water but only prolong the death agony. Nomberg-Przytyk's Esther and her baby are doomed. Such works invert the conventional symbol of pregnancy as hope and regeneration; instead, pregnancy connotes death. As students become self-conscious about their responses to these two narrative impulses, they confront their own desires for happy (if false) endings. Moreover, the real and symbolic meanings of pregnancy continue to evolve after the war. Ozick's novella *The Shawl* uses pregnancy and motherhood to explore the intersection of bereavement, trauma, and sexual shame for women victims and survivors. (See also Grossman's work on German and Jewish birth-rates after the war ["Trauma"].)

I also ask students to consider the role of the male gaze and gendered imagery in aesthetic productions. Nazi propaganda, for example, frequently depicts a lascivious, sexually rapacious Jewish man or an exotic Jewess, stock figures of European antisemitism who force or tempt Aryans into miscegenation, polluting racial purity. Steven Spielberg's film *Schindler's List* illustrates the influence of such imagery through the warning that "Jewish girls . . . cast a spell on you," and through the relationship between the camp comman-dant, Amon Goeth, and Jewish inmate Helen Hirsch. The male gaze, in its association with sovereignty and power, has other functions as well. I ask my students to note who gazes and desires and who is the object, as an index of the imbalance of power between the one free to live and to call death on the other and the one who is denied all rights. For example, in Ida Fink's story "Aryan Papers," a Jewish teenager barters her virginity for the false documents that may save her and her mother from death. In Fink's "A Conversation," a Jew-ish couple understands that for them to remain safe, the husband must yield to the sexual overtures of the woman who is hiding them. The story reverses convention, so that the farm woman, who is not the target of genocide, wields absolute power over the Jew. This privilege entitles her to gaze on him and subject him to her will.

For victims, the male gaze may represent an attempt to recuperate a remembered normalcy or to reconstitute a shattered self and a sense of autonomy. In Semprun's novel *The Long Voyage*, the male narrator shows two French nurses around Buchenwald soon after his liberation, all the while noting the "legs in the silk stockings, lips alive beneath the lipstick" (69), the "beautiful uniform that hugs the thighs" (74). Semprun's later memoir *Literature or Life* includes this episode and a similar encounter with three British soldiers. Although both episodes depict a survivor attempting to explain the essence of Nazi atrocity, there are key differences, and those differences are linked to gender. The soldiers see in Semprun an embodiment of horror; the narrative sharply contrasts his enfeebled skeleton with their hard, uniformed bodies. However, with the nurses, he emphasizes how *he* sees *them*, noting their beauty, the fit of their clothing. In other words, the narrator depicts himself as the object of the men's gaze, while the women become objects of his. This objectifying of his restores to him a degree of agency; it suggests the reemergence or reconstruction of his shattered manhood.

Fiction about perpetrators frequently links the male gaze with the power to torture and kill, linking fascism with desire and violence with Eros. Marcie Hershman's story "The Guillotine" depicts an erotic triangle involving the chief of police, his assistant, and the assistant's wife. The assistant has twinges of conscience about people tortured and killed in the police cellar, reservations his wife sees as signs of weakness. With each victim, the chief cuts his assistant's hair, symbolically emasculating him. The assistant's wife sends gifts of home-cooked food to the chief, who provides her with rare wartime luxuries reserved for those in power. Such works lead to discussions about the extent to which German women were victimized or empowered by Nazi ideology.

Exploring the debate between the historians Gisela Bock ("Ordinary Women" and "Racism") and Claudia Koonz regarding the role of women and the place of feminism in Nazism introduces students to the complexities of the issue. Koonz argued that, at the grass roots, German women were complicit with Nazism through their domestic, maternal, and political roles; they cannot be seen only as victims of sexism, because they abetted and were empowered by Nazi ideology. Bock responded that German women were victims of Nazism; they were relegated to domestic roles, their reproductive capacity appropriated by the government through compulsory sterilization and other antinatal policies that were both sexist and racist. Bock later noted that Nazi ideology was defined predominantly by racism, that some German women were perpetrators and not victims or resisters, and she cautioned against falsely equating the suffering of German women with that of their Jewish and Roma victims. Some historians maintain that the Nazi focus on Aryan family values effectively removed women from the policy-making sphere; others maintain that German women and men were equal partners in racism and genocide. Some scholars argue that in historical and literary representation, women collaborators and perpetrators have been treated more harshly than their male counterparts.

With this debate in mind, we might turn to examples of postwar German literature and film, such as Helma Sanders-Brahms's film *Germany, Pale Mother*, which develops the trope of the doubly victimized German woman: first by the sexism of Nazi ideology, then by the vengefulness of foreign men who brutalize war widows. We might view Leni Riefenstahl's film *Triumph of the Will*, noting the focus on attractive bodies and military exercises and the place of sexuality in solidifying Nazi power. These works help students consider the complex intersections of race, desire, and power in Nazi ideology.

Noting and analyzing the images of men and women in contemporary representations of the Holocaust makes visible the various meanings assigned to that past. Not surprisingly, gender analysis challenges fundamental paradigms for thinking about the Holocaust. Gender studies thus has the potential to transform our understanding of this terrible past and of our own relation to it.

Works Cited and Recommended

Bauer, Yehuda. "Gisi Fleishmann." Ofer and Weitzman 262–63.

Baumel, Judith Tydor. *Double Jeopardy: Gender and the Holocaust*. London: Vallentine Mitchell, 1998.

Bock, Gisela. "Ordinary Women in Nazi Germany: Perpetrators, Victims, Followers, and Bystanders." Ofer and Weitzman 85–100.

————. "Racism and Sexism in Nazi Germany: Motherhood, Compulsory Sterilization, and the State." Bridenthal, Grossmann, and Kaplan 271–96.

Brenner, Rachel Feldhay. *Writing as Resistance: Four Women Confronting the Holocaust.* University Park: Pennsylvania State UP, 1997.

Bridenthal, Renate, Atina Grossmann, and Marion Kaplan, eds. *When Biology Became Destiny: Women in Weimar and Nazi Germany.* New York: Monthly Review, 1984.

Delbo, Charlotte. *Auschwitz and After.* New Haven: Yale UP, 1996.

Epstein, Julia, and Lori Lefkovitz, eds. *Shaping Losses: Cultural Memory and the Holocaust.* Urbana: U of Illinois P, 2001.

Felstiner, Mary Lowenthal. *To Paint Her Life: Charlotte Salomon in the Nazi Era.* New York: Harper, 1994.

Fink, Ida. *A Scrap of Time: Stories.* New York: Random, 1987.

Frederiksen, Elke P., and Martha Kaarsberg Wallach, eds. *Facing Fascism and Confronting the Past: German Women Writers from Weimar to the Present.* Albany: State U of New York P, 2000.

Germany, Pale Mother [*Deutschland bleiche Mutter*]. Dir. Helma Sanders-Brahms. Basis-Film Verleih, Berlin, 1980.

Grossman, Atina. "Feminist Debates about Women and National Socialism." *Gender and History* 3 (1991): 350–58.

————. "Trauma, Memory, and Motherhood: Germans and Jewish Displaced Persons in Post-Nazi Germany, 1945–1949." *Life after Death: Approaches to a Cultural and Social History of Europe during the 1940s and 1950s.* Ed. Richard J. Bessel and Dirk Schumann. Cambridge: Cambridge UP, 2003. 93–127.

Heineman, Elizabeth D. "Sexuality and Nazism: The Doubly Unspeakable?" *Journal of the History of Sexuality* 11.1–2 (2002): 22–66.

Hershman, Marcie. *Tales of the Master Race.* New York: Harper, 1991.

Herzog, Dagmar. "Hubris and Hypocrisy, Incitement and Disavowal: Sexuality and German Fascism." *Journal of the History of Sexuality* 11.1–2 (2002): 3–21.

Heschel, Susannah. "Does Atrocity Have a Gender? Women in the SS." *Lessons and Legacies VI.* Ed. Jeffry Diefendorf. Evanston: Northwestern UP, 2004. 300–22.

Hirsch, Marianne. "Marked by Memory: Feminist Reflections on Trauma and Transmission." *Extremities: Trauma, Testimony, Community.* Ed. Nancy K. Miller and Jason Tougaw. Urbana: U of Illinois P, 2002. 71–91.

————. "Nazi Photographs in Post-Holocaust Art: Gender as an Idiom of Memorialization." *Crimes of War: Guilt and Denial.* Ed. Omer Bartov, Atina Grossman, and Molly Noble. New York: New, 2002. 100–20.

Hirsch, Marianne, and Leo Spitzer. "Gendered Translations: Claude Lanzmann's Shoah." *Gendering War Talk.* Ed. Miriam Cooke and Angela Woollacott. Princeton: Princeton UP, 1993. 3–19.

Horowitz, Sara R. "But Is It Good for the Jews? Spielberg's Schindler and the Aesthetics of Atrocity." *Spielberg's Holocaust: Critical Perspectives on*

Schindler's List. Ed. Yosefa Loshitsky. Bloomington: Indiana UP, 1997. 119–39.

———. "Gender, Genocide, and Jewish Memory." *Prooftexts* 20 (2000) 1: 158–90.

———. "Memory and Testimony in Women Survivors of Nazi Genocide." *Women of the Word: Jewish Women and Jewish Writing.* Ed. Judith Baskin. Detroit: Wayne State UP, 1994. 258–82.

———. "Mengele the Gynecologist and Other Stories of Women's Survival." *Judaism since Gender.* Ed. Miriam Peskowitz and Laura Levitt. New York: Routledge, 1997. 200–12.

———. "The Wounded Tongue: Engendering Holocaust Memory." Epstein and Lefkovitz 107–27.

Kahane, Claire. "Dark Mirrors: A Feminist Reflection on Holocaust Narrative and the Maternal Metaphor." *Feminist Consequences: Gender and Culture.* Ed. Elisabeth Bronfen and Misha Kavka. New York: Columbia UP, 2000. 161–88.

Karmel, Ilona. *An Estate of Memory.* Boston: Houghton, 1969. New York: Feminist, 1986.

Katz, Esther, and Joan M. Ringelheim, eds. *Proceedings of the Conference on Women Surviving the Holocaust.* New York: Inst. for Research in History, 1983.

Koonz, Claudia. *Mothers in the Fatherland: Women, the Family, and Nazi Politics.* New York: St. Martin's, 1987.

Kremer, S. Lillian. *Women's Holocaust Writing: Memory and Imagination.* Lincoln: U of Nebraska P, 1999.

Langer, Lawrence. "Gendered Suffering? Women in Holocaust Testimony." Ofer and Weitzman 351–63.

Laska, Vera, ed. *Women in the Resistance and in the Holocaust.* Westport: Greenwood, 1983.

Levi, Primo. *Survival in Auschwitz: The Nazi Assault on Humanity.* 1958. Trans. S. Woolf. New York: Collier, 1993.

Mosse, George. *The Image of Man: The Creation of Modern Masculinity.* New York: Oxford UP, 1996.

Nomberg-Przytyk, Sara. *Auschwitz: True Tales from a Grotesque Land.* Chapel Hill: U of North Carolina P, 1985.

Ofer, Dalia, and Lenore J. Weitzman, eds. *Women in the Holocaust.* New Haven: Yale UP, 1998.

Owings, Allison. *Frauen: German Women Recall the Third Reich.* New Brunswick: Rutgers UP, 1993.

Ozick, Cynthia. *The Shawl: A Story and a Novella.* New York: Knopf, 1989.

Ringelheim, Joan M. "Thoughts about Women and the Holocaust." *Thinking the Unthinkable: Meanings of the Holocaust.* Ed. Roger S. Gottlieb. New York: Paulist, 1990. 141–49.

Schindler's List. Dir. Steven Spielberg. Universal Studios, 1993.

Schoenfeld, Gabriel. "Auschwitz and the Professors." *Commentary* June 1998: 42–46.

Semprun, Jorge. *Literature or Life*. New York: Viking, 1997.

———. *The Long Voyage*. New York: Grove, 1964.

Spiegelman, Art. *And Here My Troubles Began*. New York: Pantheon, 1991. Vol. 2 of *Maus: A Survivor's Tale*.

———. *My Father Bleeds History*. New York: Pantheon, 1986. Vol. 1 of *Maus: A Survivor's Tale*.

Stephenson, Jill. *Women in Nazi Germany*. New York: Longman, 2001.

Tec, Nehama. *Resistance and Courage: Jewish Women during the Holocaust*. New Haven: Yale UP, 2003.

Theweleit, Klaus. *Male Fantasies*. 2 vols. Minneapolis: U of Minnesota P, 1987, 1989.

Triumph of the Will [*Triumph des Willens*]. Dir. Leni Riefenstahl. UFA-Filmverleih, 1935.

Weiss Halivni, David. *The Book and the Sword: A Life of Learning in the Shadow of Destruction*. New York: Farrar, 1996.

Wiesel, Elie. *Night*. New York: Bantam, 1960.

Bella Brodzki

Teaching Trauma
and Transmission

Trauma and the Holocaust are so interrelated that it may now be impossible to address one of the terms without invoking, implicating, or referring to the other. In what ways is the Holocaust traumatic? On innumerable levels, certainly. My essay focuses on three registers — the clinical, the historical, and the discursive — and in the process engages the two following questions: How is an examination of trauma relevant to the literary analysis of Holocaust texts? What do we learn about language and textuality by knowing about trauma?

Trauma comes from the Greek word meaning "wound"; in medicine it has always been defined as an injury or wound to tissue caused by external force or violence. In the 1860s physicians used the word to explain the syndrome of distress associated with the frightful experience of victims of railway accidents. Over the course of the next fifty years the concept of trauma changed from tracking the physiology of shock and began to assume its current psychological connotation. Trauma theory as we know it today derives from the work of the thinkers and physicians J. M. Charcot, Pierre Janet, Alfred Binet, Morton Prince, Joseph Breuer, Sigmund Freud, and other turn-of-the-century thinkers who employed the word *trauma* to describe the wounding of the mind—what we now call the psyche—brought about by a sudden, unexpected, shattering emotional shock. Because of the tension and slippage between the psychoanalytic and biological paradigms, between structural and thematic approaches to the identification of trauma's causes and potentially long-term effects, it is difficult to argue for a singular genealogy of trauma or of trauma studies. For literature teachers, understanding trauma and its history in broad strokes can provide a useful general framework for approaching the daunting and fraught field of Holocaust studies; it can also help them interpret specific Holocaust texts, regardless of genre—survivor narratives, oral and video testimony, film, photography, poetry, drama, fiction. The most helpful and representative introductions to trauma are Cathy Caruth's edited collection of essays *Trauma*, Judith Herman's *Trauma and Recovery* (esp. ch. 1), Dori Laub's essays in *Testimony* (Felman and Laub), Robert Jay Lifton's *The Broken Connection*, and Saul Friedländer's article "Trauma, Transference, and Working Through."

The History of Trauma

The history of trauma studies in the twentieth century has been punctuated by the wars it has seen. As Ruth Leys puts it in her account: "Just as it took World War II to remember the lessons of World War I, so it took the experiences of Viet Nam to 'remember' the lessons of World War II, including the psychiatric lessons of the Holocaust" (15). Although the term began to be commonly employed to characterize the extreme distress of World War I shell-shocked soldiers and eventually also of the survivors of Nazi concentration camps and Hiroshima, it was not until the years immediately following the Vietnam War that psychiatrists, psychoanalysts, and sociologists began to ascribe a specific set of behaviors and their sequelae and identified a condition known as post-traumatic stress disorder (PTSD). Now, however, trauma is routinely applied "to the victim of natural disaster, the combat victim, the Holocaust survivor, the victim of sexual abuse, and the Viet Nam veteran alike" (Leys 16). Thus, because *trauma* has common currency in our memory-obsessed culture—being the operative term in both popular and academic discourse on the repression, recovery, and revelation of personal and historical catastrophic experience—contextualizing the concept can help students make clearer distinctions among the various representations circulating and those they will encounter in a course addressing the Holocaust.

Theories of trauma crystallized with Freud. As an inclusive constellation of effects, traumatic experience involves intense fear, helplessness, loss of control, and threat of annihilation such that the organism's protective shield has been broken. This definition is derived from his classic psychoanalytic work on the theory of trauma, in *Beyond the Pleasure Principle* (1920). According to Freud, the problem for the traumatized organism becomes how to master the overwhelming amounts of stimulus or excitation, so that it can, presumably, return to its desired, relatively unthreatened state. Freud presents the now famous example of his grandson Hans's game of Fort-Da, by which means this one-and-a-half-year-old child masters the traumatic anxiety produced by his mother's departure. The game consists of Hans's endlessly repeating her absence in the form of a disappearing and reappearing toy and results in the child's gaining, albeit retroactively, a sense of control of a situation that would otherwise be overwhelming. The traumatic character of this experience is based on the loss of sense of control over one's life. As Freud explains, "The child playing the Fort-Da game at the outset . . . was in a passive situation—he was overpowered by the experiences; but, by repeating it, unpleasant though it was, as a game, he took an *active* part" (15). Freud's conception of the young child's ability to compensate for the loss of the missing mother by substituting an object suggests a view of trauma as foundational, as constitutive of the very conditions that produce subjectivity. In other words, as Dominick LaCapra puts it in the essay "Trauma, Absence, Loss," "Everyone is subject to structural trauma" (723). Structural trauma, he argues, is linked to originary absence. That is precisely why it must not be conflated with historical trauma and its representation, which is specific, related to particular events, and has a "subject-position associated with it" (722).

As LaCapra's assertion implies, trauma studies is a highly contested, constantly evolving field. Debates range over where—inside or outside the psyche—to locate the origins of traumatic experience. Scholars have interrogated the extent to which the trauma of the battlefield—the archetypal cause of external shock to the organism—can be linked to the trauma of early sexual abuse, for example, especially if childhood trauma, as Freud determined, is located in the realm of psychic reality as well as in actual experience. Along slightly different lines, some have questioned the degree to which Hans's response to the trauma of separation from his mother—his acting out as working through—can or should be utilized as the model for violent, historical traumatic experience or as a blueprint for its psychic overcoming. Moving in another direction, some have asked how a single, overwhelming event in a person's life, whether real or fantasized, can be likened to the experiences of massive, cumulative psychic trauma, as in the Holocaust, when vast numbers of people (including children) were subjected for months and years to loss, terror, dehumanization, and death, in a social and moral framework seemingly designed to make normal ego functioning impossible. In regard to the Holocaust, however, one can posit an analogy between the ways in which individuals and collectivities experience and work through trauma, because the victims of the Holocaust, as members of a targeted group, suffered individually *and* collectively. Furthermore, the posttraumatic condition always engages both internal and external processes of suppression and repression of memory.

Holocaust literature, especially when written from the perspective of the survivor, carries what Lifton, in an emphasis that diverges from Freud's insistence on the narcissistic injury inherent to trauma, calls "the death imprint." The survivor, Lifton explains,

> is one who has come into contact with death in some bodily or psychic fashion and has remained alive. There are five characteristic themes in the survivor: the death imprint,

death guilt, psychic numbing, conflicts around nurturing
and contagion, and struggles with meaning or formulation.
The death imprint consists of the radical intrusion of an
image-feeling of death or end to life. That intrusion may be
sudden, as in war experience and various forms of accidents,
or it may take shape more gradually over time. Of great importance is the unacceptability of death contained in the
image — of prematurity, grotesqueness, and absurdity. To
be experienced, the death imprint must call forth prior imagery either of actual death or death equivalents. In that
sense, every death encounter is itself a reactivation of earlier
"survivals." (169)

Belatedness

In a widely held psychoanalytic view, which seems to cut across most
others, crucial to traumatic experience is its belated temporality. The
impact of the traumatic event lies, Caruth says, "in its refusal to be
simply located, in its insistent appearance outside the boundaries of
any single place or time" (9). She explains in her introduction to the
edited collection of essays *Trauma: Explorations in Memory*:

> The apparent split between external and internal trauma in
> psychoanalytic theory, and related problems in other psy-
> chiatric definitions of trauma — whether to define it in terms
> of events or of symptomatic responses to events, or the rel-
> ative contribution of previous traumas to the present one —
> would all be a function, in Freud's definition, of the split
> within immediate experience that characterizes the trau-
> matic occurrence itself. (9)

Although it is generally agreed that intrinsically the process of traumatic experience cannot be fully known or assimilated — "registered"
is the term commonly used — as it occurs, Susan Brison disputes the
central assumption that the ordinary mechanisms of consciousness
and memory are temporarily bracketed or destroyed during the
trauma. In *Aftermath: Violence and the Remaking of a Self*, a personal and philosophical examination of traumatic experience, she
says, "[A]t least in the case of a single traumatic event, the event is

typically experienced at the same time and remembered from that time, although the full emotional impact of the trauma takes time to absorb and work through" (32). Alongside such challenges to Caruth's idea of unclaimed experience (*Unclaimed Experience*) endures the notion that there is a period of latency after which recognition or understanding that the trauma has occurred returns, in the form of flashbacks, nightmares, and other kinds of repetition (of the instigating events). In the wake of the Vietnam War, these phenomena were identified as the posttraumatic syndrome. Only later is the trauma signified or known, through the re-creation of the traumatic experience—often, through compulsive repetition and return, the blending (or bleeding, to invoke Spiegelman's title "My Father Bleeds History") of the past into the present, and episodes of remembering and forgetting. As Caruth formulates it, "The trauma is a repeated suffering of the event, but it is also a continual leaving of its site" (10).

Texts and Trauma

How does a reader recognize the signs of trauma in a text? How does narrative convey trauma? Can language itself be traumatized? Omission, negation, deflection, contradiction, circularity, displacement, even linguistic excess point to trauma. In all its permutations, says Sara Horowitz, author of *Voicing the Void*, silence in a Holocaust text is an index of trauma. When language fails altogether, of course, there is trauma's overlay. Thus the reader must look for traces, sometimes embodied in the trope of the mute witnesses who do not say, or cannot say, what they have seen and experienced. Some narrators are more helpful than others, as witnesses who testify to the difficulty of the enterprise.

At times, the author or narrator renders an experience of terror, horror, or shame explicitly, directly, almost didactically, perhaps using the word *trauma* itself, as in the case of Primo Levi's description in his final testimonial narrative, *The Drowned and the Saved*, of the deportees' responses to the dehumanizing conditions in the transport convoy to Auschwitz:

> For everybody, but especially for them [the inmates of the Jew-
> ish Rest Home of Venice], evacuating in public was painful or
> even impossible: a *trauma* for which civilization does not pre-
> pare us, a deep wound inflicted on human dignity, an aggres-
> sion which is obscene and ominous, but also the sign of
> deliberate and gratuitous viciousness. (111; my emphasis)

In a subsequent passage in the next chapter, which is entitled
"Useless Violence," Levi refers to the tattooing of inmates—an
iconic feature of the concentrationary universe—whose ultimate purpose was to produce the sensation of impotence:

> The operation was not very painful and lasted no more than
> a minute, but it was *traumatic*. Its symbolic meaning was
> clear to everyone: this is the mark with which slaves are
> branded and cattle sent to the slaughter, and that is what
> you have become. (119; my emphasis)

The theme of bestiality and dehumanization pervades Levi's work,
jarring with his straightforward style and commanding intelligence.
In *Moments of Reprieve*, written many years after his earlier testimonies, he directs the reader toward the cumulative effect of trauma,
its strange and estranging legacy. Situating himself in the present, in
the act of writing the very memoir, in the act of recalling a particular experience that he raises to the level of a principle, he highlights
the challenge of translating in its specific communicative context the
nonverbal lexicon of Auschwitz:

> A slap inflicted in the Camp had a very different significance
> from what it might have here among us in today's here and
> now. [P]unches and slaps passed among us as daily lan-
> guage, and we soon learned to distinguish meaningful blows
> from the others inflicted out of savagery, to create pain and
> humiliation, and which often resulted in death. . . . Among
> the many miseries in the Camp, blows of this nature were
> by far the least painful. Which is equivalent to saying that
> our manner of living was not very different from that of
> donkeys and dogs. (31)

This passage, among countless others that signal horror through
self-restraint, reveals, as Bessel A. van der Kolk and Onno van der

Hart contend in their essay "The Intrusive Past: The Flexibility of Memory and the Engraving of Trauma," "Many traumatized persons . . . experience long periods of time in which they live, as it were, in two different worlds: the realm of the trauma and the realm of their current, ordinary life" (176). What Levi shows, by way of his very simple example of the blows, is that the world of the death camps and life before and after that experience are incompatible, that the terms are fundamentally untranslatable, all the valiant efforts of the survivor-witness-narrator to bridge those worlds notwithstanding.

The incommensurability of language and traumatic experience is a paradigm of Holocaust writing. Charlotte Delbo begins the first entry of *Days and Memory*, her last meditation, written forty years after the war and shortly before her death, with the problem of "explaining the inexplicable." Delbo's analogy to the notion of two selves, an Auschwitz self and a post-Auschwitz self, is conveyed through the image of

> a snake shedding its old skin. . . . In Auschwitz I took leave of my skin — it had a bad smell, that skin — worn from all the blows it had received, and found myself in another, beautiful and clean, although with me the molting was not rapid as the snake's. . . . Along with the old skin went the visible traces of Auschwitz. . . . With the new skin returned the gestures belonging to an earlier life. . . . It took a few years to consolidate. . . . How does one rid oneself of something buried far within: memory and the skin of memory. It clings to me yet. . . . Auschwitz is so deeply etched in my memory that I cannot forget one moment of it — So you are living in Auschwitz? — No, I live next to it. Auschwitz is there, unalterable, precise, but enveloped in the skin of memory, an impermeable skin that isolates it from my present self. (1–4)

Both Levi and Delbo situate the survivor at the time of writing, calling attention to the breach between the then and the now. Another way that trauma is represented in a Holocaust text is not by announcing itself as such but through the repetition of scenes and of flashbacks to earlier events, symptomatic responses to events. In other words, repetition and return can be both formal, stylistic strategies and thematic structuring devices in a Holocaust text.

In *Chamberet: Recollections from an Ordinary Childhood*, a memoir of traumatic mother-child separation recounted decades later by
the grown child, Claude Morhange-Bégué, the site of original traumatization is the narrator's mother's arrest by the Gestapo and all its
reverberations. The scene in which the mother is taken away and the
daughter narrowly escapes being taken herself is revisited, recon-
structed, and retold, again and again, throughout the text, exhibit-
ing all the qualities of a traumatic flashback. The flashbacks display a
characteristically disjunctive relation of image and language to memory: the clarity of the visual in the child's memory is counterposed
with her inability to remember words she needs to help explain her
mother's disappearance and assuage the pain of loss and abandonment. As language fails to provide the young girl with access to
knowledge and understanding, linguistic agency becomes an obsession itself for her and a fundamental feature of the narrative, as the
narrative attempts to fill infinite emptiness. Indeed, fourteen months
later, when the child's mother returns from Auschwitz and is driven
to unburden herself "with repetitive, obsessive talk, a litany that
would graft itself upon all other speech and associate itself with any
other image" (68), the child listens, without saying a word, for days,
evenings, years. A generation later, the daughter writes the mother's
story, as well as her own.

Transmitting Trauma

A compelling recent development in trauma studies involves new
theories of how trauma or traumatic experience can be transmitted
to others. In relation to the Holocaust, this development refers to
two entirely different modes or processes of transmission as well as
to different experiences of witnessing trauma. The primary mode is
the localized transmission of traumatic experience from the generation of survivors to their children born after the war, a phenomenon
interrogated from a variety of perspectives in clinical literature and in
memoirs written by survivors' children, like Morhange-Bégué. To
gain an understanding of the complex relation between traumatic
family history and personal identity, since the 1970s numerous clinical and theoretical studies have appeared that strive to track the effects

of what may be unbound, unintegrated, unshared massive traumatization. To what degree, these studies ask, are these various modes of transmission consciously and intentionally both conveyed and received? How central is language, spoken or written, to such a legacy?

Maus: A Survivor's Tale, Art Spiegelman's double-volume, multilingual, multileveled, intimate graphic allegory, negotiates the frontiers among genres, modes, languages, cultures, and especially between the generation that suffered through and survived the Holocaust and the one that inherited it. What both connects and divides the two generations is represented by the *Maus* project's most radical, if not its most transgressive, act of transmission: Spiegelman's translation of his father's oral testimony about surviving the final solution into a comic book about catastrophe and trauma and what it means to have survived a childhood whose dominant frame of reference is that one's parents did (or did not) outlive their intended extermination. *Maus* is riddled with scenes and conversations that expose, examine, and problematize from every conceivable perspective, through every technical and intellectual resource available to Spiegelman, especially the instrument of mordant irony, the complex phenomenon of familial transmission and inheritance. Anxious, guilty, and at times overwhelmed by his inability to compete with his parents' past or with the martyred brother he never knew, Artie (the protagonist and cartoonist son) admits that his Holocaust obsession always involved his own fears of not surviving, of not having what it takes to survive. In an exemplary interaction with his wife, he plays out his version of the survivor syndrome: "Don't get me wrong. I wasn't obsessed with this stuff . . . It's just that sometimes I'd fantasize Zyklon B coming out of our shower instead of water" (*And Here* 16).

Teaching Trauma

Certainly, for the purposes of the present volume, the most diffused and potentially relevant — though not uncontroversial — mode or process by which trauma and traumatic experience are transmitted is through education, in both the broad and narrow sense. Listening to survivor accounts of extreme pain and loss and reading about the suffering experienced by victims of the Holocaust, especially under circumscribed and intensive conditions, produce a range of emotional and affective responses in the teacher and students alike. In his essay "Bearing Witness; or, The Vicissitudes of Listening," Laub alerts us to the dangers of secondary traumatization, whereby the listener erects a set of defenses as a form of self-protection against the existential confrontation with death conveyed by the narrative (72). Strong psychological and emotional responses, including paralysis, empathy, identification, outrage, and even withdrawal from extremely disturbing, painful material, should be subjected to ethical analysis. Today, we are perhaps more susceptible to the temptation to move away from what LaCapra calls the "[indiscriminate] generalization of historical trauma to the idea of a wound culture or the notion that everyone is somehow a victim (or for that matter, a survivor)" (722) by virtue of the fact that we all live in a post-Holocaust universe.

To be attentive to the intersections of the personal, the historical, and the textual with any specificity requires a special vigilance on the part of the teacher, a constant reposing of the question, What are the connections between remembering and forgetting, knowing and telling, trauma and transmission, transmission and survival in this literary text? Psychic trauma may be the greatest challenge of teaching representations of the Holocaust, in whatever form they appear, precisely because it exceeds the bounds of an individual life story, even of a generation. The notion of belatedness has overarching implications not only for cultural historians and theorists of modernity but also for analysts, literary critics, teachers, and students of Holocaust literature. The trauma of the Holocaust enacts the crisis in representation that we have come to associate with postmodernism. The question that haunts and hovers over all others in this conjecture of trauma and the Holocaust is, How to represent the unrepresentable? But the question that lurks behind it is in keeping with the belated nature of trauma itself as a transcultural phenomenon. How did it happen that trauma did not become the pervasive explanatory model for the Holocaust or the Holocaust the transformative experience of the catastrophe-ridden twentieth century, until decades after its events?

Works Cited

Brison, Susan. *Aftermath: Violence and the Remaking of a Self.* Princeton: Princeton UP, 2002.

Caruth, Cathy, ed. *Trauma: Explorations in Memory.* Baltimore: Johns Hopkins UP, 1995.

———. *Unclaimed Experience: Trauma, Narrative, and History.* Baltimore: Johns Hopkins UP, 1995.

Delbo, Charlotte. *Days and Memory.* Trans. Rosette Lamont. Evanston: Northwestern UP, 2001.

Felman, Shoshana, and Dori Laub. *Testimony: Crises of Witnessing in Literature, Psychoanalysis, and History.* New York: Routledge, 1992.

Freud, Sigmund. "Beyond the Pleasure Principle." *The Standard Edition of the Complete Psychological Works of Sigmund Freud.* Trans. and ed. James Strachey. Vol. 18. London, 1958. 7–64.

Friedländer, Saul. "Trauma, Transference, and Working Through." *History and Memory* 4.1 (1992): 39–59.

Herman, Judith. *Trauma and Recovery.* New York: Basic, 1992.

Horowitz, Sara. *Voicing the Void: Muteness and Memory in Holocaust Fiction.* New York: State U of New York P, 1997.

LaCapra, Dominick. "Trauma, Absence, Loss." *Critical Inquiry* 24 (1999): 696–727.

Laub, Dori. "Bearing Witness; or, The Vicissitudes of Listening." Felman and Laub 57–74.

Levi, Primo. *The Drowned and the Saved.* New York: Simon, 1998.

———. *Moments of Reprieve.* London: Penguin, 1986.

Leys, Ruth. *Trauma: A Genealogy.* Chicago: U of Chicago P, 2000.

Lifton, Robert Jay. *The Broken Connection: On Death and the Continuity of Life.* New York: Simon, 1979.

Morhange-Bégué, Claude. *Chamberet: Recollections from an Ordinary Childhood.* Trans. Austryn Wainhouse. Evanston: Northwestern UP, 2000.

Spiegelman, Art. *And Here My Troubles Began.* New York: Pantheon, 1991. Vol. 2 of *Maus: A Survivor's Tale.*

———. *My Father Bleeds History.* New York: Pantheon, 1986. Vol. 1 of *Maus: A Survivor's Tale.*

van der Kolk, Bessel A., and Onno van der Hart. "The Intrusive Past: The Flexibility of Memory and the Engraving of Trauma." *American Imago* 484 (1991): 425–54. Rpt. in Caruth, *Trauma* 158–82.

Eric D. Weitz

The Holocaust and Comparative Genocide in the Twentieth Century

I have never taught a Holocaust course. I have, more times than I care to count, taught the history of Nazi Germany. The students might not understand the distinction when they register for the class, but they probably come to recognize the point fairly quickly as they peruse the syllabus and see that it takes about one-third of the semester just to get the Nazis to power. I also tell them in the first minutes that my goal is to teach many aspects of the history, from high-level politics to the social lives of youth and families under the Nazi regime, from diplomatic and military maneuvers to the course of racial policies. The last third of the course focuses on war and the Holocaust, and issues of representation and memory are never far behind.

In whatever format I have taught it, as a seminar for first-year students at a liberal arts college or as a lecture course at a large public university, Nazi Germany and Hitler's Europe has been popular. Almost any course with "Hitler" or "Nazi" in the title will attract hordes of students, generally for the best reasons — because they have an intense desire to learn about a regime that systematically repressed and annihilated people and about a history that figures so prominently in our public culture.

Yet over the years I have become increasingly discontented with the nearly exclusive focus on Nazi Germany and the Holocaust in my teaching and research and in relation to public and political discussions both in the United States and in Germany. I am by training and inclination a historian of modern Germany. It is what I know best. Yet the narrowness of perspective gnaws at me, and I find unconvincing and unsatisfying the sheer unwillingness to move beyond the German national frame and the fate of Jews under the Third Reich. I need to be very clear here. The Holocaust was an atrocity of monumental proportions and the greatest tragedy in Jewish history. Yet the Holocaust was also one of a number of genocides that have occurred in the twentieth century. It had its particular characteristics, as do all historical events, as does every genocide. Those particularities had to do with Germany's highly developed bureaucratic and military culture, which constituted one (though certainly not the only) powerful strand of the German tradition. Once the Nazis had seized power, they were able to draw on and further develop bureaucratic and military practices in the drive to annihilate Jews. The other particularity had to do with Germany's great power status, which contributed to grand territorial ambitions in Europe, much grander than those of most other dictatorial systems. But there was, unfortunately, nothing exceptional in the Nazis' utopian drive to create homogeneity, nothing unusual in their deployment of the ideology of race to classify, purge, and kill defined groups of people.

Therefore, we need to be cautious about positioning the Holocaust as *the* decisive event of the twentieth century, *the* singular, exclusive "civilization rupture," to use Dan Diner's phrase. It is, of course, understandable why the Holocaust has come to play that powerful role in Western societies. It occurred in Europe in a war that involved all the major Western powers. It was unprecedented in its dimensions, so much so that even Jews in its midst could not fully comprehend what awaited them. Yet the Armenian genocide was also unprecedented. Despite past instances of violence, some of which had taken tens and hundreds of thousands of lives, nothing had quite prepared Armenians for the organized, systematic, and total attack on their very existence by the Ottoman state and emergent Republican Turkey from 1915 to 1923. Hutus and Tutsis had fought each other previously, but the 1994 genocide was also unprecedented. Never before had Hutu leaders sought the elimination in total of the Tutsi population.

No case of genocidal politics has been as extensively researched and written about as that of the Third Reich. The literature of all sorts — scholarly studies, memoirs, novels, philosophical explorations — not to speak of film and other media, is so immense that no one person can master it all. Yet at least in terms of the historiography, the singular focus on the Nazi regime and the Holocaust has probably gone as far as it can. Of course, important individual studies are still being published. Many of them draw on the newly opened archives of the former Soviet-bloc countries and are the work of a new generation of historians, many of them German, who have learned Polish, Russian, or other Slavic languages. Clearly, there will still be important debates sparked by works like Jan Gross's *Neighbors* or by continued investigations into the timing of the Holocaust. But at this point it is hard to imagine the emergence of any paradigm-shifting study. While predictions are always hazardous, it seems to me that a certain exhaustion of research is setting in, as is typical (and not to be mourned) of any field that undergoes explosive growth and inspires countless researchers to set off on the archival trail. If the founding of scholarly societies and journals constitutes one sign of maturing fields, then the establishment of the International Association of Genocide Scholars in 1994 and of the *Journal of Genocide Research* and *Zeitschrift für Genozidforschung*, both in 1999, are an indication that comparative approaches have arrived. So is the publication of a variety of books that adopt an explicitly comparative approach, such as Norman M. Naimark's important study *Fires of Hatred: Ethnic Cleansing in Twentieth-Century Europe*; the Pulitzer Prize–winning work of Samantha Power, *"A Problem from Hell": America and the Age of Genocide*; and my own *A Century of Genocide: Utopias of Race and Nation*.

The move in scholarly discussions toward placing the Holocaust in a comparative context requires some rethinking on the part of teachers, no matter what their discipline. I am not at all suggesting that we abandon courses and research on the Holocaust and on Nazi Germany. I will continue to teach my own course on the Third Reich and others that relate specifically to Germany. At the same time, I suggest that on the larger canvas of school and university curricula and of research, the singular focus on the Holocaust no longer suffices.

It is all well and good, and perhaps not even that controversial, to talk about the virtues of a comparative approach. Certainly, there have been courses for some time now at a variety of universities on comparative genocide. But the problem remains: How does one do it? What are the criteria of comparison? And how does one compare in a way that is attentive to and respectful of the particular dimensions of the Holocaust and other cases of genocide? How does one compare without falling into the trap of suggesting that, if there have been other atrocities in history, perhaps the Holocaust was not so bad, or, even worse, perhaps it was merely a defensive reaction by Germany? And how does one compare without falling into that other trap, the who-suffered-more or body-count approach to history? That approach also gets us nowhere in terms of understanding—Communism killed 80 million or 100 million and National Socialism "only" 6 million, or 38 or 50 million if we count the war as well. Those figures are facts that constitute part of our efforts to understand the tragedies of the twentieth century; they do not provide, in and of themselves, conclusions of any sort.

Let me suggest a few criteria that guide my research and teaching about genocides, the Holocaust and others.

Ideologies of Race and Nation

There exists a large, sophisticated scholarly literature on nation building and nationalism. There is another large, sophisticated scholarly literature on racial formation. One of the most general conclusions to be drawn from that literature is that nations and races are constructions and the process of making nations and races is historically contingent and never complete. At the same time, every genocide entails first the act of classification, of identifying and categorizing populations, those who are targeted for annihilation as well as those whose efflorescence is seen to depend on the removal of the dangerous group (Hilberg). Every categorization is an ideological and political act; there is nothing natural about classifications.

But when we get to the actual events of the Third Reich and other genocidal systems, we tend to abandon historicity and talk about the Germans, the Jews, and the Poles, or the Serbs, the Croats, and the Muslims, and so on, as if these were unproblematic designations for homogeneous and ahistorical collectives. At the ultimate moment of roundups, deportations, and killings, those identities have indeed become fixed. But until that moment, we need always to be attentive to the historical—and therefore contingent—nature of the categories of race and nation. The word *race* did not even exist in the European languages until the late fourteenth century, and it did not become common until the sixteenth (Conze). Race thinking emerged around 1500, with the European explorations. It developed in tandem with New World slavery and especially with eighteenth-century scientific, social, and political developments. The word *nation* has a much longer lineage, of course, but its meaning became transformed in the modern era from the French Revolution onward (Zernatto).

While there is no unmediated, direct connection between these categories and genocide—many national and racial systems are "merely" discriminatory rather than murderous, and in every case, many other historical factors have to be taken into account—they lie at the heart of the Holocaust and the other genocides of the twentieth century. In acting on the ideologies of race and nation, the genocidal regimes of the twentieth century drew on Enlightenment conceptions of human progress and nineteenth-century scientific advances that posited the possibility, indeed, the desirability, of improving society by shaping its composition. By the turn into the twentieth century, there were increasingly loud claims that some categories of the population were incapable of improvement and constituted a ballast on the well-being of the population as a whole.

Depending on who was speaking and where, the lower classes generally, promiscuous women, people of African descent, Jews, criminals, the mentally ill, or some combination of these might be identified as the threatening group. The future progress of society, in this view, depended on protecting enterprising, productive people from the negative influences of dissolute and degenerate ones (Weiner). When such ideas were linked to racial and national identities, as they so often were, entire populations could be categorized as dangers to the well-being of the dominant group. Genocide in the twentieth century was the ultimate expression of this perspective, a policy of working on the population to shape its literal character by the forced, violent elimination of groups defined as alien and threatening.

By categorizing and purging populations in this fashion, genocidal regimes function as radical simplifiers. They reduce the variety of human identities to one single form of race or religion or nation; the harmful identities are supposedly natural and eternal categories — until the enemy is removed from the face of the earth. Invariably the regimes in question employed the powerful metaphors of cleanness and purity, as well as productivity, in relation to the honored groups. *Cleanliness* and *purity* are terms that, necessarily, signify their binary opposites, the unclean and the impure. Those who were unclean were a source of pollution that threatened to contaminate the clean and the pure. For some of the powerful systems of the twentieth century, the dirt that Mary Douglas famously described as "matter out of place" was, in fact, human matter, and it had to be eradicated through political action. In excluding dirt, these systems were "positively reordering [the] environment, making it conform to an idea" (2, 36).

So the first criterion of comparison, it seems to me, is about the ideologies of race and nation. The first couple of days of my course on comparative genocides are spent on definitions of genocide, ethnic cleansing, and human rights; then we launch into two weeks of readings, discussions, and lectures on the theory and historical development of race and nation. There are a number of good anthologies that provide students with excerpts from major contemporary theorists as well as from primary sources authored by the ideologues of race and nation (Eze; Guibernau and Rex). A number of good general histories also exist, and I use Phillip Yale Nicholson's *Who Do We Think We Are?*, which serves almost as a companion piece to lectures and discussions in the first few weeks of class. Over the course of the semester, as we proceed through different cases of genocide, we examine, in each instance, how regimes constructed and enforced categories of identities. I also bring the students back to the topic of the first few weeks of class, both to remind them that race and nation are political and ideological constructions and to deepen their acquaintance with major theorists by reading excerpts from Max Weber, Ernest Gellner, and Benedict Anderson.

This procedure also enables me to follow and expand on one of Hannah Arendt's key insights in *The Origins of Totalitarianism*: that an inextricable link existed between the racism that developed with European colonial empires and antisemitism, that the Holocaust was, in some senses, the coming back into Europe of imperialism. It has taken about forty years for historians, literary scholars, and others to follow up on her insight and to start providing its empirical underpinnings. Working off Arendt's position opens up a global perspective. It enables us to explore how European ideas and political models traveled into the colonies, then back into Europe in more radicalized fashion, or how indigenous racial concepts became intermingled with European ideas about race. Examples abound: the lessons that German military and civilian officials derived from the genocide of the Herero in Southwest Africa and of the Armenians in the late Ottoman Empire, the blending of indigenous Khmer and French colonial understandings of race, the Belgians' establishment of racial categories between Hutus and Tutsis.

Revolutionary Regimes and Utopian Goals

In most twentieth-century genocides, political leaders were animated by powerful visions of the future and sought to create utopia in the here and now. To be sure, the contents of the utopias were quite different, from the explicitly Aryan future that the Nazis posited to the supposedly classless, egalitarian societies of the Soviet Union and Cambodia. But all these regimes launched massive projects, from economic development like forced collectivization, forest clearings, and canal constructions to the total restructuring of education. They were project states or, in the words of James C. Scott, authoritarian "high modernist" regimes (see Mason; Maier).

These projects entailed collective population politics on a vast scale: the refashioning of individual consciousness and the reshaping of the very composition of society. In the drive to create a homogeneous population of one sort or another, the regimes classified people sometimes by their social class background and political orientation; sometimes by religion, race, or nation; sometimes by a blending of all these categories.

By striving to remake the nature of their society so thoroughly, by utterly transforming the conditions of life for so many people, these regimes, right and left, required the organizing capacities of the modern state: its bureaucracies, which slotted people into defined categories, and its security forces, which imprisoned and killed members of the targeted populations. Because these regimes asserted total claims over society, obliterating, at least theoretically, the distinction between public and private realms that is a defining feature of liberalism, they recognized no inherent limits to their intention to remake society. The possession of state power and the ideological conviction of utopia gave them license to launch all sorts of huge projects, from the construction of dams through the massive deployment of human labor to reshaping society by granting the honored members privileged access to resources and by interning, deporting, and ultimately killing the dishonored ones (on Cambodia, see Kiernan; Chandler, *Tragedy* and *Voices*; on Rwanda, see Mamdani).

So the second criterion of comparison entails an examination of regime ideologies and structures. Mostly this examination is conveyed to students in my lectures, with extensive quotes from primary sources—political leaders from Lenin to Pol Pot and Milošević, party and state journals, images of propaganda posters. All these sources give students a sense of the regimes: What were the visions of the future that regimes sought to implement? What were their ideologies? How was the state organized to carry out its policies? To understand genocides, students (and the rest of us) need to understand something about the nature of the regimes in question. The comparative approach broadens students' horizons and is perhaps a cautionary tale, for students see a variety of formal ideological and political systems at work that carried out the worst forms of population politics.

The Crisis Situations of War and Internal Social Upheaval

Not every revolutionary regime has committed ethnic cleansings and genocides. Even the Holocaust was not predetermined, if one follows the current scholarly consensus. Some form of exclusion of Jews was inevitable once the Nazis had seized power, but not necessarily physical annihilation. For all the importance of contextual factors, a high level of contingency is present in every case of genocide. Only at moments of extreme societal crisis, often self-generated, at moments of immense internal upheaval and war, of great opportunities but also dread dangers, did regimes initiate the most extreme form of population politics and tip over from pursuing discrimination and partial killings to perpetrating the more systematic and deadly policies of genocide.

The connection between genocides and extreme societal crisis is critical, because both war and revolution break standard codes of human interaction. Revolutions by definition overthrow the legal norms of a polity and, in the process, undermine existing legal and cultural constraints on human behavior. In wartime, states typically impose emergency conditions that give officials the freedom to act in ways they would not dare venture in peacetime. The upheavals of revolution and war heighten the sense of insecurity, leading to calls for swift and forceful action to remove those who are seen as dangers to the national cause or to the creation of the new society. At the same time, wars open up vistas of pleasure in the future and create great opportunities for vast restructurings of societies and populations. Wars and revolutions are by definition also violent acts; they create cultures of violence and killing. Such cultures were created especially in the twentieth century, when total war required the mobilization of entire societies in the enterprise of violence. The battlefields of World War I set standards of violence that revolutionary states sought to replicate in their deliberate purges of defined population groups.

In every case of genocide that I teach, we move from broad analysis of the nature of regimes to the very specific political decisions that culminated in genocide. I hope that the students grasp the human dimension of these events, including the ever-present possibility that they did not have to happen. The notion of contingency is a far more unsettling perspective than, for example, Daniel Goldhagen's argument that all of modern German history was on a course to the Holocaust, that virtually all Germans wanted Jews eliminated and Hitler only implemented their deepest desires.

To introduce students to these themes, I have them read, toward the beginning, Naimark's important comparative study *Fires of Hatred*. Naimark's book is very good at identifying the broad contextual as well as immediate political factors that led to the atrocities that he studies in detail. Discussion on the book also introduces students to comparative methodology and provides concrete historical examples that allow the class to venture deeper into the problem of defining and classifying genocide, ethnic cleansing, and other forms of human rights abuses. Then there are additional sources on some (not all) of the specific cases: an edited book by Richard Hovannisian on the Armenian genocide, an excellent film produced by PBS on Rwanda (*Triumph*). I have also used memoirs, for example, Loung Ung's *First They Killed My Father*, about Cambodia, as a basis for analyzing the Khmer Rouge regime. With the students I try to work back from her account of specific incidents—the family's deportation from Phnom Penh, her younger brother's efforts to procure food for the family—to an analysis of the nature of the Khmer Rouge system.

Popular Mobilization

From something of a political science approach focused on the nature of regimes and moments of crisis, we move to social history. Genocides are the result of state policies. Genocides in the twentieth century became especially extensive and systematic because the regimes enacting them engaged massive social projects that mobilized people for all sorts of activities. The literal reshaping of the population could not simply be decreed and could not happen overnight; it had to be created by the hard work of thousands and thousands of people, whether obtained through force, begrudging compliance, enthusiastic support, or the innumerable forms in between. As Alf Lüdtke writes specifically about the Third Reich but with words that can be generalized to the other cases:

> The gruesome attraction of complicity [*Mitmachens*] operates in relation to exclusions and suppressions—and ultimately to acts of murder. Participation [*Mit-Täterschaft*] in tormenting other human beings became an integral part of the "work of domination," such that the boundary between the guilt of a few and the innocence of many blended away. (44; my trans.)

Rituals of violence became the mechanism for carrying out the deadly policies of these systems and a way of binding people to the regimes. States organized people to serve as brigade leaders, social workers, and pioneers but also as jailkeepers, guards, torturers, and killers, who devised and implemented the brutalities of genocide. In all cases, the circle of complicity extended still further to the population at large to include those, for example, who watched gleefully as the Nazis or their auxiliaries killed Jews in market squares and synagogues or as Serbian forces killed Muslims. Neighbors and bystanders seized the properties of Jews, Crimean Tatars, Chechens, Vietnamese, or Bosnian Muslims and forced them out of their homes. Genocides on the scale of the twentieth century were possible only with the participation of these many thousands, some of whom were active agents in mass killings, others of whom reaped the benefits, material and otherwise, of the removal of their neighbors.

In exploring this dimension of genocide with students, I find that literature, films, memoirs, and trial testimonies are particularly helpful. They direct attention at both state policies and the individuals who were their enactors. Memoirs describe in intricate and painful detail the herding of people into train cars, the blows that rained down on bodies, the separation of women and children from men. These kinds of sources depict the social character of genocide. They can be difficult materials to watch and to read, as we all know. But after weeks of more abstract historical and social scientific discussions, it is critical that students read and see the searing brutality of genocide. It is often the moment in the semester—hearing the stories of Armenian survivors, viewing an excerpt from the film *Shoah*, reading Loung Ung's description of life in Democratic Kampuchea—when students grasp the enormity of what we have been discussing.

Memory

Genocides are deadly to the victims; they are also events whose corrupting character travels deep into a population. The successors to the societies that have been consumed by mass violence cannot escape the legacy; they remain overburdened by the past, precisely because of the participatory nature of genocide in the modern era.

In the last two weeks of the course we discuss memory and the various forms of human rights enforcement: tribunals, military interventions, truth-and-reconciliation commissions. By this point in the semester, students have little time for extensive reading. The case-study approach has become exhausting and emotionally draining. But images of memorial sites and museums provide an important opening for discussion, as do excerpts from memoirs, novels, and poems (e.g., Akhmatova; Werfel). The very inconclusiveness of the politics of memory leaves many students unsettled, but it also impresses on them how much the events of the past continue to reverberate in individual and collective lives and in contemporary politics.

———

There have been genocides for as long as recorded history. In the twentieth century, genocides and related human rights violations, like ethnic cleansings, became more extensive, more systematic, and more deadly. The Holocaust was one case among a general class of extreme population politics carried out by modern states.

"*Vergleich ist nicht Gleichsetzung,*" as Germans say. "Comparison does not mean equivalency." Comparison heightens the attentiveness for similarities and differences in a class of common events or situations. The comparative method enables us to see how political ideas and models travel, sometimes to unexpected places. It opens up a transnational and even global perspective, an approach, a few years into the twenty-first century, more needed than ever.

Note

Some of the passages of this essay are drawn from my book *A Century of Genocide: Utopias of Race and Nation.*

Works Cited

Akhmatova, Anna H. *Requiem and Poem without a Hero.* Trans. D. M. Thomas. Athens: Ohio UP, 1976.

Arendt, Hannah. *The Origins of Totalitarianism.* Cleveland: Meridian, 1958.

Chandler, David P. *The Tragedy of Cambodian History: Politics, War, and Reconstruction since 1945.* New Haven: Yale UP, 1991.

———. *Voices from S-21: Terror and History in Pol Pot's Secret Prison.* Berkeley: U of California P, 1999.

Conze, Werner. "Rasse." *Geschichtliche Grundbegriffe: Historisches Lexikon zur politisch-sozialen Sprache in Deutschland.* Vol. 5. Ed. Otto Brunner, Conze, and Reinhard Koselleck. Stuttgart: Klett, 1984. 135–78.

Diner, Dan. *Beyond the Conceivable: Studies on Germany, Nazism, and the Holocaust.* Berkeley: U of California P, 2000.

Douglas, Mary. *Purity and Danger: An Analysis of the Concepts of Pollution and Taboo.* 1966. London: Routledge, 1996.

Eze, Emmanuel Chukwudi, ed. *Race and the Enlightenment: A Reader.* Cambridge: Blackwell, 1997.

Goldhagen, Daniel Jonah. *Hitler's Willing Executioners: Ordinary Germans and the Holocaust.* New York: Knopf, 1996.

Gross, Jan T. *Neighbors: The Destruction of the Jewish Community in Jedwabne, Poland.* Princeton: Princeton UP, 2001.

Guibernau, Montserrat, and John Rex, eds. *The Ethnicity Reader: Nationalism, Multiculturalism, and Migration.* Cambridge: Polity, 1997.

Hilberg, Raul. *The Destruction of the European Jews.* Chicago: Quadrangle, 1961.

Hovannisian, Richard, ed. *Remembrance and Denial: The Case of the Armenian Genocide.* Detroit: Wayne State UP, 1999.

Kiernan, Ben. *The Pol Pot Regime: Race, Power, and Genocide in Cambodia under the Khmer Rouge.* New Haven: Yale UP, 1996.

Lüdtke, Alf. "Einleitung: Herrschaft als soziale Praxis." *Herrschaft als soziale*

Praxis: Historische und sozial-anthropologische Studien. Ed. Lüdtke. Göttingen: Vandenhoeck, 1991. 9–66.

Maier, Charles. *Dissolution: The Crisis of Communism and the End of East Germany.* Princeton: Princeton UP, 1997.

Mamdani, Mahmood. *When Victims Become Killers: Colonialism, Nativism, and the Genocide in Rwanda.* Princeton: Princeton UP, 2001.

Mason, Tim. *Nazism, Fascism and the Working Class: Essays by Tim Mason.* Ed. Jane Caplan. Cambridge: Cambridge UP, 1995.

Naimark, Norman M. *Fires of Hatred: Ethnic Cleansing in Twentieth-Century Europe.* Cambridge: Harvard UP, 2001.

Nicholson, Phillip Yale. *Who Do We Think We Are? Race and Nation in the Modern World.* Armonk: Sharpe, 2001.

Power, Samantha. *"A Problem from Hell": America and the Age of Genocide.* New York: Basic, 2002.

Scott, James C. *Seeing like a State: How Certain Schemes to Improve the Human Condition Have Failed.* New Haven: Yale UP, 1998.

The Triumph of Evil. Prod. Mike Robinson, Ben Loeterman, and Steve Bradshaw. Videocassette. PBS Video, 1999.

Ung, Loung. *First They Killed My Father: A Daughter of Cambodia Remembers.* New York: Perennial, 2001.

Weiner, Amir, ed. *Landscaping the Human Garden: Twentieth-Century Population Management in a Comparative Framework.* Stanford: Stanford UP, 2003.

Weitz, Eric D. *A Century of Genocide: Utopias of Race and Nation.* Princeton: Princeton UP, 2003.

Werfel, Franz. *The Forty Days of Musa Dagh.* 1933. New York: Carroll and Graf, 2002.

Zernatto, Guido. "Nation: The History of a Word." *Review of Politics* 6.3 (1944): 351–66.

Alan Rosen

"Y—You Know English?": Multilingual English and the Holocaust

This volume features articles in English, penned for teachers who, whatever their capabilities, will most often teach Holocaust literature (and film) in English. Yet English was a primary language of neither the persecutors nor the victims, played a marginal role in the events, and was most generally associated with the heroic values of the Allied liberating forces. Yiddish, Hebrew, German, French, Russian, Polish, Ukrainian, and many other Continental languages were integral to the events; English was secondary, if not tertiary. How then does a teacher resolve the tension between the centrality of English to teaching the Holocaust, on the one hand, and its marginality to the events, on the other? Still further, while emphasizing that crucial writing on the Holocaust has taken place primarily in Yiddish and German, among other Continental languages, how does a teacher thereby feature English-language texts without undermining students' confidence in the authenticity of what they read?

These questions, for me, have been nurtured by the fact that I teach in a department of English at an Israeli university, where English is viewed as a modern foreign language. But conceived at the margins though they are, the questions that I raise above and in what follows have relevance for those teaching in English in lands (the United States, Great Britain, Canada, Australia) and institutions where English is (at least ostensibly) less on the margins. My essay suggests a teaching strategy for dealing with this issue by drawing on the corpus of Holocaust writing as well as on relevant theoretical material. I indicate a sequence of writings — including those authored by Opoczinski, Hersey, Ozick, and Spiegelman — that explicitly or implicitly question the status of English in relation to the Holocaust. I set these writings in the context of critical reflections on the role of languages in the Holocaust (e.g., by Primo Levi) and point to ways teachers can relate these diverse Holocaust-centered writings to more general critical strategies. Ultimately, such an approach is self-reflexive: English is used to question the feasibility and limits of English when addressing the Holocaust. But by coming to see English as a language foreign to the events of the Holocaust, students will also be led to envision the integral role of languages in general and the special role of English in particular for representing the Holocaust.

Multilingualism and the Holocaust

European Jews have had a long history of multilingualism. There was, first of all, the ongoing relevance of ancient texts: the language of the Bible was Hebrew; the language of the Talmud, Aramaic. Added to these sacred tongues were the often multiple vernacular languages spoken in the specific region where Jews resided. Jews also devised specifically Jewish languages — such as Yiddish, a Germanic tongue, or Ladino, a Spanish tongue — that were written in Hebrew script. These languages were transported to new regions when communities were forced to migrate: French and German Jews, for instance, brought Yiddish to Eastern and Central Europe, while Spanish Jews brought Ladino to Greece, Bulgaria, and Turkey when expelled from Spain. Conveyed thus to Poland, Russia, Hungary, and Romania centuries before, Yiddish in these areas at the time of the World War II numbered seven to eight million speakers—most of whom took for granted facility in other tongues as well.

Two initial readings immerse students in the thick of the Holocaust while simultaneously linking their immersion to the multiplicity of languages. Written in the ghetto, Perez Opoczinski's semiautobiographical "The Jewish Letter Carrier" chronicles the thankless labors of a mailman in the Warsaw Ghetto, the prestige he so ambiguously acquires, and the increasing devastation he witnesses as he climbs the stairwells in ghetto tenements. Often bringing money or promises thereof from relatives in Soviet Russia, letters are the lifeline for the ghetto dwellers. By the end of the story, when the *Einsatzgruppen* devastate Russia's Jews, letters no longer arrive, a development that also signals the death knell for Warsaw's Jews.

Opoczinski, like his master, Sholem Aleichem, tells the story of these Jews through the languages they speak. One group favors Polish—"they were intellectuals and read in the Polish-Jewish sheet, *The Jewish Gazette.*" A second group privileges Yiddish: "If the Hasid did differ from the intellectual it was by the demand that the letter carrier speak Yiddish" (59). The variety and contentiousness of Jewish life, even (or especially) in such close quarters, emerges through the different tongues Jews speak—and the tongues they don't. The narrator shows a hypersensitivity to who speaks what with whom. Students can thus be asked to mime the narrator, listing the languages that are spoken and accounting for the narrator's identification of them in that specific context. David Roskies's discussion of Sholem Aleichem's multilingual strategies can show exactly from where Opoczinski derives his approach (163–83); Chone Shmeruk's account of Polish Jewry's trilingual (Yiddish, Polish, Hebrew) culture can discursively drive home the fact of the importance of multiple tongues.

In the wake of Opoczinski, a teacher can then spring the question, "Where is English?" If Roskies and Shmeruk are read, it is possible to send students scrambling to hunt out the meager references to English (there are two). These references put English barely on the margins of the Holocaust map.

The second degree of immersion in the question of languages and the Holocaust comes by way of Primo Levi's essay "Communicating." Levi shows how in Auschwitz the languages that one knew — or didn't know — meant nothing less than life or death. Most crucially, since commands were issued generally in German and since survival depended on an inmate's capacity readily to carry out commands, those who knew German best fared best, those who lacked any knowledge of German fared worst. "We immediately realized," writes Levi, "that knowing or not knowing German was a watershed" (91). It was a watershed for another reason: "Whoever did not speak German was a barbarian by definition; if he insisted on expressing himself in his own language — indeed, his nonlanguage — he must be beaten into submission" (92). In a terrible inversion, Levi's essay suggests that the issue of languages was as important for the persecutors as for the victims. Reading Levi after Opoczinski, students will feel the force of a "nonlanguage," for Auschwitz brutally ravaged the nuanced attention to languages that one detected in the Warsaw Ghetto. Levi notes at the close of his remarks that he was inspired by the sight of proud English POWs who had just arrived at Auschwitz. Yet just as the English prisoners enter Levi's essay on the margins, so does the English language itself remain on the periphery of life in the concentration camp. Indeed, that English is such a rare commodity in the camps confers on it a special value — a value that, as students of the Holocaust see when they eventually come to Spiegelman's *Maus*, has immense repercussions for issues of representing the Holocaust.

But *Maus* is still some way on in the semester. A more direct response to the events of the war and the problem of English comes in postwar English-language writing on the Holocaust. My research suggests that virtually every response to the Holocaust in this period displays an anxiety toward the English in which it is written. Students might be asked at this point to imagine what it would be like to write at the close of the war in English — a language that seems so out of place when viewed in relation to these events.

John Hersey, the author of *Hiroshima*, was no stranger to

chronicling the cost of immense disaster. He was nonetheless daunted by the prospect of writing in English about the fate of European Jewry. Thus *The Wall* (1950), a large novel chronicling the rise and fall of the Warsaw Ghetto, provides a particularly rich (and articulate) example of this anxiety. First of all, Hersey has reflected on the process of composing *The Wall* in the late 1940s, emphasizing the challenges he faced when he discovered so little material in English. Hersey's remarks help set the postwar scene but also frustrate, through his obsession with the topic, easy generalizations about a lack of interest in subject ("The Mechanics," *To Invent*). At this stage I frequently direct students to bibliographies (Robinson and Friedman; Robinson), where, in a different format, they become aware of the multilingual challenges that Hersey faced.

In studying Hersey's long novel, students usually benefit from aids that list the characters and the families to which they belong. Few will miss, however, Hersey's representation of the ghetto's multiple tongues: Yiddish, Polish, German, Hebrew. Divided up in pairs, students can be assigned to catalog Hersey's ghetto languages and — served by what they know from Opoczinski and Shmeruk as well as their recent bibliographic endeavors — can speculate on the significance of any given language. Eventually, everyone can return to the novel's prologue, addressing the question, How does Hersey, about to set forth in English a six-hundred-plus-page novel on the ghetto, articulate the problem of English? The prologue offers a number of intriguing possibilities, one of which is conveyed in the following passage:

> Their [the translators'] task was very difficult: they had to try to convey in English the life of Eastern European Jews without falling into the colloquialisms, word orders, and rhythms which, as taken over and modified by the American Jewish community, have become part of an entirely different culture: the connotations would have been misleading. (11)

To interpret this passage is perhaps as difficult a task as that which faced Hersey's fictionalized translators. Indeed, the very structure of the passage — winding, seemingly without end, divided by not one but two colons — is worthy of attention. One finds that a certain kind of English can be "misleading," can falsify the experience that it attempts to chronicle. Exactly how English can mislead — and how such a consideration guided Hersey's own strategy in the work that follows — is open to conjecture. But it is precisely this kind of conjecture that Hersey wishes to set in motion by including such a bald statement of the difficulties associated with English.

Tellingly, he introduces the problem of English under the sign of translation. Translation was both problem and solution for him, a necessary task that nevertheless was fraught with the prospect of transgression. The issue of translation has shadowed the multilinguistic project of Holocaust writing generally. Faced with literature in a dozen languages, even the most resourceful students are dependent on translation. And yet they, like Hersey, have conceived of translation as a "falling into," as a foisting on these events cultural presuppositions that could "mislead." Hersey thus intuited early on that, given the multilingual embeddedness of the Holocaust, the notion of translation would be one of the figures invoked to address the challenge of representing these events. Students might (appropriately) wonder if every work written in English dramatizes the problem of English so explicitly. Most do not. Yet once set to prospecting, students can see how more covert references can thematize the problem of English.

Having read Opoczinski, Roskies, Shmeruk, and Hersey, students will come to more familiar, later writing on the Holocaust with new eyes. In Ozick's "Rosa" (written 1977, first published 1983) they will find the interplay of languages close to the surface (see Wirth-Nesher). They will knowledgeably regard the character of Rosa and her family in the context of Warsaw Jewry and its languages. They will recall from Shmeruk that Jews like Rosa who spoke only Polish constituted less than one percent of Warsaw Jewry. A series of intriguing questions emerge: Why does Ozick make such an untypical Polish Jew representative of the Holocaust survivor? Given this untypicality, how are we meant to read Rosa's adoration of Polish and disdain of Yiddish? And why does Ozick deploy such a grid of oppositional tongues to narrate Rosa's story?

The representational values ascribed to Polish and Yiddish conflate with those ascribed to English. Rosa seems to despise English in a way reminiscent of her professed antipathy to Yiddish. Does the fact that both languages are weighed down by these negative associations make of them strange bedfellows? Her contempt for English and her adoration of Polish place these languages at opposite ends of the spectrum, English connoting foreignness, displacement, "cracking of teeth," Polish connoting intimacy, familiarity, and eloquence (53). Students can be asked what Polish and English share: in terms of the circumstances of Rosa; in terms of modern Jewish history; and in terms of the narrative strategy of the story, where English is for Ozick what Polish is for Rosa.

Finally, Ozick uses as an epigraph for *The Shawl* the last two lines of Paul Celan's 1944 poem "Todesfuge" ("dein goldenes Haar Margareta / dein aschenes Haar Sulamith"). One can read the lines out loud and ask the students what they hear. This may be the moment to ask them what they feel when they hear German. Some will share candidly their negative view of German. Is it, one can ask, their version of a "nonlanguage" (see Steiner; Gilman; Horowitz; Rosenfeld; Felstiner; Felman and Laub)? They will probably be baffled to learn that Celan chose to write in German even though he had command of other languages. That will make all the more provocative Ozick's choice of the German epigraph, which she took care to set down without translation.

"Rosa" sets in motion the tension that defines the role of English: It is not a language native to Rosa and hence is unworthy (perhaps even a nonlanguage?). Yet it is the language in which the story is told. This tension receives its consummate expression in Spiegelman's *Maus* (1986 and 1991). Fixed on the graphics, enthralled by details of the story, students will nonetheless be struck by Vladek's fractured English. Yet even after the lengthy attention given to English thus far, they will be apt to see Spiegelman's strategy as simply mimetic, as reproducing a lifelike Yinglish (Yiddish-inflected English) that is appropriate to a Polish Jewish immigrant. This appreciation serves as a tribute to Spiegelman and may help some students overcome an initial (and understandable) skepticism toward this

Holocaust comic book. But such a fractured English also lends itself to the question, What does this way of representing English—as broken, uneloquent—say about representing the Holocaust? Kathryn Hellerstein's discussion of Jewish voices in American English (Cahan, Henry Roth, Malamud, Philip Roth, and Ozick) places the issue of Yinglish in a historical context of American literature and argues that the authorial decision to accent has implications beyond the mimetic. Students will see Vladek's accent in the context of many predecessors and can be asked to judge which author's strategy comes closest to that of Spiegelman. Students can also draw on their own experience, suggesting other authors for whom Yinglish (or, for that matter, other traditions of fractured English) plays a significant role.

One can sharpen the questions regarding Vladek's English by returning to the text (and, if available, *The Complete Maus* CD, on which Vladek's voice can be heard) and seeing who in addition to Vladek speaks with (or without) an accent. In the wartime chronicle of Vladek's ordeal, why does no Jew, not even when seemingly speaking languages other than English, speak with an accent?

Having considered the representational issues of English, the class can turn to the extraordinary role that English plays as a subject in Vladek's chronicle: when all seems lost in the hell of Auschwitz and Dachau, his imperfect knowledge of English obtains for him privileges that enable survival. This power of English to determine survival should move students to observe that English itself has undergone a transformation in relation to the Holocaust: once marginal to events, in *Maus* it becomes central (see Rosen). Yet Vladek's knowledge of English attains value only because English is such a rare commodity. English, in other words, retains its position as marginal. Indeed, one student will almost certainly chime in, its very success demonstrates just how marginal it is!

Critical Contexts

Especially in advanced courses, the instructor can complement this inquiry into the status of English in Holocaust writings with a discussion of various interpretive approaches (including multilingualism and postcolonialism) that examine the contested position of English in the postwar world (Sollors, "Introduction" and "For a Multilingual Turn" [includes respondents]; Shell; Ashcroft, Griffiths, and Tiffin; Bailey). Although by no means all writing on the Holocaust proceeds out of the Jewish tradition, much of it does, and that tradition is doggedly multilingual, with echoes of one language frequently layering a second or third. In addition to the works by Roskies and Shmeruk referred to above, several studies outline the history and intricacies of this multilingual predicament (Baal-Makhshoves; Niger; Weinreich), some with particular references to writings of the Holocaust (Gilman; Mintz, *Popular Culture*; Shapiro; Wisse). Such a context shows the focus of the course as an eminently logical outgrowth of Jewish writing and history.

The context of multilingualism also enables a review of the major critical works on Holocaust literature (Langer; Ezrahi; Rosenfeld; Horowitz; Young; Roskies; and Mintz, *Hurban* and *Popular Culture*). Rather than begin with the critic's introduction or the critic's commentary on a particular author, students look at the languages that are featured in (or omitted from) each critical work, scan the indexes under the heading of specific languages, and examine what the critic says about the role of language in relation to the Holocaust. Although English is here, as elsewhere, on the margins, students also check to see whether critics comment on English (Ezrahi and Young, for example, both do, minimally but suggestively) or simply imply its secondary or tertiary status. Finally, returning to the introduction and the premises set forth therein, students interrogate how the issues of language shape, guide, or determine the author's critical approach to the Holocaust.

After such intense examination of the significance of languages in relation to the Holocaust, I assign my students a concluding exercise: "Fantasize that you could write a story (or poem, or drama) about the Holocaust in any language. Which language would you choose? Given what we have read over the course of the semester, comment on why you chose this language." Their responses are inevitably searching: "Were I to write a story about the Holocaust, the most appropriate language may be German," writes a native Israeli, fluent in Hebrew and English but not German. She continues, "After all, [German] is the language that created the Holocaust, the language whose phonetic qualities (harsh, metallic, clear-cut pronunciation) correlate with the horrors inflicted by the Nazis." Read aloud to the class, this fantasy, expressed in an accented English by a native Hebrew speaker, dramatizes in a breathtaking manner the issue on which the course is focused. Yet having opted for "the language that created the Holocaust," the student was not finished: "Still, it would be impossible for me to use German. I would therefore choose Hebrew . . . the language of Jewish history and its future." One could simply let the statement end there; or, as I sometimes do, one could press further, asking what would be lost and what gained by using or abandoning, in this case, German or Hebrew. Other students are equally resourceful in their assessment, and no one language carries the day.

My students—even those who speak a native English—rarely choose English as the preferred tongue. "I still feel sometimes," says a student, drawing aptly on the idiom of host and guest, "that the English language tries to enter a lingual and cultural circle which does not welcome it." Students comment wisely on the virtues that English possesses (e.g., neutrality; see "Discussion"; Michaels; Young) but do not see it as the favored option. This attitude may of course change when the question is tendered not in Israel but in North America. But North America too has its nonnative speakers of English, and the element of fantasy permits students to try on whatever language they feel best fits. Ultimately, the in-class exercise of listening to each student comment on the student's language of choice turns into a collective assessment of the viability of languages; the exercise replays not only the sweep of the course but also the history of responses to the Holocaust.

Ideally, students come to appreciate the force of Anja's question to Vladek, "Y—you know English?" (*My Father* 16). The assumption behind this question was that one didn't know English, didn't need to know it, and hence it was a surprise to learn that a Polish Jew would know enough to pick up on a conversation in English. Yet, in Spiegelman's hands, the marginality of English in Polish Jewish culture becomes the source of its power, of its ability to communicate secrets, of its strange capacity to negotiate survival. When students come to feel that the English they speak is — in terms of the Holocaust and the study of it — a foreign tongue, they too may be in a position to harness its ambiguous power.

Works Cited

Ashcroft, Bill, Gareth Griffiths, and Helen Tiffin. *The Empire Writes Back: Theory and Practice in Post-colonial Literatures.* London: Routledge, 1989.

Baal-Makhshoves. "One Literature in Two Languages." Trans. Hana Wirth-Nesher. *What Is Jewish Literature?* Ed. and introd. Wirth-Nesher. Philadelphia: Jewish Pub. Soc., 1994. 69–77.

Bailey, Richard. *Images of English: A Cultural History of the Language.* Ann Arbor: U of Michigan P, 1991.

Celan, Paul. *Poems of Paul Celan.* Trans. Michael Hamburger. New York: Norton, 1990.

"Discussion." *The Nazi Concentration Camps: Proceedings of the Fourth Yad Vashem International Historical Conference, Jerusalem, January 1980.* Jerusalem: Yad Vashem, 1984. 716–17.

Ezrahi, Sidra DeKoven. *By Words Alone.* Chicago: U of Chicago P, 1980.

Felman, Shoshana, and Dori Laub. *Testimony: Crises of Witnessing in Literature, Psychoanalysis, and History.* New York: Routledge, 1992.

Felstiner, John. *Paul Celan: Poet, Survivor, Jew.* New Haven: Yale UP, 1996.

Gilman, Sander. *Jewish Self-Hatred: Anti-Semitism and the Hidden Language of the Jews.* Baltimore: Johns Hopkins UP, 1986.

Hellerstein, Kathryn. "Yiddish Voices in American English." *The State of the Language.* Ed. Leonard Michaels and Christopher Ricks. Berkeley: U of California P, 1980.

Hersey, John. *To Invent a Memory.* Baltimore: Baltimore Hebrew U, 1990.

———. "The Mechanics of a Novel." *Yale University Library Gazette* 27 (1952): 3.

———. *The Wall.* New York: Knopf, 1950.

Horowitz, Sara. "The Night Side of Speech." *Voicing the Void: Muteness and Memory in Holocaust Fiction.* Albany: State U of New York P, 1997. 157–80.

Langer, Lawrence. *The Holocaust and the Literary Imagination.* New Haven: Yale UP, 1975.

Levi, Primo. "Communicating." *The Drowned and the Saved.* Trans. Raymond Rosenthal. New York: Vintage, 1989. 88–104.

Michaels, Anne. *Fugitive Pieces.* New York: Knopf, 1997.

Mintz, Alan. *Hurban: Responses to Catastrophe in Hebrew Literature.* New York: Columbia UP, 1984.

———. *Popular Culture and the Shaping of Holocaust Memory in America.* Seattle: U of Washington P, 2001.

Niger, Shmuel. *Bilingualism in the History of Jewish Literature.* Trans. Joshua Fogel. New York: UP of Amer., 1990.

Opoczinski, Perez. "The Jewish Letter Carrier." 1945. *Anthology of Holocaust Literature.* Ed. Jacob Glatstein et al. Trans. E. Chase. New York: Atheneum, 1980. 57–70.

Ozick, Cynthia. *The Shawl.* New York: Vintage, 1989.

Robinson, Jacob. *The Holocaust and After: Sources and Literature in English.* Sidrah Bibliografit Meshtefet 12. Jerusalem: Israel Universities, 1973.

Robinson, Jacob, and Philip Friedman. *Guide to Jewish History under Nazi Impact.* Jerusalem: Yad Vashem; Yivo, 1960.

Rosen, Alan. "The Language of Survival: English as Metaphor in Spiegelman's *Maus.*" *Prooftexts: A Journal of Jewish Literary History* 15 (1995): 249–63.

Rosenfeld, Alvin. "The Immolation of the Word." *A Double Dying: Reflections on Holocaust Literature.* Bloomington: Indiana UP, 1980. 129–53.

Roskies, David. *Against the Apocalypse: Responses to Catastrophe in Modern Jewish Culture.* Cambridge: Harvard UP, 1984.

Shapiro, Robert, ed. *Holocaust Chronicles: Individualizing the Holocaust through Diaries and Other Contemporaneous Personal Accounts.* Hoboken: Ktav, 1999.

Shell, Marc. "Babel in America; or, The Politics of Language Diversity in the United States." *Critical Inquiry* 20 (1993): 103–27.

Shmeruk, Chone. "Hebrew-Yiddish-Polish: A Trilingual Jewish Culture." *The Jews of Poland between Two World Wars.* Ed. Yisrael Gutman et al. Hanover: UP of New England, 1989. 285–311.

Sollors, Werner. "For a Multilingual Turn in American Studies." June 1997. *Communities: Interroads Discussion List.* 2 June 2004 <http://www.georgetown.edu/crossroads/interroads/sollors1.html>. Responses from Kellman; McNamara; Lauter; Greene; Finlay; counterresponse from Sollors; postscript from Allison.

———. "Introduction: After the Culture Wars; or, From 'English Only' to 'English Plus.'" Sollors, *Multilingual America* 1–13.

———, ed. *Multilingual America: Transnationalism, Ethnicity, and the Languages of American Literature.* New York: New York UP, 1998.

Spiegelman, Art. *And Here My Troubles Began.* New York: Pantheon, 1991. Vol. 2 of *Maus: A Survivor's Tale.*

———. *The Complete Maus.* CD-ROM. New York: Voyager, 1994.

———. *My Father Bleeds History.* New York: Pantheon, 1986. Vol. 1 of *Maus: A Survivor's Tale.*

Steiner, George. "The Hollow Miracle." *Language and Silence: Essays on Language, Literature, and the Inhuman.* New York: Atheneum, 1977.

Weinreich, Max. *History of the Yiddish Language.* Trans. Shlomo Noble. Chicago: U of Chicago P, 1980.

Wirth-Nesher, Hana. "The Languages of Memory: Cynthia Ozick's *The Shawl.*" Sollors, *Multilingual America* 313–26.

Wisse, Ruth. *The Modern Jewish Canon.* Boston: Free, 2000.

Young, James. *Writing and Rewriting the Holocaust: Narrative and the Consequences of Interpretation.* Bloomington: Indiana UP, 1988.

Part II

Genres

Susan Gubar

Poetry and Holocaust Remembrance

Given the magnitude of the death and suffering inflicted by the Nazis, the idea of useful or beautiful verse about genocide strikes most people as inane at best, repulsive at worst. When Theodor Adorno famously denounced the barbarism of writing poetry after Auschwitz ("Cultural Criticism" 34), he went beyond W. H. Auden's scorn at the impotence of verse — "poetry makes nothing happen" (248) — to remind us that high sentiments, rhetorical conceits, musical phrasings, and memorable mottos facilitated the rise of fascism in a nation noted for its citizens' love of the lyric.[1] Yet, as W. B. Yeats knew when he distinguished rhetoric, our quarrels with others, from poetry, our arguments with ourselves, verse has a capacity to express the most tangled dialogues between self and soul.[2] In the context of Holocaust remembrance (and despite Adorno's injunction), poetry has a privileged place, because it enables its creators to articulate a central tension in many people's reaction to the Shoah: on the one hand, the realization that it cannot be transmitted or comprehended in its full horror and, on the other hand, the urgency of attempting to transmit and comprehend it. And inside the classroom, the formalism of this most mediated form of writing enables students to handle material that might feel too toxic, too horrific in more realistic or sustained forms of representation.

"The past can be seized only as an image," Adorno's friend Walter Benjamin explained, "and every image of the past that is not recognized by the present as one of its own concerns threatens to disappear irretrievably" (255). By abrogating narrative coherence and seizing images of the past, poets mark discontinuity, engaging the psychological and ethical, political and aesthetic consequences of the calamity without laying claim to comprehending it in its totality. In an effort to signal the impossibility of a sensible story, the authors of poetry provide spurts of vision, baffling but nevertheless powerful pictures of fragmentary scenes unassimilated into an explanatory plot. Although narratives tend to recount the past so as to account for it, poems violate narrative logic as completely as does trauma itself. Like flashbacks that cannot be integrated into ordinary consciousness by those traumatized under brutal circumstances, poetry's images testify to the truth of an event as well as to its limited comprehensibility as a piece of a larger phenomenon that itself still defies understanding. Like symptoms in the aftermath of trauma, in other words, lyrical utterance often announces itself as an involuntary return to intense feelings about an incomprehensible, incommunicable moment. But, recollected in subsequent safety, such a moment rendered in writing allows authors and readers to grapple with the consequences of traumatic pain without being silenced by it.

As it has from ancient times onward, poetry composed by survivors, eyewitnesses, and refugees uses a kind of interpretive insistence, what D. H. Lawrence termed an "act of attention" (xv) or what Robert Frost called "a momentary stay against confusion" (126), to fill in lacunae in the historical record; to curse evil, lament harm, or praise good; to testify against wrongdoing; to caution against ignorance and amnesia; to analyze specific settings or actions in the past or in accounts of them; and to underscore the central significance of what is deemed to be a decisive convulsion in culture.[3] The resistance of verse to narrative closure and the attentiveness it fosters enhance its ability to "engage with states that themselves would deprive us of language and reduce us to passive sufferers," as Adrienne Rich has suggested in a retort to Adorno (*What* 10). Curiously, that verse is read by a small audience has liberated some authors to use it for their most private, self-incriminating thoughts about the inefficacy of the aesthetic enterprise. Because of its figural and formal opacity too, verse writers can resist platitudes and clichés that block emotional responses to the Holocaust while simultaneously manifesting the representational crisis all artists, scholars, and teachers face in their approach to the Shoah. As Adorno knew it would, when he later explained that consolation necessarily finds its only outlet in art, poetry about Auschwitz exhibits the jarring dissonance between the lyric's traditional investment in voicing subjectivity and a history that assaulted not only innumerable sovereign subjects but also the very idea of sovereign selfhood. Given a devastating occurrence that has been said to have "*produced no witnesses*" (Laub 80), poets find languages through which to articulate a range of feelings about what could not be expressed within the disaster.

For teachers seeking to bring the works of survivors and refugees into the American classroom, a number of anthologies—like Milton Teichman and Sharon Leder's *Truth and Lamentation*, Hilda Schiff's *Holocaust Poetry*, and Lawrence Langer's *Art from the Ashes*—contain translations of the now canonical Yiddish, German, Hebrew, Romanian, and Hungarian verse of Abraham Sutzkever, Jacob Glatstein, Nelly Sachs, Paul Celan, Dan Pagis, and Miklós Radnóti. Perhaps Celan's "Death Fugue" and Pagis's "Written in Pencil in the Sealed Railway-Car" best exemplify some of the more general points I have made about poetry's special role in Holocaust remembrance. Since their fractured allusions receive careful scrutiny elsewhere in this volume, however, I will discuss instead the ways in which less well known poems by Sachs, Celan, and Pagis exhibit poetry's capacity to question poetry's (and, indeed, culture's) traditional faith in its own powers. In quite different ways, Sachs's "Chorus of the Unborn" (in Langer 644), Celan's "There Was Earth inside Them" (607), and Pagis's "Draft of a Reparations Agreement" (592) show how poets paradoxically elaborate on the powerful logic informing Adorno's injunction against poetry after Auschwitz, even as they furnish the inspiration for more recent poetic ventures into the perplexing subject of the Shoah.

By giving voice to those who never came into being, Sachs's "Chorus of the Unborn" constitutes a speech act that violates not simply narrative logic but normative thinking. Sachs thereby calls attention to victims of the Shoah who are sometimes overlooked: babies aborted by Nazis in the concentration camps, fetuses destroyed when their mothers were killed in the ghettos, infants who went unconceived when girls were targeted in the final solution as the potential future source of a Jewish race that had to be expunged. Goaded into language in the plural first person by a "yearning" that "plagues us," the unborn constitute a we because never given the time to individuate into separate I's. Therefore "we the unborn" address "you," as the middle stanza of this poem emphasizes not only the walls between the unborn speakers and living listeners but also the thinness of the partitions. For the unborn must not be confused with the dead: "we" yearn and so do "you"; "we" live in "your" glances; "your" breath inhales "us" so that "we mirror ourselves in your eyes / Until we speak into your ear." In the final stanza of the poem, the we of the past obtain their futurity in "you":

> We are caught
> Like butterflies by the sentries of your
> Yearning—
> Like birdsong sold to earth—
> We who smell of morning,
> We future lights for your sorrow.

A muse of sorts, the unborn who had no life in the past haunt the afterlife of the living, as Sachs mourns the loss of morning's potentialities. Her verse discloses the past as a palpably present reality, as it does elsewhere through a number of rhetorical maneuvers: for instance, the apostrophes "O the night of the weeping children! / O the night of the children branded for death!" or the erasure of human agency and the tense of "Arms up and down, / Legs up and down / And the setting sun of Sinai's people / A red carpet under their feet" (Langer 638, 640). While Celan and Pagis sometimes take a more decidedly retrospective stance toward the horrors of the

Holocaust, they too use verse to abrogate sequentiality, to insist on the ongoing pertinence of the Shoah in the present and the future.

Beginning in medias res, Celan's "There Was Earth inside Them" stresses a dreariness of repetition reminiscent of "we drink and we drink" in "Death Fugue," though here in the past tense: "They dug and they dug, so their day / went by for them, their night." Far from edifying or enlightening its subjects, inexplicable suffering in monotonous and senseless labor means that, unlike ordinary slaves, the anonymous prisoners "did not grow wise, invented no song, / thought up for themselves no language." Since the earth was "inside them," the surrealistic digging seems to involve a form of self-destruction, not the mining of ore or excavation of treasures or roots that digging signifies for earlier writers, who view the shovel or the plow as a metaphoric pen. Digging (*graben*) their own graves (*Grab*), as John Felstiner points out (*Paul Celan* 151), those who "did not praise God" remain in the past tense until a sudden "stillness" and "storm" and flooding shift the poem into the conjugating present tense of "I dig, you dig, and the worms dig too" and of the concluding stanza:

> O one, o none, o no one, o you:
> Where did the way lead when it led nowhere?
> O you dig and I dig, and I dig towards you,
> and on our finger the ring awakes.

The poet, who engages here in the quarreling with God ("Kvetchen zikh mit got") that Felstiner sees as a central source of Judaism and of Celan's artistry ("Speaking" 391, 398), calls on a divinity whose existence he doubts yet dreads to doubt, as he reduces his own poetic digging to the senselessness of forced labor in a context where wedding rings wrenched off fingers tarnish mythologies of the Wagnerian ring, where awakening rings evoke only the pealing rings of unheard cries from civilians treated like a ring of criminals encased in the senseless ring of enforced and dehumanizing routines. That the iron band of Nazi rule divided those united by marriage means the poet must wed and weld his own craft to an exhuming of the dead. While "the ring awakes," the worms dig toward

and through not their fingers but "our finger." "There Was Earth inside Them" leaves the prisoners immured like the golem in dust and
dirt, untouched by the finger of a God capable of sparking clay with
the animating spirit of breath or soul.

If in "Chorus of the Unborn" and in "There Was Earth inside
Them" Sachs and Celan seem to analyze the difficult-to-translate
German word *verschollen* ("missing," "lost without a trace"), Pagis
appears to ponder sardonically the German word *Wiedergutmachung*
("making things well again," a phrase used for material restitution).
For in "Draft of a Reparations Agreement" Pagis creates a more distanced dramatic monologue, which ironically condemns God as a
culpable bystander. "All right, gentlemen," the magisterial speaker
exclaims to interrupt "nagging miracle-makers" as he calls for "quiet!"
The rest of the poem imagines running the reels of the movie of the
Holocaust from the end to the beginning so as to right its wrongs.
What better way to undo, to wipe the slate clean, to exonerate the
living and the dead, than by imagining history as a movie and working the film backward to reverse the damages done? "Everything
will be returned to its place," the impresario persona assures those
who "cry blue murder as always."

Not only will the scream go back into the throat, the gold teeth
back into the gums, the smoke back into the chimney, and the skin
return over the bones so "you will have your lives back," but even
the yellow star will be torn from the chest and emigrate into the sky
(27). In "Draft of a Reparations Agreement," the poet bleakly jokes
at the sham of reparations, given the irreversible losses suffered. If
we take the godlike speaker to be God (what other being could make
such promises?), how seriously should the divine promise be taken?
The covenant broken in the Shoah (with innocent people who will
never get back their property, teeth, skin, or bones) hints that earlier
promises have also only been drafts, that the proposed future con-
tract between God and the Jewish people will remain just as drafty.

Wary about the futility of their own undertaking, Sachs's, Celan's,
and Pagis's texts imply that, like the word of God, the words of
poets cannot be trusted to right the wrongful calamity. Yet through
imaginings of patently impossible interventions, their works explain
why Seamus Heaney has argued, "The redressing effect of poetry

comes from its being a glimpsed alternative, a revelation of potential that is denied, or constantly threatened by circumstances" (5), why Joseph Brodsky believes that verse gravitates toward the "intuitive and the prophetic mode of revelation" (58). Heaney (considering the imagination as an agent that puts us in touch with what has not but could happen) and Brodsky (viewing the imagination as an instrument of alternative forms of thinking about what happened) appear to feel that the best poets fulfill Benjamin's definition of the most adroit historian: "Only that historian will have the gift of fanning the spark of hope in the past who is firmly convinced that *even the dead* will not be safe from the enemy if he wins. And this enemy has not ceased to be victorious" (255). The verse of Sachs's, Celan's, and Pagis's European contemporaries can help students understand how poetry seizes images of the past and rescues them from oblivion by making them central to the concerns of the present.

But studying the verse of first-generation Holocaust poets can also be "a frustrating exercise," Lawrence Langer cautions, "because much of it has been translated from a foreign tongue" (553) and translations inevitably place barriers to the primary experience of a work's rhythms, puns, innuendos, rhymes. In addition, restricting the Holocaust canon to the anthologized Yiddish, German, Hebrew, Romanian, and Hungarian poems implicitly ignores the ongoingness of this tradition in English works, which might be more accessible to students because they are written by people just as geographically and temporally removed from the 1933–45 period as they are. In addition, Holocaust poets writing in English often translate or compose texts about their precursors' works through transnational productions that, by elaborating on the accounts of eyewitnesses, function as forms of proxy witnessing. Yet the few anthologies we have of such contemporary North American and British responses tend to be out of print or inadequate in their selections of the more ambitious texts. Instructors may therefore have to place on reserve library copies of the single-authored volumes published by, say, Anthony Hecht and Gerald Stern, Michael Hamburger and Dannie Abse, William Heyen and Irena Klepfisz, Adrienne Rich (*Atlas* and *Sources*) and Jorie Graham.

Profoundly influenced by their predecessors, second-generation poets employ imagery that revolves around trains and tracks, showers and soap, brandings and burnings, thrown-away children and the living dead, discarded shoes and extracted teeth, fences and fires, ditches and smoke and stars (see Florsheim). Not through realism or comprehensiveness or logic but through intense articulations that stall, compress, or reverse historical events, much as the texts of Sachs, Celan, and Pagis do, contemporary poets drive home the paradoxical remoteness of the past as well as its proximity. Like Sachs, some North American and British poets arrest time by writing not merely for but as the casualties; like Celan, some retard temporality through recollection of and intense identification with the experiences of the victims; like Pagis, some rewind chronology through fantasies of reversing the irreversible catastrophe. To the extent that contemporary writers of verse confound normative notions of chronology, viewing the past less in linear, more in spatial terms, they clarify Adorno's resonant definition of "the poem as a philosophical sundial telling the time of history" ("On Lyric Poetry" 46). Their works can help teachers raise complex questions about the ethics of aesthetics and of the various uses to which artists put memories not their own.

As Sachs did, Celan and Pagis produced dramatic monologues spoken by the casualties, but so did many of their successors. Although teachers and students will probably be aware of the critical brouhaha over Sylvia Plath's deployment of the voices of the dead and dying (in such poems as "Getting There" [247–49], "Daddy" [222–24], and "Lady Lazarus" [224–47]), many may not be familiar with the first-person poems crafted by Randall Jarrell ("Protocols" [193]), Michael Hamburger ("Treblinka" [133] and "Between the Lines" [134]), Charles Simic ("My Mother Was a Braid of Smoke" [3]), and Irena Klepfisz ("death camp" [47]). By placing their words inside the calamity's historical moment, these poets risk appropriating the voices of the victims. For, as Elie Wiesel has argued about the dead, "no one has the right to speak on their behalf" (194).

Some readers will agree that contemporary writers ought not presume to arrogate the otherness of the deceased through a projection that might be said to profane the memory of people exterminated by the Nazis; however, the introduction of these texts into the

Holocaust classroom allows teachers to question presumptions about identity politics. Because Jews and non-Jews alike have attempted necromantic reanimations of the dead through the use of posthumous voices, such works test the common assumption of many readers that only people with a unique personal connection to the Shoah or with a particular religious or ethnic background have a license to approach the disaster. Plath's powerful works in particular raise the issue of "memory envy," a term Geoffrey Hartman coined to describe a condition "whereby those who have not gone through traumatic experiences adopt those experiences, or identify with them rather than not finding any memories at all, any *strong* memories" (230). Indeed, Plath's brilliant adoption of the voices of the victims might allow students to modify this concept so as to comprehend how "memory envy" can impel a creative writer who *has* gone through painfully strong personal events to adopt historically cataclysmic traumas and in the process illuminate them as well as her awareness of their incongruity vis-à-vis her own quite distinct crises.

Just as Celan recollected the torments of an enforced labor he endured, contemporary British and North American poets seek to document the harms inflicted in the disaster, although they tend to ground their work in earlier accounts provided by eyewitnesses. In Anthony Hecht's "More Light! More Light!," the Jewish laborers forced to dig their own graves experience what Celan's "There Was Earth inside Them" signifies when they are buried alive; however, Hecht's formal stanzas rely on the firsthand testimony of Eugen Kogan's *The Theory and Practice of Hell*. Such recyclings of earlier narratives can also be found throughout Charles Reznikoff's *Holocaust*, which consists of quotations from twenty-six volumes of postwar Nazi trials. To the extent that contemporary poets cite earlier sources, their works engage students in a consideration of whether or how the Holocaust can be responsibly remembered during a period when the survivors will no longer exist to tell their own stories. Once again, the classroom provides an arena for discussing the ethics of remembrance, for such instances of proxy witnessing can be construed either as an empathic effort to preserve the past in the present or as an instance of "stealing the Holocaust" or "consuming trauma."[4]

When a poet like Celan furnishes the impetus for verse, as for example in Carolyn Forché's "Elegy" (69), Edward Hirsch's "Paul Celan: A Grave and Mysterious Sentence" (Fishman 132–33), and Myra Sklarew's "Blessed Art Thou, No-One" (Fishman 303–04), not only the transnationalism of Holocaust literary history but also the impossibility of containing the catastrophe in bracketed dates comes into focus. Brooding on the line "Where did the way lead when it led nowhere?," Jacqueline Osherow's "My Cousin Abe, Paul Antschel and Paul Celan" approaches Celan's "brutal question" through the perspective of his schoolmate, her cousin Abe, who also lost many relatives in Transnistria. As she looks at their graduation picture, she heeds her cousin's distraught anguish at the postwar suicide: "*What could have made him do a thing like that?*" (21). Whereas Celan gripes against God's absence during the Shoah, Osherow's cousin quarrels with Celan's decision to kill himself decades after it.

Elsewhere Osherow attempts, like Pagis, to contain the past in the frames of a movie that could be rewound to the moment before catastrophe, a project replicated by poets as different as William Heyen and Robert Pinsky. Martin Amis's novel *Time's Arrow* as well as Jerome Rothenberg's verse in *Khurbn* also meditate on rewinding temporality. Perhaps the most frequently anthologized Holocaust poem, Irving Feldman's "The Pripet Marshes," best exemplifies this effort to use the imagination to put us in touch with alternative pasts or alternative ways of thinking about the past. A director of sorts, Feldman imagines his family and friends arguing in a Yiddish whose unfamiliarity thrills him as they promenade among the mists of the ghetto to which he has transported them in Ukraine. As they metamorphose into illuminated figures on the brink of some mysterious transformation, the poet tries to assert his power: "when I want to, I can be a God" (179). But his braggadocio is belied by the absurdly fragile pillowcase, handkerchief, and shoe box into which he attempts to stuff his people, as he endeavors to carry them away from the Nazis. Feldman's despair at the end of this poem — "I can't hold out any longer" — inflects his approach to aesthetic issues in his later and even more complex poems about the Holocaust, "Outrage Is Anointed by Levity; or, Two Laureates A-Lunching" and "The Bystander at the Massacre" (*All* 48–50). That these (and many of the other poems I have mentioned) have received little critical attention from Holocaust studies scholars makes them particularly resonant in the classroom, where students can forge new readings or go on to discover other neglected texts.

Elaborately extended metaphors, internal and end rhymes, symmetrical repetitions, rhythmic stanzaic patterns, complex allusions, and blatantly ersatz speakers engaged in impossible missions: what can be made from the fact that some of the translated and the English works I have discussed exhibit marked elements of formalism? At times, poets dealing with the rigid constraints imposed by the Shoah seem drawn to the rigor of structured forms. Invested with the dignity and ritual that still make verse a preferred choice for readings at weddings and funerals, meter informs readers that they are "not experiencing the real object" being imitated but are encountering "instead that object transmuted into symbolic form" (Fussell 12). Besides linking poetic expression more to mediated, less to realistic rhetorics, conventional forms like riddles, anaphoric catalogs or chants, villanelles, fugues, psalms, dramatic monologues, and sestinas subvert normative notions that a higher degree of craft decreases a text's emotional effect.

In the process, poetry about Auschwitz contests the assumption of some scholars that "Holocaust writing characteristically 'aspires to the condition of history'" or that it invariably purports to realize "historical authenticity" (Lang 19). In contrast to the transparency of realistic modes of discourse, the opacity of poetry makes the aesthetic apparent as it intensifies moral, intellectual, and sensory awareness. "Rather than betraying the historical matter or obscuring its moral import," Sidra DeKoven Ezrahi explains about Celan's most often recited and formally rigorous work, "the performed poem may actually be the only possible conduit to what cannot be faced without mediation" (274). Such logic elucidates Czeslaw Milosz's prediction about his war-torn city in his *Treatise on Poetry*: "And for your disasters this is your reward: / As a sign that language only is your home, / Your ramparts will be built by poets" (15).

A number of writers concur, as Rothenberg does, that "after auschwitz / there is only poetry   no hope / no other language left to heal" (14). "Has Adorno's question / been disposed of, interred beneath the poems / written since Auschwitz," Feldman asks in "Outrage Is Anointed by Levity," or has it been "raised again / and again like a ghost by each of them" (48)? To raise the specter of Adorno's maxim, C. K. Williams, who began his career with an extended sequence on Anne Frank, entitled a recent poem "After Auschwitz." Just as Jane Shore, Maxine Kumin, and Marge Piercy devote poems to their visits to Holocaust sites, Williams here considers his trip to the most famous concentration camp, where he felt shocked not by what he had imagined so often earlier in his life but by finding the empty barracks, crematoria, and gas chambers "bereft" compared with what he had conceived in his mind (10).

But of course the concentration camp remains peopled in his imagination, by the characters supplied by a memoirist like Primo Levi, whom Williams remembers reciting Dante to the "all but dead" and recounting the story of the about-to-be-hanged Masha, defiantly exclaiming, "I'm always all right." It is the Bavarian town where Williams sleeps, a rebuilt replica of what had been flattened by the Allies in the war, that seems "like a stage set," whereas Auschwitz remains "that other place which always / now everywhere on earth / will be the other place / from which one finds oneself." What Williams thinks Auschwitz "demands of us" is precisely what the poets provide:

> it demands of us how
> we'll situate this so
> it doesn't sunder us
> between forgivenesses
>
> we have no right to grant,
> and a reticence
> perhaps malignant, heard
> by nothing that exists,
> yet which endures, a scar,
> a broken cry, within. (10)

Notes

1. Adorno's statements for and against verse are analyzed in many scholarly books, including Rothberg's *Traumatic Realism* (25–58) and my own *Poetry after Auschwitz* (4–13).

2. Yeats's formulation is, "We make out of the quarrel with others, rhetoric, but of the quarrel with ourselves, poetry" (492).

3. See Weitzman's analysis of the uses to which verse is put in the Bible.

4. The first phrase appeared as a headline in the *New Yorker* devoted to Gourevitch's analysis of the Wilkomirski hoax; the second derives from an essay by Patricia Yaeger.

Works Cited

Abse, Dannie. *Rememberances of Crimes Past.* London: Century Hutchinson, 1990.

Adorno, Theodor W. "Cultural Criticism and Society." *Prisms.* Trans. Samuel Weber and Shierry Weber. Cambridge: MIT P, 1981. 17–34.

———. "On Lyric Poetry and Society." *Notes to Literature.* Vol. 1. Ed. Rolf Tiedermann. Trans. Shierry Weber Nicholsen. New York: Columbia UP, 1991. 37–54.

Amis, Martin. *Time's Arrow.* New York: Vintage, 1991.

Auden, W. H. "In Memory of W. B. Yeats." *W. H. Auden: Collected Poems.* Ed. Edward Mendelson. New York: Vintage, 1991. 247–49.

Benjamin, Walter. *Illuminations.* Trans. Harry Zohn. Ed. Hannah Arendt. New York: Viking, 1963.

Brodsky, Joseph. *On Grief and Reason: Essays.* New York: Farrar, 1995.

Ezrahi, Sidra DeKoven. "Seeking the Meridian: The Reconstitution of Space and Audience in the Poetry of Paul Celan and Dan Pagis." *Religion and the Authority of the Past.* Ed. Tobin Siebers. Ann Arbor: U of Michigan P, 1993. 253–84.

Feldman, Irving. *All of Us Here.* New York: Penguin, 1986.

——— "Outrage Is Anointed by Levity; or, Two Laureates A-Lunching." *The Life and Letters.* Chicago: U of Chicago P, 1994. 48–50.

———. "The Pripet Marshes." Fishman 176–79.

Felstiner, John. *Paul Celan: Poet, Survivor, Jew.* New Haven: Yale UP, 1995.

———. "Speaking Back to Scripture: The Biblical Strain in Holocaust Poetry." *Humanity at the Limit: The Impact of the Holocaust Experience on Jews and Christians.* Ed. Michael A. Singer. Bloomington: Indiana UP, 2001. 391–99.

Fishman, Charles, ed. *Blood to Remember: American Poets on the Holocaust.* Lubbock: Texas Tech UP, 1991.

Florsheim, Steward J., ed. *Ghosts of the Holocaust: An Anthology of Poetry by the Second Generation.* Detroit: Wayne State UP, 1989.

Forché, Carolyn. *The Angel of History.* New York: Harper-Perennial, 1994.

Frost, Robert. "The Figure a Poem Makes." *Robert Frost on Writing.* Ed. Elaine Barry. New Brunswick: Rutgers UP, 1973. 125–28.

Fussell, Paul. *Poetic Meter and Poetic Form.* New York: McGraw, 1979.

Gourevitch, Philip. "The Memory Thief." *New Yorker* 14 June 1999: 48–68.

Graham, Jorie. *The Dream of a Unified Field: Selected Poems, 1974–1994.* Hopewell: Ecco, 1995.

Gubar, Susan. *Poetry after Auschwitz: Remembering What One Never Knew.* Bloomington: Indiana UP, 2002.

Hamburger, Michael. *Collected Poems, 1941–1983.* Manchester: Carcanet, 1974.

Hartman, Geoffrey. "Witnessing Video Testimony: An Interview with Geoffrey Hartman." By Jennifer R. Ballengee. *Yale Journal of Criticism* 14.1 (2001): 217–32.

Heaney, Seamus. *The Redress of Poetry.* New York: Farrar, 1995.

Hecht, Anthony. *Collected Earlier Poems.* New York: Knopf, 1990.

Heyen, William. *Ericka: Poems of the Holocaust.* New York: Vanguard, 1984.

Jarrell, Randall. *The Complete Poems.* New York: Farrar, 1969.

Klepfisz, Irena. *A Few Words in the Mother Tongue: Poems Selected and New, 1971–1990.* Portland: Eighth Mountain, 1991.

Kogan, Eugen. *The Theory and Practice of Hell: The German Concentration Camps and the System behind Them.* Trans. Heinz Norden. New York: Octagon, 1973.

Kumin, Maxine. *The Nightmare Factory.* New York: Harper, 1970.

Lang, Berel. "Holocaust Genres and the Turn to History." *The Holocaust and the Text: Speaking the Unspeakable.* Ed. Andrew Leak and George Paizis. New York: St. Martin's, 2000. 17–31.

Langer, Lawrence, ed. *Art from the Ashes: A Holocaust Anthology.* New York: Oxford UP, 1995.

Laub, Dori. "An Event without a Witness: Truth, Testimony, and Survival." *Testimony: Crises of Witnessing in Literature, Psychoanalysis, and History.* By Shoshana Felman and Laub. New York: Routledge, 1992. 75–92.

Lawrence, D. H. Introduction. *Chariot of the Sun.* By Harry Crosby. Paris: Black Sun, 1931. i–xvii.

Milosz, Czeslaw. *A Treatise on Poetry.* Trans. Robert Hass. New York: Ecco, 2001.

Osherow, Jacqueline. *With a Moon in Transit.* New York: Grove, 1999.

Piercy, Marge. "Growing Up Haunted." *Telling and Remembering.* Ed. Steven J. Rubin. Boston: Beacon, 1997. 304–05.

Plath, Sylvia. *Collected Poems.* Ed. Ted Hughes. New York: Harper, 1981.

Reznikoff, Charles. *Holocaust.* Los Angeles: Black Sparrow, 1975.

Rich, Adrienne. *An Atlas of the Difficult World.* New York: Norton, 1991.

———. *Sources.* Woodside: Heyeck, 1983.

———. *What Is Found There: Notebooks on Poetry and Politics.* New York: Norton, 1994.

Rothberg, Michael. *Traumatic Realism.* Minneapolis: U of Minnesota P, 2000.

Rothenberg, Jerome. *"Khurbn" and Other Poems.* New York: New Directions, 1989.

Schiff, Hilda, ed. *Holocaust Poetry.* New York: St. Martin's, 1995.

Shore, Jane. *Music Minus One.* New York: Picador, 1996.

Simic, Charles. *The World Doesn't End.* New York: Harcourt, 1989.

Stern, Gerald. *Paradise Poems.* New York: Random, 1984.

Teichman, Milton, and Sharon Leder, eds. *Truth and Lamentation: Stories and Poems on the Holocaust.* Urbana: U of Illinois P, 1994.

Weitzman, Steven. *Song and Story in Biblical Narrative: The History of a Literary Convention in Ancient Israel.* Bloomington: Indiana UP, 1997.

Wiesel, Elie. *From the Kingdom of Memory: Reminiscences.* New York: Simon, 1990.

Williams, C. K. *Repair.* New York: Farrar, 1999.

Yaeger, Patricia. "Consuming Trauma; or, The Pleasure of Merely Circulating." *Journal X* (1997): 225–51.

Yeats, W. B. "Anima Hominis." 1971. *Essays.* London: Macmillan, 1923. 485–506.

Amy Hungerford

Teaching Fiction,
Teaching the Holocaust

Aharon Appelfeld has admonished the current generation to "transmit the dreadful experience" of the Holocaust "from the category of history into that of art" (xiv). Teaching fiction in a course about the Holocaust brings us face-to-face with the implications of that transmission. What happens to history when it is made into art? What happens to art when such history enters its purview? The question of whether one should make the history of the Holocaust into art has been debated, but it seems to me that this debate has always been after the fact. Every survivor who tells her or his story is making a kind of art, as Geoffrey Hartman has shown with his analysis of videotaped testimonies. We tell the stories of our lives using shapes found in the stories of our cultures, which means that narrative art— so central to the art of fiction—has always been part of how we understand the Holocaust.[1] We can feel confident, then, including fiction in our teaching of the Holocaust. The debates about its appropriateness take place within the space that narrative art has already given us, and the debates themselves show students the complexities of approaching not only fiction but any genre of representation.

Sara Horowitz has written that "the word 'fiction' as a synonym for 'lies' poses it antithetically to truth" (1). That opposition has been voiced by prominent people. Claude Lanzmann, the maker of the film *Shoah*, for example, has said that "fiction is a transgression" (qtd. in Hartman 84). Against such pronouncements, Horowitz joins others—including Lawrence Langer, Alvin Rosenfeld, Sidra Ezrahi, James Young, and Michael Rothberg—in taking fiction as a "serious vehicle for thinking about the Holocaust" (1).[2] One can encourage such thinking in the classroom by considering what the genre's inherent quality of imagination can—or cannot—teach us about the Holocaust. Asking students whether fiction is a kind of lying can make it more difficult for them to look for autobiography in every fiction and can keep them from taking for granted either the distance they feel from fiction (because it is not fact) or what Hartman has called its "seduction" of the reader into identification and intimacy (12).

In a course I call Literature and Holocaust, I set the stage for reading novels with two examples of how literature intersects with Holocaust history. First, we examine the chapter "The Canto of Ulysses" in Primo Levi's *Survival in Auschwitz*, comparing it with Ulysses's story in Dante's *Divine Comedy*. As students note how Primo begins that chapter underground (scrubbing the oil tank), emerges to see the snow-covered Carpathians, and then journeys with a literate and humane guide (the piccolo), they easily see how Levi has employed Dante's images—of purgatory, of the mountain of earthly Paradise, of the guide Vergil—to shape the telling of a true story. They see that facts are not separate from the kinds of language and formal structures we associate with poetic or fictional narrative.

Second, I have them read Binjamin Wilkomirski's *Fragments: Memories of a Wartime Childhood* but don't reveal beforehand that the memoir is believed to be fake. The two times I've taught this class at Yale, no student has come in knowing the book's history. I have been glad of their ignorance, since discussion of the text brings them to the same conclusion but gives their analytic skills a better workout.

Students wonder, for example, why the book is out of print. They ask questions about the exact movements of little Binjamin or the chronology of the story. I don't answer the questions; I ask the students to address them using what they have read. Because of inconsistencies in the story, discussion eventually grinds to a halt, and then someone either remembers hearing that the memoir was fake or suggests that possibility, citing the afterword (in which Wilkomirski acknowledges the irregularities of his birth certificate). Students' responses, when I tell them the whole story, vary. Some are annoyed, having felt deep sympathy for this child; they feel that they would have suffered less had they known that the incidents were fictional. Others are relieved, since the memoir's fictionality seems to justify their skepticism about the details of Wilkomirski's account. Others are astonished that a text that seemed so true to what they imagined the camps were like could be a work of fiction.

All these responses occasion useful questions. Why does one feel that sympathy is somehow less valid if the character is fictional? Since at least the eighteenth century the novel as a genre has been associated with the instruction of readers' feelings. How does writing like *Fragments* relate to the tradition of the sentimental novel? Do we always feel more strongly for a character we think has a real referent in the world? Are the facts of the Holocaust automatically more compelling than fictions based on them? Is there a relation between fictional representations of the Holocaust and Holocaust denial? These questions, which seem particularly urgent to students fresh from the Wilkomirski scandal, become an invaluable reference point when we read works that announce themselves as fiction.

Studying *Fragments* brings students quickly to philosophical questions that scholars like Berel Lang, Geoffrey Hartman, Sara Horowitz, and Michael Rothberg consider in their work on genre and the Holocaust. Indeed, it is often worth shaping students' thinking on these questions by assigning some secondary sources.[3] But as appealing as such big questions can be, the more substantial learning often takes place when the questions are grounded within a particular text. In the details of any given novel or short story, writers—and readers—wrestle with what is possible in the meeting place between fiction and the history of the Holocaust.

One writer who wrestles honorably with the possible—and the taboo—is Philip Roth. His early story "Eli, the Fanatic" or one of his two novels directly engaging the Holocaust—*The Ghost Writer* or *Operation Shylock*—would be appropriate for any course in which fiction and the Holocaust intersect. Since the Holocaust is not a persistent thematic focus in his work, it is thus possible to see how his treatment of those events is integrated into a larger artistic meditation on identity, family, fiction, and the vocation of the writer in America.[4]

The Ghost Writer is particularly useful because it meditates directly on what we call Holocaust literature, epitomized for Roth by Anne Frank's *The Diary of a Young Girl*. For those unfamiliar with the novel, I provide a short summary. Nathan Zuckerman, an aspiring young writer, has published a story based on a feud that divided his Jewish family. His parents think his story reinforces negative Jewish stereotypes and try to persuade Nathan to write fiction more flattering to the community. They enlist the help of the local Jewish bigwig, Judge Wapter, who, in a letter, challenges Nathan to choose community over artistic self-interest. The letter is accompanied by a hilarious questionnaire, which concludes by comparing Nathan to Julius Streicher and Joseph Goebbels. In a postscript the judge and Mrs. Wapter "strongly advise" Nathan to go see the Broadway production of *The Diary of Anne Frank*, as a cure for his antisemitism (103–04). In the middle of this family crisis Nathan is invited to visit the home of his idol, the older Jewish writer E. I. Lonoff. At the writer's house in the Berkshires, Nathan meets another of Lonoff's protégés, a young woman named Amy Bellette. Learning a few tidbits about Amy's past as a refugee and overhearing a strange conversation between Amy and Lonoff suggesting a love affair, Nathan falls for the young woman himself and feverishly spins a story that casts her as a surviving Anne Frank. In the story, Amy/Anne keeps her survival secret from all but Lonoff so she can continue to exist as the great dead author her diary has made her. In his fantasy, Nathan then marries her and thus solves all the problems with his family. He proves his allegiance to the Jewish community and identifies himself with the woman he calls "the most famous" (152) of Jewish writers.

Considered thematically, this novel—for all its satire of pieties

about Anne Frank—provides a passionate commentary on Holocaust literature. In the chapter entitled "Femme Fatale" (containing
Nathan's story about Amy/Anne), Anne thinks about why and how
her diary is powerful. She concludes first that it is powerful because
she is dead. She reflects:

> Were *Het Achterhuis* known to be the work of a living
> writer, it would never be more than it was: a young
> teenager's diary of her trying years in hiding . . . dead she
> had written, without meaning to or trying to, a book with
> the force of a masterpiece to make people finally see [the
> face of human suffering]. (145–46)

But soon after discovering her own fame, she gives up the idea
that her purpose is to make people more humane. Questioning
whether people will be changed for more than the time it takes to
read her diary, Anne decides that her book is for the dead, for their
memory. Then not so much for the dead as for herself—as an instrument of her rage. The book, she imagines, will make people suffer, at least a little, for what was done to her family. Finally, she
decides she must be dead, because the book has made her the "in-
carnation of the millions of unlived years robbed from the murdered
Jews" (150). It is this identity—as the dead author who represents
the dead—that Anne, in the end, wishes to preserve. The book was,
Anne says, "her survival itself" (134); writing is what survived the
camps, and writing will continue to constitute the life she survived
to live.

Anne's reflections invite the reader to consider what makes the
literature of suffering powerful. Each position Anne takes vis-à-vis
her writing makes a certain intuitive sense: she identifies first with
her audience, then with family and friends, and fixes finally on the
identity of writer. The problem of her death and the popularity of
her book thus occasion the worries of a writer. How could she ever
write something as important as the diary? While she celebrates how
it trumps the "insipid best-sellers from which real people learned
about fake people who did not exist and would not matter if they
did" (148), she worries that she can ever match the diary's significance. "Maybe if I were locked up again in a room somewhere and
fed on rotten potatoes and clothed in rags and terrified out of my

wits," she speculates, "maybe then I could write a decent story for Mr. Lonoff!" (137).

Nathan has the same worry: overhearing the suggestive conversation between Amy Bellette and Lonoff, he berates himself for his weak imagination: "Oh, if only I could have imagined the scene I'd overheard! If only I could invent as presumptuously as real life! If one day I could just *approach* the originality and excitement of what actually goes on!" (121). Of course, Roth has imagined the scene that so astonishes Nathan. What Nathan sees as life we see as fiction, and so Roth assures us that fiction really can be as original as life. But Roth's fiction is also notoriously autobiographical, and so he seems to add a caveat: fiction still draws its urgency from experience. In this sense, Roth, like Nathan, identifies with Anne Frank. Nathan, living as a young artist in New York City in the 1950s, certainly finds life—especially his sex life—a fount of excitement. His story about Anne emphasizes how life is the source of excitement for her too—especially those first stirrings of desire that she feels for Peter Van Daan. Anne's writing, unlike Nathan's, though, is shaped by deadly terror, by murderous antisemitism, and reveals the dark side of what writing can draw from life.

In imagining Anne Frank as a writer on the model of Nathan Zuckerman, Roth makes the Holocaust the limit case of life's challenge to fiction. In turn, he makes Nathan's writing both an echo and a revision of great Jewish writing on Frank's model. Nathan's writing does not take antisemitism as its subject matter or its shaping force. When Nathan's family asks that he change his art because of antisemitism, he stubbornly resists, and the solution he imagines—a story in which he marries Anne Frank—is both more brilliant and more impious than the short story that first got him into trouble. His conception of Anne as a writer first and foremost, as a young woman of awakening desire, and as a survivor who abandons her past altogether makes the ultimate writer of Holocaust literature into a human being rather than an icon. His fantasy of marrying her may secure for him the Jewish identity that his parents believe he has rejected, but, more important, it secures his identification as a writer. Since the living Anne Frank exists only in Nathan's fiction, what he marries in the end is not her but his own writing.

In Roth we find a companion for our own thinking about the relation between writing and the Holocaust. His meditations are sharpened by the fact that he has spent so much of his long career bending generic definition, playing with the boundaries between autobiography and fiction.[5] I would argue that the Holocaust is central to Roth's work insofar as it represents the ways life is stranger, more terrible, more gripping than what one can imagine. It also challenges the novelist to make that real life present in fiction. Roth's contribution to the post-1945 obsession with the relation between writer and writing, then, is informed by the suffering and the loss of persons in the Nazi genocide. Starting with Roth, one might begin to build a case for the claim that the historical experiences of the Holocaust and the possibility of nuclear war in their respective visions of genocide have a clear presence in the generic questions that shape postwar fiction. This development is revealed not only in the thematic presence of the Holocaust but also, and perhaps more important, in the philosophical difference it makes in a novel like *The Ghost Writer* or *Operation Shylock*.

There are several other novels for which one might make a similar argument. Don DeLillo's *White Noise* features a protagonist, Jack Gladney, who has founded the department Hitler Studies at a small New England college. His specialization reflects the pervasive fear of death that drives the central plot of the novel—Jack and his wife Babbette's efforts to cure their fear of death. It also reveals DeLillo's vision of American culture as permeated by a violence unassignable to a single agent. In *White Noise*, America is intimately bound up with the mass death and mass murderousness that defined the Holocaust.

Saul Bellow's *Mr. Sammler's Planet* brings the Holocaust to America in a different way, through the survivor Artur Sammler, who comes to New York as a refugee. Sammler's experience of being shot into a mass grave, then escaping from it, makes Sammler an expert on death. For Bellow it makes Sammler an expert on reading and making what he calls the "signs" that preserve human dignity in the face of death.

A novel like Martin Amis's *Time's Arrow*, though it makes the Holocaust a central theme in a way these other novels do not, also engages questions of significance to our understanding not just of the Holocaust but also of fiction. Telling the story of a Nazi doctor in reverse chronology calls into question the notion of causation so crucial to narrative structure. When time is reversed, effect becomes cause. Through this device Amis creates a post-Holocaust fictional style that reflects our sense of how attempts to explain the Holocaust logically are inadequate to account for its evil.

The way one teaches any of these novels depends, of course, on the classroom context. In my course, I teach them with other works that reflect on how modern genocide becomes a force in literary making. Additional readings include Art Spiegelman's *Maus*, Hannah Arendt's *Eichmann in Jerusalem* (I highlight the passages where she compares the trial to a play), Herman Kahn's *Thinking about the Unthinkable*, and works that engage the idea of nuclear war as it relates to reading and storytelling—works such as Ray Bradbury's *Fahrenheit 451* and the Duras-Resnais film *Hiroshima, Mon Amour*. The novels by Roth, DeLillo, Bellow, and Amis discussed above work particularly well in this context, since their more oblique engagement of Holocaust history challenges students to see how and why the Holocaust becomes central to interpretation. Novels need not be about the Holocaust to reveal its importance to literary history.

Other kinds of courses—on the history of the Holocaust, on Jewish history, or on the idea of trauma, for example—can also make use of novels, both those in which the Holocaust is a central theme and those in which it is structurally or philosophically central. A novel like D. M. Thomas's *The White Hotel*, for example, might fit into a Jewish studies course or a course on trauma. It deploys what Thomas represents as a particularly Jewish (though secular) way of seeing the world—psychoanalysis—as the means to communicate the terrible loss of the Holocaust. In imagining Freud's patient Frau Anna as, later, the victim of Nazi murder, Thomas gives us a vision of the ultimate particularity of every person who perished. Anna's eccentric and fascinating psychology as uncovered in her work with Dr. Freud becomes a world unto itself, and we feel its loss when she is killed. In Thomas's novel the victims of Nazi violence are not mere figures of innocence but striving, sensual, creative, complicated persons.

Similarly rich novels of character such as Cynthia Ozick's *The Shawl*, William Styron's *Sophie's Choice,* and W. G. Sebald's *Austerlitz* (my favorite for the beauty of its prose) are also of use in this regard. Indeed, *Austerlitz*, notable for the title character's musings on cities, train stations, and fortifications, might even be appropriately used in a specialized course on memorial architecture. Sebald's fictional mode makes these musings — seemingly secondary to the story of Austerlitz, who left Prague for England on a children's transport, never to see his parents again — in fact central to the evocation of unrecoverable personal loss.

In a history course, any novel that is about the Holocaust can serve to demonstrate how interest in the Holocaust manifested itself in the culture at certain moments. Here, the essays in *The Americanization of the Holocaust*, edited by Hilene Flanzbaum, and Peter Novick's *The Holocaust in American Life* can be helpful secondary reading. Though Novick's dismissive view of Holocaust studies has made his book anathema to some, it nevertheless accounts for how social and political forces such as the cold war and United States policy toward Israel shaped the production and reception of imaginative work about the Holocaust. The contributors to Flanzbaum's volume discuss a range of Holocaust-inflected literary and cultural artifacts in their historical context, from Art Spiegelman's *Maus* to Chicago's Niketown store to the United States Holocaust Memorial Museum. Studying Holocaust fiction in this context teaches students how collective memory and cultural imagination are formed through the push and pull between history and literature.

One of the strengths of Holocaust studies is its interdisciplinarity, and in teaching the Holocaust it is worth drawing on that scholarly strength and breadth. We certainly need to heed Hartman's caution that while "the collective memory uses and produces fictions, it must learn from art not to confuse fiction and history, and from history not to succumb to sentimental or mystical ideas about a community's 'world-historical' destiny." Hartman points out that "both historian and literary critic play a role" (49–50) in this learning process. When we teach fiction in different disciplinary contexts, that process moves forward.

Notes

1. As Susan R. Suleiman has pointed out, we also "read autobiographi-
cally," finding in the stories of others the "type" of a story we then find
in our own lives (*Risking* 199–214). On "type," see Suleiman, "Criticism" 256–61, esp. 260.

2. My *The Holocaust of Texts* also takes up the relation between fiction and
genocide, arguing that the idea of genocide—the destruction of a culture as well as persons—both enables and is itself enabled by ideas developed in literary discourses. The reading I give of Roth's *The Ghost
Writer* in the book is somewhat different from the one I give here, emphasizing instead the point that Roth marries his own writing when he
marries Anne Frank.

3. See, for example, Lang's short essay "The Representation of Limits,"
where he argues that any fictional representation of the Holocaust is
morally compromised. Lang's prose is highly abstract, but with some
help undergraduates can make use of his ideas. In *The Longest Shadow*,
Hartman writes about testimony in such a way that advanced students
might easily bring his arguments to bear on fiction. The last two chapters, "Learning from Survivors: The Yale Testimony Project" and "Holocaust Testimony, Art, and Trauma," are particularly thoughtful and
accessible. Rothberg and Horowitz both show how fiction conveys a
particular truth, having to do with the unsayable essence of trauma,
that other genres do not. The introduction to each book might make
an appropriate assignment. It should also be noted that any of the secondary works I have cited can be mined for other examples of novels in
which the Holocaust appears.

4. At least one critic contends that Roth's career does center on the Holocaust. See Steven Milowitz.

5. In his autobiography, *The Facts*, for example, Roth is addressed by
Nathan Zuckerman. In novels such as *Operation Shylock*, clearly autobiographical material—here, Roth's interviews with Aharon Appelfeld—is included in a novel that is both flamboyantly absurd and
announced, on the flyleaf, as being completely true.

Works Cited

Amis, Martin. *Time's Arrow*. New York: Harmony, 1991.

Appelfeld, Aharon. *Beyond Despair: Three Lectures and a Conversation with
Philip Roth*. Trans. Jeffrey M. Green. New York: Fromm Intl., 1994.

Arendt, Hannah. *Eichmann in Jerusalem: A Report on the Banality of Evil*.
New York: Viking, 1963.

Bellow, Saul. *Mr. Sammler's Planet*. New York: Viking, 1970.

Bradbury, Ray. *Fahrenheit 451*. New York: Ballantine, 1953.

DeLillo, Don. *White Noise*. New York: Viking, 1985.

Flanzbaum, Hilene, ed. *The Americanization of the Holocaust*. Baltimore:
Johns Hopkins UP, 1999.

Hartman, Geoffrey. *The Longest Shadow: In the Aftermath of the Holocaust.* Bloomington: Indiana UP, 1996.

Hiroshima, Mon Amour. Dir. Alain Resnais. Argos Films, 1959.

Horowitz, Sara. *Voicing the Void: Muteness and Memory in Holocaust Fiction.* Albany: State U of New York P, 1997.

Hungerford, Amy. *The Holocaust of Texts: Genocide, Literature, and Personification.* Chicago: U of Chicago P, 2003.

Kahn, Herman. *Thinking about the Unthinkable.* Introd. Raymond Aron. New York: Horizon, 1962.

Lang, Berel. "The Representation of Limits." *Probing the Limits of Representation.* Ed. Saul Friedländer. Cambridge: Harvard UP, 1992. 300–17.

Langer, Lawrence. *The Holocaust and the Literary Imagination.* New Haven: Yale UP, 1975.

Levi, Primo. *Survival in Auschwitz.* Trans. Stuart Woolf. New York: Macmillan, 1961.

Milowitz, Steven. *Philip Roth Considered: The Concentrationary Universe of the American Writer.* New York: Garland, 2000.

Novick, Peter. *The Holocaust in American Life.* Boston: Houghton, 1999.

Ozick, Cynthia. *The Shawl.* New York: Knopf, 1989.

Rosenfeld, Alvin. *A Double Dying: Reflections on Holocaust Literature.* Bloomington: Indiana UP, 1980.

Roth, Philip. "Eli, the Fanatic." Goodbye, Columbus *and Five Short Stories.* New York: Vintage, 1993. 247–98.

———. *The Facts: A Novelist's Autobiography.* New York: Farrar, 1988.

———. *The Ghost Writer.* New York: Vintage, 1979.

———. *Operation Shylock.* New York: Simon, 1993.

Rothberg, Michael. *Traumatic Realism: The Demands of Holocaust Representation.* Minneapolis: U of Minnesota P, 2000.

Sebald, W. G. *Austerlitz.* Trans. Anthea Bell. New York: Random, 2001.

Spiegelman, Art. *And Here My Troubles Began.* New York: Pantheon, 1991. Vol. 2 of *Maus: A Survivor's Tale.*

———. *My Father Bleeds History.* New York: Pantheon, 1986. Vol. 1 of *Maus: A Survivor's Tale.*

Styron, William. *Sophie's Choice.* New York: Random, 1979.

Suleiman, Susan R. "Criticism and the Autobiographical Voice." *Field Work: Sites in Literary and Cultural Studies.* Ed. Marjorie Garber, Paul B. Franklin, and Rebecca L. Walkowitz. New York: Routledge, 1996. 256–61.

———. *Risking Who One Is.* Cambridge: Harvard UP, 1994.

Thomas, D. M. *The White Hotel.* New York: Viking, 1981.

Wilkomirski, Binjamin. *Fragments: Memories of a Wartime Childhood.* Trans. Carol Brown Janeway. New York: Schocken, 1996.

Young, James E. *Writing and Rewriting the Holocaust: Narrative and the Consequences of Interpretation.* Bloomington: Indiana UP, 1988.

Jared Stark

Broken Records:
Holocaust Diaries, Memoirs,
and Memorial Books

*I have buried this under the ashes, deeming it the safest place,
where people will certainly dig to find the traces of millions
who were exterminated.*

*But lately they have begun obliterating the traces and
everywhere, where there was much ash, they ordered to have it
ground fine and to cart it away to the Vistula and let it flow
with the current. . . .*

*Dear finder, search everywhere, every inch of soil. Tens of
documents are buried under it, mine and those of other persons, which will shed light on everything that happened here.
Great quantities of teeth are also buried here. It was we, the
Kommando workers, who expressly have strewn them all over
the terrain, as many as we could, so that the world should find
material traces of the millions of murdered people. We ourselves have lost all hope of being able to live to see the moment
of liberation.*

— Salmen Gradowski, from a letter dated 5 September
1944, discovered 5 March 1945, together with a small
notebook, both written in Yiddish, in a sealed metal
canister near crematorium II at Auschwitz II–Birkenau

A Message in a Bottle

The "final solution" meant not only the murder of millions but also the obliteration of their traces. After 1.7 million Jews and over 2,000 Gypsies were murdered at the Operation Reinhard death camps — Belzec, Sobibor, and Treblinka — the camp structures were razed, the earth plowed, and trees planted. In October 1944, while the gas chambers at Birkenau were still in operation, the same crematorium ovens where bodies were burned were used to destroy truckloads of prisoner records. The genocide of the Jews was to be, Himmler declared to the SS in 1943, "a page of glory in our history which has never been written and is never to be written" (563).

The manuscript of Salmen Gradowski, a Polish Jew selected for the *Sonderkommando* or "special squad" assigned to work in the gas chambers and crematoria, thus seeks not only to provide a factual record but also to counteract Nazi efforts to erase history — to erase even the victims' deaths. If, as Primo Levi writes in *The Drowned and the Saved*, "the entire history of the brief 'millennial Reich' can be reread as a war against memory, an Orwellian falsification of memory, falsification of reality, negation of reality" (31), Gradowski's message is a call to arms, charging its reader to resist the negation of reality by learning to detect and decipher traces that would otherwise remain buried in a silent landscape.

The appeal issued by Gradowski's letter echoes throughout the first-person accounts of Holocaust victims and survivors: the wartime reports, letters, and diaries that survived the disaster as well as postwar memoirs and memorial books through which survivors seek to transmit the individual and collective impact of the genocide. To some students, witness accounts of the Holocaust may seem repetitive, even boring — broken records that endlessly play the same old tune. Others may be overwhelmed by the brutal facts these texts report, by extremities of violence that seem to remove the victims and their writings to an inapproachable and unimaginable realm, one that permits only silent awe. The testimonial appeal of these texts, however, invites and indeed demands another mode of response. For they seek not merely to describe something seen or experienced by the eyewitness. Attesting to their own fragility and insufficiency, they seek also to involve the reader in the act of witnessing, to transform the reader into a co-witness. The challenge these texts present in the classroom, I would submit, emerges most powerfully from the ethical dilemma produced by this appeal. For even as we may seek to recover the past, a text like Gradowski's also confronts us with the absence of unrecovered and unrecoverable voices and stories. In fact, of the tens of documents Gradowski urges us to find, only four others have come to light—one not until 1962, by which time over half the manuscript had become illegible. It is impossible, students realize, to make such broken records whole again. But this impossibility need not preclude a meaningful relationship to the past, both in the ways we remember the past and in the ways we depart from it.

The Appeal of Testimony

Although students may intuitively sense the unusual demands that arise from the testimonial appeal of Holocaust writing, it can be instructive to discuss texts that explicitly thematize this demand. One such moment is Levi's report, in *Survival in Auschwitz*, of a recurring dream or nightmare he had as a prisoner:

> This is my sister here, with some unidentifiable friend and many other people. They are all listening to me and it is this very story that I am telling: the whistle of three notes, the hard bed, my neighbor whom I would like to move, but whom I am afraid to wake as he is stronger than me. I also speak diffusely of our hunger and of the lice-control, and of the Kapo who hit me on the nose and then sent me to wash myself as I was bleeding. It is an intense pleasure, physical, inexpressible, to be at home, among friendly people, and to have so many things to recount: but I cannot help noticing that my listeners do not follow me. In fact, they are completely indifferent: they speak confusedly, of other things among themselves, as if I was not there. My sister looks at me, gets up and goes away without a word. . . . Why does it happen? Why is the pain of every day translated so constantly

into our dreams, in the ever-repeated scene of the unlistened-to story? (53–54)

The present tense of Levi's text places readers in the position of
the "unidentifiable friend" to whom "this very story" is told. Whereas
Levi's oneiric audience demonstrates an indifference that, in denying
the witness's existence, seems to reinstate the Nazi death sentence,
Levi's readers are challenged to compensate for this indifference: if
we can manage to hear the story properly, perhaps the survivor will
be relieved of his pain once and for all. Yet at the same time we
might question this desire to save the witness from his own story. In
his pathbreaking discussion of oral testimony, Dori Laub observes
that one of the "listening defenses" often erected by interviewers is
a "hyperemotionality which superficially looks like compassion and
caring" (73). Alternatively, when another's suffering is beyond our
control, our sense of impotence can easily generate "a sense of outrage and of anger, unwittingly directed at the victim — the narrator"
(72). Our very desire to respond, in other words, can paradoxically
obstruct our ability to respond.

Levi's dream dramatizes this dilemma. Because the dream is already, in Levi's words, a translation of his pain, already a story in itself,
readers confront two simultaneous but mutually exclusive stories: the
story Levi tells *in* the dream, to which we seek to listen, and the story
of the dream, in which the first story remains, and can only remain,
unlistened to. The dream thus exposes us to the limits of what we can
hear, to our inability to "follow" Levi into his experience. You must
turn away, you cannot help but turn away, the dream seems to say, because it is precisely in turning away that you acknowledge the unbear-
ability of what happened. At the same time, the dream warns against
any effort to turn away once and for all. We, too, must participate in
the "ever-repeated scene of the unlistened-to story."

Writing under Siege: Wartime Diaries

Perhaps nowhere is this mutual entanglement of responding and
turning away more vitally at stake than in the wartime writings of

the victims. Not only important historical sources, these documents expose students to the day-to-day impact of the as-yet-unnamed genocide in its unfolding. Rather than present the Holocaust as a past event with a known, inevitable outcome, these texts ask students to consider what it would mean to witness disaster from within. How would you recognize its signs? How can you distinguish between ordinary and extraordinary violence and suffering? What sorts of actions and reactions were, and are, conceivable or inconceivable?

The significance of these documents cannot be separated from the conditions under which they were produced and from their literary form. Whether reading excerpts from one of several excellent anthologies (e.g., Adelson and Lapides; Holliday; Langer, *Art*; Zapruder) or the work of a single diarist, students may be asked to reflect on differences between the role diaries normally play and their role for those living under imminent threat of death. Typically I keep a diary for myself, imagining myself as its eventual and even sole reader, but when a diarist is not sure to survive until tomorrow, the diary can become — perhaps must become — a testament addressed to an external reader, a form of countermemory that supplements or contradicts the official record. This element of testament is particularly strong in extant Holocaust diaries, since, with rare exceptions, those diaries that have survived (only a small fraction of the number written) were preserved deliberately, whether smuggled out of the ghettos during the war or conserved in sealed, secret archives. Though in no way assured of finding a readership, these extant diaries thus represent complex efforts to bear public witness.

The effort to convey word to the outside world, however, faced formidable obstacles. During the war, communication with the world outside the ghettos was extremely risky when not impossible. Moreover, it was far from certain that reports from the ghettos would be taken seriously: in the United States and Great Britain, early reports of Nazi atrocities provoked little reaction, whether because of skepticism, antisemitism (or, in Jewish communities, fear of exciting antisemitism), or various other cultural and political factors (see esp. Laqueur). The incomparable diary of Emmanuel Ringelblum, part of the astonishing Warsaw Ghetto archive clandestinely compiled by

Ringelblum and his Oneg Shabbat organization, is instructive in this regard. Alongside moments of elation when it appeared that news from the ghetto had reached the outside, Ringelblum's diary records the profound sense of abandonment when this news failed to result in any significant intervention.

Not only external obstacles complicated the transmission of victims' testimony. Abrupt explosions of violence, contradictory regulations, and systematic misinformation crippled the ability to comprehend one's environment. "Rigidity, terror, collapse, fear, dread—there is no word to describe all the feelings that swell in these petrified hearts that can't even weep, can't even scream," writes Jozef Zelkowicz in his Lodz Ghetto diary (208). How, one might ask, can an unprecedented reality be described? What happens when no vocabulary capable of accommodating an event is available, when the event deprives its witnesses of a language with which to grasp what is taking place? The philosopher Jean-François Lyotard asks us to imagine the Holocaust as an earthquake that destroys the very instruments one would use to measure it (56). To the extent that the genre of the diary might also be understood as an instrument of measurement, in that it serves to assess and evaluate both one's own condition and that of one's world, diaries from the ghettos embody the predicament Lyotard describes.

This predicament is particularly clear in the diary of Janusz Korczak, a pediatrician and head of the Warsaw Ghetto orphanage whose history is now inextricably linked to his refusal to abandon two hundred of his charges when they were sent to Treblinka. Combining daily observations with anecdotes, memories, dreams, and philosophical reflections, Korczak entrusts to his diary the task of integrating past and present selves into a coherent identity, of keeping track of the changes he and his world undergo as conditions in the ghetto deteriorate. It is perhaps with similar aims that he encouraged the children in his care to keep their own diaries. But two years of life in the ghetto undermine the diary's mission: "I have just read [my diary] over. I could hardly understand it. . . . It seems that I ought to be able to perceive without effort what I write about myself. Ah, but is it possible to understand one's own remembrances?"

(151). Just as he can no longer recognize himself in his diary, so too elementary tools of medical diagnosis lose their explanatory power: "Two sensible, level-headed, unbiased informants and advisers have let me down. The weighing machine and the thermometer. I have ceased to believe them. They too tell lies" (147). What ought to be the most reliable measures, the most stable guides to understanding, break down, and the diary becomes the site and symptom of a discontinuous, immeasurable rupture.

The traumatic impact of the Holocaust is transmitted not only through the content of the diary but also through ruptures in its form. In Ringelblum's diary, for instance, the datelines that precede entries gradually become more sporadic, until in the final six months chronological sequence erodes altogether. A similar breakdown occurs in the diary of Peter Fiegl, a German Jewish boy in hiding in France, for the week of 13 November 1942. "I still have no information about you," he writes, addressing his diary to his parents ten weeks after they were sent to Auschwitz. Two days later, this phrase becomes a skeletal abbreviation — "N.n.," nothing new — which the diary repeats unadorned, an eloquent stutter, for an entire week (Zapruder 75).

On the one hand, the form of the diary depends on finding something worth writing about each day, on registering change and difference. Reading the tenacious, daily acts of witnessing that Holocaust diaries record, we are forced to reconsider our retrospectively determined vision of the Holocaust: no longer a massive, single historical episode, it becomes meaningful as a series of daily incidents experienced by ordinary individuals. On the other hand, however, these diaries bear witness to events that break with chronology, that overwhelm their authors' expressive capacities, that interrupt or arrest the diary. "If my life ends," asks Chaim Kaplan in the last line of his precise, probing diary smuggled out of the Warsaw Ghetto just months before its author was sent to Treblinka, "what will become of my diary?" (400). To grasp what these diaries transmit, we must also listen for what they cannot record — their missing days, their broken endings. But this listening is also a form of not listening, since through it we seek to know, but not share, what for the diarists is a still-unwritten future.

First Person Dispossessed: Survivor Memoirs

Those who survived the Nazi death sentence, whether in hiding, in exile, or in the concentration and death camps, emerged burdened with what Terrence Des Pres calls a "debt to the dead" (37). While some survivors have borne this debt in silence, for others it has made bearing witness imperative. "In setting down this personal record," Olga Lengyel writes in one of the first published memoirs of Auschwitz, "I have tried to carry out the mandate given to me by my fellow internees at Auschwitz who perished so horribly. This is my memorial to them" (208). Conventionally, memoirs seek to bridge the gap between history, which assigns itself the task of filtering out subjective impressions in order to reveal objective historical fact, and autobiography, which gives center stage to the author's individual story. Memoirists adopt the stance of observers, drawing on their experience to portray a historical moment or milieu. Survivor memoirs, however, to the extent that they serve as memorials charged with remembering and honoring the dead, are positioned uneasily between history and autobiography. On the one hand, evidentiary concerns may conflict with the demands of memorialization. On the other hand, the story of the author's own survival, the author's autobiography, may trouble the effort to give voice to the story of the dead, and to the story of their dying.

Historical truth may seem to suffer, for instance, from efforts to derive moral lessons or to cast the victims in a heroic image. Such efforts, it has been observed, may lead memoirists to avoid the uncomfortable implications of what Primo Levi calls the "gray zone" (*Drowned* 36) or the unredeemable, meaning-shattering eruptions of the forms of anguished, humiliated, tainted, and unheroic memory charted by Lawrence Langer (*Holocaust Testimonies*). This tendency is even stronger with publishers than with the writers themselves: hence the transformation of Levi's *Se questo è un uomo* ("If This Is a Man") into *Survival in Auschwitz* for its American edition. In this vein, one can usefully ask students to compare back-cover claims about a memoir's meaning with the memoir itself. Stylistic or dramatic effects—ranging from the representation of verbatim dialogue (when such dialogue may in fact only approximate what was actually said) to the arrangement of events in a suspenseful sequence to the use of imagery that suggests allegorical or philosophical meaning—may also strain factual accuracy. Written memoirs thus come under suspicion from one direction because they may lack the verifiability demanded of historical evidence and from the other direction because they may lack the spontaneity of oral testimony, which seems to prevent the witness from crafting the past into a desired image.

Many survivor memoirs respond to these suspicions by delivering their testimony in the form of spare, chronological accounts with little if any interpretive commentary. At other times, they address these suspicions by showing or suggesting that there may be no language or form capable of representing the full truth of the Holocaust. If there were a language in which the Holocaust could "find a home," the Hungarian writer and Holocaust survivor (and recent Nobel winner) Imre Kertész speculates, "wouldn't this language have to be so terrifying, so lugubrious, that it would destroy those who speak it?" (39).

In this light, memory, because it is indirect and presupposes a lack of immediacy, emerges at the limits of history, as a way of relating to a past that cannot otherwise be accessed. Yet memory can also run up against a limit. "Even as I pen my last words," Lengyel writes, "figures rise before me and mutely plead that I tell their stories, too. I can resist the men and the women, but there are the phantoms of the little children . . ." (225; author's ellipses). The final pages of Lengyel's memoir are devoted to a group of children murdered just weeks before the final evacuation of Auschwitz. But these pages are also haunted by the other figures crowding in on her, the figures she is forced to exclude or else become absorbed into an interminable, impossible writing, one that would leave no room for life. The memoir displays a double bind: excluding certain memories threatens to betray its memorial mandate; not excluding them would subvert the survivor's ability to write.

If the task of the memoir seemed at first to erect a monument to the dead capable of standing in for, speaking for, all that was and all who were destroyed, the double bind exposed in a text like Lengyel's challenges us to think of the memoir, like the diary, as a broken record—a text that communicates in and through the ways it fractures its own form. Memoirs that appear to adhere to the simplest narrative protocols—"I remember . . ."—tend nonetheless to acknowledge or generate gaps between the experience they seek to transmit and the language and narrative forms available to accomplish this task. Wladyslaw Szpilman's *The Pianist*, for instance, which served as the basis for a film by Roman Polanski, challenges the legitimacy of its own otherwise sequential narration when Szpilman observes that in retrospect his two years in the ghetto "merge into a single image as if they had lasted only a single day. Hard as I try, I cannot break it up into smaller sections that would impose some chronological order on it" (61). In another striking instance, Cecilie Klein, in her memoir *Sentenced to Live*, explodes the conventional identification readers assume between an autobiographical narrator and the subject of the autobiography:

> Many years ago, I witnessed the massacre of my people and when my turn came, I wasn't thrown into the flames like all the others. Instead, I was chopped up into small pieces, but I refused to die. I picked up all the pieces, put them neatly together, made myself look like a person, but in fact, remained a mummy. (5)

Instead of revealing and sharing with us its writer's identity, the text appears as a mask or borrowed garment (a shroud?) assumed to make the writer recognizable to others—and to herself—but only by concealing the unhealed wounds of history. In Jean Améry's *At the Mind's Limits*, even the first-person singular loses its coherence and meaning. "I was a person who could no longer say 'we' and who therefore said 'I' merely out of habit, but not with the feeling of full possession of my self," he writes, recalling the implementation of race laws in his native Austria. "I was no longer an I and did not live within a We. I had no passport, and no past, and no money, and no history" (43–44). The dispossession of identity invalidates his given name, Hans Meier, which "no longer made much sense either" (43), leading him to adopt the pseudonym Jean Améry, which he would use as a pen name throughout his postwar life.

Students may initially approach survivor memoirs with a certain reluctance to subject them to critical analysis, a reluctance often owed to the almost sacred aura that accompanies the cultural myth of the survivor. But direct engagement with the complexities and contradictions that riddle the language and forms of testimony, particularly as these trouble conventional understandings of history and memory, can work to expose students to a way of relating to the Holocaust that sacrifices reverence for a more challenging mode of engagement, one in which, together with the survivor, we too become responsible for how the past is remembered and for what that memory will mean for the future.

Collective Legacies: Memorial and Postmemorial Books

A final form of survivor testimony to emerge in the postwar years were *yizkor* or memorial books—collectively authored volumes produced by groups of survivors, relatives, and friends. Usually published in small editions in Yiddish or Hebrew, they commemorate the prewar life of European Jewry, as well as its destruction, through compilations of stories, letters, scholarly articles, personal reminiscences, poems, town records, drawings, maps, photographs, and other documents. Recent print translations (e.g., Bisberg-Youkelson and Youkelson), an extensive online archive (*Yizkor Book Project*), and Jack Kugelmass and Jonathan Boyarin's outstanding anthology, *From a Ruined Garden*, make this important genre newly available in English. The New York Public Library also maintains a collection of digital reproductions of original *yizkor* books (*Yizkor Books Online*).

In their efforts to reconstitute the world of the shtetl in its totality, these texts serve less to provide a historically nuanced or accurate picture of prewar Jewish life—as Annette Wieviorka and Itzhok Niborski demonstrate, they tend to idealize the shtetl as a paradise lost—than to register the ways in which the Shoah cut short a tradition and history in process, producing an irretrievable, frozen image of the Jewish past. For decimated communities living in the Diaspora, these books became portable cemeteries. "No graves have been left of all those who were slain. And the surviving Koriv Jews will not be found on Koriv soil in Poland," reads one memorial book. "Beloved and precious martyrs of Koriv, we bring you to burial today! In a yizker-bukh, a memorial volume! Today we have set up a tombstone in memory of you!" (Kugelmass and Boyarin 19).

The hybrid form of memorial books also provides a way into thinking about several recent testimonial projects that emerge from collaborations between survivors and others. Art Spiegelman's two-volume graphic novel *Maus* and Alina Bacall-Zwirn and Jared Stark's *No Common Place*, for instance, foreground the process of bearing witness, the unfolding of memory, and the relationships that form as Holocaust experiences are transmitted from the eyewitnesses to their listeners. In texts such as Timothy Ryback's *The Last Survivor*, Mark Roseman's *A Past in Hiding*, or Patrick Modiano's *Dora Bruder*, survivors' stories become the occasion for investigating questions of personal and cultural identity, the politics of memory, and the ethics of witnessing. These texts—what we might call post-memorial books (adapting Hirsch's term "postmemory"; see the introduction to this volume)—lead us to ask what the legacy of the Holocaust, and of its survivors, has been, will be, or should be. They insist that witnessing can and should be a collective endeavor, an endeavor that does not simply enshrine the past but that recognizes its abiding presence.

Works Cited

Adelson, Alan, and Robert Lapides, eds. *Lodz Ghetto: Inside a Community under Siege.* New York: Viking, 1989.

Améry, Jean. *At the Mind's Limits.* Trans. Sidney Rosenfeld and Stella Rosenfeld. New York: Schocken, 1986.

Bacall-Zwirn, Alina, and Jared Stark. *No Common Place: The Holocaust Testimony of Alina Bacall-Zwirn.* Lincoln: U of Nebraska P, 1999.

Bisberg-Youkelson, Fiegl, and Rubin Youkelson, eds. *The Life and Death of a Polish Shtetl: Memorial Book of Strzegowo.* Trans. Gene Bluestein. Lincoln: U of Nebraska P, 2000.

Des Pres, Terrence. *The Survivor: An Anatomy of Life in the Death Camps.* New York: Oxford UP, 1976.

Gradowski, Salmen. Letter. *Amidst a Nightmare of Crime*. Ed. Jadwiga Bezwinska and Danuta Czech. New York: Fertig, 1992: 74–77.

Himmler, Heinrich. "Speech of the Reichsfuehrer-SS at the meeting of SS Major-Generals at Posen October 4th, 1943." *Nazi Conspiracy and Aggression*. Vol. 4. Office of the United States Chief of Counsel for Prosecution of Axis Criminality. Washington: GPO, 1946. 558–72.

Holliday, Laurel, ed. *Children in the Holocaust and World War II: Their Secret Diaries*. New York: Pocket, 1995.

Kaplan, Chaim. *The Warsaw Diary of Chaim Kaplan*. Trans. and ed. Abraham I. Katsch. New York: Collier, 1973.

Kertész, Imre. "The Freedom of Self-Definition." Trans. Ivan Sanders. *Witness Literature: Proceedings of the Nobel Centennial Symposium*. Ed. Horace Engdahl. River Edge: World Scientific, 2002. 33–43.

Klein, Cecilie. *Sentenced to Live*. New York: Holocaust Lib., 1988.

Korczak, Janusz. *Ghetto Diary*. New York: Holocaust Lib., 1978.

Kugelmass, Jack, and Jonathan Boyarin. *From a Ruined Garden: The Memorial Books of Polish Jewry*. New York: Schocken, 1983.

Langer, Lawrence, ed. *Art from the Ashes: A Holocaust Anthology*. New York: Oxford UP, 1995.

———. *Holocaust Testimonies: The Ruins of Memory*. New Haven: Yale UP, 1991.

———, ed. "Journals and Diaries." Langer, *Art* 153–233.

Laqueur, Walter. *The Terrible Secret: Suppression of the Truth about Hitler's "Final Solution."* Boston: Little, 1980.

Laub, Dori. "Bearing Witness; or, The Vicissitudes of Listening." *Testimony: Crises of Witnessing in Literature, Psychoanalysis, and History*. By Shoshana Felman and Laub. New York: Routledge, 1991. 57–74.

Lengyel, Olga. *Five Chimneys: The Story of Auschwitz*. 1946. New York: Fertig, 1995.

Levi, Primo. *The Drowned and the Saved*. Trans. Raymond Rosenthal. New York: Vintage, 1988.

———. *Survival in Auschwitz*. Trans. Stuart Woolf. New York: Collier, 1961.

Lyotard, Jean-François. *The Differend: Phrases in Dispute*. Trans. Georges Van Den Abbeele. Minneapolis: U of Minnesota P, 1988.

Modiano, Patrick. *Dora Bruder*. Trans. Joanna Kilmartin. Berkeley: U of California P, 1999.

Ringelblum, Emmanuel. *Notes from the Warsaw Ghetto*. Ed. and trans. Jacob Sloan. New York: Schocken, 1974.

Roseman, Mark. *A Past in Hiding*. New York: Picador, 2000.

Ryback, Timothy. *The Last Survivor: Legacies of Dachau*. New York: Vintage, 2000.

Spiegelman, Art. *And Here My Troubles Began*. New York: Pantheon, 1991. Vol. 2 of *Maus: A Survivor's Tale*.

———. *My Father Bleeds History*. New York: Pantheon, 1986. Vol. 1 of *Maus: A Survivor's Tale*.

Szpilman, Wladyslaw. *The Pianist.* Trans. Anthea Bell. New York: Picador, 1999.

Wieviorka, Annette, and Itzhok Niborski. *Les livres du souvenir: Mémoriaux juifs de Pologne.* Paris: Gallimard, 1983.

Yizkor Book Project. Ed. Joyce Field. 1998-2001. JewishGen, Inc. 12 May 2003 <http://www.jewishgen.org/yizkor/>.

Yizkor Books Online. New York Public Lib. Dorot Jewish Division. 27 May 2004 <http://www.nypl.org/research/chss/jws/yizkorbookonline.cfm>.

Zapruder, Alexandra, ed. *Salvaged Pages: Young Writers' Diaries of the Holocaust.* New Haven: Yale UP, 2002.

Zelkowicz, Jozef. "Days of Nightmare." Langer, *Art* 200–14.

Geoffrey Hartman

Audio and Video Testimony
and Holocaust Studies

After the Allies came upon the Nazi death camps and concentration camps toward the end of the Second World War, newspapers and magazines were filled with frightening reports and grim photos of the dead and the dying (see esp. Zelizer). Soon some of the survivors began to speak in their own voice and even to publish their experiences. The only systematic recording, however, of survivors seems to have been that by David P. Boder in displaced-person camps (established to provide a temporary refuge for a large number of homeless victims). Boder used a primitive version of the tape recorder for that purpose.[1] In addition, many written depositions were collected by historical commissions in Poland and occupied Germany. These testimonies number in the tens of thousands.[2]

While we do not have an adequate overview of the early collection of testimonies, three stages can be discerned. At first there was a flood of witness accounts from the last months of the war into the early 1950s, some of which had trouble being published. (Primo Levi's *Survival in Auschwitz* was initially rejected by an Italian publisher, and the first edition, when finally issued, sold very few copies.) Also a large amount of testimony (though mainly by Nazi officers and officials) emerged from the Nuremberg trials.[3] For complex reasons, a latency period then ensued in which, as the French put it, there was no *écoute*.[4]

Raul Hilberg's pioneering and still in many ways definitive *The Destruction of the European Jews* (1961) concentrated its attention on the perpetrators, sifting and interpreting the extant documents with great skill. Its portrayal of the victims, however, became controversial: without the benefit of a sustained analysis of survivor interviews, Hilberg gave what many considered to be an unsympathetic picture of helpless Jewish communities and a mainly ineffective or even corrupt leadership. A second wave of interest in survivor testimony came only after the widely broadcast Eichmann trial of 1961–62, although Yad Vashem, the national Holocaust memorial museum in Israel, encouraged eyewitnesses to fill out questionnaires after its founding in 1953. The shift to include for remembrance and research the experience and moral witness of the survivors was slow but did produce Terrence Des Pres's outstanding *The Survivor* in 1976.

Methodical recordings of oral testimony in the 1970s used audiotape.[5] A new phase was stimulated, however, by the TV production *Holocaust* in 1978 (see Green). While it awoke the conscience of the younger generations in Germany, it had a peculiar effect on the survivors, especially in the United States. The survivors complained that this TV version of the events sanitized and distorted what they had lived through. By this time—some twenty-five years after liberation—the survivors had in part rebuilt their families and were ready to speak in public of their ordeal, although many remained silent.

This phase saw the introduction of videotaped testimony on an organized basis. A grassroots New Haven group founded the Holocaust Survivors Film Project in 1979; and Yale University's central library accepted the project's two hundred testimonies in 1981. The Video Archive for Holocaust Testimonies (later adding the name Fortunoff for the family endowing it) was established to continue this pioneering effort by local survivors and farsighted neighbors[6] and to extend it nationally and internationally. In addition, Yale began the task of making the testimonies available for teaching and research by cataloging them and putting their summaries online. By 2002 Yale had taped 4,200 witness accounts amounting to more than 10,000 hours. Other organizations also turned to videotape,[7] and Claude Lanzmann's over-nine-hour documentary *Shoah* (released in 1985 but long in preparation), by refusing archival images and basing itself exclusively on filmed witness interviews, demonstrated how powerful such interviews could be.[8]

The last and biggest effort came in the wake of Steven Spielberg's *Schindler's List* (1992). By then many in the survivor community, less shy of publicity and the medium of video, were ready to tell their story. *Schindler's List*, moreover, hugely successful in the States among both survivors and a broader audience, gave credibility to its director as he launched his Visual History of the Shoah Foundation, which recorded over 50,000 witnesses from 1994 through 1999.[9]

Oral History, Technology, and the Pedagogical Imperative

Electronic recording has changed the mode of production, transmission, and reception of oral narratives. The stories now recorded are no longer — or not only — a filtered, even consecrated form of popular wisdom handed down in families or considered as the exclusive patrimony of local, ethnic, or national interests. The *yizker* ("memorial") books, published by regional associations (Landsmannschaften) and commemorating the destroyed Jewish communities, still reflect in their content an older tradition by combining chronicle, folklore, and *fait divers*.

Today's oral memoirs, quickly printed or directly transmitted by audiovisual media, can be infinitely reproduced and broadcast. Marshall McLuhan, the first guru of the electronic revolution, declared that a humanism wedded to technology would surpass print culture through reanimated, globally circulating words and images. In a society of communication, knowledge from whatever source becomes universal and interactive (McLuhan and Powers).

Oral traditions have indeed become more accessible. The proliferation of portable taping devices allows the proactive discipline of
oral history to join forces with a growing interest in everyday life
and to open new venues of information. Tape recorder and cam-
corder seek out native informants in our very midst. Oral history, by
interviewing not only exotic or faraway groups but people nearby—
those with extreme or else ordinary but overlooked experiences—
differentiates itself from journalism and finds its news wherever men
and women carry memories in danger of disappearing.

Memories run that danger when judged to be trivial or, at the
opposite pole, traumatic. Today they are also unexpectedly endan-
gered by our very ability to record and transmit in real time what
happens as it happens. A shadow side to McLuhan's vision appears:
both past and present, we realize, can fade or lose focus because
those same technological advances enable mechanical reproducibility. This reproducibility erodes the distinction between private and
public; removes all cult objects, religious or artistic, from the sphere
of sacred or ceremonial (Walter Benjamin, in his famous essay of
1936, already discerned what he called a loss of aura); produces a
massive influx of unfiltered data; and shines a fickle, ever-shifting
spotlight, typified by round-the-clock news, which distracts rather
than concentrates the mind. The effort to synthesize attention's over-
load becomes more exacting despite technology's promise to off-
load for later retrieval any recorded event. When we add other factors
abetting that dynamic of nervous heedfulness and willful neglect—a
negationism, on the one hand, that minimizes or even denies the
Holocaust (to be distinguished from a natural rather than malevolent reluctance to admit that a large number of our species could
have been so deluded and vicious) and, on the other hand, the need
of survivors, refugees, and immigrants to move beyond painful
memories—oblivion seems as close as ever.

Today Holocaust oral testimony rallies forces to the side of memory. More precisely, it ensures the quality of our attention to the immediate past. Systematically pursued and aware of itself as a genre, it
counteracts the media's tendency to reduce lives to bytes of information and an endless repetition of visual clichés. Video is harnessed,

because it has become a popular avenue of information and because it is playing an increasing role in schools and museums. Video testimony modifies the coldness of technology by strengthening the communal implications of the act of filming: a less artificial image is created, a representation that places the interview at the center and is not afraid of the talking-head format.

The Taped Oral Interview and Its Classroom Use

We are accustomed to think of interviews as a simple investigative device; but oral-testimony interviewing calls for an especially sensitive approach. The interview must proceed in a nonjournalistic, nonpressured manner and seek a testimonial alliance in which the interviewer becomes a partner or "midwife," an informed representative of a larger, interested community (Laub, "Bearing" 57). Given the closeness of Holocaust memories to trauma, only if there is trust can interviews elicit spontaneous moments of self-expression and unexpected returns of memory. Where this inner spontaneity develops, affective reminiscences are retrieved. They add vernacular texture and human depth to the relatively impersonal form of narration that often characterizes the professional discipline of history writing.

Each testimony is, in that respect, performative as well as informative. As in the remarkable Holocaust diaries that were saved, a sense of individuality emanates from personally observed detail and rescues witnesses from being a statistic, part of an anonymous mass. The visual dimension, too, the language of gesture captured by video, reinforces the presence of the witness. We see and hear someone who is more than a victim, who has the courage to face the past and its suffering once more.

From a pedagogical point of view, moreover, to show videotaped testimonies lessens the risk of secondary trauma in young people, despite the terrible scenes often described. For the testimonies are not photographs that burn themselves into the mind. Presented in the form of stories told by persons with whom we can try to identify, the ferocity, shame, and terror of what happened become somewhat more bearable. Interest shifts from the mystery of evil that shrouds the perpetrator to the humanity of the victim. Instead of a cinematic or other type of sensationalism—always self-defeating in the long run, for it eventually turns people off or becomes so routine that heightened doses of artificial stimuli are needed—the testimonies keep to the human face and voice, without dramatic additives.

Yet the presence of a teacher for the screening of video testimonies is essential. Their impact can often be so strong that students tend to be silent or shy about raising questions. Independent viewing and study, therefore, should in general come after a communal or classroom screening. No one should be made to feel that these are sacred documents: the survivors want their experiences to be known, and many are willing to visit classes and answer questions.

The testimonies, in short, engage the emotions as well as the intellect; in this respect they act like poetry but with a more painful directness. Care must always be taken that they stimulate research rather than substitute for it. The teacher should be ready to discuss feelings that become deeply involved, leading to the question of how objective one can nevertheless remain and the question of what one learns from viewing that is not gleaned from reading. The issue of the comparability of the Holocaust with prior persecutions, or of the persistence of genocidal episodes in history, is also bound to come up.[10] It is advisable to view the testimonies in the later part of a course, after the basic historical facts have been grasped, since a lot of information must first be acquired about a hierarchical and terroristic regime, its racist and antisemitic propaganda, the types of camps and their infrastructure, and the overall sequence of events climaxing in the planned and total genocide of the final solution.

To watch a video testimony of two or more hours from beginning to end is hard, although it should be encouraged. For teaching purposes, the shorter, thematic programs put together by the Yale Video Archive, programs that rely exclusively on testimonial extracts from survivor or bystander testimonies, can be a suitable introduction. Claude Lanzmann's *Shoah*, too, might be used, but in excerpted form. The PBS-sponsored film *Witness*, with the book that accompanies it, is another option (Greene and Kumar).[11]

The interaction, of course, between interviewer and interviewee does not always work and may be as unpredictable as a chemical reaction. Care has to be taken to neutralize any personal agenda of the interviewers. Such an agenda might bias or short-circuit the taping; it could also close off unpredictable questions and the interests of later generations. Among the essential features of an ideal interview are that the questioner remains a facilitator and does not take the initiative away from the witness; that everyone who wishes to be interviewed should have the chance, whether the person is prominent or rank-and-file; and that the focus be on the life story rather than only on the time of victimization. A good interview reveals not only the daily life and death in the camps or hiding places; it brings the entire person forward, disclosing, for instance, what was endured during the period of resocialization (the survivor's struggle for normalcy after the Holocaust) and the continuing effect of the catastrophe on the survivor's descendants. It may also cover the Jewish world before the Holocaust, the flourishing in it of Yiddish, German, and Sephardi cultures. Thus the testimonies, in audio or audiovisual format, have the possibility of combining knowledge and feeling, of enlarging our sympathy as well as making a historical, psychological, and sociological contribution.

Video Testimony's Plural Value

Both audio- and videotaped testimonies are important, but the videotaped are an especially effective teaching resource in an increasingly audiovisual culture. They play a role in documentaries or the movies, but that is not their main reason for being. As an unusually direct yet nonvoyeuristic and visually ascetic transcription of the bearing and concerns of the people interviewed, they renounce illusion and technique, everything that might steal attention from the witness.

In general, the value of oral testimony is various and cannot be confined to its historical yield alone. Oral testimony broadens the field of historical awareness. This broadening was already perceptible in Maurice Halbwachs's focus on the collective memory. His pathbreaking book, published five years after his death in Buchenwald,

characterized the collective memory as a living link between generations. He pointed to a knowledge neglected (in his time) by professional historians yet circulating from the grandparent generation to
at least that of the grandchildren. This knowledge, in the form of
family narratives, evoked lives, issues, and events that often existed
outside or on the margins of mainstream historical accounts or was
expressed in a highly poetic way. The public recovery of such knowledge depended on what was considered worthy to be recalled and
was only then termed historical.

When the history of everyday life joined with oral documentation to capture this neglected memory buzz, it provoked the much
discussed split between history and memory. For, as Yosef Yerushalmi pointed out, the methodical hygiene, vast factual detail, and
truth claim of modern scientific historiography are averse to a communal memory's inventive, mythmaking side, its healing or revanch-
ist stories. But this imaginative turn is surely also worth examining,
even should it fall more into the domain of literature, narratology,
and memory studies.

The Question of Historical Value

The suspicion that oral testimony inevitably contains fictive elements or depositions of unreliable narrators—if only because of the
frailty of human memory and the pain of recollection, especially when
these depositions are taken years after the event—is still common.
And it is certainly appropriate to remain as wary of personal witness
accounts as of official documents.[12] In each case the circumstances
under which a report was produced must be taken into consideration. Concerning Holocaust survivor testimony, Primo Levi observed
that the situation of Jews in the hierarchy of the concentration,
slave-labor, and death camps was such that practically no one could
see more than a segment of what was going on and that many victims were compelled to enter a "gray zone" of moral choice, so that
a sense of shame may have colored their recollections. That there
was often a latency period before survivors were able or willing to
talk about their experience, or before they felt they might be listened

to, also meant that whatever they had heard, read, or seen in the interim (especially through television and film) could have left its mark. Understandably, this matter of the cultural milieu's imprint on oral testimony, especially when that testimony is recorded belatedly, at different times, and in different countries or tongues, may make it less important to historians than strict factual yield. But it has a value of its own. The testimonies startle by their one-by-one-by-one distinctive identity: there was a sinister, racist denial of Jewish individuality and humanity in Nazi ideology, but the memory recovered in freedom is a plural memory, too individual to be collectivized.

Historical evidence, moreover, or its confirmation is not always the predominant reason for collecting witness accounts. By 1979, which saw plans being developed for a Holocaust Memorial Museum in Washington and also marks a new, intensive phase in the collection of survivor testimonies, a tremendous amount of quality research had been done. Oral testimony (after an initial period of debriefing and research) does not seek to turn the survivor into a historian. It enables a witness to speak who fears the passing of witness. In general, testimonial narratives have a triple audience in mind: the world that should know, the community of victims that is rebuilding, and (in a kind of self-therapy) the one who has survived to tell us.

All these motives are involved. I do not wish to slight the more direct historical contribution of many testimonies. While the great majority are belated and indirectly inform us about the workings of memory in addition to conveying the weight of what happened in a personal way, some eyewitnesses were recorded early on, during the Nazi persecution.[13] It will be clear to anyone who reads even a few pages of testimony contemporary with the events (secretly redacted chronicles like Emanuel Ringelblum's *Oneg Shabbat* [*Notes*] or Avraham Tory's *Kovno Ghetto Diary*, or poems, diaries, and other documents in such anthologies as *Lodz Ghetto: Inside a Community under Siege* [Adelson and Lapides]) how indispensable these sources are, not only from a factual point of view but also because of their unparalleled descriptive and emotional power. Later survivor and bystander accounts supplement the record by their converging perspectives as well as by documenting the aftereffects of the persecutions on the survivors. There are also aspects of the Nazi's vast kingdom of death, its smaller camps, for instance, which are fully described only in such witness accounts. The same providing of information holds for the death marches at the end of the war.

————

The establishing of important oral testimony archives over the last twenty-five years reflects the awareness that too few of the eyewitnesses passing from the scene had told their story and that the burden of instruction would soon be carried entirely by educational institutions, especially museums (increasingly aware of a pedagogical mission) and universities. Many school systems have now contracted with privately founded corporations such as Facing History and Ourselves and Spielberg's Visual History of the Shoah. The part played by witnesses visiting a classroom will soon have to be accomplished only through the taped testimonies. The best surrogate for the survivors, they provide a teaching resource as well as an object of research.

Has the time for collecting oral testimony come to an end? Given the continuing impact of the event on secondary witnesses — sons and daughters of the survivors, as well as scholars, teachers, and artists who have become adoptive witnesses — some taping should continue focusing on this group.

It has become customary to think of historians as helping us identify a usable past, but in this case, and in an era that has shown that the Holocaust was not the genocide to end all genocides, the question remains open as to whether any creative recuperation is possible. While the search may never end, it still seems crucial to take up the pedagogical challenge: How do we transmit so hurtful an image of our own species without killing hope and breeding indifference, or without rejecting historical and literary studies for simplified political remedies and a rhetoric that serves only to relieve conscience?

Notes

1. For a description of Boder and a summary of his effort, see Niewyk's introduction. Interesting statistics on French "récits de déportation" are given in Wieviorka (*Déportation*).

2. Leon Wells's *The Death Brigade* (experiences of a *Sonderkommando* survivor) was published by such a commission. More details of these collections, which remain without a bibliography, though some are in process of being cataloged, are available (see the introduction to Wieviorka, *L'ère*). The depositions of the Russian zone's Verein der Verfolgten des Nazi Regimes (Association of Those Persecuted by the Nazi Regime) may be consulted in Germany's national archive (Bundesarchiv) in Berlin-Lichterfelde. Concerning a more technical, scientific literature: in 1969 and 1970 the International Auschwitz Committee published under the title imprint "Auschwitz" and the location "Warsaw" several anthologies of articles drawn from a periodical written during the 1960s by survivors or based on their testimonies and documenting their psychological and medical state. The earliest report by survivors, the "Auschwitz Protocols," were furnished by two escapees in April 1944 (see Vrba).

3. The total bias in favor of official documents was shared by Léon Poliakov's early *Harvest of Hate*. He declares in the book, first published in French in 1951, that whenever possible, to forestall objections, the executioners were quoted rather than the victims.

4. But as Annette Wieviorka suggests in "On Testimony" (26–28), the massive outpouring of witness literature immediately after the war may have indicated not a real, let alone a large audience, but rather the lack of one, with the deportees turning to writing as a solace.

5. Among significant collections and analyses of oral survivor testimony the following should be mentioned: Gill; Epstein; and Pollak.

6. Laurel Vlock, a television interviewer and producer, recruited Dori Laub, child survivor and Yale psychiatrist, and William Rosenberg of the Farband (basically a survivor association) to found the project. See Hartman, "Learning" and "Tele-Suffering."

7. Among these organizations was the United States Holocaust Memorial Museum under its then director, Jehoshuah Weinberg. Previously the head of Beit Hatefutsoth, Israel's Diaspora Museum, he had been the first to cooperate with the Yale project abroad.

8. More information on collections of interviews, as on those in other countries (in Yad Vashem or the British Sound Archives of the British Library), can be found on the Web sites of the respective institutions. Two books focused on survivor testimonies in the Yale archive have been published: see the bibliography for Langer and for Kraft. See also Oren Stier, *Committed to Memory*.

9. Allen Nevins founded an oral history department at Columbia University in the 1950s, and Moshe Davis, influenced by Nevins, created

around 1959 what became the Oral History Division of the Institute of Contemporary History at Hebrew University. For a useful short account of the growth of oral history, especially in Israeli institutions, see Meyer.

10. A valid comparison can be made between Holocaust testimony and the Latin- or meso-American *testimonio,* although the interview partners cannot be socially typed as fixedly as in Mary Louise Pratt's discussion of testimonios as produced through the voluntary collaboration of city intellectuals and a subaltern or grassroots person. Nor, of course, while the two witness accounts often share a concern for social justice, are the principals in the Holocaust witness and the *testimonio* interviews linked by a commitment to the radical transformation of the political structure of the country that liberated them and allowed them to become citizens.

11. Information on how to obtain the Yale video programs, including the ninety-minute *Witness: Voices from the Holocaust,* can be found on the Yale Web site. Court depositions are an important special case of testimony: the Eichmann trial was filmed, and the Barbie trial (1988) videotapes are being released.

12. To determine the factual reliability of evidence is a complex matter. Much documentary evidence by the perpetrators is not above suspicion just because it was printed and officially issued. Nazi military and administrative reports are notorious for a self-serving bureaucratic and euphemistic jargon that requires decoding. It has often been remarked that history looks very different when seen from the side of the victors (or those who arrogantly foresee victory) than from the side of the suppressed. For a brief and sensible analysis of the issue, see Ritchie 92–95; for further discussion, see Kraft 14–15. The classic general description of and support for oral history remains Thompson. For an example of the belated appreciation of oral testimony, see Gross. For a good account of how difficult it was immediately after the war to overcome disbelief, see chapter 7, "Telling the Story," in Abzug.

13. Alfred Wiener collected eyewitness descriptions of the organized Nazi pogrom of 9 November 1938 that came to be called Kristallnacht (Night of Broken Glass). These records formed the basis of the Wiener library established in London and later also in Tel Aviv. Evidence for the Gypsy (Roma and Sinti) Holocaust is almost entirely dependent on the oral testimony of its survivors and has been inadequately documented. Roma testimonies, though in small numbers, are to be found in archives at Yale, the United States Holocaust Memorial Museum, and the Shoah Foundation.

Works Cited and Recommended

Abzug, Robert H. *Inside the Vicious Heart: Americans and the Liberation of Nazi Concentration Camps.* New York: Oxford UP, 1985.

Adelson, Alan, and Robert Lapides, eds. *Lodz Ghetto: Inside a Community under Siege.* New York: Viking, 1989.

Benjamin, Walter. "The Work of Art in the Age of Mechanical Reproduction." *Illuminations.* Ed. Hannah Arendt. New York: Harcourt, 1968. 217–52.

Boder, David P. *I Did Not Interview the Dead.* Urbana: U of Illinois P, 1949.

Bolkosky, Sidney, Betty Ellis Rotberg, and David Harris. *Life Unworthy of Life.* Farmington Hills: Center for the Study of the Child, 1987. Includes videotaped oral testimonies.

Browning, Christopher, R. *Collected Memories: Holocaust History and Postwar Testimony.* Madison: U of Wisconsin P, 2003.

———. *Nazi Policy, Jewish Workers, German Killers.* Cambridge: Cambridge UP, 2000.

Des Pres, Terrence. *The Survivor: An Anatomy of Life in the Death Camps.* New York: Oxford UP, 1976.

Eliach, Yaffa. *There Once Was a World: A Nine-Hundred-Year Chronicle of the Shtetl of Eishyhok.* Boston: Little, 1998.

Eliach, Yaffa, and Brana Gurewitsch, eds. *The Liberators: Eyewitness Accounts of the Liberation of Concentration Camps: Oral History Testimonies of American Liberators from the Archives of the Center for Holocaust Studies.* Brooklyn: Center for Holocaust Studies, Documentation and Research, 1981.

Epstein, Helen. *Children of the Holocaust: Conversations with Sons and Daughters of Survivors.* New York: Putnam, 1979.

Gill, Anton. *The Journey Back from Hell: An Oral History—Conversations with Concentration Camp Survivors.* New York: Morrow, 1988.

Green, Gerald. *Holocaust.* New York: Bantam, 1981. E-book (*Microsoft Reader*). RosettaBooks, 2001.

Greene, Joshua M., and Shiva Kumar, eds. *Witness: Voices from the Holocaust.* Videocassette. Stories to Remember, 1999. Fwd. Lawrence L. Langer. New York: Free, 2000.

Greenspan, Henry. *Holocaust Survivors: Recounting and Life History.* Westport: Praeger, 1998.

Gross, Jan T. *Neighbors: The Destruction of the Jewish Community in Jedwabne, Poland.* Princeton: Princeton UP, 2001.

Halbwachs, Maurice. *On Collective Memory.* Ed. and trans. Lewis A. Coser. Chicago: U of Chicago P, 1992.

Hartman, Geoffrey. ed. *Holocaust Remembrance: The Shapes of Memory.* Oxford: Blackwell, 1994.

———. "Learning from Survivors: The Yale Testimony Project." *The Longest Shadow: In the Aftermath of the Holocaust.* Bloomington: Indiana UP, 1996. 133–50.

———. "Tele-Suffering and Testimony." *Scars of the Spirit: The Struggle against Inauthenticity.* New York: Palgrave, 2002. 67–84.

Hilberg, Raul. *The Destruction of the European Jews.* Chicago: Quadrangle, 1961. Rev. ed. 3 vols. New York: Holmes, 1985.

Johnson, Mary, and Margot Stern Strom, eds. *Elements of Time.* Videocassette and guide. Brookline: Facing History and Ourselves, 1989.

Kraft, Robert N. *Memory Perceived: Recalling the Holocaust.* Westport: Praeger, 2002.

Langer, Lawrence L. *Holocaust Testimonies: The Ruins of Memory.* New Haven: Yale UP, 1991.

Lanzmann, Claude. *Shoah: An Oral History of the Holocaust.* New York: Pantheon, 1985.

Laub, Dori. "Bearing Witness; or, The Vicissitudes of Listening." *Testimony: Crises of Witnessing in Literature, Psychoanalysis, and History.* By Shoshana Felman and Laub. New York: Routledge, 1992. 57–74.

———. "Testimonies in the Treatment of Genocidal Trauma." *Journal of Applied Psychoanalytic Studies* 4 (2000): 63–87.

Levi, Primo. *The Drowned and the Saved.* Trans. Raymond Rosenthal. New York: Summit, 1988.

McLuhan, Marshall, and Bruce R. Powers. *The Global Village: Transformations in World Life and Media in the Twenty-First Century.* New York: Oxford UP, 1989.

Meyer, Ernie. "Collecting Oral History." *Jerusalem Post* 6 Apr. 1990: 16.

Niewyk, Donald L., ed. *Fresh Wounds: Early Narratives of Holocaust Survival.* Chapel Hill: U of North Carolina P, 1998.

Poliakov, Léon. *Harvest of Hate.* New York: Holocaust Lib., 1979.

Pollak, Michael. *L'expérience concentrationnaire: Essai sur le maintien de l'identité sociale.* Paris: Métailié, 1990.

Pratt, Mary Louise. "'Me llamo Rigoberta Menchú': Autoethnograpy and the Recoding of Citizenship." *Teaching and Testimony: Rigoberta Menchú and the North American Classroom.* Ed. Allen Carey-Webb and Stephen Benz. Albany: State U of New York P, 1996. 64–71.

Ringelblum, Emanuel. *Notes from the Warsaw Ghetto: The Journal of Emanuel Ringelblum.* Ed. and trans. Jacob Sloan. New York: McGraw, 1958.

Ritchie, Donald A. *Doing Oral History.* New York: Twayne, 1995.

Stier, Oren Baruch. *Committed to Memory: Cultural Mediations of the Holocaust.* 1st ed. Amherst: U of Massachusetts P, 2003.

Studies on the Audiovisual Testimony of Victims of the Nazi Crimes and genocides. Brussels: Foundation Auschwitz, Centre d'études et de documentation. 1998– .

Thompson, Paul. *The Voice of the Past: Oral History.* 2nd ed. New York: Oxford UP, 1988.

Tory, Avraham. *The Kovno Ghetto Diary.* Ed. Martin Gilbert and Dina Porat. Cambridge: Harvard UP, 1990.

Vrba, Rudolf. *I Escaped from Auschwitz: Including the Text of the Auschwitz Protocols.* Fort Lee: Barricade, 2003.

Wells, Leon. *The Death Brigade.* 1946. Washington: Holocaust Lib., 1978.

Wieviorka, Annette. *Déportation et génocide: Entre l'oubli et la mémoire.* Paris: Plon, 1992.

———. *L'ère du témoin.* Paris: Plon, 1998.

———. "On Testimony." Hartman, *Holocaust Remembrance* 23–33.

Yerushalmi, Yosef. *Zakhor: Jewish History and Jewish Memory.* Seattle: U of Washington P, 1982.

Zelizer, Barbie. *Remembering to Forget: Holocaust Memory through the Camera's Eye.* Chicago: U of Chicago P, 1998.

Web Sites

Fortunoff Video Archive for Holocaust Testimonies. 12 Mar. 2002. 24 May 2004 <http://www.library.yale.edu/testimonies>.

Oral History Holdings. British Lib. Sound Archive. 24 May 2004 <http://www.bl.uk/collections/sound-archive/holdings.html>.

Survivors of the Shoah Visual History Foundation. Shoah Foundation. 24 May 2004 <http://vhf.org>.

United States Holocaust Memorial Museum. 24 May 2004 <http://ushmm.org>.

Voices of the Holocaust. Interviews conducted in 1946 and transcribed into English by David Boder. Illinois Inst. of Technology. 24 May 2004 <http://voices.iit.edu/index.html>.

Voice/Vision: Holocaust Survivor Oral History. U of Michigan, Dearborn. 30 Mar. 2004 <htpp://holocaust.umd.umich.edu>.

Yad Vashem: The Holocaust Martyrs' and Heroes' Remembrance Authority. 24 May 2004 <http://www.yadvashem.org.il/index.html>.

Orly Lubin

Teaching Cinema, Teaching the Holocaust

More than other artistic media dealing with the Holocaust, films are vulnerable to Adorno's often misquoted cautionary injunction from 1949: "After Auschwitz, it is barbaric to write poetry" (34). Since the very first cinematic representations of events associated with the Holocaust, two major questions have focused critical discussion: first, whether film is "able to offer a representation that once and for all could 'stand in' for the Holocaust itself"; second, somewhat less demanding, "how well the film was able to produce a knowledge of the Holocaust that was adequate to the event" (Bernard-Donals and Glejzer 103). The expectation that film might enable us to grasp the actual and ethical meaning of the Holocaust emerges from the strongly mimetic reading of cinema as a medium — the belief in the true-to-life representation that moving pictures, more than other forms of art, verbal or visual, can convey.

But representing reality through artistic devices in a mimetic manner that attempts to reenact the horror might also place the spectator in a defensive and resistant mode. In his review of *Out of the Ashes*, Showtime's cinematic adaptation of the true story of Gisella Perl, a doctor who survived Auschwitz thanks to her medical abilities, Stephen Holden cautions, "Every dramatization of the Holocaust has to decide for itself at what point the depiction of unimaginable suffering becomes too much to bear, and the horror threatens to induce a defensive numbness and revulsion instead of empathy." Holocaust films oscillate between the power to lead to better understanding and to provoke empathy, on the one hand, and the danger of creating numbness, disinterest, and loss of empathy, on the other. This duality should make us cautious when we bring such films to the classroom. More often than not, the very choice of making a film about the Holocaust, the very attempt to give it a specific, closed aesthetic form, causes extreme anger and heated debates, debates that can be productively staged and reviewed in the classroom.

Ilan Avisar focuses his critiques around the contrivance of narrative itself:

> But the main problem of these narratives is not aesthetic [or] even the ethical implications of an aesthetic approach. . . . The problem is essential for it is rooted in the inherent connections between narrative, form and meaning. . . . The inherent and radical evil of Hitler's Germany is inimical to the idea of narrative development. . . . The attempt to create a dramatic figure on the basis of such atrocity [having to choose which child should die, as in *Sophie's Choice*] is an obscene violation of the most anguishing and absolutely private horrors of the victims' predicament. . . . The limits of Holocaust narratives, especially the dramatic narratives of film and theater, may reach, but not trespass, the barbed-wires of Auschwitz. ("Holocaust" 6, 7, 10, 11)

Avisar cautions against any continuous narrative of the events related to the Holocaust. He says that "in the best dramatic representations of the Holocaust we can detect a break in the narratives." Thus, in Vittorio de Sica's *The Garden of the Finzi Contini* (1970), he finds:

> [T]he narrative protagonist, who was present in every scene throughout the film, at one point completely disappears.

The cut that terminates his personal story marks the transition to the depiction of the end of the Jewish community in Ferrara. (8)

Avisar's condemnation of narrative could well be extended to other elements of aestheticization. Courses on Holocaust film need to ask from the very beginning: Does the aesthetic form given to these horrible events compromise their enormity and their horrific nature and make the Holocaust a digestible story? Are there any aesthetic forms that can create the basis for personal empathy and better understanding of its unique character? These questions arise in relation to the myriad artifices, decisions, and devices that are fundamental to cinema as a genre: the invention of a dramatic and suspenseful narrative; the creation of characters made appealing or complex or unacceptable through flowing, comprehensible, and captivating dialogue; the artistic choices that create the set, the costumes, the hairstyles, the props and the locations, making them appear realistic; the choice of lighting and filters to make the colors soft, harsh, yellowish, or shades of gray; the selection of camera angles and movements; the composition of a sound track—soft music, music that conventionally alerts us that something is about to happen, silent scenes; and, of course, the editing—cutting scenes at cliff-hanger moments, making sure that there is continuity from one scene to the next. These many decisions create something that is far more mediated than a poem written by a survivor or a testimony recorded with a static camera and no editing; but they make the era, the places, the people, the events, the encounters, and the way people lived infinitely more accessible to students several generations removed from the Holocaust. We are living in a time when the only visible remnants—piles of hair, shoes, suitcases—are already in a stage of irreversible decay and when the survivors are leaving our midst. Students who understand the duty to keep memory alive know from personal experience that film—fiction films more than documentaries—is the best medium to reach a broad audience and to touch both people's conscience and hearts.

The power of the visual image, especially the moving image,

makes the problems raised by aesthetic representation more urgent. Teaching a course on cinema and the Holocaust means dealing with that power and the dangers it entails: one can screen out the political context, forget that horrific events did in fact happen and not just on-screen, and become captivated by the beauty of the aesthetic even while watching dreadful scenes. The greatest danger is forgetting the ethical aspect of real events when they are dramatized and aestheticized, thus judging them by their appearance (a beautiful composition, a masterful movement of the camera, breathtaking acting, etc.) rather than by their moral meanings and consequences. Walter Benjamin's essay "The Work of Art in the Age of Its Technological Reproducibity" raises a number of these questions, especially in the final part, in which he evokes both the danger of fascism and the utopian hope for a revolution as possible outcomes of the artistic process.

Benjamin's essay, along with the screening of an initial representative film, can generate a list of questions that will continue to arise with each further class screening: What are the benefits and the risks involved in the use of cinema as a mode of learning about the Holocaust? Does film necessarily exploit the memories of the survivors by turning them into raw material for dramatization or, worse, for financial profit? Does the impulse to entertain flatten and degrade the memory of the victims? How does visual representation overcome the limits of language and therefore communicate beyond words? What cinematic devices might make such a deeper understanding possible? In an age that, as some claim, is characterized by the replacement of the verbal with the visual, does the very figure of the witness on-screen make the testimony more effective? Is the mediated testimony, filtered through the director's camera's lens, as real and as effective as the supposedly unmediated one?

After raising some of these questions in the context of a recently released popular film (e.g., *Schindler's List*, *The Pianist*), I move to what might appear as the most unmediated cinematic genres: video testimonies and documentaries. I then build up gradually through the dramatization and reenactment of historical events to the fictionalized story, and I end the course with the most troubling films, those that make it difficult to ignore questions of gratuitous exploitation.

Unedited videotaped testimonies, available from the Yale Fortunoff Video Archive for Holocaust Testimonies or from Stephen Spielberg's Shoah Foundation, enable students to note the time and space given to unchallenged witnesses so that they are free to shape their life stories, highlighting and expanding on details of their choosing. (See Hartman's essay in this volume for a discussion of video testimony.) The form of these testimonial videos is usefully compared with that of documentary film, particularly what one might call testimonial documentaries. (See Spitzer's essay in this volume on Claude Lanzmann's *Shoah*, one of the best known of this genre.)

Through filmed testimony, spectators have the opportunity of meeting a specific survivor, an eyewitness who is telling the story largely without the mediation of aesthetic devices. Whether released commercially, institutionally, or made for private, family consumption alone, documentary films go beyond video testimony in their levels of mediation—writing, staging, editing. They might give the impression of presenting unmediated experience, but in effect we are watching the work of the director and the editor and hearing stories told by people totally aware of the freedom of the interviewer to subject them to an artistic vision. Testimonial documentaries thus raise questions that go beyond the content of the testimony: How did the director create the desired effect—of horror or of empathy? What is the relationship of interviewer to witness, and how does that relationship inflect the film?

In many cases, the documentary is made by a son or daughter of the survivor. Sometimes it is quite clear that the stories the witness chooses to tell, and the rhetoric of the telling, are determined by this fact. The effect is easier to detect when, as Art Spiegelman does in *Maus*, the directors themselves appear in the film, and especially when they declare that one of the reasons for making the film was to sort out their relationship with their parents or parent. In *Hugo*, Yair Lev's documentary (Israel, 1989),[1] Lev appears in the film not only as interviewer but also as participant, talking about his relations with his father and reminding his parents of minor, anecdotal incidents or habits attached to his father's history. Lev shares his response with us. "This is a story I hear now for the first time," he says of an anecdote that turns out to be the most revealing of his father's behavior as a survivor. It's a story we often hear: about staying alive while someone else dies. But now it has names, faces, feelings of guilt and shame, and a concrete narrative. Both for the son-director and for the spectator it fulfills one crucial need in the struggle to understand the Holocaust: to put a face to it. The father's not very funny sense of humor, the chilling jokes, his unbelievable approach to events ("I didn't feel bad at all in Buchenwald. I spent my time there doing nothing, almost like a sanatorium. But Auschwitz was a terrible place, the food there was really lousy," he says), his self-perception and appearance as much as the look of the apartment, the dinner table, or the short comments of his wife give a sense of the banality of existence — and of going on with life. But the film also exposes the effort the father makes to comply with his son's needs: the need to understand, but also the need to make a personal, revealing film that will tell the world about himself, the filmmaker. The witness chooses stories and structures them in a way he thinks will help his son have a father with a biography, a father whose survival can be explained and was not at anyone's expense, a father who is normal.

In *Hugo*, the son is present, and his comments expose the requirements he has of his father. In contrast, in Tsipi Reibenbach's two documentaries, *Choice and Destiny* (Israel, 1993) and *Three Sisters* (Israel, 1998), the director does not appear on-screen.[2] Her voice is vaguely heard every now and then, but her presence is made palpable with the unfolding narrative, which reveals her editorial choices, especially the gendered aspect of Holocaust representation, which can provide a fruitful topic of class discussion. In *Choice and Destiny* only the father tells his stories. The mother, a survivor herself, never intervenes. She is seen constantly working in the kitchen — cooking, arranging, and especially cleaning. Late into the film, we realize that the father was a professional baker; when he cooks, taking on a feminine role, he puts on a flowered apron. Yet true to traditional gender roles, he is the one who leaves the house, whereas the mother stays inside. After being silently followed by the camera throughout the film, at the very end, the mother breaks down and starts talking: hysterically, repeating the names of the people she lost, she reiterates her decision never to talk even as she insists, "Now that I'm talking, I'll never stop." True to stereotypical femininity through her secret (as Hélène Cixous beautifully puts it in "The Laugh of the Medusa") and her hysterical responses, she is also the stronger one, keeping the past outside the home, determined to survive in an environment she is still uncertain of and uncomfortable in.

When she does not speak and even when she speaks, the mother in Reibenbach's film provides a space outside language, in Giorgio Agamben's words, "the sound that arises from the lacuna, the non-language that one speaks when one is alone, the non-language to which language answers, in which language is born" (38). Documentary film can make vivid such moments of nonlanguage, of secret words, of mumbling that provide an insight into trauma and survival. *Choice and Destiny* illustrates how editing can highlight these moments: as the mother starts speaking her refusal to speak, the camera gazes at the father, wearing his flowered apron and standing at the door of the kitchen—in Agamben's vocabulary, at the threshold—towering over his two small grandchildren, who are incapable of understanding and thus disturbed by their grandmother's Yiddish.

Testimonial documentaries like the films discussed above have the power to affirm the material presence that is repressed in the process of becoming representation—the presence of the flesh and blood, of the corporeal body. In this genre, the witness's body is not only in the center of the frame or filling it entirely but also exposed (father in a robe, mother asleep, father washing up, aunt showing her legs), discussed, and constantly fed. Cooking and eating are the ongoing activities: the eating mouth and the speaking mouth never stop; the hands are busy cleaning and cooking; and the clock ticks on, from one meal to the next.

Lev's and Reibenbach's testimonial documentaries (or films by Alan Berliner, Francine Zuckerman's film on Deb Filler's performance *Punch Me in the Stomach* [1996], Orna Ben-Dor Niv's

Because of That War [1989], Nitza Gonen's *Daddy, Come to the Fair* [1994], Steve Brand's *Kaddish* [1985], and other intergenerational documentaries, available at *Facets Multimedia*)[3] show students how cinematic devices highlight elements that may not be available in written and oral testimony or in unedited video testimony. Discussions of a father's or mother's painful recollections will thus inevitably be supplemented by an analysis of decisions made by the filmmaker and of the constraints that the interviewer-director imposes on the survivor and that finally construct any testimony.

Feature film provides the locus for another set of questions, arising from the pitfalls both of narrative and of visuality—from the public, economic, erotic, and narrative context of its making and distribution. In my courses, we examine how feature films try to avoid the spectacularization of death (e.g., the display of heaps of dead bodies) and how they try to avoid the entertainment aspects of fantasy. We revisit and deepen our awareness of the danger of lost political complexity when events are flattened into a personal, individual story; of the danger of limiting empathy to an individual, thus ignoring the suffering of the masses; and, more generally, of the danger of the ethical indifference that can come with aestheticization.

Each film deals with a different set of these problems and in different ways. In *Schindler's List*, a film I teach as a fictional extension of the documentary, since it is the dramatization of a historical character and episode, I focus on the unusual choice of filming in black and white. This is a complex choice:

> In one way, it distances; it marks this particular past as different, as elsewhere, as "another country." But in another way, it reduces distance: our images of the Holocaust are constructed in black and white, whether from newsreels or photographs, and the film resonates with this existing archive of representation; it places us immediately into that place of memory. By contrast again, our contemporary representational landscape is made from color. . . . The choice of black and white breaks us out of this indiscriminacy. It takes the Holocaust back from the television miniseries, so to speak, and in that sense defamiliarizes it, makes it strange. (Eley and Grossmann 47)

Perhaps even more important, because of the tendency of spectators to abandon their reality and become sucked into the illusion of a narrative presented on the color screen, black-and-white film constantly presents itself as artificial, reminding the audience that it is a work of art. Constantly asserting itself as a work of art, it also reminds the audience that there is a reality out there, that even though the characters on-screen are just actors pretending to die, there *was* such a reality, in which people did die. And whenever the audience gets accustomed to the black and white, enough to forget that the experience is only a movie, Spielberg inserts a glimpse of color — a candle, a red coat — again reminding us that *Schindler's List* is a film, again reminding us of the real world and of the real Holocaust, thus avoiding one of the major pitfalls of Holocaust dramatization: fictionalizing the Shoah.

Agnieszka Holland's *Europa, Europa* (Germany, 1991) is another fictional rendition of a true story that successfully avoids many of the pitfalls of fictionalization. *Europa, Europa* is the story of Salomon Perel (who plays himself as the character in old age), who survived thanks to his ability at sixteen to play different roles, himself almost confusing life with theater. He manages to run away from Germany, joins the Soviet Army as a translator, is sent to school to become an educated member of the Communist Party, falls into German hands and plays the role of a rescued prisoner of war, translates for the Germans, and is finally saved when the war is over. That the film is based on reality lends these bizarre events a truth-value without which they would seem utterly contrived. The film itself alludes time and again to the miracles responsible for Perel's survival. When Perel, as a German youth at the Komsomol school, dares suggest that God exists, his teacher challenges God to perform a miracle and to send candy from heaven. When the miracle does not happen, she then asks the party to perform the same miracle, and, sure enough, candies drop from a hole in the ceiling. Then the same call for miracles repeats itself when a prayer is answered with bombs falling from the sky, courtesy of the Allies. The final miracle occurs when an Allied soldier is ready to kill Perel as a German: Perel is identified as Jewish by a survivor still wearing the concentration camp costume. It is only now, at the end, that we remember the ironic comment at the beginning of the film. "You won't believe it," says Perel in the voice-over narration, "but I remember my circumcision." This is yet another miracle, which obviously we won't believe, as we wouldn't have believed the other ones had we not known that they are, indeed, based on historical events. One of these, a physical fact he needs to conceal, is his circumcision. Another saves his life at least once: he and Hitler have the same birthday.

This list of miracles helps explain how Perel — and others — survived: through the combination of a special talent, extraordinary resourcefulness, and circumstances. The cinematic portrayal of such events is more convincing than the written or video-testimonial portrayal, since the camera captures tiny details — a twist of the mouth, a movement of a hand, a look in the eyes, an onlooker in the background — that a verbal rendition would likely not communicate. In class, it is fruitful to catalog this plethora of visual additions and to discuss what they teach us about the environment of the hero and the power of cinematic representation. Then the discussion can move on to the narrative elements in *Europa, Europa*. This film is in fact a bildungsfilm, telling the story of growing up, albeit in unique, horrific, and unbelievable circumstances. The characterization focuses on the psychological burden to which this child and young man are subjected. When playing a role becomes more than a mask and manipulative behavior and when the need for mother, love, warmth, sex, community, even the simple ability to speak to someone without lying takes over, Salomon Perel either breaks down or identifies with his adopted identity. His now broken and fragmented sense of self is finally what helps him survive. The cinematic device of inserting his fantasies during the film, and the happy ending, enables and is enabled by the theme of growing up. The fantasies do not fictionalize the Holocaust; they are the cinematic mode of exposing both his psychological difficulties and his means of overcoming them. The happy end does not degrade the horrific fate; it shows the truth, and a belief in the power of the human spirit — a fragile promise when dealing with the Shoah. Again, even this cliché does not harm the effect of the story, since the cliché happens to be Salomon Perel's real life.

The film helps the flow of this unbelievable story of a fragmented soul by using yet another device that lets students recognize this film's artistry: the literalization of the metaphor of a flowing narrative. The flow of the narrative is simulated by the flow of water. The film opens with underwater shots of a swimming child. When Perel flees from his parent's apartment, the camera focuses on a page from the book he was reading as it floats on the bathwater; he escapes by the river and is saved from drowning. Water accompanies him and creates a visual, mental background for the spectator, who is presented with the task of putting together the pieces—and through those pieces of learning about life during the Holocaust.

It is interesting to compare *Europa, Europa* with Roman Polanski's *The Pianist* (USA, 2003): here is a story that has no amazing fateful events or totally bizarre incidents to make it entertaining as an adventure story. *The Pianist* also raises more moral questions—for example, was the choice of the hero (to survive at all costs) an ethical one? Or was his brother, critical of this choice, morally superior? And which story is the better representative of the general story of the fate of the Jews? Was the German officer who helped the hero morally superior to other Germans, or was he already thinking of the future and being opportunistic? And does it matter? Should he have been spared anyway?

The Pianist also represents a trend in recent films, to bring up moral issues about life in the ghetto or in the camp that previous films never dared raise. The danger in raising these issues is so great that most filmmakers avoid dealing with the harsh realities of the Shoah, realities that call for ethical judgment, such as the abuse of power by the inmates in the interest of survival or the relationships that developed inside the camps and ghettos—between rich and poor, powerful and powerless, men and women. These topics sometimes do appear on-screen, but often they are displaced. If the Jewish child must die, then the point of view taken in the bildungsfilm is that of his classmate watching and slowly learning the truth about the child's family and the world around the child (e.g., in Louis Malle's *Au revoir les enfants* [France, 1987]). The more recent *Out of the Ashes* (USA, 2003) dares engage with two different points of view regarding the job of a doctor inmate—was she helping as much as she could, or was she saving herself at the expense of others and abusing her position to receive bribes?

Only by taking the camera outside the concentration camp and telling the stories of bystanders can Holocaust films avoid dealing with ethical issues that are still too troubling. By moving beyond the stories of individuals to the stories of families or entire communities, one can study the effect of the different choices people had to make, the effect the events had on those who did not have the luxury of making any choices, and the interconnectedness between people affected in a variety of ways. I therefore like to include at least one feature film that deals with a family or community during the Holocaust. A family saga like Istvan Szabo's *Sunshine* (Hungary, 1999), for instance, provides such a multigenerational communal perspective. Another film depicting the environment in which the Holocaust happened is Edgar Reitz's *Heimat* (Germany, 1996), the sixteen-hour account of one family in Germany between 1919 and 1982 ("history seen from ground level," says the production note). François Truffaut's *The Last Metro* (France, 1980) is also about a group of people during the occupation, the choices they had to make, and their successful effort to save a Jew. Claude Berri's *Uranus* (France, 1990) takes us one step further, into the wider context of the behavior of the French resistance and collaboration during the occupation and after the liberation. The dating of these films is extremely important: collaboration emerges as a subject of French cinema only in the 1980s.

In this section of the course on feature film, the most difficult topic to discuss is what is sometimes perhaps too easily called Holocaust pornography. While some films genuinely investigate the sexualization of power, others eroticize death and exploit, for purposes of arousal and profit, the sadomasochistic dynamics inherent in the relations between victim and perpetrator. Students benefit from learning to analyze how easily visual media can fall into the very problems they might wish to critique. Holland's *Bittere Ernte* (*Angry Harvest* [Germany, 1986]) is exactly such an investigation of power relations and their sexual dimension: it examines the relationship between the Christian, effeminate peasant and the educated Jewish married woman whom he both hides and abuses.

Even the more controversial of such films, Liliana Cavani's *Night Porter* (Italy, 1974) or Lina Wertmüller's *Seven Beauties* (Italy, 1976), can be shown to students. They do, after all, expose the sexualization of power that was integral to the relationships between perpetrators and victims. I also like to discuss the distraction that beauty (a beautiful actress, a beautiful location, a beautiful frame) creates and, through these films, return to the conflict between ethics and aesthetics and the pornography of representation.

I like to end my course with Michael Verhoeven's *Das schreckliche Mädchen* (*Nasty Girl* [Germany, 1989]), which is a heavily stylized dramatization of a true story. A girl who starts researching her little town's history under the Third Reich stumbles onto a concealed minor event, but in order to expose it she must take the town to court, finally winning acknowledgment. Still, she refuses to stop digging for more concealed truths. I focus on the film's use of cinematic devices, such as blue screen and slides as background, its camera angles and distorted frames, its mixture of genres. The film is humorous and unassuming, but it raises issues relevant to cinematic representation of the Holocaust and to today's perspective on its history. It is a story of the commitment — initially unintended but then fully assumed — to study and confront the past. It is a story of the willingness to confront your own community's past, knowing it might reflect on you and your accountability to it, even though you were not party to its doings (a lesson to be learned in many communities nowadays). It is a story about a brave act, one in which the protagonist does not become a hero (not in the story told and not in the way she is portrayed by the film), as sometimes happens in films when the savior rather than the victim becomes the center of admiration. Most important, it is a film that exposes its own artificiality, totally self-aware of its status as fiction and the dangers entailed if it pretends to be real. Through its own self-awareness, *Nasty Girl* forces the spectators to understand what many films disguise: this is a movie, but the Holocaust was real.

Notes

1. Yair Lev's documentary can be purchased from the director, at shisha6@netvision.net.il.
2. For information about these films (or to purchase them), see Reibenbach's Web site (www.tsipi-reibenbach-films.com).
3. A source for Israeli films not easily available in the United States is the New Israeli Foundation for Cinema and Television (www.nfct.org.il/english/index.html).

Works Cited

Adorno, Theodor W. "Cultural Criticism and Society." *Prisms.* Trans. Samuel Weber and Shierry Weber. Cambridge: MIT P, 1967. 17–34.

Agamben, Giorgio. *Remnants of Auschwitz: The Witness and the Archive.* Trans. Daniel Heller-Roazen. New York: Zone, 1999.

Avisar, Ilan. "The Holocaust as Narrative: Story and Character in the Representation of the Concentration Camp Universe." *Remembering for the Future* 3 (1988): 3–12.

———. *Screening the Holocaust: Cinema's Images of the Unimaginable.* Bloomington: Indiana UP, 1988.

Benjamin, Walter. "The Work of Art in the Age of Its Technological Reproducibility: Second Version." *Walter Benjamin: Selected Writings.* Vol. 3 (1935–38). Trans. Edmund Jephcott and Harry Zohn. Ed. Michael W. Jennings. Cambridge: Belknap–Harvard UP, 2002. 101–33.

Bernard-Donals, Michael, and Richard Glejzer. *Between Witness and Testimony: The Holocaust and the Limits of Representation.* Albany: State U of New York P, 2001.

Cixous, Hélène. "The Laugh of the Medusa." Trans. Keith Cohen and Paula Cohen. *New French Feminisms: An Anthology.* Ed. Elaine Marks and Isabelle de Courtivron. Amherst: U of Massachusetts P, 1990. 99–106.

Eley, Geoff, and Atina Grossmann. "Watching *Schindler's List*: Not the Last Word." *New German Critique* 71 (1997): 41–62.

Europa, Europa. Dir. Agnieszka Holland. 1990. Videocassette. MGM-UA Studio, 14 Dec. 1999.

Facets Multimedia. 30 Mar. 2004 <http://www.facets.org/asticat>. Path: Browse Catalog; Documentary Films; Holocaust.

Holden, Stephen. "A Doctor (and Inmate) at Auschwitz." *New York Times* 12 Apr. 2003: D14.

Loshitzky, Yosefa, ed. *Spielberg's Holocaust: Critical Perspectives on Schindler's List.* Bloomington: Indiana UP, 1997.

Nasty Girl [*Das schreckliche Mädchen*]. Dir. Michael Verhoeven. 1990. Videocassette. HBO Studies, 8 Jan. 1992.

The Pianist. Dir. Roman Polanski. StudioCanal, 2002.

Schindler's List. Dir. Steven Spielberg. Universal Studios, 1993.

Christian Rogowski

Teaching the Drama
of the Holocaust

History is present, and it's a partner you didn't choose.
—Joshua [Yehoshua] Sobol

Drama can, perhaps because of its dual nature as printed play and as performance in the theater, promote a particularly direct and sustained engagement with the issues of memory and representation, of ethics and responsibility, that are crucial to the study of the Holocaust. Drama differs from other forms of aesthetic mediation (such as novels, poems, and films) in that it relies on the direct encounter between performers and audiences in a shared physical space (Bennett). In a performance, what was once an idea of, usually, a single person (the playwright) becomes an event, an experiential reality of a collective (the performers and the audience). It is this possible event that reading a play should aim at reconstructing.

Reading a play involves a sustained effort to supply what is missing from the printed text, to envisage in one's mind possible actualizations of the script. The layout of a printed drama alone — with lines of speech associated with characters, separated from other textual material that evokes the physical surroundings or specifies questions of movement, gesture, and the like — militates against the kind of skimming and scanning that all too often passes for reading, especially in the context of a course. Simply put, you cannot speed-read a play. Likewise, in performance, a play unfolds in the time span dictated by the production itself, requiring from the audience a certain degree of commitment as concerns both the time and the intellectual and emotional energy invested. The special attentiveness and energy required by reading or watching a play (let alone the effort associated with its staging) operate against the "been there, done that" mentality that prevails in today's culture. A course on the Holocaust will have accomplished much if it dispels the notion that you can do the Holocaust and then be done with it. Drama, with its emphasis on the time and energy required of each individual to engage in the issues raised, is superbly suited to initiate such an ongoing learning process.

Teaching Holocaust drama also involves developing ways to fathom and to supply what is missing in other ways, since plays that deal with the Holocaust confront issues of the linguistic and visual representation of an unrepresentable event, at the core of which stands an unimaginable loss. An analytic engagement with the plays can and should be supplemented with creative projects, dramatic exercises that encourage students to think about how that loss can be addressed in a collective experience of commemoration of the Holocaust. Analyzing, watching, and playing Holocaust-related dramas is not to be confused with naive efforts at simulating past events to make students feel what the Holocaust was like, a pedagogical approach that has provoked indignation as ultimately trivializing historical experience and mocking the unimaginable plight of the victims (Totten). Enactment should always be accompanied by discussions concerning the aesthetic and moral choices involved in efforts to represent the Holocaust. Through critical discussion and through projects that involve the analysis, performance, or creation of crafted scripts, students can experience for themselves the aes-thetic, moral, ideological, and existential problems involved in pro-viding what is missing in representations of the Holocaust.

Both the potential and the limitations of drama can be rendered productive in the classroom. For one thing, more than any other genre of artistic representation, drama involves a multiplicity of per-spectives: events tend to unfold in the interplay of various characters, with changing and often contradictory motivations, encouraging the reader or spectator to adopt shifting modes of engagement and identification. In a pedagogical context, this multiperspectivity can enable students to reach a critical understanding of the different po-sitions in the history represented (like those of victims, bystanders, enablers, or perpetrators). Students can reflect on the manifold ways in which differences involving social status, gender, ethnicity, class, or generation have an impact on how a given person thinks or acts. Another important factor is the immediacy of drama as performance. If at all possible, teachers should try to arrange for students to see a production of a play covered in a course or to get students involved in reading or enacting the play or parts of it in a kind of staged read-ing in the classroom. Students can work on creative projects associ-ated with the play, such as writing and performing scenes that fill gaps in the plot or that tell the background of a particular character and explain that character's motivation for how he or she behaved in a scene. This way, students experience firsthand the constructedness of drama and the problems involved in representing, witnessing, and remembering history. Moreover, fostering interaction among stu-dents through performance and active engagement provides an op-portunity for a different kind of learning: the focus shifts from a primarily cognitive register to a more visceral, holistic one, in which the students perhaps learn as much about themselves, their preju-dices and biases, their strengths and limitations, as they do about the subject matter. A confrontation with drama can help change the Holocaust from a merely academic topic studied at a safe distance into a directly personal concern that challenges one's existential and moral underpinnings. The question facing a teacher should not be whether or not to use drama in a class on the Holocaust but rather which plays to pick and how to integrate them into the overall ped-agogical enterprise.

In what follows, I give suggestions concerning which plays might be most useful in a course devoted to the Holocaust, high-lighting the specific thematic aspects they can illuminate. I focus on a few plays that offer particularly rich opportunities for exploring the unique ethical and aesthetic, political and psychological questions raised by dramatists' attempts to address the Holocaust. To con-clude, I provide a set of questions that can be brought to bear on al-most any play, as general guidelines that teachers can adapt to help their students confront the challenges that reading a play sometimes entail.

If one were to ask people to name a Holocaust drama, the most likely answer would be *The Diary of Anne Frank*, the adaptation of the famous Dutch Jewish Holocaust victim's writings that Frances Goodrich and Albert Hackett created for the Broadway stage in 1955 (and that provided the basis for the equally popular film of 1959). The play was instrumental for bringing the Holocaust to the attention of a wide audience, something for which it deserves con-siderable credit (Langer). Employing conventions of sentimental family melodrama, Goodrich and Hackett turned the historical Anne Frank into a kind of martyr who maintains her belief in the inherent goodness of humans even in the face of deportation and death. End-ing on such an affirmative — and ultimately reassuring — note, the play effectively obscures the horror of the subject it ostensibly seeks to address. For this reason I don't think it is a good choice for a college-level course, where a more sophisticated analytic focus is preferable. Our students need to realize that the real drama of the Holocaust, as it were, begins when Anne and her family are dragged offstage and the curtain falls.

How does one identify plays to include in a course on the Holo-caust? The sheer number and diversity of plays dealing with Nazi Germany and the persecution and mass murder of European Jews may appear bewildering. An anthology of Holocaust drama com-piled in the 1980s includes an annotated bibliography already listing more than eighty plays from various countries (Fuchs). Some ten years later, a similar list with useful short descriptions of the plots had grown to well over 260 titles (Goldfarb). To this list one must add the numerous plays that have appeared since, plays that for one reason or another did not meet the editors' criteria for what constitutes Holocaust drama, and plays not included in such listings before because they were then not readily available in English translation. A teacher must also decide which particular aspect or story of the Holocaust is best addressed with a play. A tentative typology of Holocaust drama offers the categories ghetto and martyr drama, death camp drama, survival drama, as well as a range of national perspectives, definitions that may not be too helpful (Isser). The complexities that accompany the question of choice are considerable. For instance, does the concept of Holocaust drama comprise only plays focusing on Jews as victims of genocidal violence, or does it include plays about political prisoners, such as Charlotte Delbo's *Who Will Carry the Word* (1966), and about homosexual victims, such as Martin Sherman's *Bent* (1979)? Should one consider only plays written by authors who, by whatever criterion, can be defined as Jewish, and does that status guarantee that their perspective will somehow be more appropriate than that of non-Jewish authors (Taub)? Conversely, are plays written by (non-Jewish) Germans or Austrians to be disregarded because they automatically may be suspected of pursuing a revisionist or apologist agenda? What about plays that deal with the perpetrators rather than the victims, such as Heinar Kipphardt's *Brother Eichmann* (1982)? What about plays that deal, sometimes in oblique fashion, with the historical aftereffects of the Holocaust, such as Rainer Werner Fassbinder's highly controversial play about the paradoxes of post–World War II German anti-semitism and philosemitism, *Garbage, the City, and Death* (1975)? Perhaps it is precisely plays that are considered controversial or provocative rather than emotionally involving and reassuring that provide the best basis for learning. Finally, what about plays that deal with the impact of the Holocaust on a subsequent generation? Recent years have seen a spate of plays about issues of identity and memory as they affect the children both of the victims, like Diane Samuels's *Kindertransport* (1993), and of the perpetrators, such as

Ari Roth's dramatization of Peter Sichrovsky's interviews with the children of Nazis, *Born Guilty* (1994). Such plays, addressing intergenerational conflicts informed by historical and political issues beyond the control of the individuals involved, might strongly appeal to young people who find dramas about history remote and uninspiring.

What we call the Holocaust consists of myriad stories and facets that represent a constant challenge to reassemble and redefine what one thinks one knows. Plays that merely illustrate a supposedly given fact fail to acknowledge the enormity and complexity of the Holocaust; they subsume it under stable categories. Yet does not the brutal marginalization, deportation, and quasi-industrialized murder of millions, largely carried out by a faceless bureaucratic and military machine, render obsolete notions such as interpersonal conflict, personal agency, and individual heroism, on which traditional drama is based (Rokem)? Indeed, the Holocaust challenges most, if not all, the categories we tend to hold dear. For a course on the Holocaust, a play should confront the challenge, at once aesthetic and ethical, of finding a form appropriate to the issues raised. Often this confronting means that Holocaust drama cannot remain in the confines of established literary conventions; it needs to grope toward different forms, even at the risk of failing (Skloot, *Darkness*).

The choice of play is of course dependent on what is available. Ironically, some of the most intriguing plays about the Holocaust are not easy to come by for an American readership. This problem applies particularly to the plays of George Tabori, the Hungarian playwright and director of Jewish descent who survived the Holocaust in Great Britain and first made a name for himself as a collaborator of Bertolt Brecht in the United States. His provocatively grotesque early drama *The Cannibals* (1968), included in the first anthology of Holocaust drama (Skloot, *Theatre* [1982]), explores shifting identities and impossible ethical choices. It presents four characters who reenact the grim choice that confronted their fathers in a concentration camp: whether to eat a dead fellow inmate and live or to refrain from violating a perhaps meaningless ethical taboo and die. *My Mother's Courage* (1979), the touching story of the survival of Tabori's mother in Nazi-occupied Hungary, which provided the basis for a critically acclaimed film directed by Michael Verhoeven (1995), can be found in an issue of the journal *Theater* (1999). Tabori's provocative and thought-provoking plays raise puzzling ethical questions in a constant effort to rethink and remember the interrelation between history and coincidence, necessity and human agency (Zipes). They confront us with special challenges, transforming the theater into a space for what has aptly been called "embodied memory" (Feinberg), a form of experience involving the continued presence of the past and shared by performers and audience alike.

The work of the Israeli playwright Joshua [Yehoshua] Sobol is likewise difficult to obtain in the United States. Translated into more than twenty languages, his three plays addressing the Holocaust, constituting the so-called Ghetto Triptych, are available in English translations but in scattered form: *Ghetto* (1983), *Adam* (1990), and *Underground* (1991). The first play is internationally perhaps the best-known and most well-received Holocaust drama after *The Diary of Anne Frank*. It traces the memories of a Holocaust survivor, puppeteer Srulik, from a living room in present-day Haifa back to the Vilna Ghetto, where he ran a theater company. Based on actual incidents in the ghetto, the play employs a variety of levels of fictionality, mixing songs and performances to address the role of theater and playacting in the spiritual and physical survival of the ghetto inmates. Juxtaposing past and present, it raises profoundly disturbing questions about human agency, art, escapism, victimization, complicity, and resistance.

Two documentary dramas from the 1960s are often included in courses on the Holocaust. Since they are largely based on historical documents, they could provide opportunities for research by students concerning the transformation of the historical record into drama. Rolf Hochhuth's *The Deputy* (1963), subtitled "A Christian Tragedy," examines the attitude of the Catholic Church in the Holocaust. Based on extensive research of archival materials, it pits the Italian Jesuit priest Riccardo Fontana and the renegade German SS officer Kurt Gerstein against Pope Pius XII. Despite their passionate pleas and the information they provide him with, the pope refuses to speak out publicly against the systematic mass murder of Jews. Combining extensive, somewhat awkward moral debates with symbolic scenes and a kind of martyr drama, Hochhuth's play amounts to a scathing indictment of the Vatican for complicity in the Holocaust on account of its policy of neutrality and appeasement vis-à-vis the Nazis. Some have argued that today the play is of interest more for the reaction that it provoked than for any intrinsic aesthetic or dramatic merit. Assignments for students could thus involve research into the scandal that erupted when the play first came out. Interest in the play and its theses, which have also generated an extensive and contentious secondary literature within and outside academia worth investigating, has been rekindled by the recent filmed version of the play, *Amen*, by the Greek director Constantin Costa-Gavras (2002).

Peter Weiss's *The Investigation* (1965) adopts a radically different way of dealing with historical documents. Subtitled "An Oratorium in Eleven Cantos," the play arranges excerpts from the minutes of the Auschwitz trials held in Frankfurt from 1963 to 1965. It condenses the testimonies of the accused and the witnesses into a highly stylized, quasi-liturgical form that, in combination with other documentary evidence, such as slides and charts, seeks to convey to the audience the extent of the bureaucratized, industrialized mass murder of millions. Paradoxically, the play employs both extreme veracity (relying exclusively on a montage of excerpts from the court trials) and extreme abstraction (it juxtaposes eighteen accused and nine nameless witnesses rather than individually identifiable characters). It adopts the form of an oratorio, which ends before the sentences are announced, instead of a gripping courtroom drama replete with crafty lawyers, surprising plot twists, and the triumph of good over evil, as in Abby Mann's *Judgment at Nuremberg* (1961). Class discussion here could focus on questions such as, What view of the Holocaust is created by the formal choices Weiss is making? In largely eliminating identifiable people, does he run the risk of obliterating the human dimension of the Holocaust? What type of audience address is achieved by the use of verse incantation rather than realistic dialogue? What aspects of the Holocaust does the author's essentially Marxist, anticapitalist stance illuminate or obfuscate?

Another text that addresses structural political issues (while not ignoring, as Weiss perhaps does [Cohen], the social and psychological components) is a play by a Swiss dramatist. Max Frisch's *Andorra* (1961) is the most successful and widely performed German-language drama that addresses the Holocaust. Set in an abstract, vaguely Mediterranean, provincial community (not to be confused with the actual principality of the same name), it seeks to chart the story, from ostracization to victimization, of Andri, a young man thought by his neighbors to be Jewish. The action is interrupted by a number of scenes in which various characters give a retrospective commentary in an abstract setting that implies a kind of tribunal. This dual structure, indebted to Brecht's concept of an epic theater, is aimed at distancing the audience from a direct identification. The chosen form invites a layered reading that addresses issues of increasing complexity in a manner that can be used productively in teaching the play. Frisch highlights a moral—perhaps even religious—perspective instead of attempting to visualize the horrors of the death camps.

Discussion on the main scenes could deal with the various aspects of Andri's progressive marginalization. Students, who are themselves often caught up in intense situations involving peer pressure and shifting sympathies, should find it easy to relate to the plight of a young person branded as an outsider.

In the discussion of the interspersed tribunal scenes, students should note how various characters attempt to address their personal involvement in Andri's victimization. Here, the characters' use of language should be considered first: by using abstract formulations ("What happened is regrettable," "Too bad that things got out of hand," etc.) and passive or impersonal constructions ("We were all mistaken," "Nobody could have known," etc.), they abjure any personal responsibility. Students could compare the language of these scenes with actual testimonials taken from Holocaust-related trials to see similar processes of obfuscation and denial at work. They could also work on small research projects that relate the various characters' perspectives on the issue of Andri's death to corresponding aspects of the Holocaust.

Students should reflect on the structure of Frisch's play, in which the juxtaposition of the main story line and these commentary scenes places us in conflicting positions: on the one hand, we are made to empathize with the main character; on the other hand, we recognize in the other characters' statements attitudes and prejudices that we may openly or secretly share. We are also implicitly invited to pass judgment on the characters when we hear their retrospective testimonials and can compare them against their actual behavior in the situations we witness. A tension is created that makes us oscillate among virtually all the positions involved in the Holocaust, those of victim, perpetrator (or facilitator), and judge. The play thus offers particularly rich opportunities to reflect on the Holocaust and its representation on the stage. Interestingly, today the play is sometimes performed without the tribunal scenes, presumably because they appear as an outdated Brechtian device. Students might reflect on how this omission may change the spectator's response.

Regardless of which play the teacher picks, it is helpful to provide students with some guidelines for reading a play, a literary genre with which some may not be familiar. Students should be made aware that most plays rely heavily on subtext and that *how* a character says something may be as or more important than *what* a character says. To facilitate their reading, it is helpful to ask students to take notes, which could then become the basis for written responses, classroom discussions, and paper assignments. Moreover, before assigning a play, teachers could encourage students to research its historical background. For instance, knowing something about the dilemmas faced by the *Judenräte*, the Jewish elders appointed by Nazi officials to cooperate in the administration of ghettos, will enhance an understanding of a play like *Throne of Straw* by Harold Lieberman and Edith Lieberman (1973). The play deals with the agonizing moral choices imposed on a historical figure, Mordechai Chaim Rumkowski, in the Lodz Ghetto. Likewise, students might want to read the memoirs of Fania Fenelon, a survivor of Auschwitz and Bergen-Belsen, before reading Arthur Miller's *Playing for Time* (1980), a powerful play about the bizarre challenges confronted by the women who were recruited into an orchestra formed at a death camp.

What follows are a few questions and assignments that teachers can easily adapt to a given play and that they may find useful in providing guidance to students. These questions and assignments are designed to sensitize students to the correlation between the thematic and aesthetic aspects of a play. In addition to helping students decode what a play is trying to say, the questions encourage students to reflect on how the play accomplishes this. Students should learn to recognize that a play is a construct, not simply a reenactment of a reality.

1. Where and when does the play take place? Make notes on historical, geographic, and sociological information contained both in the primary text (the utterances of the characters) and in the secondary text (the stage instructions and other forms of commentary).

2. Pay attention to the treatment of place, time, and plot. Is there only one setting, or does the action take place in a variety of places? Is the time frame continuous and forward-moving, or are there gaps or flashbacks? Is there one story line or several? If several, how are they related? Do they appear to be independent of or do they comment on one another? Think about what motivated the formal choices the playwright made. In other words, how does the form of the play reflect or convey its thematic concerns?

3. Pick a character and focus on how he or she is portrayed throughout the play. How does the play suggest to us what kind of person he or she is (through what and how the character speaks, what the character does, external signals such as clothes or body language, what we hear from other characters, other markers such as the character's name)? Does the character remain the same throughout, or does he or she undergo change? If so, what is the nature of the change?

4. Focus on a particular scene and analyze what motivates the behavior of each character in it (using the profile created by following the suggestions in the previous question). Are the characters agents of their own will, or are they subject to outside pressures?

What interests, ideas, beliefs, or values determine their perspectives, their actions or inactions? Does the language they use bespeak a hidden agenda or reveal a bias? Is there room for choice in what they do? If so, what choices are they confronted with? How do they respond to these choices and why?

5. Are there any motifs (words or images that evoke particular ideas) that recur in the play? How does the author introduce such motifs? Does their significance remain constant, or does it change? Is there a correlation between such uses of language and the ideas of the play? Are there scenes, dramatic images, or other visual devices that carry meaning along lines similar to that conveyed by language?

6. Try to act out key scenes in the classroom in a kind of staged reading.

Acting fosters classroom interaction, since it forces students to pay attention to one another; it also helps make the plays come alive by encouraging students to inhabit this or that character. The full emotional impact of scenes that may appear flat on paper but that can elicit a visceral response from the audience when performed live is brought out by asking students to act out some situations in a staged reading—for example, the famous *Judenschau* ("Jew inspection") scene in Max Frisch's *Andorra*. The frightened inhabitants of Andorra are forced to file past an inspector who supposedly can tell who is Jewish from the way a person walks. In performing the scene, students can be made to experience viscerally both the power and the ultimate absurdity of stereotyping (How does a "Jew" move? How does a "Jew's" fear differ from that of someone afraid to be thought of as a Jew?). Later in the scene, a soldier attacks Andri to remove a ring from his finger. The incident tends to strike students as particularly painful to read or watch. A subsequent discussion here could consider the question of how the scene, which technically depicts only a minor act of physical violence perpetrated on a single person, can stand in metonymically for the incomprehensible collective violence of the Holocaust. Such miniperformances highlight the unique potential that drama brings to an analysis of the Holocaust: by enacting a deeply disturbing scene of victimization in a carefully prepared and structured environment, students see that a powerful emotional experience such as this is but the faintest representation of the profound and extended horror we designate as the Holocaust.

7. In a group, pick a scene from a play (or perhaps even an episode from the historical record) and devise ways in which to create a short performance, to be presented to the class (Skloot, "Directing").

This more ambitious assignment involves discussing the problems of visualizing the printed script, an actual presentation, as well as a reflective essay that addresses questions like, What exactly happens in this episode? How can you make this scene come alive on a stage? What kind of space would be most suitable for a presentation of the scene? What does the setting look like? What objects, if any, appear onstage? How should the characters move? Which characters are involved? How do they use language (realistic dialogue, stylized verse, choruses, etc.)? What do they look like (costumes, makeup, masks, etc.)? Are there distinctions between main characters and subordinate ones, between characters seen and ones offstage? Do questions of race, gender, class, and ethnicity influence the chosen scene (both in the script and in the casting)? Does the scene aim for an immediate rendering, or would you use devices that highlight remembrance and mediation (e.g., a narrator figure, dramatic flashbacks)? What means would you use to place the scene in a larger social and historical context? Which form of audience address do you think is most appropriate? What message, if any, would you wish to convey with the chosen scene?

The project groups would have to meet on a regular basis to work on the assignment, present it to the class, and engage in postperformance discussions with their fellow students. They would have to synthesize the whole experience in a final paper that connects the project with the historical, theoretical, and artistic material covered throughout the rest of the course. At all stages, students should be encouraged to explain the choices they made as well as the options they considered but rejected. As part of an ongoing process of critical reflection, creative activity, and subsequent discussion, such combinations of miniperformance projects and critical essays provide a mode of learning that not only engages students on a cognitive level but also addresses their artistic and affective faculties, perhaps even their practical skills (e.g., when it comes to questions of set design). Through a student's engagement with the historical material, with the teacher, and—perhaps most important— with the other students, such analytic-creative projects turn the class into a community of witnesses, a collective that confronts history as a powerful continuous presence in a process of joint remembering. It is this potential of drama to "provide a communal experience of memory while contributing to the process of memorialization" (Isser 173) that renders drama a particularly effective pedagogical tool.

———

A careful critical and creative engagement with a play raises as many questions as it answers. The very limitations that drama confronts in its endeavor to represent the Holocaust may prove to be most useful when we initiate a process of reflection. Drama—as a literary genre associated with both printed text and live enactment— can open a comprehensive debate about the representability of something as enormous and complex, as overwhelming and unfathomable, as the Holocaust. Holocaust drama is a particularly good example of what I would call the homeopathic potential of literature: by exposing ourselves to carefully limited doses of a profoundly disturbing experience, we can learn in a manner that moves beyond mere cognition and that holistically involves us as human beings in an ongoing process that increases our awareness of everything humankind has been, is, and will be capable of. Drama engenders and sustains a debate that cannot and should not be closed by easy answers (Skloot, *Theatre* [1999]). Reading, performing, watching, and discussing the drama of the Holocaust thus become a kind of witnessing through cognitive, emotional, and physical engagement. Such "embodied memory" is a contribution to the labor of mourning and remembrance that is the task of all of us who are faced with the challenge of living in a post-Holocaust world.

Works Cited

Bennett, Susan. *Theatre Audiences: A Theory of Production and Reception.* 2nd ed. London: Routledge, 1997.

Cohen, Robert. "The Political Aesthetics of Holocaust Literature: Peter Weiss's *The Investigation* and Its Critics." *History and Memory* 10.2 (1998): 43–67.

Delbo, Charlotte. *Who Will Carry the Word.* Skloot, *Theatre* [1982] 267–325.

Fassbinder, Rainer Werner. *Garbage, the City, and Death. Plays.* Trans. and introd. Denis Calandra. New York: Performing Arts Journal, 1985. 161–89.

Feinberg, Anat. *Embodied Memory: The Theatre of George Tabori.* Iowa City: U of Iowa P, 1999.

Frisch, Max. *Andorra.* Trans. Michael Bullock. New York: Hill, 1964.

Fuchs, Elinor, ed. *Plays of the Holocaust: An International Anthology.* New York: Theater Communications Group, 1987.

Goldfarb, Alvin. "Select Bibliography of Holocaust Plays, 1933–1997." *Staging the Holocaust: The Shoah in Drama and Performance.* Ed. Claude Schumacher. Cambridge: Cambridge UP, 1998. 298–334.

Goodrich, Frances, and Albert Hackett. *The Diary of Anne Frank.* New York: Random, 1956.

Hochhuth, Rolf. *The Deputy.* Trans. Richard Winston and Clara Winston. New York: Grove, 1964.

Isser, Edward. *Stages of Annihilation: Theatrical Representations of the Holocaust.* Madison: Fairleigh Dickinson UP, 1997.

Kipphardt, Heinar. *Bruder Eichmann.* Reinbek: Rowohlt, 1995.

Langer, Lawrence. "The Americanization of the Holocaust on Stage and Screen." *From Hester Street to Hollywood.* Ed. Sarah Blacher Cohen. Bloomington: Indiana UP, 1983. 213–30.

Lieberman, Harold, and Edith Lieberman. *Throne of Straw.* Skloot, *Theatre* [1982] 113–96.

Miller, Arthur. *Playing for Time.* New York: Bantam, 1980.

Rokem, Freddie. *Performing History. Theatrical Representations of the Past in Contemporary Theatre.* Iowa City: U of Iowa P, 2000.

Roth, Ari. *Born Guilty.* New York: French, 1994.

Samuels, Diane. *Kindertransport.* New York: Consortium, 2000.

Sichrovsky, Peter. *Born Guilty: Children of Nazi Families.* Trans. Jean Steinberg. London: Tauris, 1988.

Skloot, Robert. *The Darkness We Carry: The Drama of the Holocaust.* Madison: U of Wisconsin P, 1988.

———. "Directing the Holocaust Play." *Theatre Journal* 31 (1979): 527–41.

———, ed. *The Theatre of the Holocaust: Four Plays.* Madison: U of Wisconsin P, 1982.

———, ed. *The Theatre of the Holocaust.* Madison: U of Wisconsin P, 1999.

Sobol, Joshua. *Adam*. Taub 268–330.

———. *Ghetto*. Adapt. Jack Viertel. Fuchs 153–230.

———. *Underground*. Adapt. Ron Jenkins. *Theater* 22.3 (1991): 9–43.

Tabori, George. *The Cannibals*. Skloot, *Theatre* [1982] 197–295.

———. *My Mother's Courage*. Trans. Jack D. Zipes. *Theater* 29.2 (1999): 109–29.

Taub, Michael, ed. *Israeli Holocaust Drama*. Syracuse: Syracuse UP, 1996.

Totten, Samuel. "Diminishing the Complexity and Horror of the Holocaust: Using Simulations in an Attempt to Convey Historical Experiences." *Social Education* 64.3 (2000): 165–71.

Weiss, Peter. *The Investigation*. Trans. Alexander Gross. New York: MacMillan, 1966. Trans. Robert Cohen. *Marat/Sade [and] The Investigation [and] The Shadow of the Body of the Coachman*. Ed. Cohen. New York: Continuum, 1998. 117–297.

Zipes, Jack D. "George Tabori and the Jewish Question." *Theater* 29.2 (1999): 98–107.

Adrienne Kertzer

The Problem of Childhood, Children's Literature, and Holocaust Representation

The syllabus for my graduate seminar on Holocaust representation includes what are likely the standard works of many courses. We begin with Alain Resnais's *Night and Fog*; we end with Claude Lanzmann's *Shoah* and Steven Spielberg's *Schindler's List*. In between are names and titles many will recognize: Anne Frank's *The Diary of a Young Girl*, Frances Goodrich and Albert Hackett's *The Diary of Anne Frank*, Elie Wiesel's *Night*, Primo Levi's *Survival in Auschwitz*, Tadeusz Borowski's *This Way for the Gas, Ladies and Gentlemen*, Aharon Appelfeld's *Badenheim 1939*, Cynthia Ozick's *The Shawl*, Anne Michaels's *Fugitive Pieces*, and Art Spiegelman's *Maus: A Survivor's Tale*. The authors of the scholarly articles included in my course pack are equally well known: Alvin Rosenfeld, Joan Ringelheim, Saul Friedländer, Dori Laub, Geoffrey H. Hartman, Henry Greenspan, and Berel Lang. But where my syllabus likely diverges from many reading lists is that we also read Anita Lobel's memoir *No Pretty Pictures: A Child of War* and Jane Yolen's young-adult fantasy *Briar Rose*.

Two pedagogical questions immediately arise. Why don't I just teach a course on children's literature about the Holocaust? Why add children's books to a syllabus that is clearly long enough without them?[1] Five of the books on my list are part of the canon of literary works considered crucial to an understanding of the Holocaust. What are Lobel and Yolen doing in this company? One answer has to do with conceptual categories, with the way that course titles determine what questions students are willing to consider. A course called Children's Literature about the Holocaust emphasizes children's literature and assumes a confidence about its identity; there is something that we recognize as children's literature whether it is about the Holocaust or not. Most often, we define this something in opposition to serious adult literature. For example, if serious adult literature explores the terrors of the imagination (madness, trauma), then children's literature offers its readers an imagination that is stripped of fear, an imagination that healthily indulges and develops children's imaginations. If serious adult literature questions the relation between representation and the world, then children's literature, taking that relation for granted, offers its readers simple, protective, and hopeful lessons about their relation to that world.

Such certainty about what children's literature is and about the binary relation between it and adult literature is undercut as soon as we think of specific children's books, including paradoxically the ones we celebrate as canonical children's books. If imagination is so pleasurable, why does the heroine in Lewis Carroll's *Alice in Wonderland* cry so much, and what is the lesson that Carroll offers his reader? In Holocaust literature, our confidence in the binary relation appears even more misplaced, and we need only consider Momik's story in David Grossman's *See Under: Love* to confront the terror in children's Holocaust fantasies. A course entitled Children's Literature about the Holocaust is false advertising; the difference between children's literature and adult works on this subject is not always clear. In addition, students who enroll in such a course are often so invested in protecting their idea of children and children's literature as a safe space, that questions about Holocaust representation become secondary. The interminable question—But is this *really* a children's book? — takes precedence over representational questions. Representational questions assume that the rupture provoked by the Holocaust — "This representational shift is like a fall" (Hartman 130) — might well unsettle our understanding of what a children's book really is.

Unable to keep children's books about the Holocaust neatly isolated and convinced that including them is pedagogically productive for my university students, I do not mention children's literature in the course title. The course focus is Holocaust representation; the children's books enter into our examination of the dilemmas of representation. Unlike students who have registered over the years in my children's literature surveys, the students who enroll in Holocaust Representation are far more willing to admit their uncertainty about what children are like and what children are willing to read. Whatever their expectations, they do not anticipate a safe space (anyone who does is quickly disillusioned after I screen *Night and Fog* in the first class). Once we agree that the Holocaust profoundly shakes our beliefs about childhood, it is easier to accept that it also disturbs our conception of children's books. If my students then turn with relief to the hopeful representations in many children's books, they do so much more aware of what those representations omit. They do not scorn the Holocaust representations in such children's books; they understand the authorial-parental-societal impulse to protect even as they acknowledge that the protection is often, but not always, inadequate for what they see and hear in our other texts.

Including Lobel and Yolen on my syllabus is strategic, a declaration that a course on the challenges of Holocaust representation requires consideration of children's literature. My pedagogy is thus grounded in a deliberately muddled and uncomfortable space: Lanzmann's *Shoah* one week, Yolen's *Briar Rose* the next. Lanzmann, contemptuous of any attempts to turn the Holocaust into a story, would no doubt be appalled to learn that Yolen wrote *Briar Rose* after watching *Shoah* and offers her readers a fairy tale in which a woman survives Chelmno. Bemused by what he might say about a course in which students spend four nights watching *Shoah* not simply because they will be discussing his film but also as preparation for the class on Yolen's *Briar Rose*, I value how this peculiar juxtaposition makes my students ask questions about both. We notice both what Yolen omits and what Lanzmann excludes.

So if my students begin puzzled that they must become familiar with the narrative patterns of children's books, I hope that they end with a more perplexing series of observations. The first is that children's literature about the Holocaust (like any other marginalized discourse) appears far more complex as soon as we pay close attention to it; the second is that many of us not only begin our lessons in Holocaust representation with children's literature, we also end there. Like many professors, I ask my students what the lesson of *The Diary of Anne Frank* is, but I also ask them what lessons we learn when we position supposedly adult works beside those we give children. What is the difference between Roberto Benigni's *Life Is Beautiful* and Lobel's *No Pretty Pictures*, a memoir that children's book lists quickly adopted because of Lobel's reputation as a picture-book artist? Students discover that her memoir is more reticent in its witnessing of Holocaust horror than Levi's *Survival in Auschwitz*, let alone the fiction of Tadeusz Borowski. Nevertheless, some of my students are hesitant. Isn't Lobel too troubling for child readers? When she describes how as a hidden child she shuns identifying herself as Jewish and how she puts her faith in the protection offered by the holy medals that her Catholic nanny gives her, won't she confuse children?

In proposing the benefits of an "interdisciplinary course in the history and literature of the Holocaust" (191), Lawrence L. Langer asserts that Ida Fink's fiction offers more insight into the Holocaust than Anne Frank's *The Diary of a Young Girl*, and I agree.[2] But when he suggests that teachers of Holocaust literature supplement Frank's *Diary* with *The Diary of Dawid Sierakowiak: Five Notebooks from the Łódź Ghetto* (Adelson), I think how much more useful it would be to assign Carol Matas's *Daniel's Story* as well. Matas's work, a children's book commissioned by the United States Holocaust Memorial Museum as a companion novel to their children's exhibit, has a protagonist who usually sounds very little like the despairing Sierakowiak. Yet it is in those few moments when Daniel does come close to sounding like Sierakowiak, and in considering why those moments are so rare, that students can discern representational issues faced not just by children's writers but by all who write about the Holocaust. How does our conception of the implied reader affect our narrative choices? What are we willing to tell? These questions, so apparent when we compare different national representations of the Holocaust, are also at issue when we imagine child readers instead of adults. If children's literature is less a question of genre than a way of reading, then what happens to our understanding of canonical Holocaust texts when we imagine child readers? Are there canonical Holocaust texts that we cannot imagine having child readers? What characterizes them?

Langer protests that narratives that emphasize "heroism, resistance, and spiritual uplift" (189) teach students little about the realities of human behavior during the Holocaust. But placing *Daniel's Story* beside *The Diary of Dawid Sierakowiak* allows students to hear two voices and to see how the pedagogical framework, the expectation that children will read *Daniel's Story* to learn a lesson, affects the representation. Reading both Matas and Sierakowiak, students not only confront the "distressing legacy" that Langer does not find in Frank (189) but also gain insight into how debates over what is permissible in children's reading affect transmission of that legacy. They discover a pattern in which, not surprisingly, what is distressing is softened and what is traumatic is made coherent; they also see how what is often regarded as unrepresentable becomes factual. Matas's protagonist, Daniel, resides for a time in the Lodz Ghetto but is then sent to Auschwitz. Narrating his memories of Auschwitz, he confides to his implied child reader that he nearly committed suicide after seeing burning bodies in a pit. This episode, "improbable" (Bosmajian 195) yet inevitable given the pedagogical framework of the children's book that Matas writes, is a passage that she insisted on retaining even after readers of the manuscript suggested that it was too much for children. Like her other attempts to complicate Daniel's voice, the passage indicates that not all children's writers conceptualize children's books as the place for simple heroism, resistance, and spiritual uplift. For Matas, the pedagogical need to inform children about the "unbelievable"—bodies burning in pits—takes precedence over the need to console and inspire the child.

Certainly, *Daniel's Story* shows multiple signs of the improbability that Bosmajian identifies, a major one being the consequence of the museum directive to Matas that her protagonist must survive. Unlike Sierakowiak then in this crucial narrative triumph, Daniel also differs in that he never once refers to Mordechai Chaim Rumkowski, the Elder of the Lodz Ghetto.[3] The university student who reads only *Daniel's Story* will not recognize this absence; the silence about Rumkowski will be glaringly apparent if the student reads both *Daniel's Story* and *The Diary of Dawid Sierakowiak*. This difference is particularly revealing, for it suggests that the gaps and ellipses that we repeatedly find in adult works also appear in children's books, but that they function in a different way. In children's books such gaps are not an abstract acknowledgment of the limits of representation but rather a cultural acceptance of the limits of what we are willing to tell children. Tell child readers about the burning bodies; do not tell them about the behavior of Rumkowski. What we regard as "unbelievable" but factual—the burning of bodies—is far more likely to be represented in a children's book than issues that we consider too morally complex for child readers.

This practice is based partly on our assumptions regarding children's ability to comprehend what Primo Levi calls "the gray zone" (42) and under which category I would include any ambiguous aspect of Holocaust experience. Particularly sensitive to the problem of talking to the young, Levi introduces his discussion of the gray zone in *The Drowned and the Saved* through an assertion about children: "The young above all demand clarity, a sharp cut; their experience of the world being meager, they do not like ambiguity" (37). But who are the young? Like Geoffrey H. Hartman— "Before Auschwitz we were children in our imagination of evil; after Auschwitz we are no longer children" (130)—Levi defines the young as those who have not yet entered the *Lager* (the German camp). With this definition, a children's literature on the Holocaust appears impossible; the child who enters the *Lager* can de facto no longer read as a child.

Despite Levi's assertion, not all of us agree that the young demand clarity. Many adults — Ernst van Alphen is just one example — commence their analysis of Holocaust representation by critiquing their memories of the stories that they were given as children. Recalling his childhood resistance to the "official war narratives" (1) forced on him by the Dutch school system, van Alphen confesses that he refused to read Frank's *Diary of a Young Girl* until he was an adult. He concludes that one reason for his resistance was that the official narratives allowed for no ambiguity. Bored by official lessons about national and masculine heroism, he admits that the images he could not make sense of nevertheless remained "haunting" (3). I cannot tell if his confession is intended to shock or impress; I can recognize how it challenges Levi's assertion about children even as it implies that something happens when children are exposed to Holocaust literature, but not always what we intend.

Perhaps our insistence that the young demand clarity and that we know what and how stories affect them are unwarranted generalizations, comparable to the many other generalizations that pervade discussions of Holocaust literature: "Whatever form Holocaust testimonies may assume . . . they *all* inhabit a haunted terrain of traumatized memory" (Zeitlin 128; my emphasis). Place this statement beside the testimonies that we give to children, and Zeitlin's description sounds less convincing, as though the process of identifying which testimonies are appropriate for children transforms their meaning. So, too, our understanding of common phrases — the limits of representation, the Americanization of the Holocaust, postmemory, and the utility of gender analysis — is qualified.[4] When we belittle the Americanization of the Holocaust and give as examples both Frank's *Diary* and *Schindler's List*, aren't we really talking about children's literature? And when we accept the inevitable failure of Holocaust representation and the equally inevitable way this "necessary failure" (Hirsch and Suleiman 102) elevates trauma narrative, do we think about how children's books fit here? Lanzmann insists that "the project of understanding" is obscene, because the "fields of explanation . . . are all true and all false" (206), and trauma theory questions the nature of witness knowledge; in children's literature, the generic demand for a coherent narrative frequently conflicts with the dislocation of Holocaust discourses valued elsewhere. Memories of traumatized childhood are much more evident in texts marketed for adults; in children's books about the Holocaust, traumatized child narrators are of limited pedagogical utility. Pedagogy often demands that children's books bear the "burden of truth in the age of denial" ("Call") and that they simultaneously reassure child readers. How can traumatized voices possibly accomplish this?

However we imagine the future of Holocaust representation, we ought not to do so without including children's books. Froma I. Zeitlin speaks of the need for new paradigms that acknowledge "the increasing distance of our age from what it feels compelled to confront and remember" (128). Zeitlin focuses on second-generation memory, but the future of Holocaust narratives may also reside in the third-generation stories that we tell children. Precisely because the Holocaust is a historical event, its representation in children's literature is not fixed. One possible future for Holocaust representation is evident in Jackie French's *Hitler's Daughter*, a children's book that is surprising and provocative not only in its title.[5] The novel focuses on the reaction of various children when a child character, Anna, announces that she will tell a story about Hitler's daughter. One child protests, "But we can't have a story about something that's not real." The other children are indifferent; as far as they are concerned, Hitler is someone that they either haven't heard of—"Who's Hitler?"—or regard as a narrative cliché, slightly better than "fairies and goldfish" (7). At the end, we learn that the story that Anna tells was once told to her by her grandmother and that Anna may have just told her listeners a story about a real person. The storyteller-granddaughter is neither traumatized by the story she has inherited nor particularly troubled by the gaps that exist in it. She is just uncertain what to make of it. Was her grandmother Hitler's daughter? Similarly, readers are left uncertain what the lesson is other than French's challenge: How do we represent the Holocaust to children to whom Hitler is no more than the villain in a television movie? Langer imagines the challenge facing a teacher "fifty years from now" (187). In *Hitler's Daughter*, it is clear that we don't have to wait that long to imagine children's books more than willing to set aside the lessons that dominate earlier children's literature about the Holocaust.

For the most part, however, we do not imagine those children's books. Blithely quoting Anne Frank, "I still believe, in spite of everything," we think that we already know what children's literature about the Holocaust is like — eternally the same, eternally inadequate, Pollyanna with a yellow star. Reading Cynthia Ozick, on why we should not read Anne Frank ("Who Owns?"), as though teachers continued to present Frank's *Diary* to children in a totally celebrating and naive manner, we mistakenly teach our students to regard the diary as the representative children's text. As a result, they remain oblivious to the growing number of children's books, books such as Cherie Bennett and Jeff Gottesfeld's *Anne Frank and Me*, that foreground the questionable effectiveness of Anne Frank as pedagogical Holocaust icon.

In "The Book of the Destruction," Hartman asks the purpose of Lanzmann's *Shoah* and observes, "Reality has displaced fantasy . . . myth and fiction may now have to be devalued to playthings" (130). Does Hartman's answer indicate that all attempts at fictionalizing the Holocaust are equivalent to a children's story, that there really is very little difference between children's and adult fiction about the Holocaust? Or does he indicate that the place for such fiction is the nursery? He is unable to reconcile the post-Holocaust knowledge that makes the viewers of *Shoah* no longer children and our need to remember "that childhood exists." Lanzmann, he observes, "elide[s] the entire issue of pedagogy" (130). In contrast, in the "Author's Note" that follows her fairy tale, Yolen addresses pedagogy by acknowledging that her text is fiction: "Happy-ever-after is a fairy tale notion, not history. I know of no woman who escaped from Chelmno alive" (202). In this way, she recognizes the limiting narrative conventions of children's literature even as she locates the genre's necessary history lesson, its burden of truth, outside her narrative.

The border between a Holocaust book for adults and a Holocaust book for children remains slippery. When Art in the second volume of *Maus* refuses to give reporters the "message" of his work (*And Here* 42), Spiegelman appears to position his work outside the conventions of children's literature, where we have always believed that there must be a message. But when Pavel, a survivor and Art's psychiatrist, responds to Art's concern that Art cannot begin to imagine what Auschwitz felt like, Spiegelman shifts to a comic-art representation that any child could understand. Mocking Art's anxieties, Spiegelman draws Pavel screaming out "BOO!" and a terrified and child-sized Art flying off the chair (46). Clearly this is not the last word (image?) in understanding the Holocaust, but it does indicate the representational possibilities of children's literature and the difficulty of establishing clear boundaries between it and other Holocaust literatures. If we place more children's books on our syllabi, we might notice how much less cheery is the voice of Anne Frank than the tagline by which we make her an emblem of the limitations of children's literature. We might further clarify the challenges of Holocaust representation if we consider how other children's books attempt to accomplish Hartman's impossible desire: "allow the limits of representation to be healing limits, yet not allow them to conceal an event we are obligated to recall and interpret, both to ourselves and those growing up unconscious of its shadow" (131). Healing, yet not concealing, *sefer hashoah* ("the book of the Shoah") as the ideal children's book.

Notes

1. The syllabus that I initially describe was assigned for a semester course (13 weeks) that I taught in fall 2000. It was taught as a double-numbered course, that is, as both a graduate and senior undergraduate seminar. The additional children's books that I discuss in the essay were on the syllabus when I taught the course as a full-year course in 2002–03.
2. Fink, like many of the authors I teach, is included in Edward T. Sullivan's bibliography *The Holocaust in Literature for Youth: A Guide and Resource Book*. In his introduction, Sullivan hopes that his bibliography will "make teachers aware that there is a lot more to the Holocaust than Anne Frank's *Diary of a Young Girl*" (5).
3. In early drafts of *Daniel's Story*, Daniel and other ghetto inhabitants

refer to Rumkowski and argue about the role of the Jewish police. The museum insisted that Matas revise these passages (see Kertzer, ch. 5).
4. Children's literature is often regarded and dismissed as a female space. In this space, women-authored memoirs dominate lists for children, whereas protagonists in children's fiction are still more likely to be male than female (see Kertzer, chs. 3 and 8).
5. The novel won the Children's Book Council of Australia Book of the Year: Younger Readers.

Works Cited

Adelson, Alan, ed. *The Diary of Dawid Sierakowiak: Five Notebooks from the Łódź Ghetto*. Trans. Kamil Turowski. 1996. New York: Oxford UP, 1998.

Appelfeld, Aharon. *Badenheim 1939*. Trans. Dalya Bilu. Boston: Godine, 1980. Trans. of *Badenhaim, 'ir nofesh*.

Bennett, Cherie, and Jeff Gottesfeld. *Anne Frank and Me*. New York: Putnam, 2001.

Borowski, Tadeusz. *This Way for the Gas, Ladies and Gentlemen*. Trans. Barbara Vedder. New York: Penguin, 1976.

Bosmajian, Hamida. *Sparing the Child: Grief and the Unspeakable in Youth Literature about Nazism and the Holocaust*. Children's Lit. and Culture 16. New York: Routledge, 2002.

"Call for Contributions in Options for Teaching Series." *MLA Newsletter* 32.3 (2000): 19.

Carroll, Lewis. *Alice's Adventures in Wonderland*. Ed. Richard Kelly. Broadview Literary Texts. Peterborough: Broadview, 2000.

Epstein, Julia, and Lori Hope Lefkovitz, eds. *Shaping Losses: Cultural Memory and the Holocaust*. Urbana: U of Illinois P, 2001.

Frank, Anne. The Diary of a Young Girl: *The Definitive Edition*. Ed. Otto H. Frank and Mirjam Pressler. Trans. Susan Massotty. New York: Bantam, 1997.

French, Jackie. *Hitler's Daughter*. Sydney: Robertson-Harper, 2000.

Goodrich, Frances, and Albert Hackett. *The Diary of Anne Frank: A Play in Two Acts*. Fwd. Brooks Atkinson. Toronto: Irwin, 1964.

Grossman, David. *See Under: Love*. Trans. Betsy Rosenberg. New York: Farrar, 1989. Trans. of *'Ayen 'erekh—ahavah*.

Hartman, Geoffrey H. "The Book of the Destruction." *The Longest Shadow: In the Aftermath of the Holocaust*. Helen and Martin Schwartz Lectures in Jewish Studies. Bloomington: Indiana UP, 1996. 116–32.

Hirsch, Marianne, and Susan Rubin Suleiman. "Material Memory: Holocaust Testimony in Post-Holocaust Art." Epstein and Lefkovitz 87–104.

Kertzer, Adrienne. *My Mother's Voice: Children, Literature, and the Holocaust*. Peterborough: Broadview, 2002.

Langer, Lawrence L. "Opening Locked Doors: Reflections on Teaching the Holocaust." *Preempting the Holocaust*. New Haven: Yale UP, 1998. 187–98.

Lanzmann, Claude. "The Obsenity of Understanding: An Evening with Claude Lanzmann." *Trauma: Explorations in Memory*. Ed. Cathy Caruth. Baltimore: Johns Hopkins UP, 1995. 200–20.

Levi, Primo. *The Drowned and the Saved*. Trans. Raymond Rosenthal. New York: Vintage-Random, 1989. Trans. of *Sommersi e i salvati*.

———. *Survival in Auschwitz: The Nazi Assault on Humanity*. Trans. Stuart Woolf. 1958. New York: Collier-Macmillan, 1961. Trans. of *Se questo è un uomo*.

Life Is Beautiful [*La vita è bella*]. Dir. Roberto Benigni. Alliance, Miramax, 1997.

Lobel, Anita. *No Pretty Pictures: A Child of War*. New York: Greenwillow, 1998.

Matas, Carol. *Daniel's Story*. New York: Scholastic, 1993.

Michaels, Anne. *Fugitive Pieces*. Toronto: McClelland, 1996.

Night and Fog [*Nuit et brouillard*]. Dir. Alain Resnais. Script by Jean Cayrol. Janus, 1955.

Ozick, Cynthia. *The Shawl*. New York: Random, 1990.

———. "Who Owns Anne Frank?" *Quarrel and Quandary*. New York: Vintage, 2000. 74–102.

Schindler's List. Dir. Steven Spielberg. Script by Stephen Zeillian. Universal Pictures, Amblin Entertainment, 1993.

Shoah. Dir. Claude Lanzmann. Aleph-Historia, 1985. Videocassette. New Yorker Films, 2004.

Spiegelman, Art. *And Here My Troubles Began*. New York: Pantheon, 1991. Vol. 2 of *Maus: A Survivor's Tale*.

———. *My Father Bleeds History*. New York: Pantheon, 1986. Vol. 1 of *Maus: A Survivor's Tale*.

Sullivan, Edward T. *The Holocaust in Literature for Youth: A Guide and Resource Book*. Lanham: Scarecrow, 1999.

van Alphen, Ernst. *Caught by History: Holocaust Effects in Contemporary Art, Literature, and Theory*. Stanford: Stanford UP, 1997.

Wiesel, Elie. *Night*. Trans. Stella Rodway. London: MacGibbon, 1960. New York: Discus-Avon, 1969. Trans. of *La Nuit*.

Yolen, Jane. *Briar Rose*. Fairy Tale Ser. New York: Tor, 1992.

Zeitlin, Froma I. "The Vicarious Witness: Belated Memory and Authorial Presence in Recent Holocaust Literature." Epstein and Lefkovitz 128– 60.

Efraim Sicher

Postmemory, Backshadowing, Separation: Teaching Second-Generation Holocaust Fiction

A growing corpus of serious literary work by "second-generation" post-Holocaust writers complicates our definition of the canon of Holocaust literature — a canon that already bursts the generic boundaries between history and fiction, autobiography and memoir, document and novel. A question at the center of debates over these writers is whether the children of survivors are, like Job's second children, "second-generation witnesses" (Berger) or, to the contrary, in Zygmunt Bauman's opinion, they have, like Alain Finkielkraut's "imaginary Jew," falsely claimed a martyrdom not their own (Bauman). The various positions on this issue may affect our recognition of a separate second-generation literature. In a study of contemporary Jewish American writers, for example, Andrew Furman suggests the second generation is expanding the definition of Holocaust literature and giving new dimension to the exploration of Jewish American identity (63).

In its recovery of the past, second-generation writing seeks its own place in history and in the chain of survival (Sicher, "Future"). These writers "represent the past through modes of enactment—even reanimation—through which the self, the 'ego,' the 'one who was not there,' now takes on a leading role as an active presence" (Zeitlin 6).

Now that most Holocaust survivors are at an age where they once more face mortality, the second generation's task of telling the story to the third generation, the grandchildren of Holocaust victims, has become all the more urgent (see Sicher, "Return"). Sometimes the survivors' obsessive telling of Holocaust stories saturated their offspring's childhood, but there were also parents who were silent about the horrors they had gone through (Epstein). In either case, for children of survivors the personal memory essential for identity formation through life narratives was absent. Absent memory nevertheless contains anxieties, neuroses, and other posttraumatic symptoms that compel the second generation to work through the unknown past, while Holocaust denial challenges a claim to that past and motivates the writing of the untold story.

There is no consensus on whether the children of survivors have a shared pathology, and it is difficult to determine how much posttraumatic stress disorder they have inherited from their parents. Generational transference of traumatic memory may be affected by national memory and local conditions: for example, the construction of a new sabra identity in Israel that negated the Diaspora, or the stigma attached to victims in the postwar United States (Fox; Hass; Bar-On). Children of survivors, like their contemporaries who are not biological offspring of survivors (e.g., David Grossman, Anne Michaels, Arye-Lev Stollman), are nevertheless forced to imagine their way from a common post-Holocaust existence into a past of which they have no personal memory. They have inherited ghosts in the family cupboard (Rosenbaum, "Memory's Ghosts"), and history, as Thane Rosenbaum put it in his 1999 novel *Second Hand Smoke*, has maimed them before their birth. Another child of survivors, the novelist Melvin J. Bukiet, comments in his introduction to a collection of second-generation writing, "For anyone who wasn't there, on either side of the barbed wire, Jew or German, thinking about the Holocaust is really an act of the imagination. All we know is how little we know" (16).

Contemplating the photographs of deceased relatives in the families of Holocaust survivors and relating their existence as spaces of lost memory to the images in Art Spiegelman's *Maus*, Marianne Hirsch distinguishes "postmemory" from "memory" by "generational distance" and from history by "deep personal connection":

> Postmemory is a powerful and very particular form of memory precisely because its connection to its object or source is mediated not through recollection but through an imaginative investment and creation. . . . Postmemory characterizes the experience of those who grow up dominated by narratives that preceded their birth, whose own belated stories are evacuated by the stories of the previous generation shaped by traumatic events that can be neither understood nor recreated. (22)

Postmemory is not empty but fills a spatiotemporal exile from a destroyed past that both distances and affirms the existence of the past (Hirsch 22–23; 244–45). Henri Raczymow, a French second-generation novelist, has formulated in the phrase *mémoire trouée* ("memory shot through with holes") a memory of a void, a memory of not remembering and of not being there. For Raczymow, in contrast to Finkielkraut, the unknown past can *only* be imagined, and it requires a cabalistic form of creation through withdrawal (*tsimtsum*) to write it into existence and achieve cosmic repair (*tikkun*; 101–02).

Teaching *Maus* and the Israeli novelist David Grossman's *See Under: Love* (*'Ayen 'erekh: ahavah*) as second-generation narratives invites students to look at how the representation of a traumatic past forms personal and collective identity. It raises questions about how we can imagine a traumatic past that we have no personal knowledge of but that affects our existence and daily lives. These signature texts for second-generation identity each address in different ways the difficulties attendant on writing memory and open up discussion of the relation of mass trauma to personal memory, of children of survivors to the post-Holocaust generation, of imagination to history. Each thematizes the representation of the Holocaust and foregrounds issues of authenticity and legitimacy.

We could start by reading Spiegelman's *Maus* not as a memoir of the survivor or a documentary-biography of Vladek Spiegelman but as an autobiographical graphic novel (Tabachnick) of the survivor's son, Art, who grows up in Rego Park, New York, overshadowed by Auschwitz. In this narrative of self-definition, the frame within the frame of Art's telling of his father's story leads Art to discover his biological origins as well as his psychological and ethnic identity as a member of the second generation, whose historical knowledge turns from being latent and unconscious to active and personal. Such a reading shows the moral and aesthetic complexities in the text's generic and epistemological status between comic book and memoir, autobiography and fiction (Horowitz).

This portrait of the artist as a child of survivors self-consciously challenges Theodor Adorno's oft-misquoted dictum that writing poetry after Auschwitz is barbaric. Art is possible and necessary after Auschwitz, it seems, even if representing an event "at the limits" transgresses the boundaries of the permissible and tests conventional representational and conceptual categories (Friedländer 2–3). For the second generation, however, the possibility of representation facilitates self-identification and helps break generational silence.

Grossman's *See Under: Love* can be usefully compared to *Maus* as a story of a second-generation artist who grows up in Israel amid the nightmares and traumatic anxieties of a family of Holocaust survivors. The first section, "Momik," is a carefully observed portrait of a child of survivors. Shlomo (Momik) has to piece the story together himself and solve the mystery of a world cursed by evil. Grossman draws on the tradition of Sholom Aleichem and uses a generic characteristic of the child's view that internalizes the coded language of immigrants from "over there" to give naive expression to the incomprehensible terror of the adult survivors (Sokoloff 153–76). In the cellar, a storeroom of memory, Momik confronts the Nazi Beast's universal threat to humanity. When he becomes an artist, Momik has to deal with the representation of the Holocaust in his imagination in order to know evil. The return to the past takes place through a rescue of Bruno Schulz from death in the ghetto in a surreal fantasy underwater with a shoal of salmon. In the re-creation of Momik's grandfather Anshel Wasserman's storytelling in the camps, Grossman insists the Holocaust can be represented but negates any redemptive narrative. In Grossman's re-creation of a lost manuscript by Schulz, messianism is envisioned as a liberating force of individuality (a plotline given a somewhat different treatment in Cynthia Ozick's 1987 novel *The Messiah of Stockholm*). However, Grossman points to the fatal consequences of an artistic utopia.

For both Spiegelman and Grossman, postmemory attempts to recover the unexperienced and unimaginable traumatic past across the generational gap. Students can track how writing life stories bridges that gap and places the children of survivors in history. The back cover of the first volume of *Maus* (*My Father Bleeds History*) displays a map of the father's prewar Poland. An inset, however, depicts Art's childhood Rego Park opposite a monochrome graphic of the father telling stories to the grown-up son, who sits listening like a little boy on the carpet. Daunted by the enormity of Auschwitz, Art will confess to his therapist an infantile incapacity to understand. On the back cover of the second volume (*And Here My Troubles Began*), an overview of Auschwitz forms the backdrop to an inset map of the Catskills, where much of the story is told. The past and the present are thus transposed. In the inside back jacket of both volumes, a despairing Art sits over his drawing book beneath posters for *Raw* magazine and for *Maus*, while outside his window a concentration-camp sentry aims a rifle at him. The artist's memoir of his father is thus framed by his own growing up in a survivor's family and, as in the anecdotal preface about a skating accident, being taught the lessons of surviving the Holocaust. The aimed rifle of an Auschwitz guard suggests that memory compels him to draw the story but prohibits that creativity, while his fame as author of *Maus* and his past history (the story of his breakdown in *Raw*, interpolated in *Maus*) remind him of his inability to represent the Holocaust adequately.

In *See Under: Love*, however, storytelling is imagined as an imperative and one fantasized as feasible inside the camps. Anshel Wasserman is a Scheherazade who tells stories to die, not to live. The commandant Neigel's nightly reward of a bullet miraculously fails to kill Wasserman, who lives on in Momik's imagination to show him how to escape from the "White Room" of traumatic memory. If, as Gilead Morahg suggests, Grossman's accomplishment is to break the taboo around the Holocaust, Grossman has also succeeded in overcoming the sanctified convention that one who was not there could not tell the story. He has given voice to the silenced survivor by putting stories into the mouth of Wasserman, whose demented gibberish is understandable only to the child. To translate the gibberish into stories, Momik decides to become a writer (*See Under* 37). Similarly, in *Maus*, Art uses his artistic skills to give a human voice to Vladek's story and to claim his place in the transmission of testimony. The voicing of both survivors' muteness will spark student discussion about the communicability of repressed memory and the efficacy of artistic ventriloquism.

Ethnic stereotyping of characters in *Maus* (Jews as mice, Poles as pigs, and so forth) manipulates our racial prejudices, but we might ask whether such externalization succeeds in enlisting our empathy for a human situation that has been rendered trivial or banal in countless films and novels. Art's mouse mask underscores the artist's futile attempt in *Maus* to distance himself from a past that victimizes him, but the mask also establishes ironic distance. Students might spot masks worn by several characters in the meta-narrative episodes that foreground the problematic representation of the Holocaust. To put on a mask suggests adopting an identity that is not inborn. But what does it mean to put on the mask of a mouse-victim in contemporary America, where, presumably, the artist does not need to be a victim? Art has apparently transposed the role model of the survivor, just as Momik in *See Under: Love* adopts the identity of the Jew-victim in pictures of the Warsaw Ghetto he sees in the library (65–70). Such transposition enacts past trauma as if it were present, bringing order to the chaos of history as well as internalizing the identities of both perpetrators and victims (Kestenberg

148–49). This internalizing risks moral relativism, but it can also open up for us Primo Levi's "gray zone" of the Holocaust (36), where there are no clear-cut ethical choices.

By drawing attention to metacritical devices, we may also show how the telling cannot be extricated from its representation: Vladek's narration forms part of the son's retelling of it, while Momik's re-creation of the unknown past exists only in his imagining of fantasy tales. In *Maus*, the self-doubting memoir writer Art is the subject of his father's biography, but he needs to establish his own identity. Students will notice that the son, in telling his father's story, includes his father's behavior toward him as a replacement child or "memorial candle" (Wardi 34–36) for the lost Richieu. Art is treated as incompetent because he has not survived the Holocaust. Even at birth, he is made to feel guilty for jerking his broken arm like a Heil Hitler salute while exiting the womb. A class might focus on how these feelings of inferiority and guilt in the artist also indicate the father's hostility toward a replacement son who will never match up to what Richieu might have been. Art complains that the competition with a blurred photograph of Richieu on the wall is unfair (*And Here* 15). When, however, Vladek calls Art "Richieu," we should not see a "mistake of identities" (Bernard-Donals and Glejzer 75–76), for Art has in a sense become Richieu through the narration of his own history.

To forget the past may be to deny the Holocaust and desecrate the memory of the victims, but to be unable to forget the past can result in becoming paralyzed and emotionally crippled by it. Momik is thrown out by the two women in his life, Ruth and Ayala, because they refuse to be tortured by his living the Holocaust decades after it ended for everyone else (Grossman, *See Under* 157). What attitude, we may ask, toward a traumatic past might enable the next generation to be free of the crippling fears they have inherited and yet bear the burden of memory? Indeed, whose past is it? It is Art who insists on having the story told and who controls the narration, thus reclaiming it as his own story (for example, he includes his father's Holocaust prewar romance after promising his father not to retell it). In answering these questions, we should examine Art's feelings of guilt toward his mother, Anja, who committed suicide, as well as his resentment toward both her overpossessiveness and the Holocaust complex that imprisons him. Art wants to reclaim his mother's memory and demands her diary, which his father has destroyed. For Art, the destruction of the diary is a form of murder — killing his story — and the first volume ends with Art's calling his father "murderer" (159).

The father's story is the son's prehistory in more than one sense. The date on which Vladek's prophetic dream of his release from a German prisoner-of-war camp comes true is the date of Vladek's marriage to Anja and Art's birthday, which, we might observe, also makes it the day of Art's bar mitzvah, a confirmation into history and into the community of a murdered people. Art's story is both told and foretold (for example, by the Gypsy fortune-teller), while as listener he is egoistically unsympathetic to his father's complaints of illness or of mistreatment.

A careful reading of the text should not miss several instances of the intertwining of the Holocaust and post-Holocaust narratives. Art's transposition of the Holocaust to his own experience (as when Art quips he has to go home before "curfew" [*My Father* 67]) or his ironic exposure of the immeasurable gap between his experience and his father's underscores the damage inflicted by the trauma beyond the historical period of the Holocaust. Art's father has in a sense "not survived" (*And Here* 90), because he is still living out camp conditions — being stingy with matches, saving needless items, or organizing an exchange of goods at the grocery store. The Holocaust has not ended for Art or for Momik in *See Under: Love* in that they are living under its shadow. Momik, moreover, must contend with the erasure of the diasporic past and rewrite his family's suppressed screams into a universal discourse of disaster. He must ask the question that historical studies of the Holocaust do not answer: What would I have done had I been there, as a victim or as a perpetrator? Grossman comments that Momik must learn to answer that question by overcoming his defenses and cowardice and by deciding whether he lives to survive or survives to live ("Personal View" 45–46). Momik does not easily learn the meaning of the empty entry in the encyclopedia of the Holocaust in the novel's appendix, "love." He must teach his son to love, not to be a survivor. Failure of love or failure to love is a constant theme in Grossman.

Neither Grossman's nor Spiegelman's perspective is neutral or unmediated. Momik has rescued Wasserman's story, but he has also rescued it from history. The retrospective narration of *Maus*, framed by Vladek telling the story on his exercise bicycle, is likewise an example of such "backshadowing," the "shared knowledge of the outcome of a series of events by narrator and listener" that is "used to judge the participants in those events *as though they too should have known what was to come*" (Bernstein 16), effectively prefiguring the present to give the past structure and meaning. This is to see Holocaust trauma as a latent *Nachträglichkeit* that reinvents the past in the writing of history (Roth; Rothberg). For example, Art frames his parents' dilemma in occupied Poland with the graphic symbol of a crossroads in the shape of a swastika (*My Father* 125) to symbolize the mousetrap in which they are caught. In another frame, the figures of Art and Vladek walk away from a ghetto fence as the cinematic transition takes us back in time. We are constantly being reminded of the present family situation, and the story ends without reconciliation between father and son. The final frame of Vladek's and Anja's joint tombstone concludes both the father's Holocaust story and the son's post-Holocaust story.

Both Momik's and Art's storytelling marks the crucial separation stage at which the child of survivors can achieve the distance from the traumatic past necessary for individuation (Wardi 214–58). In a statement accompanied by images of the Jew-mouse, real rodent, and Mickey Mouse, Spiegelman has commented that *Maus* was meant to help people digest the bitter pill, not to make them feel they were done with the story. The telling of the story was nevertheless an important stage in the artist's leaving the role of memorial candle to become a responsible and loving mouse-father (not just in a mask), shown playing with his children, overshadowed by but now separate from the hanging corpses (Spiegelman, "Saying Good-Bye"). The dedication to both Richieu and Spiegelman's daughter Nadja in the second volume of *Maus*, accompanied by the photographic image of Art's lost sibling, establishes Art's role as carrier of memory, his place between the survivors and the next generation, and the place of this text in the transmission of both family and collective memory.

Maus and *See Under: Love* ask us to imagine the unimaginable through the artifice of art. Grossman's challenge to official discourse on the Holocaust and literary conventions offers an artistic vision in which history can be known through fiction and memory can be recovered through fantasy. The comix form of *Maus,* with its jokes and puns (like "Mauschwitz" or depicting a member of the *Judenrat* as a rat), spells out the gulf between representation and the horror of the real thing. Art has compensated for the inadequacy he feels in relation to his father's experiences as a survivor by researching the historical sources and telling his father's story graphically with the skill of a draftsman. Vladek is an equivocal ghost, like Hamlet's father, spurring the son on to tell his story but also to avenge his suffering. Here, revenge comes in the form of a cartoon that defies the Nazi vilification of Mickey Mouse.

The second generation has contributed a unique perspective to Holocaust literature, which includes the story of the transmission of memory from Holocaust survivors to their descendants, thus emphasizing the distance of contemporary writers from the "vicarious past" (Zeitlin). Telling the story of Holocaust victims is, moreover, both an attempt to form selves through narrative cohesion by mastering an impossible knowledge of an event that is known only through gaps in personal history and a "labor of remembrance" that tests the limits of knowing and not knowing (Friedman). For both Grossman and Spiegelman, in a paradoxical double bind, writing out the trauma is to return to it, but it is also a prerequisite of working through immeasurable loss and coming to terms with the past.

Works Cited

Bar-On, Dan. *Fear and Hope: Three Generations of the Holocaust.* Cambridge: Harvard UP, 1995.

Bauman, Zygmunt. "The Holocaust's Life as a Ghost." *Tikkun* 13.4 (1998): 33–38.

Berger, Alan L. *Children of Job: American Second-Generation Witnesses to the Holocaust.* Albany: State U of New York P, 1998.

Bernard-Donals, Michael, and Richard Glejzer. *Between Witness and Testimony: The Holocaust and the Limits of Representation.* Albany: State U of New York P, 2001.

Bernstein, Michael. *Foregone Conclusions: Against Apocalyptic History.* Berkeley: U of California P, 1994.

Bukiet, Melvin J. Introduction. *Nothing Makes You Free: Writings by Descendants of Jewish Holocaust Survivors.* Ed. Bukiet. New York: Norton, 2002. 11–23.

Epstein, Helen. *Children of the Holocaust: Conversations with Sons and Daughters of Survivors.* New York: Putnam, 1979.

Finkielkraut, Alain. *The Imaginary Jew.* Trans. Kevin O'Neill and David Suchoff. Lincoln: U of Nebraska P, 1997.

Fox, Tamar. *Inherited Memories: Israeli Children of Holocaust Survivors.* New York: Continuum, 1999.

Friedländer, Saul. Introduction. *Probing the Limits of Representation: Nazism and the "Final Solution."* Ed. Friedländer. Cambridge: Harvard UP, 1992. 1–21.

Friedman, Michelle A. "The Labor of Remembrance." *Mapping Jewish Identities.* Ed. Laurence Silberstein. New York: New York UP, 2000. 97–121.

Furman, Andrew, *Contemporary Jewish American Writers and the Multicultural Dilemma: The Return of the Exiled.* Syracuse: Syracuse UP, 2000.

Grossman, David. *See Under: Love.* Trans. Betsy Rosenberg. New York: Farrar, 1989.

———. "*See Under: Love*: A Personal View." *Judaism* 51.1 (2002): 42–50.

Hass, Aaron. *In the Shadow of the Holocaust: The Second Generation.* Cambridge: Cambridge UP, 1996.

Hirsch, Marianne. *Family Frames: Photography, Narrative, and Postmemory.* Cambridge: Harvard UP, 1997.

Horowitz, Sara R. "Auto/Biography and Fiction after Auschwitz: Probing the Boundaries of Second-Generation Aesthetics." *Breaking Crystal: Writing and Memory after Auschwitz.* Ed. Efraim Sicher. Urbana: U of Illinois P, 1998. 276–94.

Kestenberg, Judith. "Rachel M.'s Metapsychological Assessment." *Generations of the Holocaust.* Ed. Martin S. Bergmann and Milton E. Jucovy. New York: Basic, 1982. 145–58.

Levi, Primo. *The Drowned and the Saved.* Trans. Raymond Rosenthal. New York: Vintage, 1989.

Morahg, Gilead. "Israel's New Literature of the Holocaust: The Case of David Grossman's *See Under: Love.*" *Modern Fiction Studies* 45 (1999): 457–79.

Ozick, Cynthia. *The Messiah of Stockholm.* New York: Knopf, 1987.

Raczymow, Henri. "Memory Shot Through with Holes." *Yale French Studies* 85 (1994): 102–03.

Rosenbaum, Thane. "Memory's Ghosts." *Tikkun* 14.1 (1999): 59–60.

———. *Second Hand Smoke: A Novel.* New York: St. Martin's, 1999.

Roth, Michael S. *The Ironist's Cage: Memory, Trauma, and the Construction of History.* New York: Columbia UP, 1995.

Rothberg, Michael. *Traumatic Realism: The Demands of Holocaust Representation.* Minneapolis: U of Minnesota P, 2000.

Sicher, Efraim. "The Future of the Past: Countermemory and Postmemory in Contemporary American Post-Holocaust Narratives." *History and Memory* 12.2 (2000): 56–91.

———. "The Return of the Past: The Intergenerational Transmission of Holocaust Memory in Israeli Fiction." *Shofar* 19.2 (2001): 26–52.

Sokoloff, Naomi B. *Imagining the Child in Modern Jewish Fiction.* Baltimore: Johns Hopkins UP, 1992.

Spiegelman, Art. *And Here My Troubles Began.* New York: Pantheon, 1991. Vol. 2 of *Maus: A Survivor's Tale.*

———. *My Father Bleeds History.* New York: Pantheon, 1986. Vol. 1 of *Maus: A Survivor's Tale.*

———. "Saying Good-Bye to *Maus*." *Tikkun* 7.5 (1992): 44–45.

Tabachnick, Stephen E. "Of *Maus* and Memory: The Structure of Art Spiegelman's Graphic Novel of the Holocaust." *Word and Image* 9 (1993): 154–62.

Wardi, Dina. *Memorial Candles: Children of the Holocaust.* Trans. Naomi Goldblum. London: Routledge, 1992.

Zeitlin, Froma. "The Vicarious Witness: Belated Memory and Authorial Presence in Recent Holocaust Literature." *History and Memory* 10.2 (1998): 5–42.

James E. Young

Teaching German Memory and Countermemory: The End of the Holocaust Monument in Germany

Among the hundreds of submissions in the 1995 competition for a German national memorial to the murdered Jews of Europe, one seemed an especially uncanny embodiment of the impossible questions at the heart of Germany's memorial process. The artist Horst Hoheisel, already well known for his negative-form monument in Kassel, proposed a simple, if provocative, antisolution to the memorial competition: blow up the Brandenburg Gate, grind its stone into dust, sprinkle the remains over its former site, and then cover the entire memorial area with granite plates. How better to remember a destroyed people than by a destroyed monument? Instead of commemorating the destruction of a people with the construction of yet another edifice, Hoheisel would mark one destruction with another destruction. Instead of filling in the void left by a murdered people with a positive form, the artist would carve out an empty space in Berlin by which to recall a now absent people. Rather than concretize and thereby displace the memory of Europe's murdered Jews, the artist would open a place in the landscape to be filled with the memory of those who come to remember Europe's murdered Jews. A landmark celebrating Prussian might and crowned by the quadriga, a chariot bearing the Roman goddess of peace, would be demolished to make room for the memory of Jewish victims of German might and peacelessness. In fact, perhaps no single emblem better represents the conflicted, self-abnegating motives for memory in Germany today than the vanishing monument.[1]

Of course, such a memorial undoing would never be sanctioned by the German government, and this impossibility too was part of the artist's point. Hoheisel's proposed destruction of the Brandenburg Gate participated in the competition for a national Holocaust memorial even as the radicalism of his proposal ruled out any chance of its execution. At least part of the polemic of Hoheisel's idea, therefore, was directed against actually building any winning design, against ever finishing the monument at all. He seemed to suggest that the surest engagement with Holocaust memory in Germany may actually lie in its perpetual irresolution, that only an unfinished memorial process can guarantee the life of memory. For it may be the finished monument that completes memory, puts a cap on memory work, and draws a bottom line underneath an era that must always haunt Germany. Better a thousand years of Holocaust memorial competitions in Germany than any single "final solution" to Germany's memorial problem.[2]

Like other cultural and aesthetic forms in Europe and the United States, the monument — in both idea and practice — has undergone a radical transformation over the course of the twentieth century. As an intersection of public art and political memory, the monument has necessarily reflected the aesthetic and political revolutions, as well as the wider crises of representation, following all this century's major upheavals — including World Wars I and II, the Vietnam War, and the rise and fall of Communist regimes in the former Soviet Union and its Eastern European satellites. In every case, the monument reflects its sociohistorical and aesthetic contexts: artists working in eras of cubism, expressionism, socialist realism, earthworks, minimalism, or conceptual art remain answerable both to art and to the needs of official history. The result has been a metamorphosis of the monument from the heroic, self-aggrandizing figurative icons of the late nineteenth century, celebrating national ideals and triumphs, to the antiheroic, often ironic and self-effacing, conceptual installations marking the national ambivalence and uncertainty of late-twentieth-century postmodernism.

In fact, Andreas Huyssen has even suggested that in a contemporary age of mass memory production and consumption, there seems to be an inverse proportion between the memorialization of the past and its contemplation and study (11). Once we assign monumental form to memory, we have to some degree divested ourselves of the obligation to remember. In the eyes of modern critics and artists, the traditional monument's essential stiffness and grandiose pretensions to permanence thus doom the monument to an archaic, premodern status. Even worse, by insisting that its meaning is as fixed as its place in the landscape, the monument seems oblivious to the essential mutability in all cultural artifacts, to the ways the significance in all art evolves over time. In this way, monuments have long sought to provide a naturalizing locus for memory, in which a state's triumphs and martyrs, its ideals and founding myths, are cast as naturally true as the landscape in which they stand. These are the monument's sustaining illusions, the principles of its seeming longevity and power. But as several generations of artists—modern and postmodern alike—have made clear, neither the monument nor its meaning is everlasting. Both a monument and its significance are constructed in particular times and places, contingent on the political, historical, and aesthetic realities of the moment.

Unlike the utopian, revolutionary forms with which modernists hoped to redeem art and literature after World War I, much post-Holocaust literature and art is pointedly antiredemptory. The post-Holocaust memory artist would claim not only that art is not the answer but also that after the Holocaust there can be no more final solutions. Some of this skepticism has been a direct response to the enormity of the Holocaust, which seemed to exhaust not only the forms of modernist experimentation and innovation but also the traditional meanings still reified in such innovations. Mostly, however, the skepticism stems from these artists' contempt for the religious, political, or aesthetic linking of destruction and redemption that seemed to justify such terror in the first place.

In Germany, once the land of what Saul Friedländer has called "redemptory anti-Semitism," the possibility that art might redeem mass murder with beauty (or with ugliness) or that memorials might redeem Germany's past by instrumentalizing memory continues to haunt a postwar generation of memory artists (3). Moreover, these artists in Germany are both plagued and inspired by a series of impossible questions about memorials: How does a state incorporate shame into its national memorial landscape? How does a state recite and even commemorate the litany of its misdeeds, making them part of its reason for being? Under what memorial aegis and whose rules does a nation remember its barbarity? Where is the tradition for memorial mea culpa, since remembrance and self-indictment seem so hopelessly at odds? Unlike state-sponsored memorials built by victimized nations and peoples in Poland, Holland, or Israel, such memorials in Germany are necessarily those of the persecutor remembering its victims. In the face of this necessary breach in the conventional memorial code, it is little wonder that German national memory of the Holocaust remains so torn and convoluted. Germany's Jewish question is now a two-pronged memorial question: How does a nation mourn the victims of a mass murder perpetrated in its name? How does a nation reunite itself on the bedrock memory of its horrendous crimes? These questions constitute the heart of Germany's struggle with its national memory of the Holocaust.

Nearly fifty years after the defeat of the Nazi regime, contemporary artists in Germany still have difficulty separating the monument form from Germany's fascist past. German memory artists are heirs to a double-edged postwar legacy: a distrust of monumental forms in the light of their systematic exploitation by the Nazis and a desire to distinguish the postwar generation from that of the killers through memory (see Winzen). In the eyes of postwar memory artists, the didactic logic of monuments — their demagogic rigidity and certainty of history — continues to recall too closely traits associated with fascism. How else would totalitarian regimes commemorate themselves except through totalitarian art like the monument? Conversely, how better to celebrate the fall of totalitarian regimes than by celebrating the fall of their monuments? A monument against fascism, therefore, would have to be a monument against itself—against the traditionally didactic function of monuments; against their tendency to displace the past they demand we contemplate; and, finally, against the authoritarian propensity in monumental spaces that reduces viewers to passive spectators.

One of the most fascinating results of Germany's memorial conundrum has been the advent of its countermonuments: brazen, painfully self-conscious memorial spaces conceived to challenge their very premises. At home in an era of earthworks and conceptual and self-destructive art, a postwar generation of artists now explores both the necessity of memory and its incapacity to recall events not directly experienced. Instead of seeking to capture the memory of events, therefore, these artists recall primarily their own relation to events, the great gulf of time between them and the Holocaust. For this generation of German artists, the possibility that memory of such grave events might be reduced to exhibitions of public craftsmanship or cheap pathos remains intolerable. They contemptuously reject the traditional forms of and reasons for public memorial art, seeing those memorial spaces as either consoling viewers, redeeming tragic events, indulging in a facile kind of *Wiedergutmachung* ("making amends"), or purporting to mend the memory of a murdered people. They fear that instead of searing memory and arousing public consciousness, conventional memorials seal memory off from awareness altogether; they find that instead of embodying memory, memorials may only displace memory. These artists fear that to the extent that we encourage monuments to do our memory work for us, we become that much more forgetful. They believe in effect that the initial impulse to memorialize events like the Holocaust may actually spring from an opposite and equal desire to forget them.

In the pages that follow, I recall countermonuments I have already discussed at much greater length elsewhere and add to the discussion with more examples. In this way, I refine and adumbrate the concept of countermonuments in Germany and the ways they have begun to constitute something akin to a national form that pits itself squarely against recent attempts to build a national memorial to the murdered Jews of Europe in the center of the country's reunited capital, Berlin. I find that the ongoing debate in Germany has been instructive in my own consideration of the monument's future in this decidedly antiredemptory age. I suggest that this debate be brought into classes about the representation of the Holocaust.

Widely regarded as two of Europe's most provocative artists of erasure and self-abnegation, Jochen Gerz and Esther Shalev-Gerz are still best known for their disappearing Monument against Fascism in Harburg-Hamburg, dedicated in 1986. It consisted of a twelve-meter-high lead-covered column that was sunk into the ground as people inscribed their names (and much else) onto its surface; on its complete disappearance in 1993, the artists hoped that it would return the burden of memory to those who came looking for it. With audacious simplicity, their countermonument thus flouted memorial conventions: its aim was not to console but to provoke, not to remain fixed but to change, not to be everlasting but to disappear, not to be ignored by its passersby but to demand interaction, not to remain pristine but to invite its own violation, not to accept graciously the burden of memory but to throw it back at the town's feet.[3]

These questions not only constitute the conflicted heart of Germany's struggle with its national memory of the Holocaust but also throw into sharp relief what it is monuments anywhere can and cannot do, how they remember and how they forget. Since part of teaching the Holocaust necessarily includes how these events are being remembered and passed down to the next generation, the study of German countermonuments provides an illuminating prism through which German memory and its public face might be taught and understood.

Celebrated in Germany for his hand in Harburg's vanishing monument, Jochen Gerz became a guest professor at the School of Fine Arts in Saarbrücken in 1991. In a studio class he devoted to conceptual monuments, he invited his students to participate in a clandestine memory project, what he regarded as a kind of guerrilla memorial action. The class agreed, swore themselves to secrecy, and listened as Gerz described his plan. Under the cover of night, eight students would steal into the great cobblestone square leading to the Saarbrücker Schloss, former home of the Gestapo during Hitler's Reich. Carrying book bags laden with cobblestones removed from other parts of the city, the students would spread themselves across the square, sit in pairs, swill beer, and yell at one another in raucous voices, pretending to have a party. All the while, they would in fact stealthily pry loose cobblestones from the square and replace them with the similar-sized stones they had brought along, each embedded underneath with a nail so that they could be located later with a metal detector. Within days, this part of the memorial mission had been accomplished as planned (Gerz).

Meanwhile, other members of the class had been assigned to research the names and locations of every former Jewish cemetery in Germany—over two thousand of them—that had been abandoned or destroyed or that had vanished. When their classmates returned from their beer party, bags heavy with cobblestones, all set to work engraving the names of missing Jewish cemeteries on the stones, one by one. The night after they finished, the memory guerrillas returned the stones to their original places, each inscribed and dated. But in a twist wholly consistent with the Gerzes' previous countermonument, the stones were replaced facedown, leaving no trace of the entire operation. The memorial would be invisible, itself only a memory, out of sight and therefore, Gerz hoped, in mind. As visitors flocked to the square looking for seventy out of over eight thousand stones, they too began to wonder where they stood vis-à-vis the memorial. Were they standing on it? In it? Was it really there at all? On searching for memory, Gerz hoped, the visitors would realize that such memory was already in them. This would be an interior memorial: as the only standing forms in the square, the visitors would become the memorials for which they searched. In effect, Jochen Gerz's *2,160 Stones: A Monument against Racism* returns the burden of memory to those who come looking for it.

Gerz is not the only German artist to have adapted what might be regarded as Jewish memorial motifs to recall the nation's missing

Jews. Having already designed a negative-form monument in Kassel to commemorate a pyramid fountain destroyed by Nazis in 1938 because they considered it the Jews' fountain, Hoheisel turned to the next generation of monuments with a new, more pedagogically inclined project.[4] With permission from the local public schools in Kassel, Hoheisel visited dozens of grade-school classrooms with a book, a stone, and a piece of paper. The book was a copy of *Namen und Schicksale der Juden Kassels* (The Names and Fates of Kassel's Jews). In his classroom visits, he told students the story of Kassel's vanished Jewish community, how they had once thrived in Kassel, lived in the houses where these schoolchildren now lived, and had sat at the same classroom desks. He then asked all the children who knew any Jews to raise their hands. When no hand appeared, Hoheisel would read the story of one of Kassel's deported Jews from his memory book. At the end of his reading, he invited each of the students to research the life of one of Kassel's deported Jews — where the person had lived and how, who this person's family was, how old he or she had been, what the person had looked like. He then asked the schoolchildren to visit Kassel's formerly Jewish neighborhoods and to meet the German neighbors of Kassel's deported Jews.

After this, students were asked to write short narratives describing the lives and deaths of their subjects. Then they wrapped these narratives around cobblestones and deposited them in one of the archival bins the artist had provided every school. When the bins began to overflow, new ones were furnished. In time, Hoheisel transported all these bins to Kassel's railroad station, where he stacked them on the platform from which Kassel's Jews were deported. It is now a permanent installation, what the artist is calling his *Denk-Stein Sammlung* (Memorial-Stone Archive). This memorial cairn — a witness pile of stones — marks both the site of deportation and the community's education about its murdered Jews, whose absence is now marked by an evolving memorial. Combining narrative and stone in this way, the artist and students have adopted the most Jewish of memorial forms as their own — thereby enlarging their memorial lexicon to recall the absent people. After all, only they are now left to write the epitaph of the missing Jews, known and emblematized primarily by their absence and the void they have left behind.

In another installation, the artist Micha Ullmann has also turned to both bookish themes and negative spaces to represent the void left behind by the people of the book. To commemorate the infamous Nazi book burning of 10 May 1933, the city of Berlin invited Ullmann, an Israeli-born conceptual and installation artist, to design a monument for Berlin's Bebelplatz. Today, the cobblestone expanse of the Bebelplatz is still empty of all forms except the figures of visitors who stand in it and peer down through a ground-level window into the ghostly white, underground room of empty shelves Ullmann has installed. A steel tablet set into the stones recalls that the square was the site of some of the most notorious book burnings and quotes Heinrich Heine's famously prescient words, "Where books are burned, so one day will people be burned as well" (my trans.). The shelves are still empty, unreplenished, and it is the absence of both people and books that is marked here in yet one more empty memorial pocket.

Similarly haunted by absence and skeptical of the traditional memorial's tendency to gather pervasive memory into a single spot, Renata Stih and Frieder Schnock won a 1993 competition to create a memorial in Berlin's Schöneberg neighborhood to its murdered Jews. They proposed to mount eighty signposts on the corners, streets, and sidewalks in and around the Bayerischer Platz. Each would include a simple image of an everyday object on one side and a short text on the other, excerpted from Germany's anti-Jewish laws of the 1930s and 1940s. For example, on one side of such a sign pedestrians would see a hand-drawn sidewalk hopscotch pattern and on the other its accompanying 1938 text, "Arischen und nichtarischen Kindern wird das Spielen miteinander untersagt" ("Aryan and non-Aryan children are not allowed to play together"). Or they might see a red park bench on a green lawn alongside the 1939 law "Juden dürfen am Bayerischen Platz nur die gelb markierten Sitzbänke benutzen" ("On Bavarian Place, Jews may sit only on yellow park benches") or a pair of swim trunks accompanied by the 3 December

1938 notice "Berliner Badeanstalten und Schwimmbäder dürfen von Juden nicht betreten werden" ("Baths and swimming pools in Berlin are closed to Jews") or a black-and-white rotary telepone dial with the 29 July 1940 announcement "Telefonanschlüsse von Juden werden von der Post gekündigt" ("Telephone lines to Jewish households will be cut off"; see Stih and Schnock).

With the approval of the Berlin Senate, which sponsored the memorial competition, the artists put their signs up on light posts throughout the Bayerischer Platz without announcement, provoking a flurry of complaints and calls to the police that neo-Nazis had invaded the neighborhood with antisemitic signs. Thus reassured that the public had taken notice, the artists pointed out that these same laws had been posted and announced no less publicly at the time but had provoked no such response by Germans then. At least part of the artists' point was that the laws during Hitler's Reich were as public as the memory of them in 1993. Indeed, one sign with the image of an office file even reminds local residents, "All files dealing with anti-Semitic activities [were] to be destroyed" (16 Feb. 1945), and another image of interlocking Olympic rings recalls, "Anti-Semitic signs in Berlin [were] temporarily removed for the 1936 Olympic Games." That is, for the artists, even the absence of signs was an extension of the crime. Stih and Schnock recognize that the Nazi persecution of the Jews was designed to be a self-consuming Holocaust, a self-effacing crime.

The only contemporary signs of Jewish life in this once-Jewish neighborhood are the posted laws that paved the way for the Jews' deportation and murder. As part of the cityscape, Stih explains, these images and texts would "infiltrate the daily lives of Berliners" no less than did the publicly posted laws that curtailed the daily lives of Jews between 1933 and 1945. And by posting these signs separately, forcing pedestrians to happen upon them one or two at a time, the artists can show how the laws incrementally "removed Jews from the social realm," from the protection of law (Nicolai). These places of remembrance would remind local citizens that the murder of the neighborhood's Jews happened not overnight or in a fell swoop but over time—and with the tacit acknowledgment of the community. Where past citizens once navigated their lives according to these laws, present citizens would now navigate their lives according to the memory of such laws.

For Americans watching Germany's memorial culture come to terms with the Holocaust, at least two profound lessons begin to emerge: the monument has limitations and capabilities, and any nation, including the United States, has a limited capacity to make the memory of its crimes part and parcel of a memorial legacy. As provocative and difficult as countermonuments may be, they thus seem to embody both the German memorial difficulties and the limitations of the traditional monument. The most important space of memory for these artists has been not in the ground or above it but between the memorial and the viewer, between the viewer and the viewer's memory: the memorial has been in the viewer's mind, heart, and conscience. To this end, countermonuments have attempted to embody the ambiguity and difficulty of Holocaust memorialization in Germany in conceptual, sculptural, and architectural forms that would return the burden of memory to those who come looking for it. Instead of creating self-contained sites of memory, detached from our daily lives, these artists force visitors and local citizens to look within themselves for memory and at their actions and motives for memory in these spaces. Disappearing, invisible, and other countermonuments have attempted to build into these spaces, where every new generation will find its own significance in this past, the capacity for changing memory.

The countermonument reminds us that the best German memorial to the fascist era and its victims may be not a single memorial at all but simply the never-to-be-resolved debate over which kind of memory to preserve, how to do it, in whose name, and to what end. That is, what are the consequences of such memory? How do Germans respond to current persecutions of foreigners in their midst in the light of their memory of the Third Reich and its crimes? Instead of a fixed sculptural or architectural icon for Holocaust memory in Germany, the debate itself—perpetually unresolved amid ever-changing conditions—might now be enshrined.

Notes

1. This essay is adapted from Young, *At Memory's Edge*. In it, I elaborate and expand on themes I first explored in "The Counter-monument: Memory against Itself in Germany Today." See also Young (*Texture*).
2. For a record of this competition, see *Denkmal*. For a collection of essays arguing against building this monument, see *Wettbewerb*.
3. For a detailed discussion of the Harburg countermonument, see Young (*Texture*). Also see Konneke.
4. For more on Hoheisel's negative-form monument, see Young ("Counter-monument").

Works Cited

Denkmal für die ermordeten Juden Europas: Kurzdokumentation. Berlin: Senatsverwaltung für Bau- und Wohnungswesen, 1995.

Friedländer, Saul. *The Years of Persecution.* New York: Harper, 1997. Vol. 1 of *Nazi Germany and the Jews.*

Gerz, Jochen. *2146 Steine: Mahnmal gegen Rassismus-Saarbrücken.* Stuttgart: Hatje, 1993.

Huyssen, Andreas. "Monument and Memory in a Post-modern Age." *The Art of Memory: Holocaust Memorials in History.* Ed. James E. Young, Munich: Prestel, 1994. 9–17.

Konneke, Achim, ed. *Das Harburger Mahnmal gegen Faschismus / The Harburg Monument against Fascism.* Hamburg: Hatje, 1994.

Nicolai, Bernd. "Bus Stop—the Non-monument: On the Impossibility of a Final Memorial to the Murdered Jews of Europe." *Bus Stop Fahrplan.* Ed. Renate Stih and Frieder Schnock. Berlin: Neue Gesellschaft für Bildende Kunst, 1995. N. pag.

Stih, Renata, and Frieder Schnock. *Arbeitsbuch für ein Denkmal in Berlin: Orte des Erinnerns im Bayerischen Viertel—Ausgrenzung und Entrechtung, Vertreibung, Deportation und Ermordung von Berliner Juden in den Jahren 1933 bis 1945.* Berlin: Gatza, 1993.

Der Wettbewerb für das "Denkmal für die ermordeten Juden Europas": Eine Streitschrift. Berlin: Kunst / Neue Gesellschaft für Bildende Kunst, 1995.

Winzen, Matthias. "The Need for Public Representation and the Burden of the German Past." *Art Journal* 48 (1989): 309–14.

Young, James E. *At Memory's Edge: After-images of the Holocaust in Contemporary Art and Architecture.* New Haven: Yale UP, 2000.

———. "The Counter-monument: Memory against Itself in Germany Today." *Critical Inquiry* 18 (1992): 267–96.

———. *The Texture of Memory: Holocaust Memorials and Meaning.* New Haven: Yale UP, 1993.

David Bathrick

Teaching Visual Culture and the Holocaust

Visual representations of the Holocaust have proved to be an absolutely integral but also highly contested means by which to understand and remember the Nazi atrocities of World War II. Beginning with the black-and-white photographic images emerging from the concentration and death camps in the spring of 1945, media visualizations served for some as virtual access to and knowledge of the horror; in a few cases, such visualizations even provided preeminent verification that it actually happened. The little boy with his hands raised in the Warsaw Ghetto; the starving, liberated prisoners staring gauntly into American cameras; the piles of corpses; the barbed wire; the mounds of hair; even the engineer on the train to Treblinka looking back at us in Claude Lanzmann's film *Shoah*—these are but a few of the pictorial icons by which many have sought to contain the unimaginable.

Even as these images seem to convey evidence or iconic certitude, intense concerns have arisen about the propriety, in some cases even the possibility, of visually representing the reality of the camps. In writing about the "limits" of Holocaust representation, the historian Saul Friedländer warns against "transgressing" certain "intangible" boundaries, against "banalizing" or "distorting" the record by means of "grossly inadequate representations" (3). While Friedländer's entreaty remains intentionally nonspecific, the authority of his caveat is as insistent as it is familiar in discussions of Holocaust representation: Thou shalt not . . .

Thou shalt not what? And why? This essay explores the dos and don'ts, the limits and transgressions, the aesthetic quandaries and their attempted solutions that have marked some of the creative and discursive controversies in one area of Holocaust visualization, namely, the representation of the camps and the processes of extermination. Central to my concern are questions that often prove helpful in teaching such material. In what ways have images of the Shoah facilitated or inhibited our understanding of it? How are the difficulties of pictorial visualization connected to larger issues of cultural and collective knowing and remembering? What are the potentialities and limitations of different visual media (photograph, film, television, artifact, comic book), aesthetic styles (realism, modernism, postmodernism), or genres (comedy, melodrama, documentary) in representing the Shoah? How have these issues changed as a part of the postmemorialization of second and third generations?

In the Beginning Was the Photograph

The initial photographs of the camps taken by amateur and professional photographers fighting with or accompanying the invading Allied armies have had an immediate and lasting effect on how the event is remembered *as well as* repressed. While the use of these photographs as part of the pedagogical, juridical, and political discourses immediately following the war has been debated over the years,[1] in a broader, epistemological sense they have also helped shape questions and issues at the very core of artistically representing the Holocaust.

One issue concerns the process by which photographic images of the camps have been received and interpreted, the nature of people's affective response to them, and the problems involved in properly decoding their meaning. Some have suggested that the photographs' powerful emotional impact clouds the viewer's understanding, that these "icons of destruction" (Brink) anesthetize and transfix, rendering the viewer paralyzed and incapable of critical thought. In direct contrast to such Brechtian admonishment about identification and excess emotion, Geoffrey Hartman asks, in the light of the potential deadening effect from repeated display of such images, whether "our capacity for sympathy is finite and soon exhausted" and whether we become "desensitized" over time, unable to locate the origins of our collective outrage and public remembering (152).

Such worries about emotional response and the surfeit of exposure have been countered more recently by those who point out that despite the plenitude of visual documentation, "people are becoming increasingly aware that the number of images which spontaneously come to mind when speaking of the concentration or extermination camps is seriously limited" (Brink 9).[2] And this narrowness exists despite the existence of over "two million photos in the public archives of more than twenty countries" (Milton). Why, then, with such abundant images has the visual landscape become so impoverished? And what is the impact of such redundancy on the power of these images to communicate?

In responding to these and related questions, it is important to stress to students that the photographic image was always a doubly coded one. On the one hand, it functions as index, which like filmic representation attributes "a material, physical, and thus extremely potent connection between image and referent" (Hirsch, "Surviving Images" 223). As a medium of technological duplication, photography and cinema participated in a tradition of nineteenth-century mechanically reproduced mimesis, which claimed the legitimacy of documentary, empirical verisimilitude. In this vein, the early pictures from the concentration camps were seen by many to provide unquestioned factual corroboration of a truth that spoke for itself. The pictures stood at once as a trace of the real and its self-evident interpretation; they offered information, data, and witness while accusing, arguing, warning, and even convicting.

On the other hand, as much as the images of the camps served both an evidentiary and a prosecutorial function after the war, the increased narrowing over the years of this public archive to a smaller selection of ever-repeated images transformed their status from witness into icon. Being limited in number and thereby universally legible, the repeated images achieved the status of a global language. Iconic images express an aura of timelessness and a lack of spatial specificity. They claim implicitly to tell the whole story. In the "atrocity films," as they were called at the Nuremberg trials, iconic images gradually came to stand for Nazi crimes in toto. The images, emblematically conflating concentration and death camps into an Auschwitz in extremis, represent at once the absolute telos of Nazi ideology and the Nazi practice of total annihilation. As icon, the camp photograph thus plays a vital role "vicariously" (Young 2) for second and third generations seeking to postremember and thereby reembody an experience that cannot be directly theirs. Such iconic images provide both a window of insight — points of mourning and "negative epiphany" (Sontag 19) — and a focal perspective with an unavoidably blinkered lens.

The plausible, even seductive transparency of the camp photograph as index and as icon challenges teachers and students to read against their grain of immediacy and fascination, to resist the "ideology of pure perception" (Jenks 6) inherent in positivist notions of visualization. In so doing, we accept the limits of what we can and cannot know. The information lurking in the frame of the self-evident snapshot can be excavated only by resituating and destabilizing the image.

One scholar who in the early 1950s accepted such a challenge was Hannah Arendt. In *The Origins of Totalitarianism*, she addresses what she calls "misleading" impressions imparted by many of the Allied photos immediately after the war. These photos mislead us, she contends, because they depict almost exclusively concentration camps to the west at a specific moment of chaos and disintegration in the final days of the war and not how the camps as a whole functioned for most of the three years before that. The mountains of dead and half-dead bodies were transformed by these photos into the reality of the camps, although none of them were extermination camps (Arendt 219). These images portrayed a zone of the unnatural by appealing to a set of iconic signifiers that opened viewers up to the seemingly medieval dimension of the crimes depicted, while blinding viewers to the enormity of mass industrial death found in extermination camps to the east, such as Auschwitz, Maidanek, and Treblinka.

It is important for students to understand that the photograph and film documentation used by the Americans and British for educational and juridical purposes after the war depicted the liberation of concentration camps in the borders of the Third Reich (Buchenwald, Belsen, Dachau, etc.) between mid-April and early May of 1945. Most of these images were produced by the United States Army Signal Corps, which "provided roughly one half of all the images of that much photographed war" (Barnouw 6). One must read these images as a specific moment in a vast process of destruction and breakdown. Before their liberation, camps like Buchenwald had served as pools of forced labor where inmates succumbed over time to exhaustion or illness as a result of malnutrition, debilitating labor, and brutally punitive retribution.

In Auschwitz, however, at the height of its efficiency in the fall of 1944, eight thousand to ten thousand victims a day were gassed and partly incinerated. When the Red Army arrived on 27 January 1945, there were no accumulated mountains of corpses. As visual evidence of the extermination itself, of course, there are and can be no pictures—either by the perpetrators or by the victims. It seems fitting, therefore, that one of the primary visual icons for Auschwitz situates the viewer at a distance looking down the train tracks leading to—and through—the entrance to Birkenau. Here the absence of image speaks through the silence of a metonymic photo. Beyond the gate of Birkenau there is nothing to see.

Image/Story Trouble: What Should Not and Cannot Be Seen?

The absence of image is also to be found in the epochal nonenunciation of the *Muselmann*. As described at length in the survivor literature by people like Bruno Bettelheim, Primo Levi, Jean Améry, and Ruth Klüger, the *Muselmann*, adapted from the German word for "Muslim," was the product of a policy where the SS deliberately set out to break down their victims by starving and working them to near extinction, by turning them into docile, wandering, spectral half dead. "He was a staggering corpse," wrote Améry, "a bundle of physical functions in its last convulsions. As hard as it may be for us, we must exclude him from our considerations" (9).

The *Muselmann* has remained an almost invisible figure in many representations of the Shoah. Giorgio Agamben notes that it is "a striking fact that although all witnesses speak of him as a central experience, the *Muselmann* is barely named in the historical studies on the destruction of European Jewry" (52).[3] Agamben registers a similar absence of visual representations of this figure. Describing a film clip from some documentary footage taken by the Allies in Bergen-Belson "of what seem to be living people, a group of prisoners . . . wandering on foot like ghosts," he concludes by commenting that "with the exception of a few drawings by Aldo Carpi which he did from memory, [the film clip] is perhaps the sole image of *Muselmänner* we have" (51).

The question about the void of visual portrayals of the *Muselmann*, particularly in the domain of mass-mediated culture, touches directly on the broader issue of whether and how to represent certain dimensions of the camp experience visually. Clear from the survivor accounts is the extent to which the phenomenon of the *Muselmann* is closely linked to what Primo Levi has called the "gray zone" (*Drowned* 36–69). Bettelheim and other survivors describe their mixed feelings of pity, anxiety, and revulsion at the sight of the *Muselmann*, understandably projecting onto him or her an anger or angst about their own imminent systematic transformation into a nonhuman being (Bettelheim 156). Levi goes so far as to acknowledge a kind of institutionalized complicity with the SS among prisoners for whom survival meant that, faced with a "vacillator," they would "knock [the person] aside, because it is in no one's interest that there will be one more *Muselmann* dragging himself to work every day" (*Survival* 88).

Levi's depiction of the gray zone lays bare a veritable zoology of

collaborative hierarchies and behaviors called into existence by the
rapacity of the SS. Here a teacher might ask in a classroom discussion if one can or should represent a network of camp relationships
that "cannot be reduced to the two blocks, victims and perpetrators," where survival often occurred as the result of some form of
collaboration or complicity. "The gray zone possesses an incredibly
complicated internal structure and contains within itself enough to
confuse our need to judge" (*Drowned* 42). Can one visualize as an
artist creatively, or for that matter perceive, a traumatic circumstance
and at the same time resist the "need to judge"?[4]

Difficulties that have arisen in the effort to depict cinematically
characters and narratives that inhabit the gray zone may best be illustrated through a brief discussion of Gillo Pontecorvo's 1960 film
entitled *Kapo*. This Italian-French production tells the story of the
transformation of a sensitive Jewish teenager, Edith, into a fierce and
tough-minded prisoner named Nicole. The heroine's metamorphosis
from innocent to Kapo[5] is depicted as a savage struggle for survival
at any cost. Reduced to near starvation and beaten into submission,
Nicole's ensuing behavior is a response in kind: stealing a potato
from a fellow prisoner leads to stealing socks off the feet of a murdered friend, which in turn leads Nicole to offer sexual favors to the
SS for privilege and power. As female Kapo in a labor camp for political prisoners, she indulges in particularly brutal treatment of her
underlings — until she suddenly falls in love with the Soviet prisoner
Sasha, is converted to the cause of collective revolt, and sacrifices her
life in an unsuccessful attempt at liberation of the camp.

Some have criticized *Kapo* for its overreliance on the generic
codes of Hollywood melodrama as well as for its ideologically motivated folding of the Holocaust survival story into a socialist realist
morality play about the beauty of collective death (Insdorf 156–59).
While both criticisms seem valid at a purely generic level, what remains unaddressed in this coding is the larger question about the legitimacy, indeed the possibility, of such a narrative. *Kapo*'s deus ex
machina in the final scenes foregrounds the redemptive reconversion
of the film's heroine. Nicole reassumes her Jewish identity and her
status as a loving human being. Her reconversion points also to a

structural disavowal of the issues that lie at the heart of the Kapo story, which is related by survivors, and of the larger nonnarratives of those who did not survive — regardless of where any of the victims stood on any moral ladder.

Of the *Muselmann*, Levi writes that all those "who finish in the gas chambers have the same story, *or more exactly, have no story* [my emphasis]; they followed the slope down to the bottom, like streams that run to the sea." His recounting of the prototypically "disquieting" stories of "the Kapo, the cook, the nurse, the night guard and even the hut-sweeper" is scarcely more elevating and as a potential tale of redemption highly "improbable" (*Survival* 90). Here we find a story of the end of story, told of course as part of a survival narrative. Its discursive acknowledgment of such a contradiction is itself an act of mourning.

As a counter to the *Trauerarbeit* ("work of mourning") of a book such as Levi's *Survival in Auschwitz*, we are confronted in *Kapo* with "narrative fetishism," which Erich Santner has so aptly defined as

> the construction and deployment of a narrative consciously or unconsciously designed to expunge the traces of the trauma or loss that called that narrative into being in the first place . . . it is a strategy of undoing, in fantasy, the need for mourning by simulating a condition of intactness, by situating the site of loss and origin elsewhere. (144)

Pontecorvo's story of redemptive love serves a fetishizing function by virtue of its simulated resolution of a contradiction lying at the center of the Kapo experience. Trauma, understood as the potential absence of narrative and the absence of the seen — not simply the failure of the Hollywood model — is what so often haunts the struggle for cinematic visualization of the Shoah.

Theorizing and Practicing: Acting through the Crisis of Aesthetic Representation

The question of whether to represent the Holocaust in the visual arts is inextricably linked to the issue of how one might go about it. The call by Friedländer not to transgress certain intangible borders has as much to do with choices of style, genre, medium, and aesthetics as with the thematic topics to be treated. A now canonical theoretical declaration concerning aesthetics and the Holocaust was put forth by Theodor W. Adorno in the 1950s (34), and it seems fitting to re-cover this briefly as we turn to consider developments of the 1980s and 1990s.

Adorno's often-misinterpreted injunction that to write poetry after Auschwitz is barbaric has come to serve as both prohibition and caveat. As prohibition, it has been cited, along with George Steiner's *Language and Silence,* as a call to refrain from any form of poetic representation and as a ban on images (*Bilderverbot*). Yet where Steiner's encompassing position proposes that in the post-Holocaust world language and even thought have come to occupy a different ontological status from that of authentic experience — "The world of Auschwitz lies outside speech as it lies outside reason" (163) — Adorno's hyperbolic provocation focuses more narrowly on what Adorno sees as the dangers inherent in the institutional framework of existing aesthetic experience. "Barbaric" in this reading then are the inevitable feelings of pleasure evoked by certain historically contingent aesthetic expressions — the notion, more specifically, that a transfiguration can occur and that some of the horror of the event might thereby be ameliorated.

Rethinking Adorno's thesis as one that implicitly stresses historically contextualized modes of aesthetic response and not the ontological status of the artwork itself allows us to rehear its message as admonition rather than taboo. Translated into a strategy of visual representation, such importunity cannot mean, nor should it ever have meant, the banning of images — which, given the deeply imbedded psychic investment of images in the private and public production of fantasy, is a futile effort to begin with. Rather than exorcise the visual, the point is to embrace the path to an "aesthetics of post-memory" (Hirsch, *Family Frames* 8) as a reconstructing, even a working through, of the image as fetish and as iconic staple of the collective pictorial archive so necessary for the retrieval of Holocaust memory in the first place. The power of Adorno's oracular conundrum lies thus in the challenge it poses to contemporary artists to face the problems of genre, media, and style—whether the provenance of these problems be in high modernism or mass culture, comedy or melodrama.[6]

One film that has come to represent a model for such a working through the past by repudiating and at the same time reclaiming the image is Claude Lanzmann's nine-and-a-half-hour work, *Shoah*, which refrains from using any fictional reenactment or documentary footage from the camps. For many, including the filmmaker himself, *Shoah* stands as a compelling alternative to such Hollywood productions as Spielberg's *Schindler's List* and the NBC television series *Holocaust*, both of which Lanzmann has been critical. He claims that *Shoah* is "not a documentary, it is not at all representational" ("Seminar" 96). The interviews that he conducts with survivors, perpetrators, and secondary witnesses are not directed toward recovering memory content but seek to explore the process of reconstructing and reliving the past in the present. The film offers no chronological movement or teleological plan and does not search for cause and effect.

Lanzmann considers what he creates at the visual level to be imageless images, because what we see on the screen is more the absence of an image than an attempted replica of the unspeakable deed. Gertrud Koch has referred to such an absence as "an elision which marks the boundary between what is aesthetically and humanly imaginable and the unimaginable dimension of the annihilation" (20). This image border is forcefully allegorized in Lanzmann's assertion that "the Holocaust erects a ring of fire around itself, a borderline which cannot be crossed because there is a certain amount of horror that cannot be transmitted. To claim it is possible to do so is to be guilty of the most serious transgression" ("Why Spielberg" 14).

Lanzmann's cinematic provocation represents a sustained critique of the realist claim that an artist has access to a direct and total visual rendering of the event. Here he and his film remind us that there can be no full presence but only the marking of the past as an object of reconstruction based on traces and traces of traces. The traces in *Shoah* are sites of memory in the present—the pans of the rich, green fields of Treblinka and Auschwitz today—that challenge the viewer to work imaginatively against the grain of the normalcy of these traces in order to produce or even hallucinate the horror of what was. We, as witnesses to those witnesses giving interview testimony in the film and as students and as teachers, are doubly removed and activated in the reconstruction process, forced to participate in putting together the innumerable pieces. To the degree that there can be for Lanzmann no historicist, prefilmic text—no script that maps out a pregiven path, no overriding conceptual framework— *Shoah*'s system adheres less to the generic codes of the documentary or the history film and more to those of a modern work of art, "drawing its force from the affirmation that art is not representation but presentation, not reproduction but expression" (Koch 20).

Disturbing in Lanzmann's formulations are not his modernist proclivities but the simple notion that we can get beyond representation or outside history. The problem for Adorno as well as for Bertolt Brecht is that one must work against the fetishization of image and its claim for authenticity and not that one can never abandon image in the name of pure presentation. It is a mistake to believe that, by withholding (or banning) conventional imaginings of the Holocaust, the mind is thus set free to roam where it will. This belief denies the extent to which the recycled fictions and documentary illustrations of prior visual representations continue to circulate as powerful signifiers and constitute an iconic archive by which societies remember their past. As teachers in the classroom, we must contend with these images as part of the pedagogical process of disfiguring and imagining.

The irony of course is that Lanzmann's film does cite and contend with iconic images of the Holocaust. *Shoah*'s fixation, for example, with trains confronts one of the primary tropes of Holocaust cinematic representation—not by putting us into a replication of suffering situated in a railroad car but by taking us up to the edge, by having us share, only briefly, the point of view of passengers coming into Treblinka as they observe the engineer who drove the original train looking back at them. Surely this is a moment in *Shoah* in which the film goes into dialogue with what Alexander Kluge has called "the film in our heads," by which he means "the films the spectator knows, his or her concept of cinema, genre expectation" (218).

If *Shoah*'s director stages his film as a modernist engagement with the memory of the Holocaust — a call for imageless images and pristine expression in lieu of representation — a very different strategy emerges in Art Spiegelman's two-volume comic book *Maus I* (*My Father Bleeds History*) and *Maus II* (*And Here My Troubles Began*). *Maus* as narrative is based on interviews the author conducted in the 1970s with his father, Vladek, an Auschwitz survivor. These exchanges trace the story of Spiegelman's parents' life in Poland from 1933 to 1944, which in turn is retold in the form of a comic. Thus both the father's recollections and the son's struggle to represent them constitute the focus of *Maus*.

Yet as is gradually revealed in the process of the comic character Artie's sometimes tortured retrieval, this tale of survival is less about the Holocaust as raw survivor memory than about how the second generation will repeat and thereby rework the images of a broken past, less about narrating the parents' original trauma than an attempted reconstruction of the son's location or dislocation in the family. James Young has aptly labeled the model at work here "'received history' — a narrative hybrid that interweaves both events of the Holocaust and the ways that they are passed down to us" (15). Rather than a search for an authentic, redemptive history of his parents' struggle for survival, Spiegelman's reworking is itself a historicizing process — not of the event but of the ways we recover it, what the recoverer understands and can never understand.

Artie's failure to retrieve what he thinks it is he seeks is acted out through the medium of the comic-book word-image, which enables at another register a very different if unexpected process of representation. The story is broken up by digressions and interruptions, saturated with self-reflexivity, self-irony, double narration (Artie's and his father's), and contradiction. The hybridity in *Maus* occurs on a myriad of levels, which results in a concatenation of meaning production. Modernist narrative techniques interweave with the complex montaging of comic-book image in suggestive and associational combinations. Andreas Huyssen has convincingly argued that what we have here is an estrangement effect in the service of "mimetic approximation" (35). The use of animal imagery, for instance, hints at a potential political allegorization (Germans as cats, Jews as mice, Poles as pigs), but through inversion and refiguration the imagery in the long run becomes displaced from the original context; it is not an authentic replication of the real. Approximations hover with association, and Spiegelman's drawings of the camps in *Maus* reference obliquely the photograph images familiar to us from the iconic archive: "Arbeit Macht Frei," prisoners and SS uniforms, electric fences, towers and lights, German shepherds, and so forth.[7] But it is important to emphasize to students that such references operate only obliquely. Recollection in this system of retrieval reminds those of us who come after that we have only media images, stored up, to work through — not to be banned on the one hand or fetishized on the other but to be acknowledged, resituated, destabilized, and processed as acts of memory.

While different in their aesthetic strategies, Lanzmann and Spiegelman are among a growing number of performance and visual artists committed to finding new and different ways of visualizing and thereby remembering the Holocaust. What they share at the broadest register can best be summarized as a concern more for how to present the Holocaust than for what to represent or whether to do so, a concern that is based on the realization that memory retrieval is a process of seeing and working through the past. What also links these two artists is the assumption that, in terms of the Shoah, there is no true and all-encompassing visualization and hence no mandated right way to make an image of it; there are only specific media representations of it with specific problems to be solved.

Notes

1. See Barnouw; Brink; and Zelizer, *Remembering*. Where Barnouw focuses on the impact of these images on the attitudes of Americans toward Germans, Brink concentrates on their impact on Germans, in particular those living in the Federal Republic.
2. Hirsch also speaks of "a striking repetition of the same few images used over and over again iconically and emblematically to signal this event" ("Surviving Images" 217).

3. In the standard history of the Holocaust by Michael Marrus, *The Holocaust in History*, the figure of the *Muselmann* is mentioned once (130). Similarly, in Leni Yahil, *The Holocaust*, it is mentioned briefly three times (371, 373, 569).

4. Taylor introduces the term "percepticide" to deal with a question that she formulates in the following way: "What happens to the 'witness' in a situation that forces people to participate in the production of denial?" (124). This is precisely the double bind that Levi also wrestles with and that speaks to the central problem of what it means to try to witness, in other words, to see and represent, in a situation where the seer is implicated in the perpetration.

5. Marrus defines the Kapo in the following manner: "The Nazis . . . empowered camp elders, clerks, block leaders, and so forth to supervise the inmates and assume primary responsibility for the routines of daily life" (129).

6. See Huyssen, "Of Mice and Mimesis," for an excellent discussion of appropriating Adorno for reading texts of mass culture.

7. This is a point made effectively by Hirsch ("Surviving Images" 238).

Works Cited

Adorno, Theodor W. "Cultural Criticism and Society." *Prisms.* Trans. Samuel Weber and Shierry Weber. Cambridge: MIT P, 1967. 17–34.

Agamben, Giorgio. *Remnants of Auschwitz: The Witness and the Archive.* Trans. Daniel Heller-Roazen. New York: Zone, 1999.

Améry, Jean. *At the Mind's Limits: Contemplations by a Survivor on Auschwitz and Its Realities.* Trans. Sidney Rosenfeld and Stella P. Rosenfeld. Bloomington: Indiana UP, 1980.

Arendt, Hannah. *Elemente und Ursprünge totaler Herrschaft.* Vol 3. Frankfurt am Main: Europäische, 1975.

Barnouw, Dagmar. *Germany 1945: Views of War and Violence.* Bloomington: Indiana UP, 1996.

Bettelheim, Bruno. *The Informed Heart.* New York: Free, 1960.

Brink, Cornelia. *Ikonen der Vernichtung: Öffentlicher Gebrauch von Fotografien aus nationalsozialistischen Konzentrationslagern nach 1945* [Icons of Destruction: Public Use of Photographs from National Socialist Concentration Camps after 1945]. Berlin: Akademie, 1998.

Friedländer, Saul. Introduction. Friedländer, *Probing* 1–21.

———, ed. *Probing the Limits of Representation: Nazism and the "Final Solution."* Cambridge: Harvard UP, 1992.

Hartman, Geoffrey. *The Longest Shadow: In the Aftermath of the Holocaust.* Bloomington: Indiana UP, 1996.

Hirsch, Marianne. *Family Frames: Photography, Narrative, and Postmemory.* Cambridge: Harvard UP, 1997.

———. "Surviving Images: Holocaust Photographs and the Work of Postmemory." Zelizer, *Visual Culture* 216–46.

Huyssen, Andreas. "Of Mice and Mimesis: Reading Spiegelman with Adorno." Zelizer, *Visual Culture* 28–44.

Insdorf, Annette. *Indelible Shadows: Film and the Holocaust.* Cambridge: Cambridge UP, 1989.

Jenks, Chris. "The Centrality of the Eye in Western Culture." *Visual Culture.* Ed. Jenks. New York: Routledge, 1995. 1–25.

Kapo. Dir. Gillo Pontecorvo. Vides, Zebra, Cineriz, Francinex, Lovcen, 1960.

Kluge, Alexander. "On Film and the Public Sphere." *New German Critique* 24–25 (1981–82): 206–20.

Koch, Gertrud. "The Aesthetic Transformation of the Image of the Unimaginable: Notes on Claude Lanzmann's *Shoah.*" *October* 48 (1989): 15–22.

Lanzmann, Claude. "Seminar with Claude Lanzmann, 11 April, 1990." *Yale French Studies* 79 (1991): 82–99.

———. "Why Spielberg Has Distorted the Truth." *Guardian Weekly* 3 Apr. 1994: 14.

Levi, Primo. *The Drowned and the Saved.* New York: Vintage, 1989.

———. *Survival in Auschwitz.* New York: Touchstone, 1996.

Marrus, Michael. *The Holocaust in History.* New York: Penguin, 1987.

Milton, Sybil. "Photographs of the Warsaw Ghetto." *Simon Wiesenthal Center Annual* 3 (1986): 307.

Santner, Eric. "History beyond the Pleasure Principle." Friedländer, *Probing* 143–54.

Sontag, Susan. *On Photography.* New York: Farrar, 1977.

Spiegelman, Art. *And Here My Troubles Began.* New York: Pantheon, 1991. Vol. 2 of *Maus: A Survivor's Tale.*

———. *My Father Bleeds History.* New York: Pantheon, 1986. Vol. 1 of *Maus: A Survivor's Tale.*

Steiner, George. *Language and Silence.* New York: Atheneum, 1967.

Taylor, Diana. *Disappearing Acts: Spectacles of Gender and Nationalism in Argentina's "Dirty War."* Durham: Duke UP, 1997.

Yahil, Leni. *The Holocaust: The Fate of European Jewry 1932–1945.* Trans. Ina Friedman and Haya Galai. New York: Oxford UP, 1990.

Young, James E. *At Memory's Edge: After-images of the Holocaust in Contemporary Art and Architecture.* New Haven: Yale UP, 2000.

Zelizer, Barbie. *Remembering to Forget: Holocaust Memory through the Camera's Eye.* Chicago: U of Chicago P, 1998.

———, ed. *Visual Culture and the Holocaust.* New Brunswick: Rutgers UP, 2000.

Part III

Selected Texts

Ranen Omer-Sherman

Responding to the Burden of Witness in Dan Pagis's "Written in Pencil in the Sealed Railway-Car"

I've long felt that one of the most immediate of the numerous challenges confronting me as a relatively new teacher in the Holocaust studies classroom is the question of the students' role.[1] Perhaps excepting the few students who will be initially attracted to this grim subject for the voyeuristic journey into human suffering it provides them, most students will want guidance as they consider some form of moral situatedness in relation to the narratives of atrocity that are intrinsic to studying the Holocaust. And, even in the case of the former, I have often been stirred to see that such students can be startled — on the course's very first day — into glimpsing a new paradigm of readership, as they gain insight into participating in a role that can be described as ethical witnessing for the witness, or readerly agency, particularly after a close encounter with the lyrics of Dan Pagis.

Often critically discussed alongside Aharon Appelfeld and Paul Celan, Pagis is perhaps the most accessible of a unique generation of post-Holocaust writers who were born in the polyglot and culturally rich environment of the Bukovina area of Romania (formerly Austria, now Ukraine). Born in 1930, Pagis had already experienced severe disorientation and loss even before the Holocaust, first with the emigration of his father to Palestine in 1934, then the early death of his mother not long after, culminating in his deportation at the age of eleven. Years later it emerged that, after the death of Pagis's mother, the family in Bukovina was convinced that the widower in Palestine would be unable to support the child. Because no foreign haven could be found for the boy — unlike Appelfeld and Celan, who were fortunate enough to escape the camps — Pagis was incarcerated by the Nazis for three years. He never learned the fate of his grandparents. After spending his early adolescence in concentration camps in Transnistria, Pagis reached Palestine in 1946, where he was reunited with his father (although, reportedly, years of estrangement followed into adult life) and taught school on a kibbutz. Eventually, Pagis began to write and publish poems in Hebrew, closely mentored by the Israeli poet Leah Goldberg (1911–70). Whereas it has often been argued that Celan remained committed to an enigmatic language of his own making, perhaps unsure until his eventual suicide of its destination or audience, Pagis had to cope with the challenge of Hebrew. He thus addressed a clearly defined audience of Israelis who, although engaged in a collective act of repatriation, may have been ambivalent in their response to the presence of Holocaust survivors. And yet by the end of his life, Pagis enjoyed literary celebrity as one of Israel's most popular poets, whose radical skepticism reconnected the Israeli imagination to the ever-disruptive past of the European Diaspora. Pagis died in Jerusalem in 1986.

Precisely because Pagis avoided both conventional forms of commemoration and the archetypal role of witness embodied by Elie Wiesel — and never spoke for Israel in the widely popular and officially recognized ways that Yehudah Amichai did — his poetry, as Sidra DeKoven Ezrahi, one of Pagis's most attentive and eloquent readers, argues, "blast[s] a hole in the culture so large that it exposes and undermines its deepest structures [to] claim a radical public presence" (Rev. of *Variable Directions* 37). Like Ezrahi, my students and I have gradually awakened to the disturbing awareness that Pagis's poetry denies the consolations, available in many conventional narratives, of finding security after catastrophe, not least in its radical unease over any safe definition of homeland. In this and other ways, Pagis utterly disrupts the reader's own world.

I like to teach with Lawrence Langer's *Art from the Ashes: A Holocaust Anthology*, particularly for its scope and attention to the various ways in which genre contributes to the students' encounter with narratives of trauma. Langer's anthology encompasses excerpts from ghetto diaries, essays by Primo Levi and Wiesel, short fiction by Ida Fink and many others, novels and novellas by Joshua Sobol and Appelfeld, and even haunting reproductions of art created in Terezin. But I am most impressed by the space allotted in this anthology to the often-neglected testimony of poetry, especially the judicious gleanings from Abraham Sutzkever, Celan, Miklós Radnóti, and Nelly Sachs (for more on Celan, see the essay in this volume by Baer). An additional strength of the anthology is Langer's sober-minded attention to the disparate demands that each genre makes on its grim subject matter. Teachers who may be uneasy about presenting this material for the first time will be well rewarded by Langer's cautionary approach to the relation between poetry and trauma:

> Holocaust poetry should not be mistaken for a renewal of the spirit or used as a reason for redressing the cruelty of the doom it reflects. Its true legacy is a tribute to the resilience of language and the ability of the artistic imagination to meet a chaotic challenge and with sheer inventive skill change it into durable, if often difficult and unfamiliar poetic forms. (559)

Langer's illuminating introductions to each poet provide students with engaging and informative contexts. In this regard I should add that I am especially drawn to the collection because it happens to contain the best representation of Pagis's shorter lyrics currently available in any Holocaust anthology. Although the Pagis selection appears toward the second half of the weighty volume, it is here that my class always begins.

I have been awed by the pedagogical potential that Pagis's lines offer the literature classroom—ever since encountering Sara Horowitz's collaborative explication of the poem in a Holocaust Educational Foundation workshop, where we wrestled with many of the same existential questions that the poem continues to raise for my students. I remain inspired by her creative questioning of a group of dispassionate historians on that ocassion, all unfamiliar with the poem, many of whom later acknowledged that the experience had taught them that a literary text could accomplish something vital in their classrooms, exceeding the range of conventional historical documents. Since that occasion, I have started the first or second day of class with Pagis's famous poem of incomplete witnessing, "Written in Pencil in the Sealed Railway-Car" ("Katuv b'iparon bakaron hehatum"), where humanity's sense of progress is undermined as the ominous beginnings of human community glare through present history like a murderous palimpsest:

> here in this carload
> i am eve
> with abel my son
> if you see my other son
> cain son of man
> tell him that i[2]

There are few works of art that so successfully crystallize the problem of testimony, commemoration, and conscience; no readers escape the call of this utterance for their involvement. But since the only concrete connections in Pagis's translated work are those that the individual reader creates (and of course many of our students lack biblical literacy), I like to begin by allowing students to approach it from the perspective of their unfamiliarity, in meditative isolation. Then, following that intimate first encounter, I provide classroom time for collaborating on an explication in small groups (to encourage those who are inhibited). Finally, I draw from those responses in the framework of a large class discussion. Not only does this strategy encourage students to take a direct, interpretive role (certainly an empowering paradigm for any lower-division literature classroom to embrace), but the experience — so powerfully divested of formulaic resolution — ensures that, as a community of readers, we have a powerful touchstone for experiencing the shocks of subsequent texts without anticipating consolatory conventions.

Students are naturally confused about what they are supposed to gain from the bad news that the Holocaust poem, memoir, witness account, or fictional narrative invariably delivers. Certainly I have occupied their position (and continue to do so at troubling moments). Often nearly traumatized by the bleak material they confront, they reasonably assume that they are expected, somehow, to wrest meaning from atrocity. Some students (particularly those influenced by Christian traditions) expect a form of spiritual consolation from the text — that the witness, especially the victim, will offer them a redemptive message that soothes, strengthens, or redeems their own moment in history.

In contrast to such expectations, Pagis's poem, blending the formal Hebrew of antiquity with the colloquial moment of the poem's composition, rightly places the burden of meaning on the readers, who are not merely liberated to make their own sense of the text's message but compelled to do so by the way the poet situates his unknown audience. Recently I have come to recognize that one of my most important goals in the Holocaust literature course should be to have my students grapple with creating their own version of Kaja Silverman's unsettling insistence that "if to remember is to provide the disembodied 'wound' with a psychic residence, then to remember other people's memories is to be wounded by their wounds" (189). To begin a process that might lead to a shared revelation about the unexpected forms of such commemoration, I ask my students to discuss three simple questions that the poem raises: Who is the speaker in this poem? Who is being addressed? And, most challenging, what is the message? As I mentioned, it seems to me important that, rather than immediately address this poem as a class, students work on these questions in small groups, where their ignorance of the poem's context, or of my intentions, will not inhibit discussion. It is always gratifying to learn from their responses, which, considering the poem's brevity, can be surprisingly varied.

Students immediately have to contend with the disturbing notion that someone else's utterance (someone often long dead) has made a distinct claim on them as otherwise autonomous beings: "if you see my other son / . . . / tell him that i." Thinking through these starkly open-ended lines as my students experience them, I've formed a pedagogy that embraces Emily Miller Budick's uses of Stanley Cavell's unique invocation of "acknowledgment," a trope that addresses

> the doubt of skepticism that argues we cannot "know" the world and other people in it. Rather than dismiss the skeptic's worry as either perverse or not fully intended . . . Cavell [grants] the skeptic's insight that we cannot attain knowledge as certainty. . . . According to Cavell, when we say, for example, that we "know" another person's pain we do not mean that we "know" it as a certainty. Instead we mean that we understand and respond to a claim made on us by that individual's expression of that pain. (329)

In this interpretive mode, teachers who want their students to make the most of indeterminate works like "Written in Pencil" will appreciate Budick's striking assertion that denial of "this kind would be to refuse to *acknowledge* that pain . . . not the legitimate expression of one's skepticism but what Cavell calls 'disowning' knowledge" (329). In my experience teaching the literature of the Holocaust, primarily to non-Jewish undergraduates, no other text so readily rewards their perception that the true work that awaits them is to respond to the course as if implicated. Not at all, I should hasten to stress, in the sense of a counterproductive guilt but rather as bearing the moral burden of the broken transmission of millions, of striving to form an ethical relation to fragmented texts and broken lives. The title's discomfiting reference to a "sealed railway-car" often stirs intuitive students to raise appropriate questions about the culpability of onlookers and bystanders who experienced the quotidian phenomenon of trains carrying men, women, and children to their deaths in the European countryside.

Pagis's poem is also a useful introduction to a genre often neglected in Holocaust courses. More than prose narratives, especially Holocaust memoirs, the lyrics of numerous survivor poets discourages the reader from dismissing the Holocaust as past; instead, they underscore the present, both temporally and spatially. Thinking about Pagis's searing lyric, I have found Amir Eshel's reading of Walter Benjamin's angel, bearing on the particular challenge of Holocaust poetics, to be a most instructive paradigm for students as they evaluate their own orientation toward the Holocaust as past event. Eshel comments:

> Just as Walter Benjamin's angel is "propelled" into the future while his present sight is focused on the "pile of debris," the past portrayed in this poetry is evoked from the perspective of poetic presence. Analogous to Benjamin's notion that the angel's spatial and temporal viewpoint ("His face is turned toward the past") reflects the core of Jewish remembrance (*Eingedenken*), the temporal dimension inscribed in this poetry can best be described as *facing* the Shoah . . . these particular "piles of debris" that can never be eradicated. (143)

Hence, as students come to realize, in its sheer fragmentariness it is difficult to think of Pagis's poem as a work or a text. Instead, invoking "here," it is a place they are urgently summoned to. In their own terms and language, students confront a "script" that dissolves

> the temporal and spatial distinction between "inside" and "outside," between those who are part of the events and those who "just" read about them from the safe distance and comfort usually associated with reading poetry and indulging in aesthetic pleasure. (Eshel 148)

In other words, the burden of freedom in this post-Auschwitz universe means being exposed to this closed space of exile. In my own experience, by the time students reexamine the text at the end of the course, they often discover that they have grown to appreciate Pagis's arresting triumph, conveying horror through sheer allusion, without shrillness or hysteria.

Over years of reading this poem, I have also acquired a respect for Pagis's stoic refusal to succumb to conventional constructions of the child as the quintessential emblem of vulnerability and innocence, a trope that has often generated trivialization and oversaturation of the Holocaust, in ways that, as Geoffrey Hartman warns (108), can gradually etherize our responses. The lost child of the poem certainly does not invite the easy empathy with Anne Frank or other manifestly sentimental images of vulnerability such as the well-known photograph of the Warsaw Ghetto child in a peaked cap and up-raised hands joining other Jews herded by German soldiers with automatic pistols. Instead, the missing child invoked here is Cain; both "son of Adam" and the original *ben adam*, a twentieth-century human being fully capable of unleashing atrocity. Some point after the students' first raw foray into the text, teachers will find it useful to draw their attention to the fact that the Hebrew phrase denotes, besides the son of Adam, a human or, more literally, "earth being." It is true that the immediacy of that powerful syntactic feature is lost a bit in translation. But few students will miss the way that, in its symbolic reference to the first family of humanity (chillingly collapsing the distance between the first murder and the worst atrocities of our own age), the poem effectively refutes our desire to take comfort in a linear notion of civilization's progress. Although poignantly calling out to resolve the exigency of their ephemerality ("written in pencil"), these lines etch themselves indelibly on the students' conscience.

Readers invariably awaken to the poem's moral challenge to them as a text that presupposes a community of readers who will struggle to complete its failure of transmission. After students have become acquainted with the English version in their own terms, it is worth alerting them to a critical translation problem. John Felstiner is representative of a number of critics who underscore that in English "the plural addressee of Pagis's *tagidulo* gets lost: 'tell [ye] him.'" Most students will not be aware that our English *you* was originally used nominatively as the plural of *thou*. Under the rules of contemporary usage, the translator's English can no longer inflect the verb to show that "Eve has something to tell a great many people, even unto the present generation, about her son's murder." Felstiner and other readers of the Hebrew original are well aware that, in Pagis's intertextual imagination, the "you" addressed is the second person plural; *im tiru . . . tagidu* forms an imperative that demands the moral participation of both male and female witnesses. Felstiner is discomfited by the translation of the poem's silence: "Does the silence cutting short her last words *tagidulo sh'ani*, do our questions suspended in that silence after 'tell him that i,' resound the same in English as in Hebrew?" (344).

Still, whether in English or the original Hebrew, this profoundly incomplete poem requires the intervention of a reader, who has been ethically summoned to respond linguistically. As Ezrahi memorably observes, "lack of closure here is the absolute refusal of art as triumph over mortality" (*Booking* 162). The poem disrupts too easy a resolution of the absences it commemorates. In this regard, it may be useful to raise other, related issues of public memory and commemorative space for the students' consideration. For example, some students may find it is fitting that Pagis's lines, composing one of the shortest lyrics in the modern Hebrew language, in 1995 were carved onto a transport car that is part of the Transport Memorial at Yad Vashem, Israel's national memorial to the Holocaust, to serve as a textual meditation on the foreboding surface on which they are inscribed. But for others (particularly in the wake of the brutal Israeli and Palestinian struggle over territory) it will be clear, as it is to me, that Pagis's disturbing paean to deathly silence cannot be easily confined within the monologic thrust of national or officially sanctioned commemorative narratives; indeed, it transcends any efforts to contain such narratives. For all readers, it may be worth pondering Ezrahi's sense of the manifest capacity of these lines to remain "disruptive, unassimilable, even after being 'safely' embedded in commemorative public space" (*Booking* 162).

Not only is Pagis's poem a powerful work to begin a course with; it can perform a special role at the end, as a sort of textual touchstone, at least for some approaches. Most syllabi I have seen ensure that students will encounter all sorts of writing: prose, memoir, drama, and fiction (with poetry frequently neglected). The cumulative effect of the various forms of the testimonial and witnessing process that is intrinsic to such courses is to make students more aware of the role of resilience and adaptation in the writer's act of self-representation. As Dori Laub has rightly noted, survivor narratives often stir the Holocaust classroom with the liberating "rebirth to speech . . . the very eloquence of life, with 'striking, vivid' examples of the *liberating vital function of testimony*" (58). For at the very least, Pagis's six lines deprive us of such consolation, returning us to the shadowy silences of the dead, for whom no one can speak. Rather than a triumphal sense of having worked through and overcome loss, the poem paradoxically insists on its own atrocity as an unimaginable event still to be communicated, still trapped in speechlessness. As a reminder of unspeakability, Pagis haunts us with a Holocaust that remains an event without a witness or a narrator, that depends on each reader's struggle—to witness and to narrate. Students who may have confronted their own loss of language, their startling discovery of the inadequacy of the university-trained intellect while confronting the wounding texts of Holocaust courses will understand that the polarities of both paradigms are intrinsic to the narratives of atrocity and endurance they have witnessed.

Notes

1. I am greatly indebted to the scholarly and pedagogical leadership of others, especially Sara Horowitz and Sidra Ezrahi. As a novice instructor in the spring of 1996, I was particularly inspired by the friendly collaboration and illuminating insights of Christopher Strathman into modern poetry and poetics. Strathman shared my classroom at the University of Notre Dame.
2. Although all translations of poetry contain their strengths and limitations, Stephen Mitchell, Pagis's translator, deserves significant credit for expressing the spare and tragic dimensions of the original, albeit in a resolutely universal idiom that has alienated a few readers.

Works Cited and Recommended

Alter, Robert. "Dan Pagis and the Poetry of Displacement." *Judaism: A Quarterly Journal of Jewish Life and Thought* 45.4 (1996): 399–402.
———. Introduction. Mitchell xi–xvi.
Budick, Emily Miller. "Acknowledging the Holocaust in Contemporary American Fiction and Criticism." *Breaking Crystal: Writing and Memory after Auschwitz.* Ed. Efraim Sicher. Chicago: U of Illinois P, 1998. 329–43.
Carmis, T. "Dan Pagis: Words of Farewell." *Orim* 2.2 (1987): 76–78.
Delbo, Charlotte. "Voices." Langer 77–92.
Eshel, Amir. "Eternal Present: Poetic Figuration and Cultural Memory in the Poetry of Yehuda Amichai, Dan Pagis, and Tuvia Rübner." *Jewish Social Studies* 7.1 (2000): 141–66.
Ezrahi, Sidra DeKoven. *Booking Passage: Exile and Homecoming in the Modern Jewish Imagination.* Berkeley: U of California P, 2000.
———. *By Words Alone: The Holocaust in Literature.* Chicago: U of Chicago P, 1980.
———. "Dan Pagis—Out of Line: A Poetics of Decomposition." *Prooftexts* 2.1 (1982): 78–94.

————. Rev. of *Variable Directions*, by Dan Pagis. *New Republic* 25 Feb. 1991: 36–40.

Felstiner, John. "Jews Translating Jews." *Jewish American Poetry: Poems, Commentary, and Reflections*. Ed. Jonathan N. Barron and Eric Murphy Selinger. Hanover: Brandeis UP, 2000. 337–44.

Hartman, Geoffrey H. *The Longest Shadow: In the Aftermath of the Holocaust*. Bloomington: Indiana UP, 1996.

Langer, Lawrence, ed. *Art from the Ashes: A Holocaust Anthology*. Oxford: Oxford UP, 1995.

Laub, Dori. "Bearing Witness; or, The Vicissitudes of Listening." *Testimony: Crises of Witnessing in Literature, Psychoanalysis, and History*. By Shoshana Felman and Laub. New York: Routledge, 1991. 59–74.

Mitchell, Stephen, trans. *The Selected Poetry of Dan Pagis*. Berkeley: U of California P, 1989.

Pagis, Dan. "Written in Pencil in the Sealed Railway-Car." Mitchell 29.

Silverman, Kaja. *The Threshold of the Visible World*. New York: Routledge, 1996.

Sokoloff, Naomi. "Transformations: Holocaust Poems in Dan Pagis' *Gilgul*." *Hebrew Annual Review* 8 (1984): 215–40.

Zierler, Wendy. "Footprints, Traces, Remnants: The Operations of Memory in Dan Pagis' *Aqebot*." *Judaism* 41.4 (1992): 316–33.

Ulrich Baer

Paul Celan's Stars: Teaching "Todesfuge" as a Canonical Holocaust Poem

In a note written about Paul Celan's famous Holocaust poem "Todesfuge" ("Death Fugue") before his acceptance of Germany's prestigious Büchner Prize, the poet states, "When I wrote 'Death Fugue' in May 1945, I had read at that time in the Izvestia [the Russian newspaper] the reports on the Lemberg Ghetto. . . . But this question [raised by these reports], along with many others, returns to me over and over, and so the poem is a turning back" (*Meridian* 131n419; my trans.). According to this posthumously published comment, "Todesfuge" takes its origin in newspaper reports of actual events (the Jews of Lemberg were not deported to a camp but shot outside the town) and not in firsthand experience. Celan had been interned in a labor camp in Romania and lost his parents, who had been deported to other camps. Although not based on the author's experience, "Todesfuge" is commonly considered the canonical poem about the Holocaust in any language. It frequently serves as the implicit or explicit standard for artistic responses to the Shoah. It has assumed the aura of authenticity also bestowed on the written testimonies of Anne Frank, Elie Wiesel, and Primo Levi. In the course Representation of the Holocaust, Celan's poem can serve as a pivotal text to focus general questions about the relation between fiction and testimony, language and experience, and literature and history.

The poem's poignancy and effectiveness as a testimonial rest with Celan's skillful transformation of the reality of Holocaust suffering into literature. Differently put, "Todesfuge" is a key text, and possibly the key literary text about the Holocaust, because of its decidedly poetic nature. While this is the poem's strength, its literary merit has also triggered debates about the success or failure of "Todesfuge" in representing the Holocaust and in recognizing the limits of art in the face of overwhelming suffering. Whether or not these debates have been introduced in a course, "Todesfuge" is well suited to gauge their wider scope and significance. When students are encouraged to read Celan's poem attentively rather than be awed by it or regard it as an artifact recording events available elsewhere, the discussion can serve as a transition between the primarily historiographical and the more explicitly literary segments of the course.

It is useful to provide students with background material about Celan's life. Most helpful is the information offered in the opening chapters of Israel Chalfen's and John Felstiner's biographies, in Amy Colin's book on Celan, and in entries on Celan in encyclopedias of German and Holocaust literature (e.g., see Konzett). Born in Czernowitz as Paul Antschel, Celan grew up in a German-speaking, formerly Austrian city that was annexed by Romania but whose assimilated Jewish population maintained their allegiance to German culture. For Celan, the act of writing poetry, which he began in Romanian but quickly changed to German, was an assertion of his self-understanding as a German poet and became ultimately an implicit act of resistance against the Nazi-decreed notion that to be Jewish means not to be German and against the idea that the German language and culture are inherently inhospitable and off-limits to Jewish self-expression. Despite the abyss dividing Celan's early life from their experiences, students might be encouraged to consider the issues of assimilation, minority status, multilingual or immigrant existence, and a disadvantaged group's efforts to join the mainstream, in the light of similar efforts by minoritized groups. Celan enrolled in medical school in France in the late 1930s but had to return to Czernowitz when war broke out.

After brief stops in Bucharest and Vienna after the war, Celan settled in Paris, where he married a Frenchwoman and became a naturalized French citizen. He gradually attained fame in Germany as the preeminent postwar German poet and successor to Rainer Maria Rilke and Bertolt Brecht, both of whose work he directly echoes in his verse and alludes to throughout by voicing a quasi-Rilkean insistence on interiority, with a Brechtian knack for startlingly contemporary turns of phrase. In the 1960s, Celan battled severe depression, which resulted in episodes of domestic violence and the eventual separation from his wife and young son. A brief biographical introduction could conclude with the disheartening observation that Celan's poetry appears not to have alleviated his mental anguish, despite the popular belief that the literary expression, and thus externalization, of great suffering can relieve an individual from the haunting of memory. Celan committed suicide by drowning, in 1970. Without offering an interpretation of the suicide, I raise the question with my students of whether writing poetry can be therapeutic or whether the poet's prolonged engagement with the Nazi crimes in his literary work turned him into a belated victim of its violence, analogous to the fate ascribed to Primo Levi, Bruno Bettelheim, and Jean Améry.

After this biographical sketch, I write on the board Theodor W. Adorno's famous injunction that "it is barbaric to write poetry after Auschwitz" (34). The discussion of Celan's poem takes place in the shadow of that statement. I explain briefly that the philosopher Adorno spent the war years as a Jewish refugee in the United States but returned to his native Germany after the war. In the context of discussing "Todesfuge," his statement might be read as a prohibition on poetry in the face of unspeakable crimes. But it is also an indictment of all culture, which had proved powerless in averting atrocity (part of Adorno's critique of mass consumer culture, to which poetry would potentially succumb). What is at stake in writing poetry after Auschwitz?

I then move to a reading of the poem itself (Celan, *Selected*

Poems 30). We first read the poem in English (I prefer the Felstiner translation). If possible, someone might also read the German text out loud. "Todesfuge" does not describe a specific camp but invokes an unidentified, murderous setting outside Germany where individual agency and perspective all but disappear in the tedium of forced laborers toiling on the brink between life and death. The poem's incantatory rhythm is propelled by the haunting refrain, "Black milk of daybreak we drink it at nightfall." This line emblematizes Celan's method of suspending, at the poem's beginning, the readers' knowledge of the identity of "we" and of the poem's speaker. The surrealist metaphor of "black milk," in which the life-giving, affirming nature of milk is yoked to deathly darkness, is ritually imbibed by a collective "we" that is not immediately identified as Jews. Celan's startling reluctance to identify "we" requires his readers to enter his poetic universe on the poem's terms. It also may involve readers in the poem beyond those having been addressed: since the poem is written in German, the implication is that Celan's poem includes German readers in this "we." Yet neither Jews nor Germans are named at first, and the poem's speaker remains initially unidentified. (Nowhere in Celan's poetic oeuvre is the Holocaust named.)

In "Todesfuge," "we" becomes recognizable as referring to the Jewish victims. This "we," then, is a voice on behalf of those who were brutally robbed of life and a dignified death. By speaking from the position of people who can no longer speak, Celan offers what Michael André Bernstein has called an astonishing "act of imaginative ventriloquism" that overrides the prohibition against imagining the unimaginable (104). Celan opens the realm of the unimaginable to the imagination by including himself in the "we" of the victims.

Throughout the poem, Celan adopts the high-modernist literary technique of showing an event from several emphatically subjective and divergent perspectives without achieving unity. He forgoes the desire to offer an objective representation of the Holocaust, and students can be directed toward the question of whether literature charts a special access to the kind of knowledge available to victims in the wake of overwhelming trauma. Ultimately, Celan draws attention to how the Holocaust cannot be accessed from a single vantage point and to its shattering of the notion of a unified position from which to chronicle its unfolding. To account for the Holocaust as such a rupture, he models "Todesfuge" on the baroque musical form of the fugue. In this form, constituting the apex of classicism, up to two themes are introduced and then replayed and revisited cyclically in at least three distinct voices and in various keys and rhythmic and tonal variations. Celan evokes the fugue in the poem's title as the utmost articulation of German culture, exemplified by another "master from Germany" (30), composer Johann Sebastian Bach. In keeping with a fugal pattern, "Todesfuge" repeats key phrases ("we drink it," "he writes it," "your golden hair," "your ashen hair") with only slight variations and by different speakers, not to create another masterpiece but to unsettle the notion that the Holocaust was viewed the same way by all who were engulfed in it. The fugal pattern, however, allows Celan to maintain a coherent, strongly articulated voice despite the shattering of a unified perspective.

In the poem's central, bitterly sarcastic formulation, Jewish inmates shovel their graves and play music while the commander tells them that they will find a grave in the air. Since the Jewish victims are referred to by the neutral German pronoun *man*, for "one" ("a grave in the air where *one* lies unconfined"), Celan suggests that the Germans robbed their Jewish victims of individuality even in death. But there is no clearly marked transition from the Nazis' offensive euphemism for cremation ("a grave in the air") and the Jews' own way of describing their death. Instead, Celan utilizes the fugal technique of interweaving several voices addressing one theme, to show one event from radically incompatible perspectives. Each of the poem's six stanzas contains concrete descriptions of "a man" alternately writing to his beloved back in Germany, ominously playing with snakes, whistling to his dogs, swinging an iron rod, ordering "his" Jews to shovel and sing, and shooting them dead "with perfect aim" (30). By splicing, repeating, and recombining these sentence fragments and individual words and images and thus obscuring the position and identity of the speaker, Celan reconstructs in verse a disturbingly coherent setting of death ruled by fear and suffering that is at once chaotic and yet entirely self-contained.

The poem presents both explicit and oblique references to German and Jewish literary sources. Its rhythmic structure is a modernist adaptation of a long tradition of dances of death, in works as diverse as medieval verse, the poetry of Heinrich Heine, and the lyric modernism of Georg Trakl (see Felstiner 22–42; Olschner). Although "Death Fugue" is a severe indictment of the notion of German-Jewish coexistence and the illusion that German *Kultur* could have sheltered the Jews from German violence, it refuses to renounce the achievements of German culture or to uncouple these achievements from their often Jewish sources. In the poem's final, incommensurate image, Celan juxtaposes the German camp commander's "golden-haired Margarete," taken from Johann Wolfgang von Goethe's *Faust* tragedy, with an "ashen-haired Shulamith," found in the Song of Songs. Although "Todesfuge" ends with this dissonant image, the entire poem defiantly employs even the Nazis' boundless cynicism ("a grave in the air there one won't lie too cramped" [30]) to reclaim the poet's right to address the German crimes without censoring his words or tone.

In my class, I usually play a recording of Celan reading "Todesfuge" (cassette recording available from www.hoerverlag.de) after this discussion and ask students about their impression. They frequently remark on the urgency of Celan's delivery and on how the poet's reading builds up narrative tension in a poem in which, actually, there is little unfolding and no uncertainty about the horrific ending for the Jews. In the light of Celan's strong tone in the poem and its delivery, I direct attention to his refusal to identify "a man in the house." Who could be meant by this man? Responses always include "the camp commander," and then, sometimes, "Celan." And indeed, Celan is also the writer of this poem and remains present throughout: his project is to wrest authority from the Nazis to permit the Jews to express their suffering. In these lines, the notion of writing refers at once to the act of the Jewish poet and to that of the German perpetrator, both of whom write back—to different addressees and for different reasons—to a culture of literacy that tolerated and possibly fostered the crimes committed in its midst.

To shed light on Celan's specific engagement with the question of how to bear witness to an event that is frequently considered unrepresentable, I draw attention to the rhetorical status of one of Celan's images as either literal or figurative. Placing particular emphasis on the lines "he writes it and steps in front of the house and the stars are sparkling ('es blitzen die Sterne'),'' I ask students what the sparkling stars might refer to. Invoking the preceding line, "he writes when it grows dark to Germany" 'er schreibt wenn es dunkelt nach Deutschland,' a phrase that can indicate either dusk or the writer's informing Germany of an impending darkness, students frequently suggest that the stars here refer to constellations in the darkening evening sky. This Romantic topos is surely present in Celan. But usually a student also suggests a sharply divergent reference. The sparkling stars might refer, as well, to the cloth stars sewn on Jewish prisoners' uniforms, marking each inmate as a victim of Nazi violence. How can this connotation, of a mark tagging prisoners for death, be reconciled with the Romantic image of the stars as traditional symbols for eternity, longevity, and hope? By exposing the tension between a literal and a figural dimension of the stars in "Todesfuge," students come to recognize Celan's technique of investing images from a pre-Holocaust poetic tradition with unexpected, shocking resonance.

If the poem's theme can thus be interpreted as the poet's exploration of what constitutes a proper voice and perspective in a scene of extreme violence, its language illustrates the difficulty in finding a unified voice by fusing two incompatible connotations in one image. Celan demonstrates that no single perspective can encompass the entirety of the Holocaust. As the poem takes recourse in the fugal pattern, with multiple voices, and as it overlays incompatible meanings in a single phrase, the work recognizes the Holocaust as an event that causes the splintering of all perspectives (Felman 223). The poem's opening lines spell out the realization that, to speak of the Holocaust, the poet must assume a perspective that he does not want or from which he or those on whose behalf he speaks were barred. With the poem's ending, in which Celan deliberately conjoins two figures from German and Jewish traditions, he highlights the radically disjunctive juxtaposition of two perspectives and existences.

In response to critics' suggestions, often intended as praise, that the artistic achievement of "Todesfuge" transcends all suffering, Celan insisted, in a letter in the 1960s, that all of the poem is literal description, and the "grave in the air" in "*this* poem, God knows, is neither a borrowed reference nor a metaphor" (Wiedemann 608). Celan thus defended his best-known poem against charges of unduly aestheticizing suffering and took issue with Adorno's (qualified) statement. The poet's comments notwithstanding, "Todesfuge" does not completely renounce rhetorical figures. Indeed, the highly self-conscious poem's strength results from its explicitly formal representation of horrific events and from its specific echoing of central images from the poetic traditions of which it remains a part.

Partly in response to overly formalist interpretations of "Todesfuge" that downplayed the poem's theme, Celan refused to allow the poem to be reprinted in anthologies. He was dismayed at seeing his poem in collections with poets of erstwhile ultraconservative or fascist leanings or with writers who were associated with the surrealist poet Yvan Goll's widow, who waged an unfounded campaign charging Celan with plagiarism. As discussed by Françoise Meltzer, Celan had translated some of Yvan Goll's French poetry into German in the early 1950s, and his widow claimed that Celan stole some formulations and images from her late husband's poems. In the early 1960s, Claire Goll published an open letter accusing Celan of plagiarism. When some critics did not instantly leap to his defense, Celan detected, not wholly without grounds, a conspiracy against him waged by the German literary establishment. He began to suspect antisemitism in anyone who did not support his cause. Claire Goll's charges quickly subsided, but Celan never recovered from the attacks. His mental suffering in the 1960s is inseparable from the Goll affair, which he experienced as a traumatic continuation of his persecution under the Nazis.

Celan's lifelong struggle to achieve a personal form of expression in the face of brutal attempts to deprive him of his identity might resonate for American students who are familiar with the struggles of minority-group members to assert themselves. Students' realization might prompt a general discussion of lyric poetry as a subjective form of human expression. In a short speech Celan gave on receiving a literary prize, he said that

> language, remained, not lost, yes in spite of everything. But it had to pass through its own answerlessness, pass through a frightful muting, pass through the thousand darknesses of deathbringing speech. It passed through and gave back no words for that which happened; yet it passed through this happening. Passed through and could come to light again, "enriched" by all this. (*Selected Poems* 395)

Celan's startling capacity for rhetorical irony is apparent here: the German language, for him, had been "enriched" ("angereichert") by the crimes committed during the reign of the Reich.

The initial question whether "Todesfuge" represents the kind of poetry that triumphs over what has been considered unspeakable can now be modified as we draw attention to Celan's technique of layering incompatible meanings in one image (of "the stars," for instance). Instead of opposing poetry to history, suffering to art, and language to silence, "Todesfuge" demonstrates how history shapes our understanding of poetry, how veiled references transform images culled from different traditions and introduce an almost palpable sense of dread, and how poetry can make use of these effects to testify to a reality whose truth cannot be contained by one perspective.

Works Cited

Adorno, Theodor W. "Cultural Criticism and Society." *Prisms.* Trans. Samuel Weber and Shierry Weber. Cambridge: MIT P, 1967. 17–34.

Bernstein, Michael André. *Five Portraits: Modernity and the Imagination in Twentieth-Century German Writing.* Evanston: Northwestern UP, 2000.

Celan, Paul. *Der Meridian: Endfassung, Vorstufen, Materialien.* Frankfurt: Suhrkamp, 1999.

———. *Selected Poems and Prose of Paul Celan.* Trans. John Felstiner. New York: Norton, 2001.

Chalfen, Israel. *Paul Celan: A Biography of His Youth.* Trans. Maximilan Bleyleben. New York: Persea, 1991.

Colin, Amy. *Paul Celan: Holograms of Darkness.* Bloomington: Indiana UP, 1991.

Felman, Shoshana. "The Return of the Voice: Claude Lanzmann's *Shoah.*" *Testimony: Crises of Witnessing in Literature, Psychoanalysis, and History.* By Felman and Dori Laub. New York: Routledge, 1991. 204–83.

Felstiner, John. *Paul Celan: Poet, Survivor, Jew.* New Haven: Yale UP, 1995.

Konzett, Matthias, ed. *Encyclopedia of German Literature.* Chicago: Fitzroy Dearborn, 2000.

Meltzer, Françoise. *Hot Property: The Stakes and Claims of Literary Originality.* Chicago: U of Chicago P, 1994.

Olschner, Leonard. "Fugal Provocation in Paul Celan's *Todesfuge* and *Engführung.*" *German Life and Letters* 43.1 (1989): 79–89.

Wiedemann, Barbara, ed. *Paul Celan: Die Gedichte.* Frankfurt: Suhrkamp, 2003.

Gary Weissman

Questioning Key Texts:
A Pedagogical Approach
to Teaching Elie Wiesel's *Night*

No work testifying to the horror of the Nazi camps is taught more frequently in American middle schools, high schools, and colleges than Elie Wiesel's *Night*. Indeed, *Night* is the key literary text through which the destruction of the European Jews is contemplated not only by most students of the Holocaust but also by a great many teachers. Consequently, much has been written on teaching *Night*, most of it by and for secondary school teachers, as those in higher education have seldom addressed the practical matter of how to teach this book in the college classroom.[1] Scholars have, instead, produced a vast corpus of commentary on *Night*, much of which describes the book as an incomparable work that resists literary categorization and critical analysis.[2] This scholarship serves foremost to affirm Wiesel's authority as the living memorial to the Holocaust and to elucidate his moral and theological "messages to humanity." It also encourages pedagogical approaches to *Night* that focus on teaching these messages without examining how they are shaped by the act of writing.

This essay proposes that teachers employ a more critical stance when teaching Wiesel's book to college students. It identifies and challenges some assumptions that underlie traditional approaches to *Night*, while describing the alternative path I followed in my literature course Auschwitz Memoirs: Reading and Writing on Holocaust Testimony. Needing to assemble a manageable reading list for this course and wanting to highlight the variety of literary approaches taken to render a shared experience — while emphasizing how vastly different this experience was for Jews and non-Jews, men and women, teens and adults, members of different nationalities, and prisoners assigned to various kinds of work — I decided to limit the readings to six memoirs set largely at Auschwitz.[3] I began the course with *Night* to engage students' prior understanding of how Holocaust memoirs should be read. Because of their familiarity with a conception of the Holocaust that has entered American culture largely through Elie Wiesel, this understanding — that the proper response to survivor memoirs is a kind of self-effacing reverence — was shared even by students who had not previously read *Night*.

Wiesel's influence on Holocaust remembrance is difficult to overestimate, as he has largely defined the terms in which the Holocaust is contemplated and discussed — even establishing *Holocaust* as the common term for the Nazi genocide (Garber and Zuckerman 202). "I remember having chosen the word because of its mystical and religious connotations," he has said (qtd. in Lewis 156). In books, speeches, and newspaper articles, Wiesel describes the extermination of the European Jews as a sacred mystery, central to which is the question of God's role in the tragedy. He contends that the Holocaust transcends history and defies comprehension and comparison to other events; it can be represented through survivor testimony alone, for only the survivors know what it was like, yet even their testimony is incapable of fully revealing the event. The survivors are duty-bound to testify; as for the rest of us, our proper response is one of deferential silence before the ineffable. We are not to understand or explain the Holocaust; we must listen to the survivors and remember.

Even students unfamiliar with Wiesel will have internalized a sense of the Holocaust as an event of intimidating, mystical-religious magnitude. This sense is manifested in students' understanding that survivor memoirs compel an ethical response of awe, grief, or silence. In my classroom the articulation of these responses was the starting point rather than the goal of discussion. Rather than have students respond to writing about the Holocaust as if responding to the Holocaust itself, I wanted them to recognize Holocaust memoirs as writing that can be read critically—in a way that involves not fault-finding but stepping back to reexamine a text from a fresh perspective. This meant putting aside a conception of the Holocaust that grants survivor memoirs the aura of sacred testimony, discouraging inquiry and analysis as irreverent.

James E. Young has persuasively argued that survivor testimony should be valued not for providing factual evidence but for identifying "the kinds of understanding the victims brought to their experiences and . . . the kinds of actions they took on behalf of this understanding" (10). Still, critical readers are faced with an added complexity, for the extent to which survivor memoirs provide historical understanding of how their authors perceived events during the Holocaust is questionable. After all, a survivor's retrospective perception of events may differ substantially from the understanding that shaped his or her comprehension of and response to events as they occurred. Yet, far from detracting from what this literature offers, the fact that the memoirs can testify to how survivors' worldviews have changed since the Holocaust adds a deeply meaningful dimension to what we can learn from reading them. Instead of thinking in terms of "the collective voice of the survivor" (Fine 105), we can explore how surviving victims' distinctive voices continue to develop after Auschwitz, despite many scholars' efforts to ground survivors' worldviews and voices in the extreme experience of the Holocaust, making that experience definitive.

As the structure of my Auschwitz Memoirs course suggests, I believe that the Holocaust is best taught not through authoritative key texts but through a number of texts that make smaller claims to being decisive or representative. This view conflicts with a pronounced tendency among Holocaust commentators to lay claim to key texts through which the horror of the Holocaust is laid bare. Not long ago this tendency led to the debacle involving Binjamin Wilkomirski's *Fragments: Memories of a Wartime Childhood*. Praised as a Holocaust memoir on a par with *Night*, *Fragments* accrued numerous awards and speaking engagements for its author before it was revealed to be a fraud, a work of fiction by a Swiss-born, non-Jewish writer impersonating a Holocaust survivor. Early doubts about the veracity of the book were discouraged by suggestions that one would be revictimizing Wilkomirski, impugning the memory of child survivors, and lending credence to deniers by questioning the truthfulness of his memoir (see Eskin 139–53).

The rush to make *Fragments* the newest key text on the Holocaust discouraged critical readings that might have shown that Wilkomirski's book could not be what it professes to be even if its author were a survivor of the Nazi camps. "I am not a poet or a writer," writes Wilkomirski, who claims to recount events not as the survivor-writer remembers them decades later but as they are held in his "child's memory" (4–5). This is the long-silenced, almost preverbal memory of a child so young that little or no social or linguistic understanding predating the camps impinged on his perception of horrific events as they unfolded. In claiming to let this memory speak directly, without the intervention of adult interpretation or the writer's hand, *Fragments* offers readers the fantasy of a Holocaust memoir unmediated by any reshaping of the past.

While as a counterfeit work of Holocaust literature *Fragments* seems an anomaly, it reveals a resistance to critical reading that often accompanies efforts to celebrate key Holocaust texts and defend them against heretical interpretations. This resistance arises from efforts to ground Holocaust testimony in something more authentic and authoritative than writing—which is shaped, on the one hand, by the survivors' subjective and mutable understanding of past experiences and, on the other, by rhetorical decisions regarding such matters as literary approach, narrative voice, and audience. These efforts lead to the creation of mythic origins, such as the grounding of *Fragments* in the unadulterated purity of a child's memory. As the validity of these mythic origins might not stand up to analysis, scholars' commentary on key texts often has the effect of forestalling rather than encouraging critical inquiry. Survivor testimony, when treated as "holy," tends to be read through practices that, as Young has noted, ignore "the ways in which Holocaust literary testimony is . . . constructed and interpretive" and focus instead on "finding meaning in the events it relates" (21–22).

This criticism certainly applies to *Night*, which, more than any other work of Holocaust literature, has given rise to an elaborate mythos regarding its origin. Even readers unfamiliar with commentary on *Night* may encounter it, as my students did, in François Mauriac's foreword, where Wiesel is described as having the look of "a Lazarus risen from the dead,"[4] and in Robert McAfee Brown's preface to the widely available Bantam paperback edition. At the core of this mythos is a mystical-religious sense that the Holocaust has made Wiesel its singular, most authoritative witness. Brown writes, "Among the few who survived . . . was Elie Wiesel, whose deliverance condemned him to tell the story to an unbelieving and uncaring world." He goes on to describe Wiesel as the medium through which we may come closest to the Holocaust, stating that "between us and the fiery furnaces where they burned babies alive stands the presence of Elie Wiesel; his presence casts a shadow from within which we can see, in dimmest outline, the reality he saw and touched and tasted directly" (vi). Here Brown manages to describe how we "see" the Holocaust through Wiesel in terms that make no mention of reading or writing.

Night is, of course, a written text; but myths concerning how *Night* came into being suggest that the book's authenticity lies in its resistance to whatever is potentially distancing and fictionalizing about writing. These myths, often recited by Wiesel and repeated by scholars, base *Night*'s authenticity and authority in the absence of words, in a mystical-religious silence. One myth concerns Wiesel's vow of silence: in 1945 he vowed to wait ten years before writing about the Holocaust, "to be sure that what [he] would say would be true" ("Talking" 274; see also Wiesel, "A Jew Today" 18). Another myth placing the writing of Wiesel's book in the context of a far greater silence involves the paring down of *Night* from eight hundred pages to a slim volume closer to one hundred pages. Wiesel has written:

> To bring back at least a certain fragment of the truth the writer becomes responsible not only for the words but for the white spaces between the words, not only for the language but for the silence. Therefore, the less you write, the more true the message and the story. ("How" 65)

One need not refer to noteworthy Holocaust memoirs that are much longer than *Night* or that were written just after the war to cast doubt on these myths of what guarantees truth in representations of the Holocaust; the question is why Holocaust scholars who write on Wiesel have so often embraced the myths. While the young Wiesel may have taken a vow of silence, the story becomes myth when read as evidence of his memoir's truthfulness or authenticity. No doubt there are compelling reasons why he waited years to write about the camps. Perhaps he was too traumatized to dwell on his experiences with the intensity required by writing; perhaps it took him years to feel confident enough as a writer to address them. Such conceivable explanations do not bear on the truth-value of what he eventually did write; instead, they relate to the demands of writing. Surely Wiesel's book is the result not of a purifying ten-year vow of silence but of a complex writing process that began with his decision to write, one day, about the camps. How are students to analyze the book, when the Holocaust's mystical-religious gravity, *Night*'s exalted status as *the* classic memoir of the Holocaust, and Wiesel's stature as *the* survivor of the Holocaust all conspire to dissuade them from considering *Night* as writing that can be read critically?

In my course, students were introduced to the critical reading of Holocaust memoirs through what can be regarded as a heretical reading of *Night*: Naomi Seidman's essay "Elie Wiesel and the Scandal of Jewish Rage." When discussing the essay in class (after we had read and discussed *Night*), many students expressed surprise, if not relief, that a survivor memoir could be closely analyzed and questioned — and without dishonoring the victims or denying the Holocaust. Seidman's essay reintroduced students to *Night* as a text with an elaborate history as a revised, edited, translated, and published piece of writing. It redirects our attention to this writing by comparing *Night* (really *La nuit*, the French work from which *Night* is translated)[5] with an earlier memoir that Wiesel wrote in Yiddish and published in 1956, two years before *La nuit*. This memoir, titled *Un di velt hot geshvign* (And the World Remained Silent), is frequently omitted from discussions of Wiesel's oeuvre and from commentary on *Night*, which is typically referred to as Wiesel's first book. When *Un di velt* is mentioned, it is described in passing as a longer, unrefined version of *Night*. Seidman, by contrast, approaches this "unread ghost" (18) as a book in its own right, a memoir telling a story related to, but different from, the one told in *Night*.

Seidman's critical reading of *Un di velt* is also a critical rereading of *Night*. Her focus is on how Wiesel wrote his memoirs for two different audiences — one of Yiddish-speaking Jews, the other of Christian readers. She finds the differences between the two memoirs best conveyed by the books' contrasting images of the survivor. In *Night* the image is portrayed in the book's oft-cited last lines, where Eliezer, hospitalized in Buchenwald after the camp's liberation, looks in a mirror: "From the depths of the mirror, a corpse gazed back at me. The look in his eyes, as they stared into mine, has never left me" (109). Innumerable scholars have commented on the significance of this image without knowing that it was not Wiesel who chose to end *Night* here but his French editor, Jérome Lindon, who also cut sixty-seven pages from the Yiddish memoir to produce the slim volume he and Wiesel titled *La nuit* (Wiesel, *All* 319; Diamont 260). Whereas *Night* ends with the image of the survivor as corpse, the Yiddish memoir continues: "I saw the image of myself after my death. It was at that instant that the will to live was awakened. Without knowing why I raised a balled-up fist and smashed the mirror, breaking the image that lived within it" (qtd. in Seidman 7).

According to Seidman, the "Jewish rage" that compels the survivor to shatter the reflection of the skeletal camp prisoner also compels him to write about the camps — and "not ten years after the events of the Holocaust but immediately upon liberation as the first expression of his mental and physical recovery" (7). The Yiddish memoir presents an alternative mythic origin for Wiesel's testimony, in which the authenticity of his testimony is based not in silence but in its claim to having originated there in the camps. "I stayed in bed for a few more days, in the course of which I wrote the outline of the book you are holding in your hand, dear reader," writes Wiesel. He sees that "ten years after Buchenwald" the world is forgetting what happened to the Jews and fears that "the naïve world" will come to believe the lies of "Germans and anti-Semites" who deny the Holocaust. He concludes, "I thought it would be a good idea to publish a book based on the notes I wrote in Buchenwald" (qtd. in Seidman 7).

Here writing comes across not as a mysterious struggle to represent the unrepresentable but as a practical means of resistance (only later could Wiesel say, "Writing lies within the domain of mystery" [*All* 321]). "The Yiddish survivor is filled with rage and the desire to live, to take revenge, to write," states Seidman (7). The French survivor, by contrast, does not smash the mirror or write notes for a book he will publish to counter the lies of Germans, antisemites, and a naive world. Why not? Seidman argues that in order to appeal to a wider audience of Christian readers, Wiesel and his French publishers reshaped his story, transforming "the survivor's political rage into his existential doubt" directed at the Jewish God (15).

My point in assigning Seidman's essay was not to replace the mythic reading of *Night* with the "true" reading. In fact, since teaching Auschwitz Memoirs, I have come across a highly negative response to her essay that I would recommend assigning alongside it. The essay, by Eli Pfefferkorn and David Hirsch, "Elie Wiesel's Wrestle with God," sets out to refute what the authors see as "Ms. Seidman's attempt to undermine the authenticity of *Night* as witness testimony" (21). The authors contend that her "revisionist essay," written in both bad faith and righteous fury, grossly exaggerates differences between *Un di velt* and *La nuit* or *Night*. Although I find their arguments largely unpersuasive, their response to Seidman's argument allows students to see the critical reading of *Night* as the subject of an ongoing conversation in which they, too, can take part. Whether or not one agrees with Seidman's reading of *Night*, the real value of her essay for teaching is that it allows students to see the importance of approaching survivor memoirs as texts that are written for specific audiences, that employ various literary strategies, and that express particular interpretations of experience.

Following our discussion of Seidman, and before turning to the memoirs we would read, the class looked at a passage from Wiesel's 1995 memoir, *All Rivers Run to the Sea*, to consider how he might have reinterpreted his experiences since *Night* was published. (A more approachable text may be the 1997 *New York Times* op-ed piece "A Prayer for the Days of Awe," in which Wiesel writes that he now realizes he never lost faith in God, "not even over there," at Auschwitz.) The passage from *All Rivers* describes experiences in Auschwitz that bear no mention in *Night*: Eliezer and his father wake before roll call to strap on tefillin and recite blessings; Eliezer says his prayers every day and hums Shabbat songs on Saturdays (82). Having reexamined *Night* through Seidman's essay, students were prepared to discuss how Wiesel might have reshaped the image of his past, and the image of the survivor, to match his present worldview. That is, they considered how as Wiesel's crisis of religious belief has given way to a growing reaffirmation of Jewish faith, his depictions of Jewish experience at Auschwitz have changed accordingly.

Although I have described an approach using Seidman's essay to introduce students to issues involving the construction and reception of *Night* and of Holocaust memoirs generally, teachers may apply Seidman's insights without necessarily assigning her essay. For instance, teachers can ask students to compare the endings of *Night* and *Un di velt* as well as passages in *Night* and *All Rivers* concerning religious practice in the camp. Through discussion of these passages' stylistic and thematic differences, students may come to their own realization of the complex, nontransparent, evolving relation between experience and writing. In addition to highlighting Wiesel's treatments of certain themes (Jewish identity, the image of the survivor, silence), teachers can ask students to consider how the particular time and language in which each of the three accounts was written bear on the decisions Wiesel made as a writer.

Seidman remarks, "It is a measure of the profundity of the influence of *Night* on the discourse of Holocaust literature that its distinctive tone and approach has come to seem simply inevitable, the only response imaginable" (3). No doubt, *Night*'s mythic status has served to make it a useful tool for teaching the Holocaust to young people, as it encourages teachers to believe that they can adequately cover the Holocaust with this single, short book. In an essay written for teachers, Margaret A. Drew writes that since young people's knowledge of the Holocaust is often limited to what they learn from reading only one book, that text must be "good history as well as good literature" (11). "One of the few books that can meet the criteria in both history and literature is Elie Wiesel's *Night*," she states, adding that it presents "a personal experience that can be multiplied by 6 million" (15–16). Carol Danks similarly recommends *Night* to high school teachers, noting that it "presents accurate historical information, has an authentic narrative voice, seems approachable to students, and can be taught in limited classroom time" (101).

Having been introduced to the Holocaust as a child by reading an autographed copy of *Night*, I can attest to its great educational value. Treated as a window onto the Holocaust, *Night* allows young readers to gain a valuable introductory understanding of what European Jews experienced in the Holocaust. But all texts, and key texts in particular, need to be read differently at different levels. At the college level, *Night* is a key text through which teachers can encourage students to move past an uncritical mystical-religious conception of the Holocaust, toward a deeper understanding of how survivors have translated their experiences into writing. There may be real value in treating Wiesel's book as a text that teaches itself by emotionally affecting younger readers, just as younger students may benefit from reading *Night* as a transparently authentic voicing of accurate historical information, expressing the experience of all victims. But for mature students, a deeper appreciation of Holocaust literature lies precisely in questioning the earlier reading.

Notes

1. Many Web sites offer lesson plans and activities for teaching *Night* to middle and high school students; several can be accessed at *Web English Teacher* (www.webenglishteacher.com/wiesel.html). For published writings see, for example, Danks; Drew; Greenbaum; Totten, "Entering."

Totten, a professor of curriculum development, provides one of the more comprehensive guides for teaching *Night*; however, his approach, like many others, suggests that only Wiesel provides the means for "grappling with Wiesel's story and the ramifications that the Holocaust has for humanity today" (239). Totten suggests that students, in addition to "writing a letter to Elie," take a final exam that asks them to respond to the "validity and significance" of Wiesel's statements by using "examples and additional quotes from Wiesel's *Night* to support their position and arguments" (224, 239). Diamant persuasively argues that for literary scholars as well "it is Wiesel himself who is largely responsible for generating the terms in which he is read" (118).

2. *Night*'s literary genre is strangely unresolved. "Described as an autobiographical narrative, a fictionalized autobiography, a nonfictional novel, the work defies all categories," writes Fine (114). For a discussion of *Night*'s literary status, see my *Fantasies of Witnessing*. For a brief discussion of the resistance to subjecting *Night* to literary considerations, see Rosen (1321) and Davis, who also offers a valuable discussion of the book's literary construction. For a concise sampling of scholarship on *Night*, see Mass; for a succinct overview of this scholarship, see Rosen (1321–24).

3. Besides *Night*, readings included *The Yellow Star*, by Simcha Bunem Unsdorfer; *Auschwitz: True Tales from a Grotesque Land*, by Sara Nomberg-Przytyk; *None of Us Will Return*, by Charlotte Delbo; *Auschwitz: A Doctor's Eyewitness Account*, by Miklos Nyiszli; and *Eyewitness Auschwitz: Three Years in the Gas Chambers*, by Filip Müller. We began with "Auschwitz—an Overview," by Yisrael Gutman. (For more on Delbo, see the essay in this volume by Greenberg.)

4. For contrasting evaluations of Mauriac's foreword, see Fleischner; Langer (142–44); as well as Seidman's more thorough consideration of Wiesel and Mauriac's relationship.

5. There are, of course, significant differences between *La nuit* and *Night*, but these fall outside the purview of Seidman's essay. For a consideration of these differences, see Diamant, in which she notes material that has been added to the English translation (287).

Works Cited

Brown, Robert McAfee. Preface. *Night*. By Elie Wiesel. 25th anniversary ed. New York: Bantam, 1986. v–vi.

Danks, Carol. "Using the Literature of Elie Wiesel and Selected Poetry to Teach the Holocaust in the Secondary School History Classroom." *Social Studies* 87.3 (1996): 101–05.

Davis, Colin. "How Wiesel Tells the Story That Can Never Be Told." Mass 78–85.

Delbo, Charlotte. *None of Us Will Return*. Trans. John Githens. Boston: Beacon, 1978.

Diamant, Naomi. "The Boundaries of Holocaust Literature: The Emergence of a Canon." Diss. Columbia U, 1992.

Drew, Margaret A. "Teaching Holocaust Literature: Issues, Caveats, and Suggestions." Totten, *Teaching* 11–23.

Eskin, Blake. *A Life in Pieces: The Making and Unmaking of Binjamin Wilkomirski.* New York: Norton, 2002.

Fine, Ellen S. "The Surviving Voice: Literature of the Holocaust." *Perspectives on the Holocaust.* Ed. Randolph L. Braham. Boston: Kluwer-Nijhoff, 1983. 105–17.

Fleischner, Eva. "A Letter to Question *Night*'s Preface." Mass 157–60.

Garber, Zev, and Bruce Zuckerman. "Why Do We Call the Holocaust 'The Holocaust'? An Inquiry into the Psychology of Labels." *Modern Judaism* 9.2 (1989): 197–211.

Greenbaum, Beth Aviv. *Bearing Witness: Teaching about the Holocaust.* Portsmouth: Heinemann, 2001.

Gutman, Yisrael. "Auschwitz—an Overview." *The Anatomy of the Auschwitz Death Camp.* Ed. Gutman and Michael Berenbaum. Bloomington: Indiana UP; Washington: United States Holocaust Memorial Museum, 1994. 5–33.

Langer, Lawrence L. *Preempting the Holocaust.* New Haven: Yale UP, 1998.

Lewis, Stephen. *Art out of Agony: The Holocaust Theme in Literature, Sculpture, and Film.* Toronto: CBC Enterprises, 1984.

Mass, Wendy, ed. *Readings on* Night. San Diego: Greenhaven, 2000.

Müller, Filip. *Eyewitness Auschwitz: Three Years in the Gas Chambers.* Trans. Susanne Flatauer. Chicago: Dee, 1999.

Nomberg-Przytyk, Sara. *Auschwitz: True Tales from a Grotesque Land.* Trans. Roslyn Hirsch. Chapel Hill: U of North Carolina P, 1985.

Nyiszli, Miklos. *Auschwitz: A Doctor's Eyewitness Account.* Trans. Tibère Kremer and Richard Seaver. New York: Arcade, 1993.

Pfefferkorn, Eli, and David H. Hirsch. "Elie Wiesel's Wrestle with God." *Midstream* Nov. 1997: 20–22.

Rosen, Allan. "Elie Wiesel." *Holocaust Literature: An Encyclopedia of Writers and Their Work.* Ed. S. Lillian Kremer. Vol. 2. New York: Routledge, 2003. 1315–25.

Seidman, Naomi. "Elie Wiesel and the Scandal of Jewish Rage." *Jewish Social Studies* 3.1 (1996): 1–19.

Totten, Samuel. "Entering the 'Night' of the Holocaust: Studying Elie Wiesel's *Night*." Totten, *Teaching* 215–42.

———, ed. *Teaching Holocaust Literature.* Boston: Allyn, 2001.

Unsdorfer, Simcha Burem. *The Yellow Star.* New York: Yoseloff, 1961.

Wiesel, Elie. *All Rivers Run to the Sea: Memoirs.* New York: Schocken, 1995.

———. "How Does One Write?" *Against Silence: The Voice and Vision of Elie Wiesel.* Ed. Irving Abrahamson. Vol. 2. New York: Holocaust Lib., 1985. 65.

———. *A Jew Today.* Trans. Marion Wiesel. New York: Vintage, 1978.

———. *Night.* Trans. Stella Rodway. Fwd. François Mauriac. New York: Bantam, 1986.

———. *La nuit.* Paris: Minuit, 1958.

———. "A Prayer for the Days of Awe." *New York Times* 2 Oct. 1997: A16.

———. "Talking and Writing and Keeping Silent." *The German Church Struggle and the Holocaust.* Ed. Franklin H. Littell and Hubert G. Locke. Detroit: Wayne State UP, 1974. 269–77.

———. *Un di velt hot geshvign.* Dos Poylishe Yidnòtum 17. Buenos Aires: Tsentral-Farband fun Poylishe Yidn in Argentina, 1956.

Weissman, Gary. *Fantasies of Witnessing: Postwar Efforts to Experience the Holocaust.* Ithaca: Cornell UP, 2004.

Wilkomirski, Binjamin. *Fragments: Memories of a Wartime Childhood.* Trans. Carol Brown Janeway. New York: Schocken, 1996.

Young, James E. *Writing and Rewriting the Holocaust: Narrative and the Consequences of Interpretation.* Bloomington: Indiana UP, 1990.

Jonathan Druker

A Rational Humanist Confronts the Holocaust: Teaching Primo Levi's *Survival in Auschwitz*

At Auschwitz, Primo Levi encountered a world that was as improbable and unbelievable as it was brutal. In his death camp memoir, *Survival in Auschwitz*, he reports being plagued, while in captivity, by a recurring dream in which he tells "this very story," the one the reader has in hand, and is not believed by his audience (60). Now, on a different continent and in a new century, American college students at a large public university in the Midwest are, if anything, too credulous when reading Levi, too convinced that his lucid, restrained prose captures, in one-to-one correspondence, the single reality of the death camp. Of course, they need not doubt the authenticity of this canonical Holocaust text, written immediately after the war, in 1946, but they do need to develop sensitivity to the particular cultural lens through which any memoirist views experience. Autobiographical writing does not imitate the world but constructs a personal and approximate version of it subject to the limits of language and ideology. Even students familiar with these principles of critical reading are likely to set them aside in the case of Levi's testimony, because the Holocaust, especially when represented in this genre, has a nearly inviolable status in mainstream America. Yet, despite being firsthand accounts of enormous suffering and profound ethical searching, Holocaust-survivor testimonies demand the same scrutiny that careful readers accord to other literary texts. Therefore, when teaching *Survival in Auschwitz*, the instructor has the pressing task of helping students recognize the significant extent to which Levi's cultural assumptions inform his representation of the camp, giving it shape and contour. This essay offers a reading that pays attention to the text's cultural and ideological frames of reference and outlines specific strategies for making them evident to students. Naturally, this rich and complex book supports a variety of other theoretical and thematic approaches that lend themselves to sound pedagogies.[1]

With some knowledge of European history, the canny reader of *Survival in Auschwitz* deduces much about Levi's background that is confirmed by other sources, such as his largely autobiographical volume *The Periodic Table*. Levi grew up in a secular, bourgeois family in the thoroughly acculturated Jewish community of Turin, which had endorsed, and benefited from, Enlightenment principles of equality and universal rights. Having received a solid education in the canonical Western texts and having completed a university degree in chemistry, Levi deeply imbibed the values associated with science and humanism. The narrator of *Survival in Auschwitz* effectively identifies himself, in order of importance, as a man, an Italian, and a chemist; his Jewish background is rather insignificant to him but not, of course, to the Nazis and to the Italian Fascists who adopted antisemitic racial laws in 1938. Levi's commitments determined the categories and parameters that he draws on when registering his impressions of Auschwitz and representing himself as a survivor; in short, he writes as a rational humanist who has faith in the efficacy of both secular ethics and the scientific method. Thus, it is self-evident to him that Nazi ideas about race, based on irrational hatred and specious science, are simply false and must be resisted. Even at Auschwitz, where he, like all the victims, underwent an almost unimaginable dehumanization at the hands of other human beings, his trust in humanist culture and rational thought continued to exist on some level.

Since the United States is, for the most part, heir to these ideas, it is not surprising that Levi's rational humanism contributes to the tendency of students to produce uncritical readings of the memoir. For many readers, his perspective appears natural, neither tendentious nor selective, and therefore beyond critique. Indeed, Levi's book draws enormous strength from unquestioned moral universals and seemingly unassailable propositions: that nothing is more valuable than human life and that every life is of equal worth; that inhumane action can have no rational basis and can never be justified; that differences in race, religion, and ethnicity are much less significant than what unites humanity; that divine powers do not decide human affairs. With the possible exception of Levi's atheism, virtually all American students will endorse his values and confirm how fundamental they are to our idea of civilization. Nevertheless, students can be made to understand that these values have their own genealogy and are not neutral. Encoded in them are specific ideas about what it means to be human, ideas that met their greatest challenge during the Holocaust.

Auschwitz, as represented in Levi's memoir, was designed not only to exterminate enemies of the Third Reich but also to contest the validity of rational humanist concepts that coalesce around the words *human* and *man* (*man* understood by Levi as a genderless abstraction). The memoir's governing idea, at moments obscured by numerous factual details that fulfill an invaluable documentary function, is that Auschwitz obliterated the humanity of both the oppressed and the oppressors. "The personages of these pages are not men," Levi writes. "Their humanity is buried, or they themselves have buried it, under an offence received or inflicted on someone else" (*Survival* 121). Early chapters carefully explain how the newly arrived death camp prisoner, stripped of community, family, possessions, dignity, and even his name, becomes "a hollow man, reduced to suffering and needs, . . . a man whose life or death can be lightly decided with no sense of human affinity" (27). For Levi, the creation of Auschwitz expresses "the resolution of others to annihilate us first as men in order to kill us more slowly afterwards" (51).

The importance of this theme, the fragility of human identity in a death camp designed to expunge it, is brought front and center in the epigraphic poem that evokes powerful images of physical and psychological dehumanization (11). In keeping with Levi's secular humanism, the poem, elsewhere titled "Shemà," after the fundamental prayer in Judaism (itself drawn from Deut. 6.4–9), supplants the Jews' commitment to monotheism with a menacing curse on those who fail to acknowledge the humanity of the suffering victims (see Levi's *Collected Poems* 9). Drawn from a line in the poem, the memoir's original Italian title, *Se questo è un uomo* (If This Is a Man), although both hesitant and ambiguous, offers no promises of survival but foregrounds questions about the definition of the word *man* and the conclusions or obligations (the "then") that may flow from the "if" statement. Not surprisingly, students are misled by the book's American title, which markets death camp survival as a kind of redemption. However, Auschwitz produced very few survivors; it produced, rather, an inconceivable number of people who, according to Levi, were so drained of physical and mental vigor as to be only hollow shells. (In the death camp jargon, these prisoners were known as *Muselmänner*, a term of uncertain origin that perhaps refers to the supposedly fatalistic attitude of Muslims toward whatever Allah wills for them. See Agamben 41–86 for a probing discussion of the significance of the *Muselmänner* as represented in texts by Levi and other authors.) In large measure, it is the death camp's ferocious assault on humanity at large, not just individuals, not just the Jews, that spurs Levi to write his testimony. This assault is hauntingly embodied in the image of the "non-man," who, for Levi, is the emblematic image of "all the evil of our time" (90).

With some help from the instructor, students will recognize the important role of the "non-man" in Levi's conception of Auschwitz as a "world of negation" (122), opposed to all that is positive and good. A productive classroom exercise is to have students generate binary pairs that incisively contrast Levi's values with the negative ones privileged in Auschwitz. Starting from man, effectively the memoir's own starting point, pairs emerge in which the first term identifies ideas Levi defends against the second term, which figures significantly in his representation of Auschwitz and its functions: man or human versus animal or non-man, mind versus body, rational thought or consciousness versus instinct or madness or absence of thought, science versus myth, language versus unintelligible Babel or silence, freedom versus slavery, ethical obligation to the other person versus Darwinian survival of the fittest. These binary terms provide the basis for a practical pedagogical approach to the text that helps students recognize several important themes that together give form to Levi's rational humanist conception of the camp. After the binaries have been presented, the students' assignment, as they read, is to identify qualities that, for Levi, confer humanness on humans; to note how Auschwitz works to undermine these qualities; and to consider what avenues Levi and the other prisoners might have for resisting dehumanization.

The contested status of rational thought in Auschwitz is a key theme in the memoir, and it will serve here as an example of how Levi's cultural assumptions organize his experience of the Holocaust. In broad terms, he represents the death camp as a giant, mind-emptying machine that efficiently produces the unvarying non-man "on whose face and in whose eyes not a trace of thought is to be seen" (90). The prisoners are "automatons": "they do not think and they do not desire, they walk" (51). If they think anything, it is that they have become no more than "hunger, living hunger" (74). Levi's own encounter with the camp's crushing assault on thought is summed up pithily by a camp guard who tells the new arrival, "'*Hier ist kein warum*' (there is no why here)" (29). Levi does not take this remark to mean that rational analysis necessarily falters in the face of irrational violence or that Auschwitz is a nihilistic void so profound as to be beyond our comprehension; rather, it means that the camp's function is to diminish the prisoners' humanity by denying their capacity for understanding. Indeed, "one loses the habit . . . in the Lager . . . of believing in one's own reason" (171). The camp's brutal regime demands instinctual response, not speculation: two weeks after his arrival, Levi has concluded that "it was better not to think" (37), as it took too much energy and evoked painful memories of all that was already lost to him. Later, in a moment of self-criticism, he accepts that he is "not made of the stuff of those who resist [death]," that he is "too civilized" and "think[s] too much" (103). Thought and civilization are inexorably linked for him, just as madness is an inherent feature of the barbarous world of Auschwitz (20).

Although Levi eventually includes himself among the senior prisoners who know the wisdom of "not trying to understand" (116), he could not have written so thoughtfully after his liberation from the camp had he not constantly observed and analyzed his surroundings and the behavior of his fellow prisoners in ways that had no immediate utility, except perhaps as an affirmation of his own durable human qualities. Every page of *Survival in Auschwitz* seeks to affirm the value of rational thought and the scientific method, the very habits of mind that Auschwitz almost completely eliminated in its victims. Thus one can surmise that thinking about the camp, its function and its meaning, was a modest form of resistance to Nazism and also a process for turning negative experience into positive knowledge. "No human experience is without meaning or unworthy of analysis," Levi asserts; "fundamental values, even if they are not positive, can be deduced from this particular world we are describing" (87). For Levi, as a scientist, there is always a what and a why, always something to learn. By turning Auschwitz into a complex problem for analysis, he resists the system designed to diminish the very abilities, such as rational thought, that in his view distinguish human beings from animals. Moreover, he refuses to mystify the Holocaust, to relegate it to a realm beyond comprehension.

An important dramatization of the humanizing value of preserving thought and gaining knowledge in the death camp occurs when Levi recites the Ulysses passage in Dante's *Inferno* to a French friend (112–15). Only now does Levi understand what he memorized as a schoolboy, the lines of Ulysses's famous speech to his sailors: "you were made men, / to seek after knowledge" (113). Spoken inside the death camp, this humanist creed acquires profound meaning for Levi. These several pages of the memoir lay out a complex scene about cultural memory and the literary canon, language and translation, and teaching; for my present purpose, however, what is significant is the analogy Levi draws between Ulysses's audacious voyage and the audacity of the prisoners, Levi and his friend, who "dare to reason" in this place (114). The idea that thinking and knowing confer humanness is again put forward when, through his knowledge of organic chemistry, Levi convinces an unsympathetic German chemist that he is not a "something" that it is "opportune to suppress" but a man whose individual identity "is impossible to doubt." He feels a "lucid elation" resulting from the "spontaneous mobilization of all [his] logical faculties." Indeed, he "seem[s] to grow in stature" as his intellectual prowess is recognized (106).

Another key element in Levi's rational humanism finds expression in the memoir's ethical discourse. Students understand that Levi conceives of Auschwitz as a world without ethics, but they need help recognizing, and then articulating, the ways in which the memoir stages a confrontation between his secular ethics and the Nazis' murderous social Darwinism. While the basis of Levi's ethics is Judeo-Christian, the commitment to these principles does not originate in a covenant with God; rather, in a Kantian fashion, one is ethically obligated to other persons, friend or foe, because they are rational beings. Levi understands Nazism as having supplanted the ethical obligation to others with Darwinist thinking, which renders moral questions irrelevant: whoever survives is fittest, and being fit is the only virtue in this system of thought.

According to Levi, Auschwitz, as a microcosm of the Nazi realm, is governed by "a pitiless process of natural selection," where "the struggle to survive is without respite, because everyone is desperately and ferociously alone" (89, 88). With the total breakdown of community among the prisoners, each is compelled to disregard the humanity of the others. The survivors, "the saved," suppress all compassion for, and even exploit, "the drowned," another term Levi uses to describe the non-men. Indeed, the common trait among four survivors vividly portrayed in the memoir is their loathsome selfishness (92–100). At this point, it becomes clear that Levi has ironically inverted the typical moral terminology: "the drowned" (i.e., the damned) in Auschwitz are innocent and "the saved" (i.e., the survivors) are sinners. No matter what moral shortcomings they possessed, the non-men are absolved because they are complete victims, while the survivors of this Darwinian world inevitably appear morally corrupt when judged by the standards of everyday life. Still, some students miss the significance of Levi's remark about the rarity of survival "without renunciation of any part of one's own moral world" (92). They may do so, in part, because they implicitly believe in heroic individualism, a concept not at odds with humanism, and also because Levi praises the ingenuity of some survival schemes (145–48). In linking physical and moral survival in their mistaken reading of Levi's representation of Auschwitz, these students tend to see the survivors as worthy, since they have the will and courage to survive, and the non-men as unworthy, since they lack the ability to save themselves. The instructor can head off this misapprehension and even use it to engage in a larger discussion about survivor guilt, or what Levi calls "shame" (150). For a substantive engagement with the topic, students can also read Levi's short essay "Shame," found in *The Drowned and the Saved*. Teachers who wish to focus on the difficult questions Auschwitz raises about ethics and justice might assign "The Gray Zone," another essay from that collection, which describes how the structure of the concentration camp blurred the distinctions between victims and victimizers, producing an ambiguous world in which the simple hero-villain binary comes apart.

One last pedagogical suggestion applies to courses in which students read other survivor memoirs aside from Levi's: comparing Holocaust testimonies can sharpen students' thinking about the importance of a memoirist's cultural lens. For example, the Auschwitz of Elie Wiesel's *Night* threatens the very possibility of faith in God and, therefore, the basis of the Jewish religion and identity (for more on *Night*, see the essay by Weissman in this volume). In contrast, the Auschwitz of Levi's memoir threatens to refute the Enlightenment's idea of humanity. Wiesel tends to focus on the particularity of the victims, European Jewry; Levi, discounting the ultimate significance of ethnic or racial difference, dwells instead on Nazism's affront to humanity at large. The point for students to appreciate here is that historical events, including the Holocaust, have no unitary, inscribed meanings; rather, all meanings, constantly various and shifting, are constructed with the aid of specific cultural and ideological frames of reference.

Having thus far encountered Levi on his own terms, in an effort to understand the categories of thought that produced and limit his concept of Auschwitz, I find it worth mentioning that his rational humanism can be fruitfully critiqued by using the ideas of posthumanist thinkers, such as Max Horkheimer and Theodor Adorno, who assert that fascism was not simply humanism's enemy but also its logical offshoot. In this view, genocidal violence is not antithetical to modernity, as Levi would have us believe, but one of its constitutive elements. With the instructor's help, students in advanced undergraduate courses can begin to develop a posthumanist critique by using the memoir itself to deconstruct the binaries that, for Levi, distinguish his normal world from the negative world of Auschwitz. Some of the following points might be made:

1. Levi defends the claims of Enlightenment universality whereby Nazism's attack on a single person, regardless of his or her cultural identity, amounts to an assault on the very idea of humanity. However, Horkheimer and Adorno argue that the principle of universality—that every human being is essentially the same— also oppresses the individual and crushes cultural and ethnic difference of every kind, producing forms of intolerance like antisemitism (13, 169).

2. Levi insists on the humanizing function of rational thought and contrasts it to the madness or absence of thought that characterized the death camp. Yet even if Auschwitz worked toward irrational ends, it used rational administration to systematically dehumanize the prisoners, as the memoir demonstrates in depressing detail. This observation about the Holocaust lends support to Horkheimer and Adorno's contention that instrumental reason and the technology it produces are not only progressive forces but also tools for domination in the hands of the powerful.[2]

3. A similar tension is evident in the memoir's embrace of the scientific method and knowledge, as expressions of human dignity,

and its rejection of the social Darwinism used to justify the creation of Auschwitz. The dilemma for the rational humanist is that Darwin's potent theory, a credit to the perspicacity of the human mind, actually dethrones human beings, transforming them into animals subject to exploitation and even natural selection.[3]

4. In *Survival in Auschwitz*, Ulysses seems to affirm his humanity by audaciously pursuing knowledge; for Horkheimer and Adorno, the figure of Ulysses in Western culture embodies aspects of fascism in that he conceives of knowledge as power and uses language and reason cunningly for self-preservation (60–61, 91). Indeed, both the Nazis and the Italian Fascists believed that they were the true inheritors of the noble Hellenic culture Ulysses represents. As a heroic survivor who refuses to bend before overwhelming forces, Ulysses has a role, in the memoir, that might thus be at odds with Levi's larger claim that survival actually diminished one's humanity and debased one's ethical principles.[4]

These points established, the instructor may invite students to consider whether the humanist ideas that Levi draws on are to some degree complicit in the Holocaust and, further, whether the Holocaust reveals something essential about the character of Western civilization. The goal is not to resolve these issues but to enable students to weigh claims that the Holocaust is unique against broader concerns about the recurring role of genocide and ethnic cleansing in the discourses of culture and science. Regardless of whether one embraces posthumanist ideas, a useful teaching strategy is to maintain a nonpartisan stance in the classroom. In setting forth without prejudice humanist and posthumanist interpretations of the Holocaust's relation to modernity, the instructor not only introduces two important philosophical traditions that have been used to situate the Holocaust in history but also enacts an effective, open-ended pedagogy that keeps students thoughtfully engaged.

Notes

1. Gordon's book, which covers Levi's entire output, has three intelligent chapters on *Survival in Auschwitz*, concentrating on ethics and the sight of the other, memory and the obligation to testify, and language

and silence. Agamben's intellectually demanding book argues persuasively, after Lyotard, that Levi testifies to the unrepresentable essence of Auschwitz. Langer's essay finds in Levi confirmation that the Holocaust constitutes a rupture in history from which no redemption and no knowledge can be recovered.

2. "The fallen nature of modern man cannot be separated from social progress. On one hand the growth of economic productivity furnishes the conditions for a world of greater justice; on the other hand it allows the technical apparatus and social groups which administer it a disproportionate superiority to the rest of the population" (xiv; see also 24, 30, 37).

3. "Knowledge, which is power, knows no obstacles: neither in the enslavement of men nor in the compliance of the world's rulers. . . . What men want to learn from nature is how to use it in order to dominate it and other men. That is the only aim" (Horkheimer and Adorno 4).

4. These ideas for a posthumanist critique are borrowed from my fuller treatment of such an approach in "The Shadowed Violence of Culture: Fascism and the Figure of Ulysses in Primo Levi's *Survival in Auschwitz*."

Works Cited

Agamben, Giorgio. *Remnants of Auschwitz: The Witness and the Archive*. Trans. Daniel Heller-Roazen. New York: Zone, 1999.

Druker, Jonathan. "The Shadowed Violence of Culture: Fascism and the Figure of Ulysses in Primo Levi's *Survival in Auschwitz*." *Clio: An Interdisciplinary Journal of Literature, History, and the Philosophy of History* 33.2 (2004): 143–61.

Gordon, Robert S. C. *Primo Levi's Ordinary Virtues: From Testimony to Ethics*. Oxford: Oxford UP, 2001.

Horkheimer, Max, and Theodor Adorno. *Dialectic of Enlightenment*. Trans. John Cummings. New York: Herder, 1972.

Langer, Lawrence L. "Legacy in Gray." *Memory and Mastery: Primo Levi as Writer and Witness*. Ed. Roberta S. Kremer. Albany: State U of New York P, 2001. 197–216.

Levi, Primo. *Collected Poems*. Trans. Ruth Feldman and Brian Swann. London: Faber, 1988.

———. *The Drowned and the Saved*. Trans. Raymond Rosenthal. New York: Random, 1989.

———. *The Periodic Table*. Trans. Raymond Rosenthal. New York: Schocken, 1984.

———. *Survival in Auschwitz: The Nazi Assault on Humanity*. Trans. Stuart Woolf. New York: Simon, 1996.

Lyotard, Jean-François. *The Differend: Phrases in Dispute*. Trans. Georges Van Den Abbeele. Minneapolis: U of Minnesota P, 1988.

Wiesel, Elie. *Night*. Trans. Stella Rodway. New York: Bantam, 1982.

Pascale Bos

Reconsidering Anne Frank: Teaching the Diary in Its Historical and Cultural Context

It is said that after the Bible, Anne Frank's diary is the most widely read text in the world. Thirty-one million copies of the diary have been sold, and it has been translated into more than sixty-five languages. In the United States, Anne Frank has been one of the central figures in Holocaust education for at least two generations, as her diary is used in almost all courses (and course sections) dealing with the Holocaust on the elementary and secondary education levels. To support this educational effort, great volumes of teaching materials have been created, suggesting a variety of approaches to teaching the diary. Considering the central presence of Frank, one may wonder what more could be said about the diary's use in the classroom. Quite a lot, in fact: while the use of Frank's diary (or the 1955 screenplay based on her journal) has largely gone undisputed among secondary school educators, the ubiquitous presence — some would argue overuse or misuse — of Frank's journal and her legacy in Holocaust education has led to pronounced discomfort among some cultural critics and academics. For this reason, many college professors would not even consider teaching Frank's diary in a course on Holocaust history or literature. This essay briefly discusses the prolific, varied critiques of the pedagogical uses of Anne Frank's diary and persona that have emerged over the past two decades and suggests an approach that takes into account these objections.

The numerous critiques of the use of Frank's diary tend to revolve around the following issues: the neglect or even erasure of Anne's Jewishness and/or the specific historical circumstances under which her family lived and died (as German Jewish refugees who hid in Amsterdam and who were betrayed by Dutchmen), the sanctification of her in a way that erases the complexity of her work and her self-representation, the attempt to mitigate the horrors of the Holocaust through an emphasis on her optimism and/or on the family's helpers (while ignoring the family's murder in concentration camps), and a universalizing of her experience of persecution to such a degree that it applies to all kinds of injustices in the world (which positions the Holocaust as less than unique and renders the actual circumstances of her life and death almost irrelevant).

A number of these problematic uses can be attributed to the figure of Anne herself and to the nature of her journal: that she came from an assimilated Jewish background rather than an observant one, for example, explains the less than pronounced Jewishness of her perspective. Her optimism, in contrast, needs to be understood as a result of the fact that she was hidden from the horrors of the Holocaust initially and that the diary ends before she would come to know its ultimate horrors firsthand. In other ways, however, the questionable approaches to her diary may have resulted from misconceptions about people in the age group to which most of the teaching material about her has been directed (eighth to twelfth graders rather than college students) and from the particular pedagogical goals these materials tend to have.

Anne Frank Universalized

In middle school and high school curricula, the Frank text is often used precisely for its potential to serve as a universal example of victimization as the result of racism. While the goal may be to teach about the Holocaust specifically, the larger goal is to have young students understand racial (and other forms of) discrimination, its roots, and its ultimate consequences (mass murder) and to educate them to be vigilant and to be aware of personal choice and responsibility.[1] These curricula thus frequently present the diary without a thorough-enough analysis of the specific national and historical context of which it is a product and only broadly situate it as a Holocaust text (perhaps within the context of a few class hours discussing the background of World War II and National Socialism).

De-emphasizing the diary's historical specificity allows young students to identify with a victim "just like them," a girl who struggles with common adolescent issues: her parents, youthful infatuation, burgeoning sexuality, and a need for independence. In this approach, the drama of the diary (or the stage play or the film versions) stems from Anne's insightful adolescent descriptions of interfamilial conflicts playing themselves out in the pressure cooker of the secret annex while the Nazis terrorize the Jews of Europe on the outside. Through this relatively harmless exercise in identification, it is hoped, students may gain a deeper insight into, and interest in, the experiences of those who were persecuted for their race or belief; it is the empathy they feel for Anne that brings the Holocaust back to a manageable, human scale. Once her diary is covered, many curricula shift from the Holocaust and Jewish persecution to discrimination and (racial) oppression in general, leading to discussions on contemporary conflicts in the United States or on wars and genocide and on broader moral lessons about human behavior and individual choice.

At times, the use of Anne's diary in teaching about the Holocaust also clearly serves to mitigate the horror of the Holocaust. Many of the curricula suggest, for instance, that the diary can be used to introduce even very young students to this difficult topic, for Anne's idealism and her hope in the fundamental goodness of people balance out the bleakness of Holocaust history. While the drama of her life is heightened if students also learn about her death in Bergen-Belsen, their overall impression should be that good ultimately triumphs over evil.

Although it is easy to see how such a broad and general treatment of this text and the Holocaust is problematic and particularly inappropriate for college-age students and although much criticism has indeed been directed toward such generic readings, few critics have suggested what a more useful approach to Frank's diary would look like.

I propose that the text should be brought back to college classes precisely because Frank's persona and diary are already familiar to most American students. Both the journal and the writer, therefore, lend themselves to an analysis that demythologizes what students have learned so far about the book, the persona of its author, and the Holocaust more generally. I suggest an approach that emphasizes the story's very particularity instead of its supposed universality: a study that places in context her assimilated German Jewish background and her life as a member of an upper-middle-class German Jewish refugee family under Nazi occupation in Amsterdam. Students can look at both the German Jewish context and that of the Jews in the Netherlands during the Nazi occupation. A second approach, which can be developed separately or in conjunction with the first, is to examine the wealth of new critical literature on the use and misuse of Anne Frank and to make the adaptation and marketing of this text over the past five decades, and in different national contexts, a topic of investigation. Analyzing how the diary and Anne Frank herself came to have the iconic status they now have can serve as an interesting case study in the power of Holocaust representations.

There are, then, two different ways to recontextualize the text historically and culturally. First, the diary can be used to explore the Frank family's unique predicament as a German Jewish family whose sense of Jewish identity was both historically specific and class-specific, that was unexpectedly confronted with antisemitic persecution (see Blasius and Diner; Kaplan; Moore, *Refugees*; Mosse). By understanding the Franks' German Jewish identity, students can consider Anne's writing as a particular cultural response that was not unique to her or to her family but was indebted to a German Jewish cultural tradition that continued in the family after their emigration to the Netherlands. Students can come to understand this culture by reading passages in the diary that deal with Anne's sense of religious and cultural identity and then gathering relevant background information (Mosse). From this activity students will learn that middle-class and upper-middle-class Jews in Germany were steeped in the nineteenth-century German ideal of *Bildung*—that is, of a culture based on a classically informed humanism rather than on religion or nationality. Anne's awareness of her own experience of persecution—as a human being first, and as a Jew second—can be read as stemming from this cultural tradition, as can her ideas about what may resolve such conflicts in the future. Whereas her views are less religiously or traditionally Jewish than what we as (in particular, American) readers may expect to find in the diary of a persecuted Jewish teenager, they mirror quite faithfully the cultural background in which Anne, as an assimilated German Jew, was raised. Furthermore, the marketing of the diary after the war by Anne's father, Otto, and his choice of cuts and elisions can be understood, from this perspective, as conforming to an ideal of assimilation in which Jewish, Christian, and humanist values informed German Jewish life equally.

Such an explanation thus takes into account the assimilated nature of the Frank family and their relationship to Judaism, which would become contested in the American reception of the diary and the ensuing theater and film production. Understood in historical context, Anne's particular sense of Jewish identity and Otto Frank's postwar choice of editorial cuts and the marketing strategy of his daughter's work and her legacy as a universal (not necessarily Jewish) figure of oppression become comprehensible. Seen this way, the diary clarifies, in turn, the ways in which Anne's life and writing were more traditionally Jewish than those who treat her book as a testimony to universal human suffering wish to suggest but certainly less traditionally Jewish than those who would present her story primarily as one of religious persecution would like to see.

Placing the Franks in their Dutch context, to look at the relatively unfamiliar story of the Dutch Jews and of German Jewish refugees under Nazi occupation in the Netherlands, is revealing as well (see Blom; Colijn and Littell; Hirschfeld; Jong; Moore, *Victims*; Presser). For the Franks' privileged life as prosperous German Jewish emigrants in Amsterdam who would successfully hide as a family in the city for over two years was, in fact, unusual. The story of most Jews in the Netherlands was considerably more grim. The majority of the refugees in the Netherlands were able neither to integrate culturally nor to become stable financially, and they were the first to be caught when the Nazis occupied the country. Furthermore, finding a place to hide was difficult for all Jews, and most were quickly betrayed (only 10% survived in hiding, almost always separated from their families). It is thus important to enhance students' understanding of the diary by providing background reading that shows that it was the Frank family's end—their betrayal, deportation, and death—rather than their life in hiding that was typical of the Dutch experience. Discussing in some detail the Dutch Jewish death rate will be revealing, as this record is astonishing: the Nazis succeeded in deporting over 82% of the Jewish population of the Netherlands, and less than 5% of the deportees survived, resulting in a Jewish death rate of over 75%. Emphasizing that this murder rate of Jews is by far the highest of any Western European country and studying the complex reasons for these numbers will deepen students' interaction with the text.

For readers keeping in mind Anne's diary images—in which she notes the help the family receives; in which Dutch collaborators are scarcely mentioned; and in which the family's eventual betrayal, deportation, and her death cannot be foreseen—the extent of the Dutch Jewish extermination tends to shock and surprise. Discussing the diary as a representation of the Dutch historical experience—despite no tradition of antisemitism in the Netherlands, it includes a high collaboration rate, little participation in resistance, and a substantial rate of betrayal of Jews in hiding—allows students to question what role accommodation and collaboration played in the success or failure of Nazi deportations in different European nations and how national war myths as deceptive as that of the Dutch develop.

That the myth of the Dutch as a righteous nation and the

Netherlands as a liberal haven emerged and perpetuated itself in relation to Anne's diary is particularly instructive. Some American critics have accused the Dutch of manipulating Frank's image to construct a more favorable image of their role in the war, so that Frank serves as "Holland's unofficial patron saint" (see Miller 95). However, an analysis of the development of this image suggests that it derives from Otto Frank's editorial cuts and more specifically from the American play and film adaptation of Anne's diary, neither of which can be attributed to a deliberate attempt on the part of the Dutch to falsify their own image. Indeed, if Frank's iconization suggests anything, it is that the American investment in the myth of the Dutch as an upstanding people who hid Jews like the Franks and thus resisted the Nazis may be as strong as that of the Dutch.

This observation brings me to the final suggestion for teaching the diary: to discuss Frank's work and its legacy critically, tracing the publication and reception of the diary itself, with its reprints, reedits, and stage and film versions. Such an activity offers insight into the marketing and reception of Holocaust texts and the evolution of a Holocaust literary genre more generally, of which the Frank text is one of the earliest and most popular examples.

It has been well documented that, notwithstanding its later success, Otto Frank initially had great difficulty finding a Dutch publisher for his daughter's diary. Once he did, the diary appeared in a shortened, edited version. Through an analysis of the original and later editions of the diary (again, use the *Critical Edition* [ed. Barnouw and van der Stroom], in which the different versions and editions of the diary can be found side by side), students can examine the editorial choices Otto Frank and the Dutch publisher made for the first publication of the work, choices that were then repeated, with interesting additional revisions in the German and other translations. Those changes reveal a desire to have Anne portrayed a certain way. By deleting the passages that dealt with her conflicted relationship with her mother, her sexual development, and her anger toward the antisemitism in Dutch and German culture, her father and the original publisher could underplay the more complex aspects of her personality and her Jewish background — facilitating, in turn, her transformation into an idealized, universal figure of martyrdom.

The transformation of the diary became even more dramatic after the American edition was published. Its enormous success led to the creation of a theater version by the Hollywood screenwriters Frances Goodrich and Albert Hackett. The story of the creation of this play is a fascinating one, as it illustrates what occurred in the repackaging of Frank's story for an American audience of the 1950s. The play, first performed in the United States in 1955 and in Europe in 1956, became a huge hit. By 1959, a film had been made of the play (for which the screenplay was itself modified), and Frank's life became even more widely known.

Much has been written on the marketing of Frank that took place by means of these rewritings, and a reading of some of the background material and a student's comparison of the diary in its different versions with the play and the film serve as a good exercise to gain insight into the Americanization of Frank's literature and the Holocaust more broadly. In the 1970s and 1980s, some critics have argued, Anne Frank's legacy in the United States went through a radical transformation once more: while her persona had once been universalized, it was now placed exclusively in a Jewish and Holocaust context. As such, Anne became the quintessential Holocaust victim and the central focus of Holocaust education. An analysis of the transformations provides a framework in which to discuss the larger social and political forces at work in the American literary establishment's early and more recent attempts to represent the Holocaust and the public's attempt to come to terms with it through the persona and diary of Anne Frank.

Finally, to understand more broadly the Anne Frank industry that emerged in the United States as well as in the Netherlands and elsewhere since the initial publication of the diary, one should also examine the various Frank organizations, their histories and philosophies.[2] Looking at the educational initiatives these organizations have developed over time, the books and films they have produced, and in particular the international exhibits they have put on suggests the different contexts in which Anne Frank's legacy is placed and offers insight into the meanings her memory has taken on in the participating nations.

The approaches outlined here thus attempt to take into account most if not all of the critiques directed at the use of the diary. Both the erasure of Anne's Jewishness and the opposite tendency, to make her stand in for all Jewish children murdered in the Holocaust, can be addressed through an analysis of her specific background and experiences as a German Jewish refugee. Furthermore, by looking at the complexity of the Frank family's sense of Jewish identification, we gain insight into the assimilated German Jewish cultural tradition Anne's writing should be seen in, if we are to resist a universalizing of her work. Discussing the Dutch historical context in detail allows for a much needed adjustment of the commonly held, overly positive views of gentile wartime behavior toward the Jews in the Netherlands and elsewhere. The analysis also leads to an awareness of accommodation and collaboration more generally in occupied nations, complicating the story of simple heroism sometimes presented through Frank's diary.

Finally, Frank's work should be discussed not as either typical or exemplary, I believe, but rather as one of the many texts Jews created while living through the Holocaust. It is one, however, that, for a number of specific cultural and historical reasons, managed to exude an unequaled power to engage its audiences. In addressing its popularity, we should first look at Anne's writing itself. After sixty years, it still sparkles, amuses, moves, and engages. When we also look at the various diary editions and in particular at the theater and film adaptations, however, we can see the transformations that led to the author's subsequent iconization. Analyzing these adaptations and her phenomenal, enduring popularity allows us to look at what purpose her persona and her work have served over the past decades and still serve for us now and to evaluate our own goals and motivations in Holocaust education.

Notes

1. See, for example, the questions that are part of the online Anne Frank Center USA teaching guide. Students are asked to define the terms *stereotype* and *scapegoat* and examine how nationalism and national identity have "been used to justify discrimination and war." Students are then encouraged to organize "a campaign to promote racial, religious, cultural understanding in their school" (*Teacher's Guide*).

2. There are six organizations that officially represent the Frank legacy and propose extensive curricula: Anne Frank House in Amsterdam (Anne Frank Foundation); Anne Frank Center USA (founded in 1977 "to educate people about the causes, instruments and dangers of discrimination and violence through the story of Anne Frank"—see www.annefrank.com); Anne Frank–Fonds in Basel, Switzerland (established in 1963 by Otto Frank, "to promote charitable work and to play a social and cultural role in the spirit of Anne Frank"—see www .annefrank.ch/e); Anne Frank Zentrum in Berlin (the German partner organization of the Anne Frank House in Amsterdam); Anne Frank Educational Trust UK (which aims to "educate against all forms of racism and discrimination by explaining the history of Anne Frank and the Holocaust"—see www.afet.org.uk); and Anne Frank Youth Center, Frankfurt am Main (which presents an exhibition and organizes activities "for the promotion of understanding between different cultures, nations and religions"—see www.jbs-anne-frank.de/indexen.htm).

Works Cited and Consulted

Barnouw, David, and Gerrold van der Stroom, eds. The Diary of Anne Frank: The Critical Edition. Prepared by the Netherlands State Inst. for War Documentation. New York: Doubleday, 1989.

Cole, Tim. Selling the Holocaust, from Auschwitz to Schindler: How History Is Bought, Packaged, and Sold. New York: Routledge, 1999.

Colijn, Jan G. "Toward a Proper Legacy." Rittner 95–104.

Frank, Anne. The Diary of a Young Girl: The Definitive Edition. Ed. Otto Frank and Mirjam Pressler. Trans. Susan Massotty. New York: Doubleday, 1995.

Goodrich, Frances, and Albert Hackett. The Diary of Anne Frank. New York: Random, 1956.

Kniesmeyer, Joke. Anne Frank in the World, 1929–1945. Amsterdam: Bakker, 1985.

Miller, Judith. One, by One, by One: Facing the Holocaust. New York: Simon, 1990.

Moger, Susan. Teaching the Diary of Anne Frank: An In-Depth Resource for Learning about the Holocaust through the Writings of Anne Frank. New York: Scholastic, 1998.

Rittner, Carol, ed. Anne Frank in the World: Essays and Reflections. Armonk: Sharpe, 1998.

Rosner, Hedda. Understanding Anne Frank's The Diary of a Young Girl: A Student Casebook to Issues, Sources, and Historical Documents. Westport: Greenwood, 1997.

Teacher's Guide to the Exhibit: Anne Frank: A History for Today. Anne Frank Center, USA Online. 2000. 13 Apr. 2004 <http://www.annefrank.com/download/material_guidetoexhibit.doc>.

Suggested Reading

Anne Frank in German Jewish Context

Blasius, Dirk, and Dan Diner, eds. *Zerbrochene Geschichte: Leben und Selbst-verständnis der Juden in Deutschland* [*Shattered History: Life and Self-Definition of the Jews in Germany*]. Frankfurt: Fischer, 1991.

Kaplan, Marion A. *Between Dignity and Despair: Jewish Life in Nazi Germany.* New York: Oxford UP, 1998.

Moore, Bob. *Refugees from Nazi Germany in the Netherlands, 1933–1940.* Dordrecht: Nijhoff, 1986.

Mosse, George. *German Jews beyond Judaism.* Bloomington: Indiana UP, 1985.

Anne Frank in Dutch Jewish Context

Blom, J. C. H. "The Persecution of the Jews in the Netherlands in a Comparative International Perspective." *Dutch Jewish History: Proceedings of the Fourth Symposium on the History of the Jews in the Netherlands.* Vol 2. Ed. Jozeph Michman. Assen, Neth.: Van Gorcum, 1989. 273–89.

Colijn, Jan, and Marcia S. Littell, eds. *The Netherlands and Nazi Genocide: Papers of the Twenty-First Annual Scholars' Conference.* Lewiston: Mellen, 1992.

Hirschfeld, Gerhard. *Nazi Rule and Dutch Collaboration: The Netherlands under German Occupation, 1940–1945.* Trans. Louise Willmot. Oxford: Berg, 1988.

Jong, Louis de. *The Netherlands and Nazi Germany.* Erasmus Lectures, 1988. Cambridge: Harvard UP, 1990.

Moore, Bob. *Victims and Survivors: The Nazi Persecution of the Jews in the Netherlands, 1940–1945.* London: Arnold, 1997.

Presser, Jacques. *The Destruction of the Dutch Jews.* New York: Dutton, 1969.

Young, James. "The Anne Frank House: Holland's Memorial 'Shrine of the Book.'" *The Art of Memory: Holocaust Memorials in History.* Ed. Young. New York: Jewish Museum, with Prestel, 1994. 131–37.

Critical Readings of Anne Frank's Diary and Legacy

Bettelheim, Bruno. "The Ignored Lesson of Anne Frank." *"Surviving" and Other Essays.* New York: Knopf, 1979. 246–57.

Doneson, Judith. "The American History of Anne Frank's Diary." *Holocaust and Genocide Studies* 2.1 (1987): 149–60.

Graver, Lawrence. *An Obsession with Anne Frank: Meyer Levin and the Diary.* Berkeley: U of California P, 1995.

Langer, Lawrence L. "The Americanization of the Holocaust on Stage and Screen." *From Hester Street to Hollywood: The Jewish-American Stage and Screen.* Ed. Sarah Blacher Cohen. Bloomington: Indiana UP, 1983. 213–30.

———. "The Uses—and Misuses—of a Young Girl's Diary: 'If Anne Frank Could Return from among the Murdered, She Would Be Appalled.'" *Forward* 17 Mar. 1995: 1, 5.

Melnick, Ralph. *The Stolen Legacy of Anne Frank: Meyer Levin, Lillian Hellman, and the Staging of the Diary.* New Haven: Yale UP, 1997.

Ozick, Cynthia. "Who Owns Anne Frank?" *New Yorker* 6 Oct. 1997: 76–87.

Rosenfeld, Alvin H. "Popularization and Memory: The Case of Anne Frank." *Lessons and Legacies: The Meaning of the Holocaust in a Changing World.* Ed. Peter Hayes. Evanston: Northwestern UP, 1991. 243–78.

Judith Greenberg

Surviving Charlotte Delbo's *Auschwitz and After*: How to Arrive and Depart

So harrowing, immediate, and visceral is the experience of reading Charlotte Delbo's trilogy, *Auschwitz and After* (*Auschwitz et après*), that one emerges from its pages numb and haunted. Granting no emotional distance, its mixture of poetry and prose brings the reader directly into what Delbo calls *la mémoire du sens* or "sense memory": the unbearable wound of the Holocaust. If we must be made to see — *il faut donner à voir*, as Delbo says (see Langer x) — then how do teachers assume the responsibility of transmitting such knowledge?

Titles and Arrivals

A class may find itself speechless in the wake of reading Delbo. The trilogy's title, *Auschwitz and After*, and the titles of the three books that it comprises, *None of Us Will Return, Useless Knowledge,* and *The Measure of Our Days* (*Aucun de nous ne reviendra, Une connaissance inutile,* and *La mesure de nos jours*), can provide gates of entry for discussion. For instance, the words of the trilogy's title, when reversed without the *and* ("After Auschwitz"), introduce the problems of postwar poetry raised by Theodor Adorno and allude to discussions surrounding the very possibility of aesthetics and representation in the wake of Auschwitz. But the words of the title are not positioned in the familiar succession. Rather, the phrasing "Auschwitz and after" calls attention to the issue of chronology. It invites students to reflect on how Delbo herself lives and writes after Auschwitz. While it may seem that one necessarily writes testimony from a retrospective position, the text problematizes a clear temporal structure of before, during, and after. Students may observe the impossibility for Delbo, as witness to the deaths of her husband and so many others, to arrive at an after. What is the possibility of an aftermath, they can ask, when one cannot escape the memories of Auschwitz? The words of the first volume emphasize this paradox. As a future-tense verb, *reviendra* ("will come back"), implies a future, and yet the *ne* ("not") denies the possibility of its existence. The title thus presents an imagined but unrealizable state, a kind of apocalyptic destruction. As Michael Rothberg writes, "The paradox becomes how to represent survival when return has been deemed impossible" (156). The impossibility for survivors to return to a pre-Auschwitz state of mind means that they never escape Auschwitz. The horrors Delbo witnessed possess her. Well after her return from Auschwitz, she can still sense its smells, chills, hunger, thirst, and abuse. The ambiguous phrase *aucun de nous n'aurait du revenir* ("none of us should have returned"), at the end of the volume, further underscores the paradoxical condition of return. Yet the echo here is slightly altered. Instead of predicting sure extinction, the phrase acknowledges that, while impossible, the future did appear for some. The wording conveys defiance. We shouldn't have returned, and yet we did; we defied the Nazis, our bodies, and the limits of the possible. It can also signify the difficulty of life in the aftermath — none of us should have returned, because our lives after Auschwitz are fraught with painful memories.

Such close analysis of the words *after* and *return* creates an opportunity to introduce what Delbo calls *la mémoire profonde* or "deep memory": the inescapable and persistent presence of the Holocaust. "Deep memory" describes the impossibility for the survivor to set herself apart from her experiences during the war. In her final book, *Days and Memory*, Delbo writes:

> Auschwitz is so deeply etched in my memory that I cannot forget one moment of it. —So you are living with Auschwitz? —No, I live next to it. Auschwitz is there, unalterable, precise, but enveloped in the skin of memory, an impermeable skin that isolates it from my present self. . . . In this underlying memory sensations remain intact. (2–3)

To help students explore the idea of deep memory, teachers can provide some background on trauma. (See the essay by Brodzki in this volume.) Specifically, they may discuss how trauma can break down the ability of normal memory to distinguish past from present. Trauma disrupts the ability to fit memories into a cohesive narrative of the self.

For Delbo, traumatic, or deep, memory may reside side by side in the survivor with *la mémoire ordinaire* or "common memory" (see Langer). "Common memory" consists of normal experiences and belongs to an order utterly different from deep memories of the camp. For example, in a passage from a section called "One Day," Delbo interweaves her pre-Auschwitz childhood memories—of the death of her dog, Flac—with a memory from Auschwitz of a woman killed by a Nazi dog for breaking ranks to swallow snow. She blurs the association of dog and death, common to those who have lost a pet and experienced this normal sense of grieving, with the absurd, unbelievable association that exists in the camp:

> She sucks the snow. Now we understand why she broke rank, the resolute expression of her face. She wanted clean snow for her swollen lips. . . . Her back hunches, shoulder blades protruding through the worn fabric of her coat. It's a yellow coat, like that of our dog Flac which had grown thin after being ill, whose whole body curved, just before he died. . . . This woman is going to die. . . . The SS has his dog on a leash. Did he give an order, make a sign? The dog pounces on the woman—without growling, panting, bark-

ing. All is silent as in a dream. The dog leaps on the woman, sinks its fangs in her neck. And we do not stir, stuck in some kind of viscous substance which keeps us from making the slightest gesture — as in a dream. The woman lets out a cry. A wrenched-out scream. A single scream tearing through the immobility of the plain. We do not know if the scream has been uttered by her or by us, whether it issued from her punctured throat, or from ours. I feel the dog's fangs in my throat. I scream. I howl. No sound comes out of me. The silence of a dream. (*Auschwitz* 27–28)

The passage shows the dissolution of boundaries between dreams and reality, between Delbo's identity and that of the dying woman, and between the past and the present. The floodgates of association open and blur the separate times of normal and concentration camp worlds.

Common memory is also what allows Delbo to reemerge from the nightmare. As Langer says, common memory "urges us to regard the Auschwitz ordeal as part of a chronology, a dismal event in the past that the very fact of survival helps to redeem. It frees us from the pain of remembering the unthinkable" (xi–xii). Students can think about the ways in which Delbo forges a new self to rejoin the normal world after Auschwitz.

For one, if the postwar self is to write about Auschwitz and *donner à voir*, then she must join the world that enables her to sit with pen in hand. She must also depart from the camp emotionally, to have the presence of mind to write. She depends on *la mémoire externe* — "external memory" or "thinking memory" — to convert the pain of the experience into a story. Delbo explains: "Because when I talk to you about Auschwitz, it is not from deep memory my words issue. They come from external memory, if I may put it that way, from intellectual memory, the memory connected with thinking processes" (*Days* 3). Shifts among various kinds of memory are central to Delbo's poetics, as exemplified by the following passage:

Standing, wrapped in a blanket, a child, a little boy. A tiny, shaven head, a face with jutting jaws and a salient superciliary arch. Barefoot he jumps up and down ceaselessly with a frenzy like that of some barbaric dance. He also waves his arms to keep warm. The blanket slips open. It's a woman. A female skeleton. She is naked. He ribs and pelvic bones are clearly visible. . . .

Presently I am writing this story in a café — it is turning into a story. A break in the clouds. Is it afternoon? We have lost all notion of time. The sky appears. Very blue. Hours have passed since I succeeded in not looking at the woman in the ditch. Is she still there? She has reached the top of the slope — how was she able to do this? — and stopped there. Her hands are drawn by the glittering sun. (*Auschwitz* 26–27)

Students can analyze what it means for Delbo to interrupt the description of the woman in the snow to remark on her own act of writing. Delbo makes explicit the turning of sense memory and deep memory into narrative: "Presently I am writing this story in a café — it is turning into a story." This sentence highlights the difficulty of stepping out of the pain of sense memories and the immediacy of deep memories in order to write. The word *presently* stresses how the activity of writing requires a jump in time away from the memories. Yet how should one interpret the line "A break in the clouds. Is it afternoon?" Did this observation occur in the past, at the camp, or does it happen in the present, at the café? The next line underscores the temporal confusion: "We have lost all notion of time." What kind of "hours have passed" since Delbo looked at the woman in the ditch? Does she refer to hours while in Auschwitz or the hours upon hours that have passed since her return? Or does deep memory collapse the hours spent at Auschwitz into the hours spent in the aftermath and render such distinctions irrelevant? The text transmits to its readers the loss of "all notion of time."

If readers here encounter an example of the temporal confusion facing the survivor, then many passages explore the role of reading in a new era. Analyzing each word of the title in relation to reading addresses how Holocaust stories are transmitted to future generations. Students read *Auschwitz* and accompany Delbo on her journey of memory. Writing refuses to stand silent, and reading keeps the past from slipping into obliteration. Yet students also read *after* and cannot truly experience the past.

Close reading of other titles provides rich analytic material as well. For instance, the meaning of the pronoun *us* in *None of Us Will Return* raises a multitude of references and questions. As a pronoun that embraces others, *us* opens a question of address: Who belongs to "us"? And what does it mean to have a plural rather than a singular first-person pronoun in the title? Students may remark on the dissolution of individual identity. They may explore the ways in which this testimony is collective, the survivor speaking for a multitude of mute voices. Indeed, Delbo writes *The Measure of Our Days* through the voices of some of her fellow survivors, giving this work a feeling of collective testimony of their experiences of return.

Students may propose that "us" refers to Delbo's fellow prisoners in Auschwitz—and perhaps prisoners of the other camps as well—particularly to the fate of most of the men, women, and children, who literally will not return, dying in the camps. The title may imply that Delbo writes for those who did not return and cannot speak. But if "us" refers to the dead, students can consider why Delbo includes herself, a living writer, among them. The discussion may lead to an exploration of the ways in which Delbo identifies with the dead. How does trauma involve an encounter with death and confuse the boundaries between life and death? Delbo asks a question, on her return to Paris, that can be presented to the class: "If I confuse the dead and the living, with whom do I belong?" (236). A teacher may ask students to consider how Delbo herself becomes a kind of ghost, both dead and alive, first after she witnesses her husband's murder and then in Auschwitz. They may remark on how prisoners in the camps in general become automatons, walking skeletons. In the hell of Auschwitz, dead bodies surround the living: the threat, stench, and image of death are omnipresent. And the living resemble skeletons; they are breaths away from the fate of most of the others. Apart from the physical torture the prisoners endured, one can ask students about the psychological effects of witnessing the suffering and deaths of others. The living become emotionally dead or numbed in order to resist madness. They also experience a contradictory impulse that brings its own form of death: survivors identify deeply and feel death through witnessing.

After considering the blurring of the difference between life and death in the camp, students may recognize the role of the life force in keeping the survivors going. One of the most difficult conditions of survival is that the living must turn away from the dead so as not to join them. While a survivor may identify so deeply with the dying that she feels the dog's fangs on her throat, she must resist the pull of death. A class can explore the departures taken by the living. A prisoner who dies must be left behind, abandoned in her final painful moments in order for the living to avoid being killed by the Nazis for trying to help. For instance, Delbo remembers the woman left to die in the snow. She observes the bewilderment in the woman's eyes on realizing that no one will help her in her final moments: "Help me. Pull me up. Lean in my direction. Stretch out your hand. Oh, they don't make a move" (25). The living run away from the dead, no matter how beloved, in order to stay alive. Similarly, students may observe their own need to depart, or turn away from, the text at times, in order to retain a level of composure. There are limits to the collectivity of this embrace.

"Us" also introduces the specifics of Delbo's fate. The pronoun can refer to the women in the car that deported Delbo, one of 230 Frenchwomen, on 24 January 1943, from the French camp of Romainville to Auschwitz. Only 49 of the women returned. The group with which one arrives in hell becomes a part of one's identity. In this context, "us" may extend beyond the group of 230 deportees to the group of women prisoners, as distinct from men, who spend their days with Delbo in Auschwitz. This sense of "us" offers students a point of arrival into the women's side of the barbed wire, for Auschwitz separated, usually permanently, husbands from wives, mothers from sons, fathers from daughters, and brothers from sisters. It wrenched apart the "us" of families. For instance, while the women at Auschwitz could witness the abuse and torture done to the men, they remained removed from them. In a section called "The Men," whose title emphasizes the separation of the sexes, Delbo can only imagine that the men have "a better charnel house than ours, probably slightly less awful" (95).

The women also form a kind of "us" because they are deprived of any privacy and autonomy. A class may examine one passage that portrays how the women's individual and pleasurable bodies disappear into a bizarre mass defined by pain:

> It is a tangle of bodies, a melee of arms and legs and, when at last we believe we grasped something solid, it is because we knocked our heads against the planks we sleep on and everything vanishes in the shadowy dark where Lulu's leg is moving, or Yvonne's arm, and the head resting heavily on my chest is that of Viva so that awakened by the feeling that I am on the edge of the void, on the edge of our tier, about to go tumbling down into our passageway . . . (55)

Detached from the possession of their own bodies, the women breathe (or suffocate from) the bodies of the others. The individual dissolves into the composite of dying bones. Identification among prisoners has a physical as well as an emotional dimension. Delbo describes the exhausting nights in which women die alone "squeezed against the others who are still in the throes of struggling" (57). Delbo's body will continue to hold this sense memory. The individual body stores not only its own wounds but also those of the other women — "us."

But this primarily negative grouping among the women has a "positive" side. In the midst of the dehumanization, Delbo describes how women prisoners nurture one another and attempt to keep a sense of community to sustain them. For instance, a class can examine one horrific experience in which the prisoners are forced to run fast in the snow and those who cannot keep up "disappear." The women worry about the survival of the others. Delbo witnessed one mother get stopped by a guard and tell her daughter, "Take off. Run. Leave me" (38). The mother did not return. In another instance, one sister says to the other: "If something like this were to happen again, please don't bother about me. Run along. Think only of yourself. Please promise me, won't you? You swear?" (39). After this tortuous ordeal, the surviving women try to keep count of the living. They recite the names from each group, inquiring particularly about the aged, the sick, or the weak, who would have had a harder time surviving the run. Their own accounting (as distinct from the SS accounts) is an effort to sustain bonds of compassion. One may point out how *The Measure of Our Days* performs the same kinds of roll calls: Delbo entitles sections with the names of the women in her group. In testifying to the horrors of their experiences, she tries to restore a sense of their identities.

Teachers can ask what a sense of "us" provides the women. Without the others, Delbo writes, no one believes that she will return. They need one another to imagine a future; they "mother" one another. Every morning during the ritual of roll call, Delbo almost surrenders to death, but her blockmate Viva slaps her back to life: "When I come to, it is from the shock of the slaps Viva imprints on my cheek with all her might, lips tight, eyes averted." During this daily ritual, in which Delbo struggles with the choice between continued suffering and the abandon of death, she "cling[s] to Viva like a child to its mother" (65). Thus while identification with others can be suffocating, it prevents an isolation that would promise death.

Delbo's yearning for a maternal figure illustrates one of the most painful absences in Auschwitz. Not only does the camp dispossess women of their bodies and sexuality; it also rips them from the role of mother. Delbo describes how her yearning for and dreams of her mother sustain her through the horrific nights. But access to that primary loving and nurturing bond is wrenched in unimaginable ways. "Here mothers are no longer mothers to their children" (12). Students can discuss the profound desecration of the maternal body enacted on the women by cutting open their wombs. One section describes the arrival of the SS doctor who signals grave danger:

> Further on, he halts at the ranks of the Greek women and asks: "Which are the women between twenty and thirty who have given birth to a child?" They must renew their supply of guinea pigs in the medical-experiment block. The Greek women have just arrived. As for us, we have been here much too long. We are too thin or weak for them to cut open our bellies. (53)

The horror of imagining what the Nazis enact on fetuses, infants, and children is too hard to bear. It becomes a relief for women to have lost their procreative identities.

Students may interpret how the title *None of Us Will Return* refers not only to Auschwitz's alteration of one's mental state but also to the impossibility of restoring the body to its health and, perhaps, procreative capacity. A passage studied earlier highlights the desexualization that was part of the dehumanization at Auschwitz. Only when the blanket slips is it clear that Delbo has mistaken a jumping body for a boy. Every trace of sexuality has been stripped from this woman, as from all the women prisoners, through starvation and forced shaving. Indeed, Delbo, in another section, explains that women are sterilized in the surgical ward (95). Torture morphs the women into new beings.

But if these meanings of "us" seem to address women exclusively, the class can also consider whether there is a larger reference for the pronoun. Can "us" embrace all who can no longer return to an identity or conception of the world before the Nazis—both those who witnessed the horrors of the war and humanity in general, after Auschwitz? If so, then "us" embraces the reader. Readers can join Delbo's "us" and arrive at Auschwitz on opening the pages of the book.

Departures

If we readers are included in the title's embrace, then we can look at the dynamics of "us" as a class that arrives at the gate of Auschwitz together. The "us" of the class becomes complicated as students with divergent backgrounds read differently. Delbo renders problematic the ability to create distance from the other. She demands that we look at the demons in our own history. For instance, she holds her Christian faith up to inspection:

> You who have wept two thousand years
> for one who agonized for three days and three nights
> what tears will you have left
> for those who agonized
> far more than three hundred nights and three hundred days
> how hard
> shall you weep
> for those who agonized through so many agonies
> and they were countless

They did not believe in resurrection to eternal life
And knew you would not weep. (10)

This condemnation of the behavior of Christians who ignored and ignore the suffering of the victims of the Holocaust may create conflict for students and cause fissures in this "us."

In the context of the Nazi logic that divided Aryan from Jew, "us" from "them," "us" may imply a "not us" or "them." This division invites an examination of how a class may separate as students read as Jews and non-Jews. For Delbo both underscores the radical difference between Jew and non-Jew during the war and blurs the division. She recognizes the increased chance of her own survival as a non-Jew, however slight. Cattle cars of Jews were exterminated immediately on arrival. For them, arrival meant only the end. Non-Jews had a marginally greater chance of survival. Even so, Delbo suffered the same cold, hunger, humiliation, fear, and trauma as the Jews at Auschwitz. How students position themselves in relation to the text requires self-examination, a confrontation with the significance of nationality and ancestry in their conceptions of identification and identity.

No matter what their background, all students encounter the obligation to transmit memory. Delbo and her husband, Georges Dudach, returned from their safe positions in South America to join the French resistance. In a similar call to ethical duty, Delbo begs the "muscular" living to "do something"; "justify your existence . . . because it would be too senseless / after all / for so many to have died / while you live / doing nothing with your life" (230). Ultimately, the text asks us, How do we as readers walk with the dead? It positions the useless knowledge of the Holocaust not on a distant shore but within us.

But even as students incorporate Delbo's memories as part of their own knowledge, they cannot truly enter the gates of Auschwitz. The railroad car that takes the class to the camp is purely metaphoric, as Delbo is aware when she writes at the café, "it is turning into a story." *Auschwitz and After* confronts departures as much as arrivals—the many ways in which readers cannot know the nightmare of Auschwitz, no matter how much they read. As Marianne Hirsch has asked, "Can bodily memory be transmitted once survivors are dead?" This question is at the heart of Delbo's text. If students can use the titles to arrive at Auschwitz, then they can also locate the departures of language and the places where they cannot go. Silences and blank spaces appear throughout and point to the impossibility of conveying the pain. Gaps in stories, and places we as readers are not permitted to see, remind us of the limits of knowing the horrors. For instance, one barrack in the women's camp is set apart as even more terrifying than the usual torturous landscape. Delbo describes looking at Block 25, where the crazed and weak are sent. No one returns alive from Block 25. Like Delbo, the reader does not know what actually transpires there. All we see are the corpses thrown out of the cellblock. All women fear being put there. Students can discuss how Block 25 can represent the spaces that words cannot fill, the magnitude of horrors that we cannot know as readers, and all who cannot return.

Works Cited

Delbo, Charlotte. *Auschwitz and After*. Trans. Rosette C. Lamont. New Haven: Yale UP, 1995.

———. *Days and Memory*. Trans. Rosette Lamont. Marlboro: Marlboro, 1990.

Hirsch, Marianne. "Public Sentiments: Memory, Trauma, History, Action." Conference at Barnard Coll., 16 Feb. 2002.

Langer, Lawrence. Introduction. Delbo, *Auschwitz* ix–viii.

Rothberg, Michael. *Traumatic Realism: The Demands of Holocaust Representation*. Minneapolis: U of Minnesota P, 2000.

Susan Rubin Suleiman

The 1.5 Generation: Georges Perec's *W or the Memory of Childhood*

The concept of generations is well established in Holocaust studies, largely because of the increasing interest in the second generation—children of Holocaust survivors, born after the war, whose lives are indelibly marked by their parents' traumatic experiences but whose own relation to those experiences is that of "postmemory" (Epstein; Hirsch). Attention to the specific experience of the second generation has been encouraged by the appearance of major literary and artistic works by members of that generation—perhaps the best known of these being Art Spiegelman's *Maus,* which became a classic the moment the first volume, *My Father Bleeds History,* was published (1986).

In a course on representations of the Holocaust, I think it is worth devoting specific attention to yet another generation, which I call "1.5"—child survivors of the Holocaust, too young to have had an adult understanding of what was happening to them but old enough to have been there during the Nazi persecution of Jews. Unlike the second generation, whose most common shared experience is that of belatedness—perhaps best summed up in the French writer Henri Raczymow's rueful statement "We cannot even say that we were *almost* deported" (104)—the 1.5 generation's shared experience is that of premature bewilderment and helplessness. Almost without exception, Jewish children in Europe during the war experienced the sudden transformation of their world from at least some degree of stability and security to chaos. We know the statistics: only 11% of those children were still alive in 1945 (Dwork xxxiii).

There are an impressive number of contemporary writers who experienced the Holocaust as children or adolescents and who have dealt with that experience in their works. Among the best known are Aharon Appelfeld, Imre Kertész (who won the 2002 Nobel Prize for Literature, the first Hungarian writer and the first Holocaust survivor to do so), Georges Perec, and Elie Wiesel. But many others have produced at least one important work relating to their childhood in the Holocaust, including Louis Begley, Berthe Burko-Falcman, Magda Denes, Saul Friedländer, Elisabeth Gille, Ruth Klüger, Sarah Kofman, Régine Robin, and Lore Segal. Some write directly about their experience, while others transpose it into fiction; all have given powerful accounts of what it felt like to be a child or adolescent during the Holocaust, encountering loss, displacement, terror. I discuss in detail only Perec's book here, but the works-cited list at the end of this essay includes one work by each of these authors that deals with the subject. If time allows in a course, at least two such works should be read, so students can see commonalities as well as variations in childhood experience as well as in the literary choices made by the adult writer looking back on the past.

While all Holocaust survivors underwent trauma, the specific experience of children was that the trauma occurred before the formation of stable identity that we associate with adulthood and in some cases before any conscious sense of self. In thinking about child survivors of the Holocaust in the context of personal and collective memory, we can consider eleven to be a useful age boundary, one on which psychoanalysts and cognitive psychologists agree: for the former, it marks the move from latency to early adolescence; for the latter, it signals an important stage in the capacity for logical reasoning.

Another, earlier age boundary would seem necessary as well, below which there are no conscious memories at all and little or no vocabulary available to the child at the time of the trauma. We can therefore delineate three discrete groups: children too young to remember (infancy to around 3 years old); children old enough to remember but too young to understand (approximately ages 4–10); and children old enough to understand but too young to be responsible (ages 11–14). By "responsible" I mean having to make choices (and to act on those choices) about their own or their family's actions in response to catastrophe. Adulthood is the state in which one is both capable of naming one's predicament and responsible for acting on it in some considered way.[1]

In *W or the Memory of Childhood*, Georges Perec creates a compelling literary representation of childhood trauma and offers, at the same time, a complex reflection on how to write about such trauma many years later. I teach this book in a course on war and memory, focusing on it specifically as a work by a child survivor of the Holocaust whose experience — like that of most child survivors in France, who were not in ghettos or camps — was that of a hidden child. One of France's most innovative writers, whose stature has grown exponentially since his premature death in 1982 (four days short of his 46th birthday), Perec was born in Paris in 1936, to Polish immigrants who had arrived in France during the 1920s. He was four when his father, who had enlisted as a foreign combatant at the outbreak of World War II, was killed by advancing German troops not far from the capital, in June 1940. A year and a half later, the five-year-old boy said good-bye to his mother at the Gare de Lyon railroad station, joining a trainload of children who were being evacuated by the Red Cross: he was on his way to a village in the foothills of the Alps near Grenoble, where two of his aunts and their families had found refuge. He never saw his mother again. She was rounded up by French police in January 1943 and taken to the transit camp at Drancy, outside Paris, from which she was shipped to Auschwitz a month later. Georges was brought up in the family of his paternal aunt, Esther Bienenfeld.[2]

When *W or the Memory of Childhood* was published in 1975, it took many readers by surprise. Perec, a well-known (albeit often impoverished) writer, was associated with the group of experimental novelists and poets who went by the name Oulipo (short for Ouvroir de Littérature Potentielle ["workshop of potential literature"]). The Oulipo writers—including Raymond Queneau, who is quoted in the epigraphs to the two parts of *W or the Memory of Childhood*—were known for their interest in difficult word games (palindromes, anagrams, crossword puzzles of various kinds) and mathematical games, such as the Japanese game of Go, all of which they often used as the basis for their work. Perec, a champion player with words, had accomplished a tour de force in 1969 when he published a full-length novel from which the letter *e*, the most commonly used vowel in French, was absent: appropriately, the title of this work (whose hero is a man named Anton Voyl, a play on the French word for "vowel," *voyelle*) was *La disparition*, "the disappearance."[3] Most readers thought of Perec as simply a playful writer; and since his name sounds like many typical Breton place-names and family names ending in *ec* or *ecq*, few readers knew of his Polish Jewish family history, marked by the Holocaust.

W or the Memory of Childhood does not break with Perec's experimental mode of writing; but in this book, what appeared as purely formal experimentation in earlier works takes on a profound existential significance: doubling, splitting, discontinuity, absence, substitution become not only signs of the work's formal ambition but also signifiers imbued with personal and historical meaning, related to the nature of childhood memory and to traumatic separation and loss experienced by child survivors of the Holocaust.

Doubling and Splitting

W or the Memory of Childhood—doubleness is already present, indeed twice present, on the cover of the book. The capital letter *W* (which in French is pronounced "double V," not "double U") is itself doubled by the appositional phrase "the memory of childhood." To complicate matters, the conjunction *or* leads to two possible interpretations. According to one, "memory of childhood" is synonymous with "W," as in some classic titles: Voltaire's *Candide; or, Optimism*, Molière's *Tartuffe; or, The Impostor*. But *or* can also indicate difference, an alternative between two divergent entities: in that case, "W" is not another version of the memory of childhood but an alternative to it. Perec plays on both these meanings. The book consists of two apparently independent narratives told in alternating chapters: the W series (19 chapters, set in italic type) tell a story inspired by the novels of Jules Verne and other science fiction adventure tales, narrated in the first person by a character named Gaspard Winckler; the other chapters, which can be called the memory series (18 chapters, set in roman type), are also in the first person, but the speaker here is Perec himself, and the discourse is not fictional but autobiographical. Yet another doubling, then: two narrators who say "I" and two narrative genres, two modes of discourse — adventure *or* life story, fiction *or* autobiography.

In teaching this book in a course on the Holocaust, one may be tempted to skip the adventure tale and focus on the child who lost his parents and had to hide his Jewishness to survive. Most commentators are fascinated by the autobiographical story, which begins (ch. 2) with the provocative statement "I have no childhood memories," then proceeds to tell, with repetitions, hesitations, and frequent self-corrections, the memories that nevertheless remain from the author's early childhood, as well as a few later recollections he associates with his parents — for example, his visit to his father's grave in a military cemetery in the 1950s and his receiving his mother's death certificate from French authorities in 1958. (The certificate erroneously, or more likely euphemistically, lists the place of death as Drancy, when in fact she was shipped out of there in February 1943 and died in Auschwitz.) But to read only the autobiographical story, skipping the alternating chapters, is of course to read only half the book. The first question one might ask students to think about, therefore, is, What is the relation between the two series, the two stories?

Perec himself answers this question, but in characteristically equivocal fashion, in the first autobiographical chapter (ch. 2):

When I was thirteen I made up a story which I told and drew in pictures. Later I forgot it. Seven years ago, one evening in Venice, I suddenly remembered that this story was called W and that it was, in a way, if not the story of my childhood, then at least a story my childhood . . . : it was about the life of a community concerned exclusively with sport, on a tiny island off Tierra del Fuego. . . .

Later I came across one of the drawings I had done around the age of thirteen. With their help I reinvented W and wrote it, publishing it as I wrote, in serial form, in *La Quinzaine littéraire* between September 1969 and August 1970.

Today, four years later, I propose to bring to term—by which I mean just as much "to mark the end of" as "to give a name to"—this gradual unravelling. W is no more like my Olympic fantasy than that Olympic fantasy was like my childhood. But in the crisscross web they weave as in my reading of them I know there is to be found the inscription and description of the path I have taken. (7)

The "crisscross web they weave" is one way of thinking about the two series that constitute *W or the Memory of Childhood*. While different in genre and discourse, the tale of W and the autobiographical fragments crisscross at several points: Gaspard Winckler, the fictional narrator, shares with the autobiographical I (Perec) an uncertainty about his own history. Thus Winckler writes in his first chapter, "For years I sought out traces of my history, looking up maps and directories . . . I found nothing" (3). Like the autobiographer, Winckler has the feeling of being the "sole depository" of the tale he tells, since all those he writes about have disappeared. Perec will say, in a later chapter, that his writing is conditioned, in its very possibility, by his parents' disappearance: "I know that what I say is blank, is neutral, is a sign, once and for all, of a once-and-for-all annihilation" (42). There are numerous other details that underline similarities between the two stories and the two narrators: Winckler lives under an assumed identity, not unlike the child Perec, who had to pretend not to be Jewish while hiding from the Nazis—furthermore, the adult Winckler has assumed the identity of a child also named Gaspard

Winckler. This is a doubling inside the fiction, itself in a doubling relation with the autobiography.

These examples suggest a metaphoric relation between the two
series. There are also metonymic details that migrate from one series
to the other. Venice, for example, crops up in both stories, as do
pretzels: Winckler, when offered pretzels with a drink, declines them,
saying, "I never eat pretzels" (16); three chapters later, Perec notes
that his family name, when pronounced in Hungarian, means "pret-
zel" (35). Whether metaphoric or metonymic, such details confirm
the image of the "crisscross web" between the two stories, as if each
was somehow linked to the other. There is another possible relation
between the stories, suggested by Perec in the first part of the long
passage quoted above: not a crisscrossing but a juxtaposition, not an
interconnected web but parallel lines that unfold without any point
of contact or similarity. The story of W that he invented at age thirteen was, Perec writes, "a story" (not "the story") of his childhood —
but exactly how it was that story remains undefined. For one thing,
he no longer has any memory of the story he invented at age thirteen; at best, he has reinvented it on the basis of drawings from that
time — but the W he has reinvented "is no more like my Olympic
fantasy than that Olympic fantasy was like my childhood." Whereas the
image of the web suggests connection — whether based on proximity
or similarity, metonymy or metaphor — and hence a kind of integration, the emphasis here is on nonconnection or on a connection that
remains unknowable. The two series coexist; that is all. In the last
pages of the W series (end of ch. 36), it becomes clear that the
"Olympic" island is in fact a metaphoric double of a concentration
camp, with its cruel Masters and starving slaves — but this equivalence was obviously elaborated in the adult reinvention of the childhood fantasy. Whether in its original (forgotten) form or in its adult
reinvention, the story of W is a story of Perec's childhood in a
double sense: it was invented by him during childhood, and it describes or corresponds to his childhood, although only in a displaced
way that is not explained.

Doubling, then, can take the form of repetition or duplication;
it can also take the form of splitting, a fragmentation into discon-

nected parts. *W or the Memory of Childhood* suggests that these two processes may occur at the same time, or that they may be two aspects of a single phenomenon. Perhaps most tellingly, in the context of childhood and identity, Perec explores the doubleness of names, his own and his parents': his father's name was Icek or André; his mother's, Cyrla or Cécile—the one Jewish-Polish, the other non-Jewish, French. The drama of Jewish identity and desire for assimilation, both before and after World War II, played itself out, for many Jews, on the terrain of names: "Gallicization" of their names was a way to elide their Jewishness, and during the war it became necessary for survival (see Lapierre). Jewish children who passed for Christian during the war often had to adopt Christian names: Saul Friedländer became Paul Ferland (Friedländer); Sarah Kofman became Suzanne (Kofman); Claude Langmann (now famous as the filmmaker Claude Berri) became Claude Longuet (Berri). As for Perec, his first name was French, and his last name was already double, a Polish name that, pronounced in French, sounded Breton. He therefore didn't have to adopt a new name, but he nevertheless knew, even at age four, that he had to play a double game. In June 1940, at the time of the mass exodus from Paris in advance of the Germans' entry, he was taken by a friend of his grandmother to a neighboring town for safety.

> She told my aunt that she hid me under the eiderdown each time there was a raid, and that the Germans who occupied the village liked me a lot and played with me. . . . She was very afraid, she said to my aunt who subsequently told me, that I might say something I shouldn't say and she didn't know how to get me to understand the secret I had to keep. (52)

Evidently, she didn't have to tell him: he already knew.

It is characteristic of the autobiographical narrative in this book that Perec recounts the episode not as a straightforward memory but as a recollection told to him later by his aunt, who herself heard it from the grandmother's friend. Memories from such an early age are necessarily incomplete or erroneous; this crucial episode, where the young child knew enough to keep the secret of his Jewishness, did not remain with him but had to be told to him by others. Much of the metanarrative commentary in *W or the Memory of Childhood* is concerned with the problematic nature of all childhood memory: Does one remember or invent one's childhood? Perec's radical version of this universal experience is similar to that of many other children who lost their parents in the Holocaust—the sudden, violent separation from parents literally cuts off the child from the continuity of transmission that constitutes family memory. For Perec, the presence of his aunt and older cousins attenuated this loss to some degree.

Another important doubling that occurs in the book in the context of identity concerns religion. After the child had been permanently separated from his mother, his aunt put him in a Catholic boarding school in the village near Grenoble where they were hiding, and he was taught the catechism and was baptized. He received, as a baptism present, "a kind of picture in relief of the Virgin and Child in a gilded frame, which I contemplated piously all afternoon at the back of the classroom, . . . and which that evening I hung over my bed" (95). The Jewish child is doubled by the newly baptized Christian child, and his lost mother is doubled (but also, perhaps, replaced and therefore made symbolically present) by the Virgin Mary.

In dealing with a writer as exquisitely attuned to the French language as Perec was, we should stress that the doubling and splitting linked to names and to religion went hand in hand with a doubling of languages: Perec's parents, like those of Régine Robin and Sarah Kofman, spoke Yiddish at home. One of the earliest memories Perec mentions (ch. 4) is of himself at age three identifying a Hebrew letter, to the great delight of his family (Yiddish, although very different from Hebrew, is written in the same characters). But the letter he actually reproduces (13) is hard to identify, and it is clear that he does not really know the Hebrew alphabet, let alone Yiddish. The doubling and then the erasure of the mother tongue in immigrant families is, of course, not uncommon. But again, in *W or the Memory of Childhood* it takes on a heavier freight: for what was erased in Perec's childhood was not only the language of the mother but the mother herself.

Absence and Void

Perhaps the most memorable page in *W or the Memory of Childhood* consists of almost nothing: a blank separating parts 1 and 2, with only a wordless line in the middle of the page, consisting of three ellipsis points and a parenthesis in bold face: (. . .). Warren Motte, in his perceptive essay on the book, calls the item "an eloquent figure of nullity" and reads it as "the key statement of the book" (247, 246). The statement implies absence, specifically the absence of the mother; it also signifies the inability (or the refusal) to speak. Perhaps "statement" is not the right word, because what this graphic figure represents is precisely the absence of words, the very opposite of a statement. This nonrepresentation does not mean, of course, that the figure has no meaning; but the meaning it suggests is that the importance or consequence of certain losses cannot be stated, only conveyed in various ways, none of which can adequately express or replace what has been lost, in the sense in which a sign is said to stand for something. Paradoxically, the sign in this instance (the figure of ellipsis in parentheses) stands for silence and bracketing; but what the silence and bracketing themselves stand for can only be suggested, not stated.

One might point out, in teaching this book, the multiple ways in which Perec suggests absence — and the corollary of absence, a sense of radical loss — without explicit statement. Here again, the relation between the existential and the literary (or rhetorical) dimensions of the work is beautifully articulated. As a start, note that the break between parts 1 and 2 occurs after chapter 11, a W chapter — and note, too, that Perec's mother was deported in the convoy of 11 February 1943, the date that figures on her death certificate and that Perec mentions in the longest autobiographical chapter of part 1 (ch. 8, p. 41). After the break, furthermore, the alternating pattern of odd and even chapters (odd for W, even for autobiography) reverses, in a chiasmus: chapter 12, which opens part 2, unexpectedly resumes the W narrative instead of switching to the autobiography. (The W narrative itself shifts radically, for the first-person narrator disappears, and we have a series of impersonal descriptions of the island society.) It's as if the whole book swiveled on its axis or crossed in the middle of an X or in the middle of a swastika—Perec shows, in a subsequent chapter, that the letter *x* can in fact be re-composed into the Nazi symbol. For a young child, the violent separation from parents is like being turned inside out, a psychological state that may be suggested by the trope of chiasmus.

Perec has recourse to other tropes as well, notably to metaphor, and more generally to substitution. In the final autobiographical chapter before the break (ch. 10), he recalls the last time he saw his mother, when she accompanied him to the train station. In his memory, she bought him a magazine showing "Charlot" (Charlie Chaplin) hanging by his suspenders from a parachute; and in his memory, his own arm was in a sling, and he may have been wearing a hernia brace or truss. But he tells us right away that the arm sling was a false memory, for his aunt and cousins have assured him that his arm was fine. Independently, David Bellos has shown that the Charlot image on a magazine cover was probably from much later, after the war (58). Clearly these elements of the memory were imagined, and Perec himself gives an explanation:

> A triple trait runs through this memory: parachute, arm in a sling, hernia brace: it involves suspension, support, almost artificial limbs [*prothèses*]. In order to be, you had to be propped [*Pour être, besoin d'étai*]. Sixteen years later, in 1958, when, by chance, military service briefly made a parachutist of me, I was able to read, at the very instant of jumping, the deciphered text of that memory: I was thrown into the void; all the threads were broken; I fell, alone and without support. The parachute opened. The canopy unfurled, a fragile and firm suspense before the controlled descent [*la chute maîtrisée*]. (55; trans. modified)

The "triple trait"—in fact a triple metaphor—that Perec deploys here suggests both terrifying loss (amputation, free fall without support) and the possibility of attenuating it through substitutions, prostheses, props (the sling, the truss, the parachute). The generalization, almost a maxim, "In order to be, you had to be propped," suggests the possibility of losing one's very being, or self, at such a moment of separation; luckily for Perec, the props existed. The second half of the passage, which reads the childhood memory through his later recollection of an actual parachute jump, introduces a literary dimension: the childhood memory is a "text" to be "deciphered," both written and read. If we wanted to be optimistic, we could suggest that the transformation of a terrifying free fall ("I fell, alone and without support") into a "controlled descent" (the French is even stronger: a "mastered fall") is a function of writing, as if the deployment of writing is what saved Perec from falling apart.

But that interpretation would, I think, exaggerate. There is certainly a suggestion, here and elsewhere in the book, that writing is a form of substitution for loss and a form of commemoration. But such affirmations are accompanied, sometimes in the same sentence, by the contrary sense that writing can never replace, cover over, or otherwise compensate for the void left by the death of his parents:

> I write because we lived together, because I was one amongst them, a shadow amongst their shadows, a body close to their bodies. I write because they left in me their indelible mark, whose trace is writing. Their memory is dead in writing; writing is the memory of their death and the assertion of my life. (42)

At most, such writing is a trace, the sign of something that once was but has disappeared: an assertion of the writer's life, yes, but also a reminder of death, of an irreparable—and, as the central ellipsis suggests, an unsayable—absence or disappearance.[4]

A good place to end a discussion of *W or the Memory of Childhood* is with the page that immediately precedes part 1—that is, with the very first page of the text. Forming a pendant to the almost blank page before part 2, it too contains a single, very brief line, this time with writing: "Pour E," which is impossible to translate in a single phrase. "For E," says the English translation—but it also means "for them," *pour eux. Eux*, the unnamed "them," or *e*, the letter that disappeared from a book that has not disappeared, *La disparition*. In life, as in writing, the void is not filled; but its place is marked, it is not nothing.

Notes

1. For an extended theoretical discussion of the concept of the "1.5 generation," see Suleiman, "1.5 Generation."
2. For these and other biographical details about Perec, see the authoritative biography by David Bellos.
3. The English translation, appropriately, is devoid of *e*'s: *A Void*, trans. Gilbert Adair.
4. For an earlier discussion of writing in this book and in other Holocaust memoirs about childhood loss, see Suleiman, "War Memories."

Works Cited

Appelfeld, Aharon. *Tzili, the Story of a Life*. Trans. Dalya Bilu. New York: Dutton, 1983. Trans. of *Ha-Kutonet veha-pasim*.

Begley, Louis. *Wartime Lies*. New York: Knopf, 1991.

Bellos, David. *Georges Perec: A Life in Words*. Boston: Godine, 1993.

Berri, Claude. *Le vieil homme et l'enfant*. N.p.: Solar, 1967.

Burko-Falcman, Berthe. *L'enfant caché*. Paris: Seuil, 1997.

Denes, Magda. *Castles Burning: A Child's Life in War*. New York: Norton, 1997.

Dwork, Debórah. *Children with a Star: Jewish Youth in Nazi Europe*. New Haven: Yale UP, 1991.

Epstein, Helen. *Children of the Holocaust: Conversations with Sons and Daughters of Survivors*. New York: Putnam, 1979.

Friedländer, Saul. *When Memory Comes*. Trans. Helen R. Lane. New York: Farrar, 1979. Trans. of *Quand vient le souvenir*.

Gille, Elisabeth. *Shadows of a Childhood: A Novel of War and Friendship*. Trans. Linda Coverdale. New York: New, 1998. Trans. of *Un paysage de cendres*.

Hirsch, Marianne. *Family Frames: Photography, Narrative, and Postmemory*. Cambridge: Harvard UP, 1997.

Kertész, Imre. *Fateless*. Trans. Christopher C. Wilson and Katharine M. Wilson. Ann Arbor: U of Michigan P, 1992. Trans. of *Sorstalanság*.

Klüger, Ruth. *Still Alive: A Holocaust Girlhood Remembered*. New York: Feminist, 2001.

Kofman, Sarah. *Rue Ordener rue Labat*. Trans. Ann Smock. Lincoln: U of Nebraska P, 1996.

Lapierre, Nicole. *Changer de nom*. Paris: Stock, 1995.

Motte, Warren. "Georges Perec and the Broken Book." *Auschwitz and After*. Ed. Lawrence D. Kritzman. London: Routledge, 1994. 235–49.

Perec, Georges. *A Void*. Trans. Gilbert Adair. London: Harvil, 1994. Trans. of *La disparition*.

———. *W or the Memory of Childhood*. Trans. David Bellos. Boston: Godine, 1988. Trans. of *W ou Le souvenir d'enfance*. Paris: Denoël, 1975.

Raczymow, Henri. "Memory Shot Through with Holes." Trans. Alan Astro. *Yale French Studies* 85 (1994): 98–105.

Robin, Régine. "Gratok." *L'immense fatigue des pierres: Biofictions.* Montreal: XYZ, 1996.

Segal, Lore. *Other People's Houses.* New York: Harcourt, 1964.

Spiegelman, Art. *My Father Bleeds History.* New York: Pantheon, 1986. Vol. 1 of *Maus: A Survivor's Tale.*

Suleiman, Susan Rubin. "The 1.5 Generation: Thinking about Child Survivors and the Holocaust." *American Imago* 59.3 (2002): 277–95.

———. "War Memories: On Autobiographical Reading." *Risking Who One Is: Encounters with Contemporary Art and Literature.* Cambridge: Harvard UP, 1994. 199–214.

Wiesel, Elie. *Night.* Trans. Stella Rodway. New York: Hill, 1960. Trans. of *La nuit.*

Nancy K. Miller

Ruth Klüger's *Still Alive: A Holocaust Girlhood Remembered*: An Unsentimental Education

Readers of nineteenth-century autobiography, in fiction or fact, are accustomed to finding themselves solicited by the author: "Reader, I married him," Jane Eyre, the heroine of her own story, announces with a tone of triumph (395). "Reader," Harriet Jacobs warns at the end of *Incidents in the Life of a Slave Girl*, "my story ends with freedom; not in the usual way, with marriage." *Still Alive* is neither a novel nor a slave narrative, of course. But this Holocaust memoir engages directly with us, almost as if the story we are reading of a young, feisty, intellectual Jewish girl deported from Vienna at age ten required a user's manual. "Dear reader, don't wax sentimental," Ruth Klüger admonishes us as she describes the relationship among her mother, herself, and Susi, an orphan her mother informally adopts in Birkenau. "We are a family," Klüger explains, "which means we are like other families, only perhaps a bit worse" (123). She insists that whatever the depredations of life in occupied Vienna, the so-called ghetto of Theresienstadt, the camps of Birkenau and Christianstadt, *Still Alive* is nonetheless a recognizable, even familiar (because familial) narrative. Talking back to people who, on hearing her story, feel sorry for her, for the loss of her childhood, Klüger, the adult writer, maintains the contrary: "But I say, this, too, was childhood. I grew up, and I learned something, as every child does who grows up, who grows older" (122). The pattern of this childhood owed its design to the almost uncanny meshing of Alma Klüger's psyche with the internal logic of Auschwitz. If Auschwitz "was not run on reasonable principles" (104), Alma Klüger instinctively understood how it worked. Arguing against Bruno Bettelheim's claim that a sane person ought to be able to adjust to living with the horrors of a concentration camp, Ruth Klüger counters that because her mother was not often sane, she was especially well equipped to save the lives of this trio:

> I think that people suffering from compulsive disorders, such as paranoia, had a better chance to pick their way out of mass destruction, because in Auschwitz they were finally in a place where the social order (or social chaos) had caught up with their delusions." (104)

Klüger's insistence on the ordinariness of her family story depends on this paradox: they resembled other families except for her mother's fear of persecution, a fear that shaped the daughter's life in and outside the camps.

Still Alive can't be understood outside the knot of this mother-daughter entanglement—a relationship of ambivalence that resembles in many ways the antagonistic mother-daughter pairs in twentieth-century autobiographical writing by women. The subtitle of Maxine Hong Kingston's *The Woman Warrior*—*Memoirs of a Girlhood among Ghosts*—comes eerily close to the title in English, as well as the themes, of Klüger's coming-of-age story, including the memory ghosts of the dead that haunt her ("I wish I could write ghost stories," Klüger says, thinking about her vanished father [34]). Like *Still Alive*, Vivian Gornick's *Fierce Attachments*, Carolyn Steedman's *Landscape for a Good Woman*, Annie Ernaux's *A Woman's Story*, and Simone de Beauvoir's *A Very Easy Death* are all structured around the difficult bonds linking mothers and daughters. Klüger did not bring out an English-language version of her memoir (published in German in 1992) until her mother's death, not wishing to wound her with her portrayal. Situating *Still Alive* in the context of a tradition of contemporary women's family memoirs illuminates those aspects of the book that resemble forms of writing conceived outside the nightmare world of the Holocaust.

In the section of *Still Alive* that deals with Vienna, Klüger heaps scorn on the assumption that the hardship incurred during the Hitler regime solidified family feeling — especially among the young. This belief is denounced as "sentimental rubbish": "In our heart of hearts, we all know the reality: the more we have to put up with, the less tolerant we get and the texture of family relations becomes progressively more threadbare" (52). As the narrator of her own — and her mother's — story, Klüger is determined to steer clear of that kind of rubbish: "The main characteristic of sentimentality is deception, including self-deception: the inclination to see something other than what's in front of you" (96). This determination to see clearly, a kind of emotional realism, we could say, is crucial to Klüger's goal in the memoir, a goal of all Holocaust literature: to bear witness no matter how painful or distasteful the evidence. The question then becomes: How does testimony that emerges from the standpoint of a girl and her mother differ from the acts of witness recorded in earlier Holocaust literature?

The difference of emphasis becomes clear in the account of the Birkenau episode that Klüger herself refers to as a "turning point" (108; a common feature in autobiographical narrative): the selection, a matter of life or death. In *Still Alive*, women between the ages of fifteen and forty-five are to be chosen for a labor camp. Klüger's mother wants her twelve-year-old daughter to add three years to her age. The daughter resists — who would believe this lie? As she passes before the table of the SS official, his young female clerk (also a prisoner) gives her the same advice. Ruth says she is fifteen and in a moment of incredible good fortune is signed up for the work detail. Klüger interprets "the intervention of the stranger" who saved her life as an example of "moral freedom at its purest" (108–09). It's only when the stranger intervenes that Ruth performs the lie and that an "act of grace" occurs. Why deem the stranger uniquely responsible for an outcome that was at least partly the result of maternal advice? As the adult Klüger recounts the episode, it is thanks to the prisoner's wholly unexpected charitable impulse that the girl Klüger was survives. But as she also acknowledges, family is not about justice but about emotional truth: "(I repeat: my mother and I were very unfair to each other)" (105). Despite her insistence, as narrator, on the mutual unfairness that characterized their relationship, Klüger notes her mother's capacity to acknowledge the suffering of others. She relives in memory a scene from the transport to Auschwitz in which an old woman urinated on her mother's lap. "I still see the tense look of revulsion on my mother's face in the slanting twilight of the car, and how she gently pushed the woman from her lap. . . . It was a pragmatic, humane gesture" (92).

Each critical moment in the narrative is framed by some version of the mother-daughter relationship. Two other crucial moments demonstrate the phenomenon. The first is the mother's reluctance to send Ruth (who remembers wishing she could leave) on a children's transport that would take her safely out of Vienna; Alma Klüger refuses to contemplate the possibility of separation: a "child and its mother belong together." This is a negative event (it fails to happen) yet has a powerful effect: "But I never forgot that brief glimpse of another life which would have made me a different person." A cloud of doubt and uncertainty surrounds this decision, as does the family's delay in leaving Vienna. "And I still ask: Why didn't we get out in time?" (57, 58). The question remains unanswered.

In the equally fateful decision to escape from the labor camp, the daughter's, not the mother's, judgment prevails. Ruth, her mother, and Susi decide to run away from the death march. "My mother," Klüger writes, "wanted to wait for the next bread ration," but Ruth insists that this is the moment to act: "My mother still hesitates, then agrees, albeit reluctantly: yes." As in the selection, Klüger pauses over this crux (the second major turning point in her narrative) and analyzes the stakes of making a life-and-death decision: the "feeling of what it means to reconstitute yourself, not to be determined by others, to say yes or no as you like, to stand at a crossroad where there had been a one-way street, to leave constraint behind with nothing in front, and call that nothing good" (130). Her meditation on these critical junctures joins a long tradition in Holocaust literature of trying to determine why some survived and others didn't. Did it matter what you did? Or was death merely random? Did the best survive and the worst perish?

In *Still Alive*, the conundrum of survival is cast as a problem of narrative. How do you tell a survival story? And whose story is it? "My mother irritates me," Klüger complains about a camp encounter, "because she stylizes herself at my expense: she is the potential heroine, unlikely as it may seem, and reduces me to poor-little-victim status" (127). The daughter wants to be the heroine of her own story.

Klüger describes the experience of having the numbers tattooed on her arm as an occasion to understand how her younger self reacted to the humiliations of camp life. "The tattoo," she declares, "produced a new alertness in me." The memories of woman and child combine to produce a response that the memoirist imagines will inspire distrust in younger readers, who will shake their heads and say, "This is a bit unbelievable, even in a girl who was as hung up on the written word as I was." But Klüger argues against the disbelief of readers who were not in her situation that she could welcome the tattoo's inscription as "incontrovertible evidence" of the horrors lived in the camps because the evidence meant that she would live to tell her story—with the proof written on her body. This projection of selfhood into a future time operated as a motor of hope and even confidence: "I wouldn't perish here, not I" (99).

Throughout *Still Alive* Klüger incorporates the resistance of readers, anticipating their reactions to her narrative. What happens when you evoke an experience that overflows the boundaries of acceptable conversation? What comparisons are valid? "Should we treat a transport to Auschwitz like a stuck elevator . . . ?" (93). If acceptability is an issue between Klüger and her German friends, for whom the sites of Holocaust history lie within their national borders, how does it affect American students, for whom horror is experienced mainly on television, in the movies, or in books—about the Holocaust or not—and usually on foreign soil? Klüger offers the metaphor of bridges—modes of connecting the memories of Holocaust suffering to the history of those who have lived in very different, often entirely protected, circumstances. Since September 11, our students may well make the connection between images of people jumping from the Twin Towers out of fear of being burned alive, victims of the disaster finding themselves caught in stairwells, trampled by others, and the intolerable conditions of organized claustrophobia in the freight cars. But again, can we compare an accident or a single act of terrorism with a sustained plan to eliminate an entire group of people? The notion of bridges touches on the vexing argument at the heart of Holocaust studies: Should the Holocaust be seen as unique, outside all parameters of comparison? Without analogy, however, how can we produce comprehension, educate new generations?

As she reflects on the story she is telling and frames the description of the freight car that took her and her mother to Auschwitz, Klüger worries about its interpretation: "All I can do is warn the reader not to invest in optimism vouchers and not to give credit, much less take credit, for the happy end of my childhood's odyssey— if indeed simple survival can be called a happy end" (91). The writer's anxiety about genre is part of survivor guilt; but the fact of survival is also a problem of pedagogy. The actual moment of exit from the labor camp is posed in those terms:

> Without meaning to, I find that I have written an escape story, not only in the literal but in the pejorative sense of the word. So how can I keep my readers from feeling good about the obvious drift of my story away from the gas chambers and the killing fields and towards the postwar period, where prosperity beckons? (138)

Should teachers warn their students as Klüger warns her readers, Don't think it wasn't all that bad just because I made it out? As in slave narratives, one lucky escape does not diminish the death and suffering of those who remained behind.

It is in part for this reason—the comfort produced by narrative forms—that the filmmaker Claude Lanzmann has maintained that Holocaust experience should remain beyond representation. Klüger believes in the power of words to convey history, without consigning degradation to the ineffable. For example, the female prisoners were subjected to a humiliating body search. In recounting the violation, she does not want to recast her discomfort (even in her role of narrator fifty years later) as "traumatic experience." When in the course of her literary studies Klüger came on a comparable scene in *Candide*, she felt a kind of relief: "Any event you can turn into literature becomes, as it were, speakable" (119).

Still Alive is divided into four parts, which correspond to places where Klüger lived on her journey. The last two sections of the book—located in postwar Germany and New York—take up the problem of the aftermath. How do you survive survival? (This is the question at the heart of Art Spiegelman's *Maus* and also the third part of Charlotte Delbo's *Auschwitz and After*.) She is not telling, Klüger reminds the reader, "the story of a Holocaust victim" (138); the real victims have not escaped the silence of death. Because she is still alive, she has the task of testifying to what she has seen—and of writing critically what she thinks about what she has seen. The second half of the book follows the pattern of the female bildungsroman: the coming-of-age narrative of a woman leaving childhood behind, a woman who wants to be a poet and who ultimately becomes, after a slightly haphazard education, a professor of German (who still writes poetry). It's no less the familiar tale of immigration and Americanization through public education. At the end of the New York period, the daughter finally leaves her mother's house—a rupture cast in literary terms: "At the end there was my betrayal: I had become Shylock's Jessica, abandoning an unloved parent" (202). It is not surprising that becoming the woman she wanted to become required cutting herself off from the mother who bound her too tightly and too close to her madness—who, like Shylock, wanted her pound of flesh.

The German version of the book ends here. But in English the epilogue, written after Alma Klüger's death, produces a twist that ties the autobiographical knots differently and that returns us to the question I raised earlier: How is women's experience of the Holocaust distinct—distinguishable—from that of men? This is a question some critics and scholars feel cannot, should not, even be asked.

Faced with extermination, what difference does gender make? Classic texts of Holocaust literature, like *Maus* and Elie Wiesel's *Night*, portray the camps from the perspective of a father-and-son relationship; Primo Levi's *Survival in Auschwitz* describes the sustaining friendship between adult men. Not since *The Diary of Anne Frank* have we had so powerful a female vantage point from which to perceive Jewish suffering during the Nazi regime. In addition to the mother-daughter relationship, *Still Alive* represents female networks within the camps but also, once Klüger emigrates to the United States, friendships among women in college and summer school. (Thinking back over her time in Christianstadt, she makes the controversial claim, evocative of a certain phase of difference feminism, that "Nazi evil was male, not female" [115]. Whether this "gender gap" [116] can be documented is of course open to debate, but we might ask why she wishes to take this position.)

In the epilogue Klüger explains that the readers of *Still Alive: A Holocaust Girlhood Remembered* are dealing with not so much a translation as a "parallel book" to *Weiter leben: Eine Jugend*, written for her children and American students (210). The titles reflect a difference of emphasis: childhood (*Jugend*) lacks the mark of gender present in girlhood; and living on (*weiter leben*), unlike *still alive*, which evokes the defiance of Holocaust survival, suggests the persistence of memory. The German book, moreover, written in the 1980s, was addressed to friends who had been loyal to the author in the aftermath of an accident (still alive) and through them, presumably, a wider audience of Germans willing to deal with their history — although the word *Holocaust* does not appear in the original title. Many of the political asides to the reader have resonances in Germany that will either pass unnoticed by American readers or be interpreted differently; nor will the stylistic effects of Klüger's much-remarked-on Viennese German become palpable in American English.

When in the last part of the memoir, during her summer in Vermont, Klüger becomes close to three other women, she begins to understand what it's like to live in the skin of someone unlike you instead of "running in circles within an idiosyncratic enclosure of barbed wire," locked into the camp in your mind. To connect to chosen friends is to remake oneself in the company of others: "Family members, by contrast, share your genes; they don't expand your vista, except by chance" (195). Yet despite the stated importance of this newfound intimacy among friends, the epilogue returns to bloodlines: to what connects a child to her great-grandmother, binding Klüger's granddaughter and her mother. "I look at a snapshot of the two of them rubbing noses, a smile of total affinity on both their faces. . . ." The four-year-old child finds a way to connect beyond language—through signs and gestures of affection. The book ends with the little girl's loss—as she stands bewildered at her great-grandmother's funeral. *Still Alive* is dedicated to the memory of the author's mother. Either path leads back to women.

The last two words of *Still Alive* in the English version leave intact the ambivalence at the heart of the memoir: "Perhaps redeemed" (214). The choice of ambiguity in "perhaps" is a final rejection of the sentimental. Like *Still Alive*, women's memoirs constructed around the heat and intensity of mother-daughter bonds tend to resist the seduction of the happy end; they may flirt with forgiveness and sometimes come close, proposing metaphors of collaboration, but the past is often still too alive to manage true reconciliation. If they move beyond blame and accusation, of necessity the memoirist daughters protect their version of history (it's their memory, after all, however revised).

Yet it might be possible to read in this ending the glimmer of an unconscious empathy between daughter and mother through loss. In the final paragraph, Klüger portrays her mother as an "old adult who had once lost a teenage son to anonymous murderers" (214). She says early in the memoir that the death of her brother was her "first great loss"; like the afterlife of traumatic experience (*trauma* is my term, not hers), "every subsequent loss has seemed a replay of that first"; the death of her brother also meant losing her role as "little sister" (28). Just as the Holocaust continues its work in lives and in memory long after the events (living on?), the two survivors, mother and daughter, never ceased mourning, however separately, that brutal loss.

In writing about her mother's last days, Klüger observes that the "thing that says 'I' gradually steals away" (211). Earlier in the epilogue, describing the psychological effects of her accident in Germany, she explains that it was "as if burglars had been in my head" (207). But theft becomes restoration when the physical damage of the accident brings to consciousness girlhood memories of a dislocated past and self. In the end, it's the daughter who can still say "I"; who, true to her childhood wish, has remained alive to bear witness to injustice; who owns the secrets of death, which, once the province of the grown-ups, are now hers to tell.

Works Cited

Beauvoir, Simone de. *A Very Easy Death*. Trans. Patrick O'Brian. New York: Pantheon, 1965.

Brontë, Charlotte. *Jane Eyre*. Ed. Richard J. Dunn. Norton Critical Ed. 2nd ed. New York: Norton, 1987.

Delbo, Charlotte. *Auschwitz and After*. Trans. Rosette C. Lamont. New Haven: Yale UP, 1995.

Ernaux, Annie. *A Woman's Story*. Trans. Tanya Leslie. New York: Seven Stories, 2003.

Frank, Anne. The Diary of a Young Girl*: The Definitive Edition*. Ed. Otto Frank and Mirjam Pressler. Trans. Susan Massotty. New York: Doubleday, 1995.

Gornick, Vivian. *Fierce Attachments: A Memoir*. Boston: Beacon, 1997.

Jacobs, Harriet. *Incidents in the Life of a Slave Girl*. Ed. L. Maria Child. Introd. Julie. R. Adams. 14 Feb. 2004. 14 Apr. 2004 <http://xroads .virginia.edu/~HYPER/JACOBS/hjhome.htm>. Path: Site Index; Ch. 41.

Klüger, Ruth. *Still Alive: A Holocaust Girlhood Remembered*. Fwd. Lore Segal. New York: Feminist, 2003.

———. *Weiter leben: Eine Jugend*. Göttingen: Wallstein, 1992.

Levi, Primo. *Survival in Auschwitz: The Nazi Assault on Humanity*. Trans. Stuart Woolf. New York: Simon, 1996.

Spiegelman, Art. *And Here My Troubles Began*. New York: Pantheon, 1991. Vol. 2 of *Maus: A Survivor's Tale*.

———. *My Father Bleeds History*. New York: Pantheon, 1986. Vol. 1 of *Maus: A Survivor's Tale*.

Steedman, Carolyn Kay. *Landscape for a Good Woman: A Story of Two Lives*. New Brunswick: Rutgers UP, 1987.

Wiesel, Elie. *Night*. Trans. Stella Rodway. New York: Bantam, 1986.

Michael G. Levine

"Toward an Addressable You": Ozick's *The Shawl* and the Mouth of the Witness

The Shawl: A Story and Novella, by Cynthia Ozick, is often read in courses on Holocaust literature in conjunction with Elie Wiesel's *Night*. Wiesel's testimony describes in painful detail the murder of his beloved father as well as the humiliations to which the father-son bond was itself subjected in Auschwitz. Ozick's work is divided into two parts. The brief story, "The Shawl," focuses on the plight of a mother who is made to look on helplessly as her infant daughter is hurled into an electrified fence in an unnamed camp. The novella, "Rosa," set approximately forty years later in Miami Beach, is in many ways the story of the surviving mother's ongoing psychological imprisonment in the camp in general and in this scene of witnessing in particular. In contrast to the poignant eloquence of Wiesel, the fictive survivor of Ozick's story, Rosa Lublin, is painfully inarticulate. Like so many of the actual witnesses interviewed by the Shoah Foundation and the Fortunoff Video Archive for Holocaust Testimonies at Yale, Rosa speaks a broken immigrant English, and it is through the cracks, lapses, and perseverations in her speech that fragments of "deep memory" surface in the narrative.[1]

We should also examine *The Shawl* in relation to *No Common Place: The Holocaust Testimony of Alina Bacall-Zwirn*, a hybrid text combining transcripts of the survivor's video testimony given at the Yale archive; fragments of her late husband's unpublished manuscript, "One Small Candle," composed with the help of a ghostwriter; and taped interviews with Jared Stark (Bacall-Zwirn and Stark). Like *No Common Place*, *The Shawl* draws particular attention to the act of bearing witness, inviting us to view testimony less as a finished product, less as a story at the disposal of the witness and accessible to her conscious recall, than as a fragmentary, ongoing, interminable process. Very different in genre and narrative perspective, the two works are stories of mothers who have never come to terms with the loss of their infant children in the camps and who cling desperately to fantasies of their miraculous survival. Both texts, too, are very much concerned with the status of the mother tongue, with the question of what it means to bear witness not only in a foreign language but also — what is more problematic — from a space between languages.[2] In short, both lead us to examine the way deep memory may unwittingly emerge in an idiom the witness does not know she speaks, in an unconscious discourse of the other, foreign to all mother tongues.

In teaching these texts, we should also focus on the connections they draw between the traumas of birth and of death. Not only are both these survivor narratives very much stories of life in death, stories of a survivor's struggle to emerge from the enduring frozenness of an ongoing present — from what Ozick's protagonist refers to as the time frame of the "during" — but both figure the act of witnessing itself as a process of deferred parturition. The metaphoric connection between childbirth and testimony draws attention to the active role played by the listener or interviewer in the act of bearing witness, leading us to ask how the "witness to the witness" is positioned not merely as a recipient of the survivor's story but as a kind of midwife assisting in its delivery.[3] As Dori Laub, analyst and cofounder of the Yale video archive, has noted, "The emergence of the narrative which is being listened to—and heard—is . . . the process and the place wherein the cognizance, the 'knowing' of the event, is given birth to. The listener . . . is a party to the creation of knowledge *de novo*" (57). In *No Common Place* the role of listener, or second-degree witness, is assumed by the cosignator of Bacall-Zwirn's testimony, Stark. In *The Shawl* this role is delegated to Rosa Lublin's acquaintance Simon Persky.

The mother-daughter story that Ozick tells is in many ways a traditionally gendered narrative. In it the violence directed against a woman takes the form of a rape. That violence is in turn perpetuated in the form of an unwanted child the victim is made to conceive and bear. In the end, a man appears on the scene bringing help and possible redemption to the woman in distress. Yet Ozick significantly complicates these familiar gender roles in casting Simon Persky less as a discrete male character than as a stand-in for a host of haunting figures who never appear as such. In speaking both to and through Persky, Rosa indirectly addresses the ghosts of her all-too-present past.

"Before is a dream. After is a joke. Only during stays. And to call it a life is a lie," Rosa tells Persky (58). For her, the struggle to bear witness is itself an effort to emerge from this life-in-death state of suspended animation. In seeing her words fall repeatedly on deaf ears, she reexperiences her traumatic muting at the moment of her rape and at the time of her daughter's death. "Whoever came [into my store in New York]," she laments, "they were like deaf people. Whatever you explained to them, they didn't understand" (27).

Like Rosa's untransmittable story, the unbearable pain she carries inside her has nowhere to go. Lacking any verbal outlet, demanding and yet resisting translation into words, the pain remains pent up in her traumatically estranged and anesthetized body. "The Shawl" ends with the protagonist's "swallowing up the wolf's screech" that had been "ascending . . . through the ladder of her skeleton" (10); the beginning of the novella reads like a belated repetition of this scene. Only here what erupts in place of the suppressed outburst is an act of self-violence directed at a surrogate body. Thus the second part begins, "Rosa Lublin, a madwoman and a scavenger, gave up her store—she smashed it up herself—and moved to Miami" (13). Taking an ax to this junk shop specializing in "antique mirrors" (26), Rosa not only vents her frustration at not being heard by those who came into her store but seeks, through this self-destructive violence, to release the stored-up memories and choked-back screams lodged in her body.

While Ozick's protagonist is quick to ridicule the women she meets in Miami for their naive belief "in the seamless continuity of the body" and prides herself on being able to "see everything they were not noticing about themselves" (28), she is painfully lacking in self-awareness. Indeed, it is no exaggeration to say that she is someone who can see herself only in the mirror of those surrounding her, who can speak about herself only as though talking about somebody else, who can hear her most repressed thoughts only when they return to her in the voice and through the mouth of another. When, in "The Shawl," her niece, Stella, blurts out the unspeakable truth of the paternity of her daughter, Magda, referring to the child as an "Aryan," Stella's mouth metamorphoses before her aunt's eyes from an organ of speech into an omnivorous oral cavity seemingly bent on consuming the very person spoken about: "and Rosa thought how Stella gazed at Magda like a young cannibal. And the time that Stella said 'Aryan,' it sounded to Rosa as if Stella had really said 'Let us devour her'" (5).

Rosa is so insistent in her denial of her daughter's true paternity because she herself cannot connect feelings of maternal love (always presented, in the text, in a highly idealized, spiritualized, and sanitized form) with the circumstances of Magda's conception. While Rosa admits to having been "forced by a German . . . and more than once," she nevertheless insists that she was "too sick to conceive." Like the protagonist, who has no direct, unmediated access to the traumatic scene of her rape, students usually have difficulty finding traces of it in the text. Such problems are very much a part of the narrative, since it is precisely this story that Rosa herself does not possess. Indeed, because she constructs an immaculately whitewashed account of the conception of her daughter to replace the version she has repressed ("Your father," she writes to her dead child after the war, "was the son of my mother's closest friend" [43]), students are constantly put in the position of having to read what she says against the grain, to treat what she remembers as a screen memory.

This situation holds as well for the scene of Magda's murder. Although Rosa clearly sees her child being picked up by a camp guard and thrown into an electrified fence, the depiction of this traumatic moment is so abstract, so highly aestheticized, as to make it read less like an eyewitness account of Magda's flight through the air than like an unwitting description of Rosa's own psychic flight from the scene. "All at once Magda was swimming through the air. The whole of Magda traveled through loftiness. She looked like a butterfly touching a silver vine" (9–10). As often happens in *The Shawl*, such lofty language bears witness to Rosa's own departure, to the way a pointedly aestheticized screen memory is made to stand in for what Rosa could not bear to witness. Students are therefore obliged to read through these screens toward other versions of a story that is never recounted as such.

Whereas we might usually expect the third-person narrator to be of help in assessing the truth of the protagonist's words or in providing access to knowledge denied her, Ozick's use of free indirect style has a way of extending Rosa's individual sense of disorientation to the narrative as a whole. This device makes it extremely difficult for the reader to assume a position of mastery with regard to Rosa or her story. Indeed, without an objective third-person narrator to depend on for guidance, we are made to participate all the more in this Polish Jewish refugee's struggle to orient herself in the aftermath of the Shoah, in a foreign language and in an alien world.

The greatest challenge in teaching *The Shawl* is to get students to understand how, in the text, birth trauma and death trauma are related and why these traumas associated with the beginning and the end of life are made to pass for and through each other. One way to bring this problematic relation into focus is to trace the familiar equation of silence with death in the first part and then ask why Magda seems to come to life only after the fact, emerging from her deathlike silence and "spilling a long viscous rope of clamor" (8), evocative of an umbilical cord, at the very moment she is about to be killed. How, we might ask, does this moment of birth as death repeat Rosa's own sense of having died at the time of her violent conception of her daughter? Once the overlapping and repetitive relation has been established, we can point students to the second part of the story, where traces of these intimately related traumas continue to wash up in bits and pieces on the shoreline of Miami Beach. It is here, moreover, that the doubling of birth as death, the repetition of the one trauma through the other, returns as a movement of deferred parturition, as the very structure of the survivor's struggle to bear witness to—and from—her indefinite suspension at the limit of life and death.

Such a limit takes various forms in *The Shawl*, appearing as the static time frame of the "during" (58); "the margin of the arena" (9) from which Rosa is made to witness her daughter's murder at the end of the first part; and the shoreline of Miami Beach, on which she finds herself stranded throughout much of the second. As though to stress the identity of these seemingly unrelated places of suspension and the movement from threshold to threshold that the survivor is fated to trace, Ozick plays on the etymological derivation of the word *arena*, from the Latin *harena*, meaning "sand" or "sandy place." Moving from New York to Miami at the beginning of the novella, Rosa thus finds herself still standing at the margin of a place and in the enduring frozenness of a point in time she never left. Her struggle to bear witness to and from this place of suspension impels her to move in two opposing directions at once—back to the sameness of the past and toward the possibility of a different future.

The best way to show how the two related traumas of the first part of *The Shawl* resurface in the second is to begin with a scene set in the Laundromat near Rosa's hotel. Students may be asked to consider the very banality of the setting. How, for example, is it indicative of Rosa's precarious hold on the present, of her vulnerability to a past that may return to haunt her at any time—even in the most seemingly benign circumstances? "[S]he sat on a cracked wooden bench and watched the round porthole of the washing machine. Inside, the surf of detergent bubbles frothed and slapped her underwear against the pane" (16–17). Here, teachers might point out how the sense of violence hinted at in this spectacle of underpants being beaten against the glass is reinforced not only by the pun on *pane* but, more generally, by the ties connecting this scene to two others around which it may be seen to revolve. While already anticipating a later moment, set literally at the edge of the surf in which Rosa's pursuit of her missing underwear will gradually dissolve into a hallucinatory reenactment of her rape, the scene echoes an earlier description of Magda's death, the moment when the child is seen "swimming through the air" before being "splashed against the fence" (9–10).

While waiting for this infernal machine to finish, Rosa first notices an elderly man, Simon Persky, sitting next to her. They get to talking, and he invites her to have tea with him in a local cafeteria. There Persky glimpses something white on the floor near Rosa's laundry cart: "a white cloth. Handkerchief. He picked it up and stuffed it in his pants pocket" (26). When Rosa returns to her hotel room, she unloads her laundry only to find that she is missing one pair of underwear. Later, as the sun goes down over Miami and the houselights of the present and the world of consciousness dim, Rosa sets out in search of her missing panties. As this theater of the unconscious now fades in, the nouns *pants* and *underpants* start to sound more and more like the verb *to pant*, used a number of times in the preceding pages to describe the protagonist's actions. In a text that plays so often on Latin etymologies and is replete with allusions to classical texts—most notably *The Aeneid*, "the whole first half" of which, Rosa claims, her father knew "by heart" (69)—it is useful to have students return to Vergil, paying particular attention to the figures of Dis and the Minotaur and the text's descriptions of the Cretan labyrinth. Instructors should also focus on the etymology of the verb *to pant* derived from the Vulgar Latin *phantasiare*, meaning "to be oppressed with nightmare, to gasp or pant with nightmare."[4] Bearing this pivotal term's history and multiple senses in mind, students may then be invited to do a close reading of the following crucial passage, in which Rosa, wandering out onto the beach, asks herself:

> If someone wanted to hide—to hide, not destroy—a pair
> of underpants, where would he put them? Under the sand.

Rolled up and buried. She thought what a weight of sand would feel like in the crotch of her pants, wet heavy sand, still hot from the day. In her room it was hot, hot all night. No air. In Florida there was no air, only this syrup seeping into the esophagus. Rosa walked; she saw everything, but as if out of invention, out of imagination; she was unconnected to anything. She came to a gate; a mottled beach spread behind it. It belonged to one of the big hotels. The latch opened. At the edge of the waves you could look back and see black crenellated forms stretching all along the shore. In the dark, in silhouette, the towered hotel roofs held up their merciless teeth. Impossible that any architect pleasurably dreamed these teeth. The sand was only now beginning to cool. Across the water the sky breathed a starless black; behind her, where the hotels bit down on the city, a dusty glow of brownish red lowered. Mud clouds. The sand was littered with bodies. Photograph of Pompeii: prone in the volcanic ash. Her pants were under the sand; or else packed hard with sand, like a piece of torso, a broken statue, the human groin detached, the whole soul gone, only the loins left for kicking by strangers. (47–48)

At the edge of the waves Rosa again finds herself doubly marginalized, closed out on the one side by the towered hotel roofs' black "merciless teeth" biting down on the city and on the other by the forbiddingly open expanse of the sea across which the sky is said to breathe "a starless black." Stranded on the beach, Rosa hears nothing but the sound of a certain panting. No longer coming from the mouth of a single, identifiable person or suggested by the use of a specific verb, the panting is now associated with a diffuse, pervasively insistent p sound: "a pair of underpants, where would he put them? . . . Photograph of Pompeii: prone in the volcanic ash. Her pants . . . under the sand . . . packed hard with sand, like a piece of torso." Thematically linked to Rosa's blind, groping search for a piece of her shattered self, the sound's painfully probing rhythms are ones to which the reader has become gradually attuned in the preceding pages through the repetition of related phrases such as "Persky had her underpants in his pocket" (34).

The sound of panting is very much a part of the sexually charged atmosphere of the beach onto which Rosa has strayed. Indeed, the bodies with which the sand is said to be "littered" are those of naked gay couples she nearly steps on, "double mounds in the sand" (48) whom she later taps with her shoes in order to ask for directions out. Finding herself thus trapped on the beach surrounded by indistinct panting noises that seem to come from everywhere and nowhere at once, from the present as well as from the past, Rosa begins to pant, "to be oppressed with nightmare," as the scene of her rape now returns to take her back to the place she never left.

In addition to being haunted by the visual and acoustic images associated with Rosa's being "forced . . . and more than once," the scene set "at the edge of the waves" returns her, in effect, to the "margin of the arena," where she was left at the end of "The Shawl." The sense of immobilization associated with both earlier moments is experienced now in the scene on the beach as a feeling of confinement. "When she came back to the gate, the latch would not budge. A cunning design, it trapped the trespasser. She gazed up, and thought of climbing; but there was barbed wire on top" (48). As though standing still again in the camp, Rosa sees in the locked gate topped with barbed wire looming before her the electrified fence into which Magda was thrown and hears in the noise resounding in her ears, its electric voices. Only now instead of the cries of "Maamaa, Maaamaaa" (9) that those voices had once "all hummed together," she seems to hear the "paapaa, paaapaaa" of Magda's anonymous fathers all panting together. More generally, it might be said that to be suspended in this way on the shore's sandy margin is to find oneself exposed once again to the violence of more than one traumatic experience, to the repeated violation of experiences belatedly breaking into and resonating through one another, to the violent shattering of an undelimitable traumatic scene that from the very first will have been more and less than one.

Students may be asked at this point to recall how the cry of "maaaa—" is said to spill from Magda's mouth like "a long viscous rope of clamor" in the first part of *The Shawl*. The simile marks a threefold connection in the text: the tenuous attachment of mother and daughter in the process of separating; the conjunction of the lips above and those below at the moment of parting; and the sounding together of an infant's first cry with its last. In the second part of *The Shawl*, the verbal bridge of the perseverating *p* sound associated with Persky's dental work and the hotel roofs' "merciless teeth" joins the panting above to the underpants below to reinforce the link between Rosa's estranged lower parts and that which goes on, as it were, sub rosa, under the seal of silence. What returns as one panting refrain echoing through another, as the reverberation of pants within pants, are the remains of a traumatic violation heard through the deafening sound of its violent muting.

The persistence of this acoustic trace resonates with Rosa's sense of being suspended in a time and place she never left, with her sense of entrapment in a series of interrelated, ongoing moments whose pain she can neither express nor silence. It should further be emphasized that the violence here is associated not merely with the content of the protagonist's repressed memories but also with the repressive act of silencing. While Ozick leaves unnamed the camp in which Rosa loses her daughter, a number of indications in the text suggest a connection between it and the *Lager* known as Maidanek. In pursuing this connection, instructors may wish to refer to historical and eyewitness accounts of what transpired there on 3 November 1943. On that day the popular German tune "Rosamunde, Give Me a Kiss" was played incessantly over the camp's loudspeakers "to muffle the sounds of the shooting and the cries of the dying" as the SS carried out the largest single mass execution in the history of the camp (Feig).[5] The last name of Ozick's protagonist may be read as an allusion to this uniquely urban camp located 4.8 kilometers from the center of the Polish city of Lublin, while her first name and the text's intense focus on the mouth may recall the aestheticized violence associated with the playing of "Rosamunde."

Rosa's panting and the haunting repetition of the *p* sound through which it is made audible are evidence of her ongoing imprisonment in the past. The repetitions, however, are also associated with a movement in another, future-oriented direction, with a desperate search for an instance that Paul Celan (whose poem "Todesfuge" is cited in the epigraph to *The Shawl*; see also Baer's essay in this volume) refers to in his 1958 Bremen speech as the place of "something standing open, occupiable," of "an addressable you" (35; trans. modified). Such an instance is most closely identified with the figure of Persky, and Rosa's stuttering may be understood as an unwitting effort to seek him out; to address him; and, in doing so, to involve him as a listener to her heretofore untransmittable testimony. As Laub has observed:

> Bearing witness to a trauma is . . . a process that includes the listener. For the testimonial process to take place, there needs to be a bonding, the intimate and total presence of an *other*—in the position of the one who hears. Testimonies are not monologues; they cannot take place in solitude. The witnesses are talking *to somebody*: to somebody they have been waiting for for a long time. (70–71)

Persky may in one sense be viewed as the long-awaited addressee of Rosa's testimony. Yet, in another, more enigmatic sense he stands merely as the placeholder of an other still to come, of an other whom Rosa seeks to address in speaking not to but through him. To bring this point into focus, instructors may direct students to the scene in which Rosa's would-be suitor, a retired button salesman also originally from Warsaw (though, as the now destitute but still class-conscious daughter of a highly assimilated bourgeois family constantly reminds Persky, "Your Warsaw isn't my Warsaw" [22]), first shows up at her hotel. He arrives unexpectedly in place of Magda—or, rather, in lieu of the long-awaited delivery of her precious shawl, which Rosa's niece, Stella, had promised to send from New York. "Her room was miraculously ready: tidy, clarified" (55). As though to underscore Persky's role as a stand-in, Rosa does not dare open the box containing the shawl when it finally arrives. Instead, she has Persky act on her behalf. "What her own hands longed to do she was yielding to a stranger, a man with pockets" (59). In delegating such an important task to this "stranger," Rosa is no doubt testing Persky to see whether he is truly capable of functioning as a supplementary witness to the witness, of entering her pantingly phantasmatic underworld in which something as insignificant as the unwrapping of a small package can be experienced as a scene of labor and delivery.[6]

To understand why survivors may require the participation of a second-degree witness, we should turn to a scene, toward the end of the text, in which Rosa recalls seeing the "most astounding thing" from her vantage point on the pedestrian bridge connecting one part of the Warsaw Ghetto to the other:

> that the most ordinary streetcar, bumping along on the most ordinary trolley tracks, and carrying the most ordinary citizens going from one section of Warsaw to another, ran straight into the place of our misery. Every day, and several times a day, we had these witnesses. Every day they saw us — women with shopping sacks; and once I noticed a head of lettuce sticking up out of the top of a sack — green lettuce! I thought my salivary glands would split with aching for that leafy greenness. (68)

That this woman with the head of lettuce is singled out not just as an eyewitness ("Every day . . . we had these witnesses. Every day they saw us") but as one in possession of the "leafy greenness" of nourishment suggests that the act of witnessing she had been in a position to perform was — and still is — as vital to Rosa, as desired by her, as sustenance itself. It is therefore significant that this woman — and others like her — not only failed to bear witness to Rosa's ordeal but failed every day. Indeed, it is this quotidian violence, this daily humiliation of seeing herself not being seen, of gradually being made to view herself as invisible that returns to haunt Rosa in her store in New York and again in Miami.

Like the woman with the lettuce, Rosa is herself a potential witness. Yet, having internalized the anonymous others' disregard for her, she cannot testify alone. The point of these overdetermined identifications is thus to suggest that there can be no witness without a witness to the witness, without the vital accompaniment of another, without someone prepared to listen with "leafy" fresh ears to what in a sense had "been there" the whole time — like the "missing underwear" Rosa eventually finds "curled inside a towel" (61) — to hear in what had been said time and again an unheard-of difference. Her salivary glands seem about to "split with aching," but what Rosa ultimately longs to taste are her own words, through the ear of the other, through an act of listening that might belatedly bring something unexpected in her speech to life. In "The Interlocutor," an essay to which Celan's thinking about the place of "an addressable you" is greatly indebted, the Russian poet Osip Mandelstam writes:

> When I speak to somebody, I do not know with whom I speak, and I do not wish, I *cannot* wish to know him. There is no lyric without dialogue. Yet the only thing that pushes us into the arms of the interlocutor is the desire to be surprised by our own words, to be captivated by their novelty and unexpectedness. (62–63)

Rosa's return in her final letter to a Warsaw that will never have been exactly hers or Persky's seems in the end to open another space, another portal in the present through which the witness to the witness may enter once again as if for the first time. "He's used to crazy women," Rosa tells the Cuban receptionist in her hotel, "so let him come up" (70).

The other whose place Persky holds and indeed holds open may be said to stand for a new psychic opening in Rosa. It stands, in other words, for a repositioning of her desire with respect to Persky the man and, more important, to what he represents in her libidinal economy. In the course of the text, Persky is cast in two related roles: either he is belittled as an uncultivated, déclassé, insignificant button salesman; the sexually frustrated husband of a crazy woman; and the embodiment of all the "teeming Mockowiczes and Rabinowiczes and . . . Finkelsteins" (66) Rosa had been lumped together with in the Warsaw Ghetto; or he is feared as a lascivious predator "with pants in his pockets," as a revenant of the thieves who had raped her and stolen her life. By the end of the text, however, Rosa begins to see, through him, someone she never saw before. In the mirror of this perpetually displaced stand-in, what may be glimpsed is a remobilization of her traumatically fixated desires, the fragile opening of a more vulnerable version of herself.

Discussions of *The Shawl* may conclude by a return to the initial comparison of Wiesel's and Ozick's texts. While Wiesel's Holocaust testimony is carefully framed by two very different scenes of reflection (the one metaphoric, the other literal) placed at opposite ends of the text, Ozick uses the figure of the mirror throughout *The Shawl* to bring into focus questions of doubling and repetition. In the last haunting words of *Night* Wiesel relates how three days after the liberation of Buchenwald he stood before a mirror, transfixed by the ghastly gaze of the corpse he saw staring back at him. The scene suggests a total collapse of the space of reflection through which the young Elie had at the outset sought to approach the infinite. It testifies as well to the infinitesimal reduction of the very notion of "eternity" described in the opening pages of *Night* as "that time where [human] question and [divine] answer would become *one*" (17). It is this temporal horizon that contracts in the end into a ceaselessly repeated moment of shock and disbelief registered in the split between first person and third person in the last line: "The look in his eyes, as they stared into mine, has never left me" (116).

In *The Shawl* Ozick uses the uncanniness of the mirror to much the same effect, while at the same time employing it to help us see repetition in an entirely new way—as a double and divided compulsion, as an unconscious drive impelled to move in two opposing directions at once, both backward to the sameness of the past and forward to the possibility of a different future. It is in attuning ourselves to the stammerings, perseverations, and pantings of *The Shawl* that we begin to view repetition not simply as a compulsive acting out of the past but as an equally unconscious way of working through it toward, in Celan's words, "something standing open, occupiable, an addresable you, perhaps, an addressable reality." To move beyond traumatic fixation in the teaching of Holocaust literature, we should, Ozick's text suggests, go even further in the direction of the unconscious toward a more complex, conflictual understanding of repetition and the vital, if heretofore unforeseen, possibilities pulsing within it.

Notes

1. On the notion of "deep memory," see Lawrence Langer's pioneering study of video testimonies (1–38).
2. In both works, Polish is the mother's tongue and American English the language adopted after the war.
3. The Holocaust scholars Henry Greenspan and Sidney Bolkovsky describe

the testimonial interview as a "collaboration in the sense of a laboring together. The essence of that labor is a shared commitment to bring forth, as fully as they may be retrievable, that survivor's tellable memories of the destruction. Expressions like 'labor' and 'bringing forth' are deliberately used because there is a kind of birthing and midwifery that goes on here—a creation that required more than one person at the start and needs more than one person all along the way." See also James Young's description of Art Spiegelman as "the midwife to and eventual representer of his father's story" (686).

4. In current usage, *to pant* means "1. To breathe hard or spasmodically, as when out of breath; to draw quick laboured breaths, as from exertion or agitation; to gasp for breath. . . . 2. To gasp (for air, water, etc.); hence figuratively to long or wish with breathless eagerness; to gasp with desire; to yearn. . . . 3. To throb or heave violently or rapidly; to palpitate, pulsate, beat. . . . 5. To utter gaspingly; to gasp *out*."

5. See also Trepman's eyewitness account.

6. The word *package* echoes the Yiddish *Paekel*. See in this regard Hartman's discussion of the Holocaust testimony of Bessie K., a mother who, like Ozick's Rosa, wraps her baby in a coat so that it appears to be a bundle. As she tries to smuggle it by a German guard, the baby, who is choking, makes a sound; the guard summons her back and asks for "the bundle." Hartman obseves that "when she admits she gave the officer the baby, she does not say 'the baby' but 'the bundle' (a natural metaphor, sad and distancing, yet still affectionate, perhaps a Yiddishism, the 'Paekel.'"

Works Cited

Bacall-Zwirn, Alina, and Jared Stark. *No Common Place: The Holocaust Testimony of Alina Bacall-Zwirn*. Lincoln: U of Nebraska P, 1999.

Celan, Paul. *Collected Prose*. Trans. Rosemarie Waldrop. Riverdale-on-Hudson: Sheep Meadow, 1986.

Feig, Konnilyn G. *Hitler's Death Camps: The Sanity of Madness*. New York: Holmes, 1981.

Greenspan, Henry, and Sidney Bolkovsky, "When Is an Interview an Interview? Notes on Listening to Holocaust Survivors." The Contribution of Oral Testimony to Holocaust and Genocide Studies. Fortunoff Video Archive Conf., Yale U, 6 Oct. 2002.

Hartman, Geoffrey. "Holocaust Testimony, Videography, and Education." Marvin and Celina Zborowski Endowment Lecture. Center for Jewish Studies, Queen's Coll., Flushing, NY. 2 May 2001.

Langer, Lawrence. *Holocaust Testimonies*. New Haven: Yale UP, 1991.

Laub, Dori. "Bearing Witness; or, The Vicissitudes of Listening." *Testimony: Crises of Witnessing in Literature, Psychoanalysis, and History*. By Shoshana Felman and Laub. New York: Routledge, 1991. 57–74.

Osip Mandelstam: Selected Essays. Ed. and trans. Sidney Monas. Austin: U of Texas P, 1977.

Ozick, Cynthia. *The Shawl: A Story and Novella.* New York: Knopf, 1989. Vintage, 1990.

"Pant." *The Oxford English Dictionary.* 2nd ed. 1989.

Trepman, Paul. *Among Men and Beasts.* Trans. Shoshana Perla and Gertrude Hirschler. South Brunswick: Barnes, 1978.

Wiesel, Elie. *Night.* Trans. Stella Rodway. New York: Hill, 1960.

Young, James E. "The Holocaust as Vicarious Past: Art Spiegelman's *Maus* and the Afterimages of History." *Critical Inquiry* 24 (1998): 670–97.

Leo Spitzer

"You Wanted History, I Give You History": Claude Lanzmann's *Shoah*

> *. . . Mr. Suchomel, we're not discussing you, only Treblinka.*
> —Claude Lanzmann, *Shoah*

"You start the course with *Shoah*?" a colleague from another institution asked us skeptically. "Does that work? Do the students have enough background to tap into this long film and appreciate its complexities, depth, and range?"

We do indeed start with Claude Lanzmann's nine-and-a-half-hour *Shoah*—a 1985 film that its French filmmaker edited down from over 350 hours of interviews and that took more than ten years to make. It is one of two long filmic texts around which our interdisciplinary undergraduate course on representations of the Holocaust is organized; the other is Marcel Ophüls's *Hotel Terminus* (1989). Our course, limited to forty students, is team-taught (we are in history and comparative literature) and meets in two-hour modules twice a week, with an *x*-hour available for additional use. Although we occasionally give short lectures, we largely teach our classes in a discussion format. In our first session, we introduce the course and the film and view approximately one hour of it with the students. They are then expected to see the rest of *Shoah* in four two-hour out-of-class sessions over the next week and a half; each session is scheduled at least twice for the sake of flexibility. Copies of the video version of the film are on reserve in the audiovisual section of our library.

By the time we hold our first scheduled discussion of *Shoah*, we expect students to have completed a series of readings to contextualize and complement the testimonial approach of the film. We assign selections from works by Ronnie Landau, Michael Marrus, Dan Pagis, Miklós Radnóti, Paul Celan, Avraham Tory, Ida Fink, Dori Laub, and Primo Levi. These works not only provide the students with historical background and interpretation but also introduce them to a range of short autobiographical and fictional accounts of individual experiences in ghettos and camps, as well as to critical analyses of testimony and listening. For example, Levi's essay "The Gray Zone" challenges and complicates any unambiguous differentiation between notions of good and evil that students may have brought into the course and deeply probes many of their unexamined moral assumptions. Together, *Shoah* and the readings offer students a multifaceted introduction to the difficult, disturbing issues and the varied approaches they will encounter in our course.

There are, of course, practical and what we might term "generational aesthetic" difficulties in teaching *Shoah*—and in placing it so early in the course. Quite apart from its daunting length, it is a film that fundamentally differs in sensibility and approach from the type of films our students have grown up with and normally watch. They have become used to viewing rapidly paced films and videos, replete with dynamic, dramatic action, multichannel sound effects, fast cuts, speedy plot development. They are, after all, of the generation of *Schindler's List*, *Saving Private Ryan*; *Run, Lola, Run*—of channel and Web surfing. *Shoah*, in contrast, is an intensely quiet and slow-moving film—one that can be frustrating in the deliberate way it handles differences in languages, translations, and subtitles. Lanzmann explains:

The languages that I did not understand, such as Polish, Hebrew, and Yiddish, were translated into French in the body of the film itself (and then translated into English [subtitles] for the American edition). The interpreters . . . are themselves present on the screen. (vii)[1]

Shoah, moreover, is not a documentary film in the traditional sense. Unlike Alain Resnais's *Night and Fog*, for example, it makes no use of archival footage from the 1930s and 1940s. It employs no PBS-style documentary voice-over narration, no musical accompaniment for dramatization or highlighting. Nor is it a dramatic, fictionalized reenactment of what might have occurred, such as *The Wannsee Conference* or the made-for-TV *Warsaw Ghetto Uprising*. Nor, for all its rich historical content, is it in any sense a chronological history of the Holocaust.[2]

But we do require students to view *Shoah* in its entirety so early in the course because, in a very real sense, it not only makes testimony, witnessing, and what James Young has termed "received history" central to its concerns; it also illustrates and performs many of the fundamental questions about Holocaust representation that our course wishes to address. "The film is made around my own obsessions," Lanzmann admitted in a lecture at Yale University in 1990 (Symposium). The almost obsessive thrust of *Shoah*, its primary goal, is to bring to memory and to record the workings of the Nazi machinery of destruction—to detail its operations and lethal course, from the ghettos, to the transports and trains, to the selection in the extermination camps, to mass murder in gas vans and gas chambers, to the burial and burning of the corpses. The film penetrates both the procedural and the psychic dimensions of this process: the secrecy that enabled it to function, the collusions that both actively and passively aided and sustained it, and the apathy of a world that stood by in silence and allowed it to happen. Lanzmann's primary witnesses for this daunting project, the persons he interviews most fully, are those who were closest to the process and mechanics of extermination—those in and around the deepest pits of hell. They include survivors of the special work details in the concentration camps, a number of Polish bystanders who lived and worked near the killing centers, and several German perpetrators.

On the basis of the testimony elicited from these witnesses, *Shoah* is built on the confrontation of past and present and on the representation of the past through layers of mediation — the core pedagogical goal of our course. The past is recalled often at the very sites of past crimes — Chelmno, Sobibor, the train station in Berlin from which Jews were deported. At other times, the voices of witnesses — surviving victims, bystanders, and perpetrators — recorded in Tel Aviv, New York, Germany, or Switzerland are heard while the camera pans over the present views of Birkenau or Treblinka. "It is hard to recognize but it was here," Simon Srebnik, one of only two survivors of Chelmno, the first extermination site of World War II, says softly near the beginning of the film. "Yes, this is the place. No one ever left here again. . . . I can't believe I'm here. No, I just can't believe it. It was always this peaceful here. Always . . . It was silent. Peaceful. Just as it is now" (5, 6). Srebnik's unequivocal statement of identification and recognition haunts the entire film. As we look at other sites — sunny fields, dark forests, endlessly repeated train tracks — we project onto them past scenes of destruction that they both reveal and conceal. It is here, it is the same, it was always this peaceful; and, at the same time, it is different, hard to recognize, concealed: it has to be dug up. And in being dug up, literally before our eyes through the testimony of survivors, empty, unreadable landscapes are reinscribed with a memory that the Nazis worked hard to erase.

In juxtaposing the past with the present site of memory, *Shoah* thus undoes two sets of erasures: the gradual and ordinary fading caused by the passage of time and the deliberate erasure attempted by the Nazi perpetrators. But Lanzmann's method goes beyond the actual return of witnesses to the places where it happened. Even where such a return does not occur physically, Lanzmann often manages to reimmerse witnesses into the past emotionally and psychologically so as to elicit from them their deepest feelings and their most traumatic memories. While *Shoah*, therefore, is not a reenactment in the sense of employing actors to play events and speak text from the past, Lanzmann does stage scenes in order to stimulate witnesses to bring forth testimony. He hires a railroad train that was used in bringing victims to Treblinka, and he films the train's journey into the *Lager*'s station, driven by the same engineer who drove such trains to the death camp. He asks a Treblinka guard, SS Unterscharführer Franz Suchomel—whom he films surreptitiously in his house in Germany—to recall the song the Nazi guards and prisoners used to sing together at the camp. And, as he does so, we can see that Suchomel is suddenly transported back, in an uncanny enthusiastic reverie, to the site of the experience: "Satisfied? That's unique. No Jew knows that today!" Suchomel brags after performing the song (Lanzmann 106). Lanzmann interviews a barber, Abraham Bomba, one of the Jewish survivors who had been made to cut women's hair inside the undressing rooms of the Treblinka gas chambers, and purposely films the interview in a barber shop in Israel (where Bomba lives) while his witness is cutting hair. He does this in order to bring the barber to recall the deepest, most repressed bodily memories of that horrific past:

Bomba: . . . I can't. It's too horrible. Please.
Lanzmann: We have to do it. You know it.
Bomba: I won't be able to do it.
Lanzmann: You have to do it. I know it's very hard. I know and I apologize.
Bomba: Don't make me go on please.
Lanzmann: Please. We must go on. (117)

This is no longer simply recollection, memory, witnessing. It is acting out a traumatic past in front of the camera, reliving it. Unlike relatively unmediated video testimonies, such as many of those collected in the Fortunoff Video Archive for Holocaust Testimonies at Yale University or in Steven Spielberg's Survivors of the Shoah Visual History Foundation project, Lanzmann's interviews, and the situations and settings in which they are carried out and seen by the viewer, are driven by the filmmaker himself. His questions, his curiosity, his passion, his insistence shape the film.

Throughout *Shoah*, Lanzmann wants details, particulars, specifics about the operation of the machinery of extermination ("How far?" "What color?" "How long?" "How wide?" "Can you describe this . . . precisely?"). He is relentless in his quest. In posing such precise questions, he seems deliberately to be rejecting larger, more encompassing moral and philosophical inquiries. And, to be sure, as details are piled on details, not in any chronological order, we and the students in our class learn an immense amount about the Nazi war years and the enabling mechanisms of the final solution. We also learn about survival and how witnesses have processed their terrible knowledge and managed to live with it, more or less successfully. Most important, perhaps, we learn about how the past lives on in the present.

But if Lanzmann's approach allows him to get at and lay bare stories and elicit knowledge that cannot be obtained otherwise—if it drives him to challenge what Shoshana Felman has called the paradox of witnessing about "the-event-without-witness"—that approach does not appeal to everyone (227). Our class discussions on this topic—on the need to elicit testimony versus the ethics of doing so—are generally animated, intense, even impassioned. Some students will be caught up in Lanzmann's obsessive pursuit of detailed information and strongly defend its no-other-choice necessity. How else but through surreptitious means could anyone have managed to get a perpetrator like Suchomel to reveal what he revealed about Treblinka? How else could one access traumatic memory— "deep memory," in Charlotte Delbo's words (3)—without pushing some witnesses insistently, as he did with Bomba, through a barrier of horrific pain?

Other students, however, will find Lanzmann's questions intrusive, his manner bullying, and his interviewing techniques unethical. Where should one draw the line between the desire for testimony and factual knowledge and the reluctance, or unwillingness, of the individual witness to tell? Isn't there a danger that those who have been victimized, like Bomba, may be retraumatized by the very act of witnessing that Lanzmann demands from them? Is Lanzmann's secretive filming of Suchomel, and his blatant, pitiless lying to him, a lesson in necessary technique—in a way to elicit truth from an otherwise silent or deceitful perpetrator-witness? Or does it, in a castigating but also problematic manner, echo (although certainly not repeat) the dissimulation that the Nazi perpetrators performed on their victims? And what about Lanzmann's dealings with his third group of witnesses, Polish bystanders? Isn't there often mockery, if not cruelty, in the manner in which he interviews and exposes them?

Shoah stimulates discussion questions such as these—questions that students recall and engage throughout the term in their journal entries and in relation to other readings and visual materials in the course. But as a pedagogical instrument, the film is also important for what it does not do. For one, despite its lengthy testimonial examination of conditions in the Warsaw Ghetto and its conclusion with the words of Simha Rottem, one of the surviving leaders of that ghetto's uprising, *Shoah* is not a film about Jewish resistance or heroism. Long segments with participants and eyewitnesses render few if any details about matters like the Sobibor rebellion or the activities of Jewish partisans or the escape from Auschwitz by Rudolf Vrba—one of the film's most articulate narrators and one of the few persons ever to have escaped from this concentration camp. To learn about such events and actions we must examine other accounts—published memoirs, diaries, even Lanzmann's more recently released filmed interviews.[3] Why were these interviews not included in the nine and a half hours of *Shoah*?

Shoah, moreover, virtually eradicates gender differences among the victims of the final solution. Perpetrators and bystanders, inasmuch as they figure in the film, represent a range of groups, male and female, farmers and tradespeople. But among the Jewish survivors who speak and give their accounts in the film, the erasure of differences and particularly the almost complete absence of women's testimonies is striking. It is almost as if, for Lanzmann, gender is irrelevant to the death machinery on which he focuses with such relentless energy—a machinery designed to render subject into object, to degender, to declass, to dehumanize, and to exterminate and destroy the traces.[4] Or is it that Lanzmann privileges testimonies from men in his project? Certainly, only men worked in the *Son-*

derkommando special work details that constitute Lanzmann's primary witnesses, persons who were closest to the process and mechanics of extermination. And yet other parts of the film (the story of the Warsaw Ghetto, the story of the Theresienstadt "family camp" in Auschwitz, for example) could have included more sustained testimonies from women.

When we urge students to recognize such omissions in *Shoah*, broader representational issues are highlighted for discussion. The representational choices not only in Lanzmann's work but in all else we read and see in the course—including the course itself, its syllabus, and the selections we made in drawing it up—stimulate members of the class to understand the ways in which historical understanding is necessarily constructed. Each omission brings with it important reading skills and permits some reference to the growing critical literature on the presence or absence of Jewish resistance and on gender and the Holocaust.

It would be wrong to end any discussion of *Shoah* by highlighting its omissions. Watching and discussing the film prepares students to engage the study of the Holocaust at the most humanly immediate and theoretically sophisticated levels. Basically it is a film about witnessing and transmission. Many of the film's witnesses were slated for extermination, but against all odds they were able to survive and to tell. In their faces and eyes, we get an inkling about what it means to live with the past we have inherited from them. As we watch *Shoah*, we ourselves become witnesses to these narratives. We come to share a knowledge that must be further divulged and spread.

Notes

1. All *Shoah* quotations are from Lanzmann, *Shoah: An Oral History of the Holocaust*.
2. The five-videotape boxed edition of *Shoah*, marketed by New Yorker Films, comes with a teaching guide that includes a chronology of the Holocaust keyed to places and events mentioned in the film. It also comes with a glossary of terms. We reproduce both of these useful aids and make them available to the students. A four-disc DVD edition is also now available in France and the United States. The French set includes a transcript of the film's text, which is keyed to correspond to

each of the discs. The United States set includes a key that sequentially identifies speakers in each disc.

3. See memoirs by Richard Glazar; Filip Müller; and Rudolf Vrba; as well as Lanzmann's *Sobibor.*

4. For a fuller discussion of this aspect of *Shoah*, see Hirsch and Spitzer.

Works Cited

Films and Film Texts

Claude L.: Testimony (HVT-700). Interviewed by L. Dori Laub and Laurel Vlock. Yale U, Video Archive for Holocaust Testimonials, 1986.

Hotel Terminus: The Life and Times of Klaus Barbie. Dir. Marcel Ophüls. MGM Home Entertainment, 1989. 2 videocassettes.

Lanzmann, Claude. *Shoah: An Oral History of the Holocaust. The Complete Text of the Film*. New York: Pantheon, 1985.

Night and Fog. Dir. Alain Resnais. 1956. DVD. Criterion Collection, 2003.

Shoah. Dir. Claude Lanzmann. New Yorker Films, 1985. 5 videocassettes (VHS).

Sobibor: 14 octobre 1943, 16 heures. Dir. Claude Lanzmann. Paris: Cahiers du cinéma, 2001

The Wannsee Conference. Dir. Heinz Schirk, 1984.

Warsaw Ghetto Uprising. Dir. Jon Avnet. NBC miniseries. 2001.

Associated Readings

Celan, Paul. "Death Fugue." Langer 601.

Delbo, Charlotte. *Days and Memory*. Trans. Rosette Lamont. Marlboro: Marlboro, 1990.

Felman, Shoshana. "The Return of the Voice: Claude Lanzmann's *Shoah*." Felman and Laub 204–83.

Felman, Shoshana, and Dori Laub. *Testimony: Crises of Witnessing in Literature, Psychoanalysis, and History*. New York: Routledge, 1992.

Fink, Ida. "The Key Game" and "A Spring Morning." Langer 242–48.

Glazar, Richard. *Trap with a Green Fence: Survival in Treblinka, Jewish Lives*. Evanston: Northwestern UP, 1995.

Hirsch, Marianne, and Leo Spitzer. "Gendered Translations: Claude Lanzmann's *Shoah*." *Gendering War Talk*. Ed. Miriam Cooke and Angela Wollacott. Princeton: Princeton UP, 1992. 3–19.

Landau, Ronnie S. *The Nazi Holocaust*. Chicago: Dee, 1994.

Langer, Lawrence, ed. *Art from the Ashes: A Holocaust Anthology*. New York: Oxford UP, 1995.

Laub, Dori. "Bearing Witness; or, The Vicissitudes of Listening." Felman and Laub 57–74.

———. "An Event without a Witness: Truth, Testimony, and Survival." Felman and Laub 75–92.

Levi, Primo. "The Gray Zone." 1986. *The Drowned and the Saved.* Trans. Raymond Rosenthal. New York: Summit, 1988. 36–69.

———. "Shame." Langer 215–33.

Marrus, Michael. *The Holocaust in History.* Hanover: UP of New England, 1987.

Müller, Filip, *Eyewitness Auschwitz: Three Years in the Gas Chambers.* Chicago: Dee, 1999.

Müller, Filip, Helmut Freitag, and Susanne Flatauer. *Auschwitz Inferno: The Testimony of a Sonderkommando.* London: Routledge, 1979.

Pagis, Dan. "Written in Pencil in the Sealed Railway-Car." Langer 588.

Radnóti, Miklós. "Root," "Forced March," and "Razglednicas." Langer 631–34.

Sereny, Gitta. *Into That Darkness: An Examination of Conscience.* New York: Vintage, 1983.

Symposium on the Films of Claude Lanzmann. Yale U. 5 Apr. 1990.

Tory, Avraham. "Memoir." Langer 215–33.

Vrba, Rudolf, and Alan Bestic. *I Cannot Forgive.* New York: Grove, 1964.

Young, James. "Toward a Received History of the Holocaust." *History and Theory* 36.4 (1997): 21–43.

Adam Zachary Newton

Not Quite Holocaust Fiction: A. B. Yehoshua's *Mr. Mani* and W. G. Sebald's *The Emigrants*

"The Holocaust is ultimately about the abandonment of an entire people to the murder machine of a powerful state" (Bartov 33). Even when translated into a program for literary fiction, that straightforward definition would seem to exclude a text like the genre-defying *The Emigrants*, by W. G. Sebald, or the antisaga novel *Mr. Mani*, by A. B. Yehoshua. Only obliquely could each be classed as Holocaust fiction—a vexed and strange locution if there ever was one. And yet it is precisely in situating themselves on the oblique, in "side-shadowing" (Bernstein 1), that these two acts of literature teach a lesson in the ethics and problematics of representation.

If the section in the present volume on selected texts attests to something like a canon, then works like Sebald's or Yehoshua's oblige us to step back and consider what the rubrics "Holocaust fiction" and "imagining the Holocaust" should mean,[1] descriptively and programmatically. Indeed, saying as much is how I typically begin the two- or three-week segment devoted to these books, in courses on the European novel (Sebald) and modern Jewish poetry and

prose (Yehoshua). By favoring margin over center, by plotting themselves extraterritorially, by shunting themselves onto what Bruno
Schulz calls "branch-tracks of time," *The Emigrants* and *Mr. Mani*
locate themselves extragenerically as well—in the literary province
of the not quite. Their narrative business lies not with the event but
(following Schulz again) rather with "events that have been left in the
cold, unregistered, hanging in the air; homeless, and errant" (131).

How does one tell generalized calamity? Whose particular story
instructs or marks us? What are the "rights of history and the rights
of imagination," and what are the concomitant aims of each (Ozick,
"Rights")? How to make these two rights commensurate, or, if not,
to differentiate between them? Such questions are placed at the de-
centered center by *The Emigrants* and *Mr. Mani*, whose signal virtue
in this context becomes their very obliquity—the slanted way with
which they pose the task, engage the trust, of imagining or fictionalizing as authorizing aims. Both could be said to parry Theodor
Adorno's perhaps too-famous interdicting thrust about poetry after
Auschwitz, but not because they interpret its *trompement* to signify
an anti-aesthetic; rather, they take its challenge to mean: no more
literary genres as usual. If writing, as the narrator of *The Emigrants*
puts it, is always already "a questionable business" (230), then texts
like Sebald's and Yehoshua's, which actively question that business
in the process of transacting it, are ideally suited to take the measure
of representing the Shoah in the first place.

Yehoshua's *Mr. Mani* was received, on its publication, as a cultural phenomenon in Israel, and by any reckoning it is one of the
most important late-twentieth-century novels. It is typically the first
text with which I begin the course on modern Jewish literature from
the end of the nineteenth century to the end of the twentieth. Students quickly realize that such back-to-front logic suits the structure
of the text precisely, since Yehoshua's novel narrates its plot in pur-
poseful retrograde: five generations in a Sephardic family proceeding
backward from 1982 (Israel's incursion into Lebanon and the beginning of the first Palestinian intifada) to 1848 (the "springtime of
nations").

Each of the novel's five segments is plotted according to a specific temporal-spatial axis (1. Athens to Jerusalem, 1848; 2. Kraków to Jerusalem, 1899; 3. Jerusalem, 1918; 4. Heraklion, 1944; 5. the Negev and Jerusalem, 1982); war looms ever present for each; and the core event inflecting all the crossroads of modern Jewish history as terminus ad quem and terminus a quo, both their national telos and their vanishing point, is the Shoah. Yet in Yehoshua's peculiarly Israeli twist on modernist narrative technique, the fate of Europe's Jews at mid-century is envisioned sidelong, under Eastern-Sephardi rather than Ashkenazi eyes; athwart both Zionism and Diasporism, Sephardism is perhaps this book's ultimate *kivun negdi* or counter-move. Completing the text's decentering design, the individual stories of each section are narrated in half conversation, with the interlocutor's half of the dialogue strategically omitted.

An "anti-family anti-saga" (Shaked 227), *Mr. Mani* is thus also anti-plot, anti-conversation, and (to play on a book title by Emmanuel Levinas) "otherwise than History; or beyond Necessity," in the sense that it compels readers to consider, alongside modernity's actual unfolding, the unrealized and alternative possibilities for Jewish national destiny at its most fatidic moments. In one passage that students invariably seize on, one of the novel's Mr. Manis says, minutes before his suicide, to two young Polish Jews on their way back from the Third Zionist Congress, "Well, well . . . so there is a railway line here too. Who knows, perhaps in a few years you will be able to take a train straight from Jerusalem to that Oświęcim of yours without having to brave the sea!" (283). It is just this kind of linkage in multiple senses that Yehoshua's novel prompts readers to work out for themselves. For, of course, had there been such a branch track of counterfactual time and place, conceivably some of the trainloads dispatched for Auschwitz, as Bernard Horn puts it (137), would have journeyed to Palestine instead.

Mr. Mani is engineered in such a way that students must intervene and realize it in the act of reading much more than they might another work: by unraveling the inverse plot structure; by completing the conversations; by coordinating its five temporally connected stories through a network of repeated motifs; by teasing out its theory of psychocultural transference; most of all, by letting themselves be taught by its counterlesson in historical consciousness. This last operation—because it compels a reckoning with the depredations of the Shoah as they inflect the choices that Jews as a people have made about home, nation, and state—seems to me invaluable for students' grasp of the complex relation between literature and history, between fiction and the Holocaust.

Yehoshua's novel offers students a unique template for interrogating all those narrative, literary, or extraliterary verities they tend to take for granted. Because it obliges them to ask questions they perhaps did not know they had, the work goes to the very root of literary representation as inquiry rather than inquest. If history (and plot) are to be understood linearly, then their direction will be forward; *Mr. Mani* proposes regress instead. As the Shoah took place in Europe, then its ramifications, one might think, must be confined to Jews of Germany, Poland, Russia, France, Belgium, et alia; *Mr. Mani* proposes a Sephardic genealogy, through Ottoman lands, instead. What has been called, after Bakhtin, the dialogic imagination necessarily involves the intersection, overlap, even abrasion, of two heard voices; *Mr. Mani* supplies, at each integral juncture, only one. Most pertinent for the present context, a Holocaust fiction will inevitably have the Shoah at dead center, an axial point of reference; *Mr. Mani* substitutes periphery—an oblique angle in place of locus, matrix, or hub.

Last, as a contemporary Israeli novelist who claims multigenerational family roots in Jerusalem, Yehoshua presents students with a crucial refraction of the parallel tracks of Zionism and Nazism in a world literature that, contrary to their expectations perhaps, had for a long time held the Shoah at a discreet distance.[2] With the exception of Aharon Appelfeld's oeuvre and Yoram Kaniuk's 1975 novel *Adam Resurrected*, it was really not until the 1980s that Israeli writers began to write Holocaust fictions in earnest; David Grossman's *See Under: Love* is the most acclaimed. But slantwise, Yehoshua's *Mr. Mani* breaks new ground.

An idiosyncratic testament to obliquity and therefore also not strictly a Holocaust fiction, W. G. Sebald's *The Emigrants* is a work, like *Mr. Mani*, that ripostes Adorno by countervailing readers' customary notions about genre. Troubling the divide between history and the literary imagination, between record and fiction, it presents another kind of template through which students can begin to formulate basic questions about the politics and poetics of representation, indeed about the politics of reception as well (especially in the wake of cases of literary counterfeit, like Wilkomirski-Doesseker's *Fragments* and Hans Koeppen's *Jakob Littner's Notes from a Hole in the Ground*).[3]

Generically composite — novel, memoir, elegy — Sebald's book asks readers to perform concurrent acts of deciphering. What do the four stories of emigrants — not all of them German or Jewish or directly impinged on by the Shoah — have to do with one another? Is there a sequential logic to their presentation? As with *Mr. Mani*, does the repetition of theme and motif synthesize disparate elements or merely impose a deliberately artifactual unity? And perhaps most immediately, how does one parse the interpolation into a complex, layered text of eighty-six photographs — portraits, landscapes, inscriptions, objects? At carefully chosen junctures in the narrative, each (often albumlike) photograph seems to offer ocular proof for a corresponding textual referent. And yet such evidence often provides corroboration only obliquely, through an always intricate occultation that refuses to cede the seeing eye its full autonomy. The text as a whole works this way, too, since one of its overarching thematic burdens is the pathos of visibility in counterpoint with an ethos of voice: each piece of evidence is kept partly shaded or muffled from us, even when we most want to learn the truth.

In line with Ozick's criterion, a manifest boundary (and bargain struck) between telling and showing in *The Emigrants* ensures that the rights and aims of history and of the imagination will be reciprocally tensed in the name of each. If, as for one of the four emblematic protagonists, the very divulging of personal history risks a kind of ruination and decay, then, by exposure to imaged face or landscape at the level of the discourse, Sebald's readers are similarly made aware of vision as willed grasp, point of view as neither innocent nor ever neutral, seemingly benign travelogue as compelled (and compulsory) escort. Obliquity, then, is this work's topic; its method; and, analogous to *Mr. Mani*, its logic of instruction.

I insinuate two tacks that students can pursue with the text; the approaches interdepend, but they are also separable, each provoking its own set of questions. The first has to do with the ethics of narration. As a way of defining an "ethics of Holocaust writing," Daniel Schwartz, in *Imagining the Holocaust*, preliminarily distinguishes between possible Jewish and non-Jewish responses to such literature according to a criterion of identification: having been "protected by accidents of geography," Jewish American readers possess the advantage of seeing themselves "in these ghetto places, these streets . . . deported and [made to] suffer the horrors of these camps" (5). Sebald, a non-Jewish German expatriate, constructs a generalized readership along very different lines, as students establish for themselves, even after an attempt to gauge differentially sectarian responses to *The Emigrants* from reviews by André Aciman and Cynthia Ozick ("Posthumous Sublime"), on one hand, and James Wood and Anthony Lane on the other.

More immediately, though, the narrator's tentative, self-critical relationship to the four stories he tracks so assiduously models a hermeneutic attitude the book wants its readers to inculcate: that the four Holocaust narratives — which are severally, albeit to varying degrees, darkened by the shadow of German-Jewish relations — are to be held deliberately at a distance. Their aim is not identification (or worse, appropriation) but, rather, the keen sense of remanded proximity, as if to say, "This close but no farther."

Here is where the second tack comes in, the crucial role played by the text's photographs. I have used two kinds of secondary materials in both graduate and undergraduate classes in this regard, to different effect. One consists of the *yizker* ("memorial") book that provides a record of the Polish shtetl of Strzegowo, where my father's family lived; I show the photographs of my grandfather and his brothers, I tell their brief stories, and then I ask students to talk from Sebald's text about the gap between the personalizable and the personated.[4] Unmediated, direct access to story, even to the manifestly evidentiary, is the real fiction, *The Emigrants* implies. This not-at-all easy lesson in noncommensuration, in the order of mimesis, is the elemental one to convey to students (prone, as they often are, to uncritical leaps of projected equivalence) through a text like this.

Additionally, I assemble a small packet of meditations on photography by Benjamin, Barthes, and Luc Sante, who may be the least known of the three but whose remarkable feat of narrative recuperation, *Evidence*, sorts particularly well with Sebald's method. Sante writes:

> Through the act of looking, we own these pictures, or, rather, they thrust themselves upon us. . . . The responsibility of witness that is thrust at us is too grave: when such a thing comes from a stranger, it is as if we had been entrusted with his or her existence. . . . The terrible gift that the dead make to the living is that of sight, which is to say foreknowledge; in return they demand memory, which is to say acknowledgment. (63)

But perhaps the most effective strategy for working through the meaning of the photographs was taught to me by one of my students, who in effect created a composite version of Sebald's text through a selection of passages and photostated reproductions of its pages. That is, he rubbed the text (to borrow a metaphor from Levinas [*Nine* 46]) in the knowingly vain hope of having it bleed a little more and thus grant his expropriative wishes.

A final though by no means inconsequential point to be made about both Sebald's book and Yehoshua's book, which is always indistinctly grasped (if at all) by students who are reading a translation, is that the prose executes its own stunning performance of obliquity. Sebald's prose is close to Kafka's in its precise, coruscating quality while layering on itself a uniquely threnodic and elegiac timbre that one hears in the nineteenth-century writers Gottfried Keller and Adalbert Stifter.[5] Each of the five conversations in *Mr. Mani* voices a different Hebrew, four of which are intended to simulate another tongue: German, English, Yiddish, and Ladino (Judeo-Spanish); thus even (and especially linguistically) the text imaginatively resists the very vocal center through which it speaks. Both texts, finally, remain at a calculated distance from home.

This effect results, in no small part, of course, from the decidedly oblique positions of their authors in relation to the Shoah: a non-Ashkenazi Israeli, with no familial tie to the European theater of World War II, and a non-Jewish German émigré whose subject is the spoliation endured by modern German Jewry. Sebald's 2001 death in a car accident introduces a final threshold, in a work centrally about thresholds: a kind of black border, like a bereavement notice, that surrounds the writing, containing but also distancing it from us. Thus, at some subtensive remove from testimony on the one side and full-fledged Holocaust fiction on the other, Sebald's and Yeshoshua's texts summon students to perhaps the most pressing question that such writing presupposes: What are the boundaries of fiction, what exactly lies contained within them, and what is stranded without?

Notes

1. The latter phrase is the title of a recent critical study by Daniel Schwartz. Sebald registered his own discomfort with the rubric of Holocaust fiction, in an interview with Arthur Lubow published in the *New York Times* four days before Sebald's death.
2. See Shaked; Sicher; Morahg.
3. On Wilkomirski, see Ozick's "The Rights of History"; Maechler; Alter; and the essay by Weissman in this volume. On Koeppen, see Franklin.
4. Hirsch's *Family Frames* is a helpful gloss in this regard.
5. One of the most helpful of recent analyses traces a distinctly Romanticist legacy in Sebald's writing. See the essay by Chandler and also Mc-Cullough's volume.

Works Cited

Aciman, André. "Out of Novemberland." *New York Review of Books* 3 Dec. 1998: 42–43.

Alter, Robert. "Arbeit Macht Fraud." *New Republic* 30 Apr. 2001: 35–38.

Barthes, Roland. *Camera Lucida: Reflections on Photography*. Trans. Richard Howard. New York: Noonday, 1982.

Bartov, Omer. "The Anti-hero as Hero: Review of Tzvetan Todorov's *The Fragility of Goodness*." *New Republic* 13 Aug. 2001: 33–38.

Benjamin, Walter. "Little History of Photography." *Selected Writings*. Vol.

2. Trans. Edmund Jephcott and Kingsley Shorter. Cambridge: Belknap–Harvard UP. 507–30.

Bernstein, Michael André. *Foregone Conclusions: Against Apocalyptic History*. Berkeley: U of California P, 1994.

Chandler, James. "About Loss: W. G. Sebald's Romantic Art of Memory." *South Atlantic Quarterly* 102 (2003): 235–62.

Franklin, Ruth. "Speak Not, Memory." *New Republic* 20 Aug. 2001: 30–39.

Hirsch, Marianne. *Family Frames: Photography, Narrative, and Postmemory*. Cambridge: Harvard UP, 1997.

Horn, Bernard. "The *Shoah*, the *Akeda*, and the Conversations in A. B. Yehoshua's *Mr. Mani*." *Symposium* 53 (1999): 136–50.

Lane, Anthony. "Higher Ground." *New Yorker* 29 May 2000: 128–34.

Levinas, Emmanuel. *Nine Talmudic Readings*. Trans. Annette Aronowicz. Bloomington: Indiana UP, 1990.

———. *Otherwise than Being; or, Beyond Essence*. Trans. Alphonso Lingis. Pittsburgh: Duquesne UP, 1998.

Lubow, Arthur. Interview with W. G. Sebald. *New York Times* 11 Dec. 2001, sec. E: 1.

Maechler, Stefan. *The Wilkomirski Affair: A Study in Biographical Truth*. Trans. John E. Woods. New York: Schocken, 2001.

McCullough, Mark. *Understanding W. G. Sebald*. New York: Columbia UP, 2003.

Morahg, Gilead. "Israel's New Literature of the Holocaust: The Case of David Grossman's *See Under: Love*." *Modern Fiction Studies* 45 (1999): 457–79.

Ozick, Cynthia. "The Posthumous Sublime." *New Republic* 16 Dec. 1999: 33–38.

———. "The Rights of History and the Rights of Imagination." *Commentary* Mar. 1999. Rpt. in *Quarrel and Quandary*. New York: Knopf, 1999. 22–27.

Sante, Luc. *Evidence*. New York: Noonday, 1992.

Schulz, Bruno. *Complete Fiction*. Trans. Celina Wieniewska. New York: Walker, 1989.

Schwartz, Daniel. *Imagining the Holocaust*. New York: St. Martin's, 1999.

Sebald, W. G. *The Emigrants*. Trans. Michael Hulse. New York: New Directions, 1997.

Shaked, Gershon. *Modern Hebrew Fiction*. Bloomington: Indiana UP, 2000.

Sicher, Efraim. "The Return of the Past: The Intergenerational Transmission of Holocaust Memory in Israeli Fiction." *Shofar* 19 (2001): 26–46.

Wood, James. "The Wrong Thread." *New Republic* 6 July 1998: 38–42. Rpt. *The Broken Estate*. London: Cape, 1999.

Yehoshua, A. B. *Mr. Mani*. Trans. Hillel Halkin. New York: Harvest, 1993.

Part IV

Classroom Contexts

Marcia D. Horn

Winning Support for a Multidisciplinary Holocaust Course at a Small Liberal Arts College

Ferrum College is a small, Methodist-affiliated liberal arts college in rural southwestern Virginia with about nine hundred and fifty students, very few of whom are Jewish. Over the last fifteen years, at no time has the college had more than four Jewish faculty members. Almost twenty percent of Ferrum's students are African American. Most students coming to Ferrum know little about Judaism or the Holocaust. In this somewhat unlikely setting, Ferrum College has succeeded in not only initiating but also sustaining and building a course on the Holocaust. Essential to its success has been the help of Holocaust survivors, the resources of the United States Holocaust Memorial Museum, professors in Holocaust studies, community members in the greater Roanoke Valley and beyond, speakers and grants from the Roanoke Jewish community, a supportive administration, and a creative and committed faculty.

My background is in Renaissance English literature, with a specialty in Shakespeare. While I continued teaching English, three crucial experiences pointed me in a new direction—the decision to initiate a Holocaust course at Ferrum College: participating in a 1994 National Humanities Center seminar on cultural memory led by Leo Spitzer and Marianne Hirsch, which focused on the Holocaust and African slave narratives; learning that my grandparents in the late 1930s had saved two boys from the Holocaust; and, in spring 1996, listening to a guest speaker at Ferrum College, Susan Cernyak-Spatz, describe her experiences in Auschwitz. After hearing this address, a colleague and I turned to each other and said, "We need a Holocaust course at Ferrum College." Cernyak-Spatz agreed to be the first of several mentors to help us in the initial stages of this project. I started corresponding with and later met both former children my grandparents had helped save, visiting one in Berkeley while I was on sabbatical in 1998. After my return, I contacted special mentors from the United States Holocaust Memorial Museum and faculty members from local high schools, colleges, and universities who were teaching the Holocaust.

"The Holocaust touched every aspect of life." The words of survivor Sophie Miklos, whom I had also met on my sabbatical, have never left me. I called my faculty friends who were interested in teaching the Holocaust from the approach of their own specialty. Thus, we developed the multidisciplinary perspective that is the essential feature of our course. I became coordinator, and The Holocaust: Past, Present, and Future was first offered in spring 1999 with eight professors coteaching. Since 2000, ten faculty members have taught the course each year. This number is about one-seventh of Ferrum's full-time faculty.[1] Thirty-five students registered for the spring 2002 Holocaust course. In the same year, a redesigned Web site was added: www.ferrum.edu/holocaust.

Over the years, the Holocaust faculty members have brought their expertise to the subject matter of the course. For example, the religion professor surveys the religious history of antisemitism from pre-Christian times to the present, providing resources through his own Holocaust Web site. The European history professor traces the historical development of antisemitism, including the development of racial-superiority theories, and raises questions about intentional-ist and functionalist approaches in accounting for the rise of Nazism and the Final Solution. The sociology professor uses her part of the course to ask the big question, Why?, introducing students to social-justice concerns and the theories of discrimination, racism, and genocide. The Spanish professor focuses on the contrast between the flourishing culture of pre-1492 medieval Spain, when Muslims, Christians, and Jews for the most part coexisted, and the cultural decline initiated by the Inquisition and the expulsion of the Jews. The psychology professor presents a film on the Milgram experiment, which shows how ordinary people (college students in the experiment) readily agree to hurt others when they are asked to do so by authoritative figures. The Russian history specialist examines the atrocities committed in the Soviet Union during the Stalinist era and invites comparison and contrast with the Nazi regime. The art professor discusses the complex ways in which art functioned in this period as propaganda and as memorial. The two music professors play examples of music as propaganda for, protest against, and memorialization of the Holocaust. As the literature professor, I use both memoirs and fictional texts to explore first-person accounts of trauma, deep memory, and forgiveness.

The special challenge for the faculty is to provide coherence. Thus, the course is divided into a number of general themes that help connect the disciplines: "Introducing the Issues," "Understanding the Complexities of the Horror," "Resistance, Rescue, and Survival," "Remembering, Reacting, and Responding" (including current examples of genocide). Within these broad topics, specific disciplines are introduced in subtopics: people of faith, historians, psychologists, and artists ask, Why? All Holocaust faculty members attend the first and last class; otherwise, according to their teaching style and the nature of the material, they choose to present either individually or in teams of two or three. As coordinator, I attend every class; other faculty members attend when their schedules allow.

Ferrum is a small college with generally small classes, and the flexible-credit options encourage ample enrollment. The Holocaust course is open to sophomores through seniors (first-year students are allowed only by special permission). Students choose to take the course as an elective, as part of a sophomore-level English require-ment, or—if they are juniors or seniors—as an upper-level topics course in their major or minor. (Juniors or seniors who take the course for upper-level credit work with the faculty specialist in a par-ticular field, who assigns all their papers. The course coordinator as-signs the papers for the other students.) In their first week, students complete a special multipart registration slip, signed by their adviser or division chair, according to the type of credit they wish to earn. Copies of the signed forms are then returned to the registrar, the ad-viser, the course coordinator, and the student.

Many of Ferrum's students are first-generation college students; therefore, it is important to broaden the course's appeal by not only providing flexible credit but also offering a variety of disciplines. The multidisciplinary concept answers this need. Given the background of many of our students, it is also vital to balance a cognitive style of teaching with a relational style in order to reach them—to have enough historical background and to provide materials that will elicit immediate, visceral responses. Early in the course, we discuss the central role of racism in Nazism and read some excerpts from Hitler's speeches. When the students visit the Holocaust Memorial Museum in Washington, DC, virtually all of them notice the racial charts, the measurements, and the consequences of race theory. Dur-ing the last week of class, we discuss more recent examples of geno-cide, such as in Rwanda, the Sudan, and the former Yugoslavia. In our 2002 class, we also discussed the Milošević trial and held a special session on the September 11 attacks, terrorism, and anti-semitism. Our 2004 class held special student-led discussions on the Israeli-Palestinian conflict and some implications of antisemitism and anti-Arab sentiment.

Although Ferrum has very few Jewish students, the college cur-rently has three Jewish faculty members, all of whom teach the Holo-caust course. Survivors, hidden children, liberators, and rescuers have been invited from the Roanoke Jewish community and from as far as Rye, New York, to share their experiences with our class and the col-lege. In spring 2001, for example, the liberator Sid Franklin, a member of Temple Emanuel in Roanoke, came to class to give an intensely personal account of the shock he experienced as a young man unprepared for what he would encounter at when he arrived at Buchenwald. As he told his story, he wept, and the students were so moved they wrote to him individually to let him know how much his talk had meant to them. They asked him to return to Ferrum every year. In spring 2003, the rescuer Tina Strobos shared her story with the Holocaust class and college community of how she and her family saved a hundred Jews in Amsterdam by hiding them and securing credentials for their escape. Dramatists, professors teaching Holocaust courses at other universities, and researchers from the Holocaust Memorial Museum have also enriched the class. In spring 2001, the museum researcher Scott Miller addressed both the class and the college community on the issue of the United States as bystander and of the complexities of the search for the survivors of the SS *St. Louis.* Special guests have been audiotaped or videotaped so that the college can keep a firsthand record of these visits. Several excerpts are available to our students on our Holocaust course Web site under the Resources link.

The Holocaust course requires deep commitment, hard work, and special responsibilities. In addition to writing three papers, students keep journals, consult articles on closed reserve and electronic reserve, use material on the Web site, and watch videos. They are required to view *Schindler's List* and *Night and Fog* and to see excerpts of other videos during class or outside class to complete journal assignments. A film on the Milgram experiment, for example, is an integral part of the psychology presentation, which concludes with a journal assignment. The video *The Wave,* which is shown near the end of the semester, has proved particularly powerful in sparking discussion of how easy it is to shape hate and yield to peer pressure; students write about this video too in their journals. Every student is responsible for an individual oral report. All students take a one-day bus trip to the Washington Holocaust museum, consult original documents, and use online sources. For the past four years, students in the course have planted seeds in the special Holocaust Memorial

Garden that has been established in a central part of campus. The garden's inscription, created by one of the students in the course, reads, "Because they lived it, we teach it."

We consider student evaluations an important part of the course process. Each year, Holocaust faculty members have met to review the evaluations and to make course changes. For example, in spring 2000, evaluations alerted us to students' difficulty with the critical examination of the role of Christianity during the Holocaust. For some, this material was upsetting and painful; for others, it was enlightening ("I had no idea" or "I never knew"). Our challenge as faculty members was to turn an obstacle into an opportunity—a teachable moment. This subject was vital to understanding the historical background of antisemitism, but it was difficult for devout Christian students in a Methodist-affiliated college. Introducing some of the recent attempts by Pope John Paul II toward reconciliation led to eye-opening class discussions and deep and very moving personal accounts in students' journals. Students had to look inward at their own beliefs and examine what Margot Stern Strom's resource book, *Facing History and Ourselves,* calls the self confronting "the *other*" (65). In the next version of the class, the faculty members discussed more thoroughly and carefully the role of Christianity during the Holocaust.

Student evaluations as well as biannual Holocaust faculty meetings have enabled us to keep the syllabus flexible and creative. Class quizzes, a regular policy of the first year, were abolished the second year (largely because there was such a time crunch with so much material from so many disciplines). Instead of taking quizzes, students, either individually or as a team, are now responsible for a fifteen-minute class presentation on a topic discussed during that week. One popular student-team presentation is a discussion and debate of intentionalism versus functionalism.

The reading list has also changed. The first two years, students used the same texts: Donald Niewyk's *The Holocaust,* Varlam Shalamov's *Kolyma Tales,* Hana Volavková's *I Never Saw Another Butterfly,* Elie Wiesel's *Night,* Simon Wiesenthal's *The Sunflower,* and Jane Yolen's *Briar Rose.* Two years ago, David Engel's *The Holocaust: The*

Third Reich and the Jews was added to the course. Excerpts from Shalamov's text replaced the entire book. The discussion of *Night* has been one of the more powerful classes each year, and Wiesenthal's *The Sunflower* has inspired probing questions about forgiveness. (Sunflowers have become one of the popular choices for the Holocaust Memorial Garden.) The students have also found Engel's succinct volume to be extremely helpful for final-exam review; its original documents and maps make fine topics for discussion and journal questions.

In spring 2001, the Holocaust psychology professor asked students to complete new evaluation forms—not only the traditional departmental evaluation used in the first two years of the course but also a three-part questionnaire, which asked the students to compare their conceptions of the multidisciplinary format before and after they had taken this course. As far as we could determine, this kind of multidisciplinary format of the course is unique, so the faculty member was especially interested in the students' responses. We found that students appreciated the roles of subjects they had previously thought had little relevance to the Holocaust, such as art, music, and Spanish history. In addition, we discovered that this approach helped them understand that what they were learning in this class was related in some way to what they had learned in the past or were learning in other classes.

When students were asked what they liked best about the course, they cited most often the museum trip and the speakers, followed closely by the reading assignments, journals, and films. They liked the way faculty members worked with students. One student said, "Thank you! You've really changed my life." Students also had suggestions for course improvement, such as more emphasis on psychology and sociology; more equal teaching time among the professors; a reduction in the number of required out-of-class events, such as films and speakers; and more emphasis on the topic of resistance and uprisings. Overall, they thought the course should continue to be taught yearly.

One of the positive effects of building this course has been community outreach. Senior citizens from the local community enroll in the class at no charge. Evening presentations by special Holocaust speakers are open to the public at no charge. Holocaust faculty members and students have presented Holocaust issues at local churches and in outreach programs in local temples and synagogues. Articles in local papers featuring upcoming speakers and events have also helped publicize the course. Ferrum has networked with other colleges, sharing speakers and sometimes (with Lynchburg College) sharing faculty presentations. Success in funding many of these programs has added to the course's continued strength.[2] Some faculty members have initiated a special Holocaust session at the South Atlantic Modern Language Association, and in 2001 two presented on the local cable-channel station a trip to Holocaust sites in Poland and the Czech Republic. All the above efforts help not only strengthen ties between the community and college but also sustain awareness of the Holocaust.

In this course, students have had the rare opportunity to work closely with faculty members from different disciplines on the central issue of the Holocaust and questions it raises in contemporary life. And one reason that ten faculty members have bonded so effectively in this course has been the ability to work together in the same classroom and learn from one another's perspectives in examining the Holocaust.

Thus, learning has occurred in a unique way on different levels in and outside Ferrum College. Extensive campus programming has helped the college and greater community increase awareness about the Holocaust and its implications. Professors have learned from students how to improve the course. And the students, some of whom in turn may become teachers, will perhaps use the lessons learned in the Holocaust course in their own classes and in their own lives.

Notes

1. Ten professors teach the Holocaust course: Ed Cornbleet (Spanish), Rachel Denham (art), Gary Evans (music), David Howell (religion), Susan Mead (sociology), Samuel Payne (political science), Erma Rose (music), Milt Rowan (history), Sharon Stein (psychology), and the coordinator Marcia Horn (literature).
2. Essential to sustaining the Holocaust course has been the variety of

funding resources. The Roanoke Jewish Community Council has contributed yearly for start-up videos and materials, trips to the Holocaust museum, and transportation expenses for several speakers. The Roanoke Jewish community has volunteered speakers (survivors, liberators, and former hidden children), who made guest appearances at the college. Funding from the Virginia Commission for the Arts enabled Claudia Stevens to come to campus and reenact the life of Fania Fenelon, the first of Stevens's three appearances dramatizing Holocaust subjects at Ferrum. The campus Integrated Programming Board and the chairs of three divisions financed the Mill Mountain Players trip to Ferrum to perform a play on Anne Frank. The Center for Advanced Holocaust Studies at the United States Holocaust Memorial Museum paid for my attendance at a two-week summer program of study and research. In addition, the college administration has supported the course not only by funding the Holocaust faculty members for overtime pay but also by providing me with faculty-development grants — to fund a trip with Erma Rose to Holocaust sites in the Czech Republic and Poland and to fund travel expenses related to establishing a special session on the Holocaust at the South Atlantic Modern Language Association (SAMLA). An Appalachian College Association (ACA) grant, available through the college, also helped fund the SAMLA trips. In October 2002, an ACA group Award for Best Intra-Institutional Collaborative Course Website provided the Holocaust course with additional financial resources. Finally, in April 2003, the Lasko Charitable Fund awarded the course a grant to help finance speakers and programs in spring 2004.

Work Cited

Strom, Margot Stern, ed. *Facing History and Ourselves Resource Book: Holocaust and Human Behavior.* Brookline: Facing History and Ourselves Natl. Foundation, 1994.

Renée A. Hill

Teaching the Holocaust in a Genocide Studies Framework at a Historically Black University

Setting and Background

Even after attending a weeklong seminar with other faculty members from historically black universities at the United States Holocaust Memorial Museum, I did not immediately consider teaching a course on Holocaust studies. The topic was too big, and I felt dwarfed by it; the villainy was too egregious, the pain and suffering too engulfing, the result too catastrophic, the mission too grandiose. Wipe a people off the face of the earth? It was hard to imagine shrinking down this kind of apocalyptic epic to a syllabus manageable in fifteen weeks and forty-five hours.

In the end, the magnitude and complexity of the events kept pulling my attention. How can a society rebuild on a foundation of such malevolent ashes? How can it put itself back together after being rent apart in such violent ways? As a political philosopher, my interest has long been in problems of justice, and the idea of embarking on a scholarly journey with a few committed students, in which we would sit around a seminar table together, debating punishment, compensation, obligation, responsibility, and how we would demarcate a postgenocidal society, became more and more provocative. Although my interest was sparked by studying about the Holocaust, as a philosopher I am interested in looking at global principles and seeing how aptly theory can apply to reality—whether theory illuminates or complicates a situation, transforms a situation or is transformed itself, or whether it simply proves inadequate to handle a situation. To examine such multiple scenarios, I opened the course content to the study of genocides taking place in the last century. When thorny issues of definition or application arose, the paradigmatic example of a genocide was repeatedly the Holocaust. My seminar was entitled Justice after Genocide, and I eventually ended up with a class of ten students, eight black and two white. By the close of the course, my students and I had agreed that the name of the seminar was a bit naive. A more accurate name might have been How Would One Go About Gesturing at Justice after Genocide?, or even Genocide. Now What?

I teach at Virginia State University, a historically black university of about five thousand students. We are located at the northern edge of Petersburg, Virginia, about two hours south of Washington, DC. Although we are located in the South, we have a large number of students from large urban areas along the northeast corridor. It is this mix of East Coast, largely urban, African American students that I teach in my introduction to philosophy courses and to whom I appealed when I was considering putting together a course on genocide.

How would one teach a course in Holocaust studies at a predominantly black university? The seminar I attended at the United States Holocaust Memorial Museum hosted thirteen faculty members from historically black colleges and universities and was aimed at giving us some of the tools we would need to teach Holocaust studies at our respective schools. The seminar began by attempting to deflect defensiveness on the part of those caught up in a "who suffered worst" contest. Was the Holocaust the worst tragedy ever inflicted by human beings on one another? Worse than the Middle

Passage and the American form of slavery? Doris Bergen turned us away from that potential quagmire to focus on the conditions leading up to the Holocaust and to present a wealth of information and resources for our edification and future teaching purposes. The seminar also offered some course content that might be of special interest to an African American audience: discussion of how the Nazis persecuted black Germans. In general, however, the seminar was devoted to giving us (especially those of us who were not historians) a broad background on which to base a course on the Holocaust.

I designed my course to highlight the general philosophical principles that I wanted the students to reflect on and discuss. The "who suffered worst" question, or irritation that the Holocaust receives more attention than American slavery, never surfaced in class. I mentioned the mistreatment of black Germans as part of the ubiquitous torture of others practiced by the Nazis. I also opened with a reading about the genocide in Rwanda and the story of a victim of rape. But I do not believe that I needed to include the castration, rape, and imprisonment of black people to engage my students. They were engaged from the beginning, gripped by the story and tragedy of so many.

The course considered genocides other than the Holocaust, but that event remained the standard for what constitutes a genocide. We thus came back to the Holocaust over and over as we measured other atrocities against it. Were I to teach the course again to an audience primarily made up of gays and lesbians or of Roma, I would probably include some examples of the maltreatment of those groups, just as I included examples of the denigration of black Germans, but the overall content would remain the same. I did not feel the need to customize the content because my class was predominately black, nor did I focus on genocide in general rather than the Holocaust because I had no Jewish students. Any topic worthy of study has a universal lesson and appeal. Whether teaching a course exclusively on the Holocaust or more generally on genocide, I would design a class with the same general goals regardless of the ethnic makeup of the students. The only difference is that I would expect more background knowledge of upper-level students with a relevant major, such as history, than of a general first-year population.

The students in my course self-selected for interest in the topic, ability to think abstractly, and enjoyment of philosophical issues. There were a few characteristics shared by many, although not all. I hesitate to generalize from this small group to the entire population at my university, and even less to other historically black universities, but these shared characteristics were a lack of historical background, strong retributivist leanings, and empathy for the victims. I came to the class assuming that the students would be cognizant only of the Holocaust and not of other twentieth-century genocides, for example, actions taken against the Herero and the Armenians. Although my students knew the broad outlines of the crimes perpetrated by Nazi Germany, they were largely unfamiliar with the details of what the Jewish population suffered and even with the existence of other victims. When we came to the section of the class on punishment, most of my students were emphatically retributivist, ready not only to punish but also to torture and maim perpetrators of genocidal crimes. Perhaps driving this vehement "arm, leg, and eye for an eye" approach to punishment was the deep sense of empathy toward those who suffered. The class field trip to the Holocaust Memorial Museum in Washington no doubt heightened the sense of connection to the victims, but whatever the causes, my students were deeply affected by the stories of the victims.

I underestimated the emotional impact the subject and narrative would have on my students. As stated in the editors' introduction to this volume, it is crucial in teaching the Holocaust that support mechanisms be put in place, but I did not recognize that need at the time. Fortunately, most of my students either knew one another or knew me well enough to drop by my office to talk if they were overwhelmed. But one student was new to me and to the other students in the class, and when she disappeared for a couple of weeks, it did not occur to me to think that she was having trouble with the subject matter. It was only when she came back and confessed that she had been too depressed to attend class that I found out the problem.

In the future, I will make sure that I have everyone's e-mail address or phone number, announce that I am always available for conversation in my office if someone wants to discuss the class, and check on everyone from time to time to make sure that they are not sinking underneath the burden of horrors that people inflict on one another.

Components of the Course

There were three objectives of the class: to grapple with the problems of defining *genocide* and establishing necessary and sufficient conditions for categorizing a situation as genocide, to become familiar with the genocides in the twentieth century, and to examine thoughtfully the problems associated with bringing about as just a response as possible after a genocide has taken place.

We began by struggling with definitions of genocide. We looked at the international legal definition of *genocide* and John G. Heidenrich's consideration of its definition in *How to Prevent Genocide* (1–20), read some of Raphael Lemkin's thoughts on genocide (Power 17–85), and then brainstormed about elements of genocide ourselves. Should genocide be distinguished from democide? Should rape and sexual assault be included? Should planned extermination of political groups or socioeconomic groups be included? What about groups identified by sexual orientation? How many people have to be killed to constitute genocide? Should only killing of people count? What about other features marking cultural eradication? Is intent a necessary condition? Does one have to have the power to actualize that intent?

As we considered these questions, we read "What a Tutsi Woman Tastes Like," by Elizabeth Neuffer; "Bury My Heart in Committee," by David Van Biema; and "Genocide, Victimization, and America's Inner Cities," by Charles Green. The Neuffer article emphasized the victimization of women in recent criminal acts like those in Rwanda and Bosnia. The articles about Native Americans (Van Biema) and African Americans (Green) stimulated discussions about whether the United States had engaged in genocidal practices against its native population and kidnapped Africans or, later, African Americans. Finally, students were required to develop their own definitions of genocide. They were then each assigned a case of mass killing from the last century, asked to report on the details of the mass killing to the class, and then required to apply their definition of genocide to determine whether or not their assigned crime met that definition. We classified (sometimes without universal agreement) mass killings in South Africa (against the Herero), Turkey (against the Armenians and Kurds), Iraq (against the Kurds), Bosnia, Rwanda (against the Tutsis), Russia (by Stalin), and Cambodia (by the Khmer Rouge). One interesting by-product of our discussion was the realization that some students felt as if the crime they were reporting on was belittled if not declared genocidal. A personal investment developed: students wanted their crime be designated genocide, as it is the superlative with reference to injustice; there is no other criminal appellation so damning.

The second portion of the course dealt with raising the problem of the manipulation of the national narrative, another issue needing to be accommodated as we moved toward developing a just response to genocide. The students read from *Genocide and the Politics of Memory* by Herbert Hirsch and "Genocide and Denial" by Roger Smith. The manipulation of the national narrative to foment, excuse, or deny genocidal action is an important component of the crime. How this history-making subtext forms part of the genocidal act and must be part of the just response deserved more time than I had to devote to it. An extended discussion of the national narrative and its support of hierarchy and social stratification would have been insightful. A fertile area for future examination and comparison could be examining the work of the Truth and Reconciliation Committee in South Africa and its attempts to correct bias and fill in lacunae in the South African historical story.

After wrestling with definitions of genocide, we turned to philosophical readings about theories of punishment and compensation. I chose two articles on punishment by Joel Feinberg, a political philosopher. His "The Classic Debate" explains the difference between utilitarian and retributive theories of punishment. As a part of my goal to apply theory to reality, I tried to push my students to understand the social purposes and consequences of punishment. Feinberg's

"The Expressive Function of Punishment" expands the ways in which we can think about punishment and its uses in society: punishment is significant beyond condemning certain actions and making wrongdoers pay for their malfeasance. One of Feinberg's expressive functions of punishment, "absolution of others," would be especially important in a genocide like that in Rwanda, where a large segment of the society was complicit in the iniquity. Such punishment could serve, in the postgenocidal society, to sort out those who were and were not murderers (595). Feinberg lays out his ideas clearly and often offers examples that help readers follow the application of his theory.

Extension of the use of and justification for punishment is continued in Jean Hampton's article "The Moral Education Theory of Punishment," in which she argues that punishment is a type of "moral communication" (120). Her argument is more theoretical and her article longer than either of Feinberg's. She, with Feinberg, helped move the students away from simplistic views of punishment toward more varied and sophisticated reasons for sanctioning or reinforcing behavior. We also read "The Politics of Memory" by Jane Kramer, which raises issues about commemoration and asks who is really being honored if a glitzy monument to mark a crime is erected by descendants of the perpetrators in the perpetrators' land.

The articles assisted us as we pondered difficult postgenocidal questions concerning the objectives of punishment, compensation, and commemoration. Whom should we punish, and to what end? What if, as in Rwanda, there are great numbers of people committing the crime in a massive sadistic frenzy? What if, as in Turkey, the government never admits to genocide? What if the perpetrators are dead or cannot be found? What if stolen artifacts and goods are now in the hands of innocent bystanders? Does there need to be an apology? Does it need to be sincere?

It was here that my students' retributivist leanings revealed themselves. I pointed out some lines from Heidenrich's book:

> Can any legal penalty for the crime of genocide truly fit the crime? Millions of Adolf Eichmann's victims were murdered by prolonged torture, starvation, medical experi-

ments, gassed while pressed together naked, or literally worked to death. After these crimes no form of punishment could "rehabilitate" Eichmann — but the Israeli judges who sentenced him could not bring themselves to order his death by any of these inhumane methods. (64)

Most of my students had trouble understanding this point of view. Punishment to them was simply to hurt the one who had hurt others, and even the retributivist canon of punishment proportionate to the crime went by the board as the students learned more and more about the ruthlessness of those implementing genocide. Many students' final papers described ingenious forms of punishment designed to cause painful death to the perpetrators.

Our closing discussion was on how individual responsibility today could prevent genocide in the future. This was another area that deserved more development. By this section of the course we were running out of time, and I did not have the space to prompt the students to reflect on personal and societal tendencies toward stereotyping or scapegoating.

Looking Ahead

Often an instructor receives from a class as much as or more than does the typical student. My students struggled with what would be the right, the good, the healing thing to do after such oppressive crimes. They thoughtfully evaluated motive, judged behavior, and weighed consequences as they searched for solutions to problems with no good solutions. I constantly hear complaints about the apathy, materialism, and narcissism of the generation I teach. Teaching a class on genocide, where one is dealing with subject matter that makes you stare into the abyss, caused me to be inspired and reassured by the sympathetic suffering, moral indignation, and commitment to making things better evinced by my students.

Works Cited

Feinberg, Joel. "The Classic Debate." Feinberg and Gross 613–17.
____. "The Expressive Function of Punishment." Feinberg and Gross 592–602.

Feinberg, Joel, and Hyman Gross, eds. *Philosophy of Law.* 5th ed. Boston: Wadsworth, 1995.

Green, Charles. "Genocide, Victimization, and America's Inner Cities." *Genocide, War, and Human Survival.* Ed. Charles B. Strozier and Michael Flynn. Lanham: Rowman, 1996. 111–23.

Hampton, Jean. "The Moral Education Theory of Punishment." *Punishment: A Philosophy and Public Affairs Reader.* Ed. A. John Simmons, Marshall Cohen, Joshua Cohen, and Charles R. Beitz. Princeton: Princeton UP, 1995. 112–25.

Heidenrich, John. *How to Prevent Genocide: A Guide for Policymakers, Scholars, and the Concerned Citizen.* Westport: Praeger, 2001.

Hirsch, Herbert. *Genocide and the Politics of Memory: Studying Death to Preserve Life.* Chapel Hill: U of North Carolina P, 1995.

Kramer, Jane. "The Politics of Memory." *New Yorker* 14 Aug. 1995: 48–65.

Neuffer, Elizabeth. "What a Tutsi Woman Tastes Like." *The Key to My Neighbor's House: Seeking Justice in Bosnia and Rwanda.* New York: Picador, 2001. 271–92.

Power, Samantha. *"A Problem from Hell": America and the Age of Genocide.* New York: Basic, 2002.

Smith, Roger W. "Genocide and Denial: The Armenian Case and Its Implications." *Armenian Review* 42 (1989): 1–38.

Van Biema, David. "Bury My Heart in Committee." *American Indians and U.S. Politics: A Companion Reader.* Westport: Praeger, 2002. 117–22.

David Scrase

Building a Holocaust Studies Program for Both Town and Gown

When it comes to teaching the Holocaust, one factor distinguishes the University of Vermont from all other state universities: the presence on our faculty for over thirty years of Raul Hilberg. There have, accordingly, been courses on the Holocaust at this institution since the 1960s. Everything that we now do is influenced to some degree by this past history and by the example and achievement of Hilberg. Our excellent library holdings in Holocaust scholarship and the readiness of scholars to visit us stem from his presence on campus.

In 1991, a symposium was organized to mark Hilberg's retirement. The six speakers were Yehuda Bauer, Christopher Browning, George Steiner, Alvin Rosenfeld, Richard Rubenstein, and Claude Lanzmann. A tribute to Hilberg was given by Herman Wouk. This event was a fitting end to the teaching career of a person of Hilberg's stature, but it also ushered in a program in Holocaust studies, which since then has blossomed and grown.

The office of the dean of the College of Arts and Sciences pro-vided start-up money and modest continuing support. With the as-sistance of our institution's office of development, we have been able to find generous financial help from our alumni, which has en-abled us to do all that we planned and more.

From the outset, we saw our mission as twofold: we would not only be educating our own undergraduates but also be reaching be-yond campus to the general population, which seemed particularly important since we are a state and a land-grant university. Further-more, town-gown relations have been strained over the years. Any-thing we could do that might help alleviate this situation seemed positive, and I think the program in Holocaust studies has been very successful in fostering better relations between the academic com-munity and the local inhabitants.

As for our campus needs, we were fortunate to be able to hire a historian (filling the slot previously occupied by Hilberg in political science) specializing in German history and the Holocaust. This po-sition, first held by Doris Bergen, is currently occupied by Jonathan Huener, a specialist on German and Polish history with an interest in the history of the Auschwitz camp and memorial site (see his *Auschwitz*). From my German and Russian department, I have been able to offer regular courses on literature and film that related to the Holocaust. The films I use vary from documentary-type movies such as *Night and Fog* or *The Longest Hatred* to feature films like *The White Rose*, *Europa, Europa*, and *The Nasty Girl*. Initially, I did not show Steven Spielberg's *Schindler's List*, on the grounds that stu-dents already know the movie and that the addition of an unfamiliar title on the syllabus is preferred. Eventually, however, there was a new generation of students who had seen Roman Polanski's *The Pi-anist* but not Spielberg's film. What I teach evolves from year to year, according to circumstances.

Similarly, I teach lesser-known literary works. I do not teach *The Diary of Anne Frank* or *Night*. I attempt to show survival through passing—a boy's experience of passing in Louis Begley's *Wartime Lies*, a girl's in Nechama Tec's *Dry Tears*. A woman's experience of Auschwitz is dealt with through Sara Nomberg-Przytyk's *Ausch-*

witz: True Tales from a Grotesque Land; a man's experience of a variety of camps, including Mauthausen and its notorious work camp, Gusen II, is dealt with in Bernard Gotfryd's "*Anton the Dove Fancier" and Other Tales from the Holocaust.* To explore the aftermath of the Holocaust, I usually teach Cynthia Ozick's *The Shawl.*[1]

Several other faculty members have developed courses that center on various aspects of the Shoah. Together, these courses, taught in the departments of history, German and Russian, political science, and religion, are sufficient for us to offer a minor in Holocaust studies. This minor is, in fact, a significant departure from the Hilberg era, which started with one essential course in political science and a second in English. The minor has prerequisites of one year of German and a course in modern European history. A further six courses in Holocaust studies complete it. Students will usually take The History of the Holocaust, The Holocaust through Literature and Film, Religious and Moral Perspectives on the Holocaust, and The Holocaust and the Humanities and choose from several other courses that treat the Holocaust or genocide. Course offerings are dependent on the presence or addition of faculty members whose interests and qualifications revolve around particular Holocaust-related topics. I am now, for instance, helping a new member of the Romance languages department set up a course on French film and the Holocaust. An incoming professor of history who has qualifications in international law will offer a course based on the Nuremburg trials that deals with genocide and international law.

To reach out to the general public, we used a strategy that derived from the resources available to us. A local high school teacher, Robert Bernheim, taught a yearlong course on the Holocaust at his school; further, he had previously designed and run a summer seminar for schoolteachers on teaching the Holocaust. He then introduced a similar course that we, in conjunction with our continuing-education program, offered during the summer. A three-credit course, it was taught by Bernheim and with faculty members from the university and made good use of a small but dedicated group of survivors, liberators, and rescuers living in the area. We have continued to offer this course every summer.

Another local resource proved to be Michael Schaal, a second-generation survivor who came up with the idea for a gathering of survivors and survivor families, which addressed the situation of such families and developed strategies for dealing with any problems or questions survivors had.

For both events we invited guest speakers from out of state, scholars and survivors. Such lectures and presentations were open to the general public and attracted, on average, an audience of about seventy. The major lecture offered each fall is, however, the Raul Hilberg Lecture. For this popular event (attracting a mixed audience of 200–300 local citizens, professors, and students), we invite scholars; past guests have included Gerhard Weinberg, Yaffa Eliach, Ian Kershaw, and Peter Hayes. We also invite visiting scholars for a week or more to campus. Visiting Raul Hilberg Scholars usually give a public lecture and presentations in our classes. Previous visiting scholars have been Saul Friedländer and Christopher Browning.

In addition to lectures by major figures in Holocaust studies, exhibitions, concerts, and performances are often arranged on an irregular basis either by us or by other departments (of music, theater, and art, for example) and cosponsored by us. The most recent cosponsored exhibition was of photographs by Jeff Gusky of Jewish sites in present-day Poland. Our musical offerings included a concert given by faculty members of Holocaust music and a piano-and-voice recital of Holocaust music at nearby Saint Michael's College, which we cosponsored. The most recent musical event (also with Saint Michael's College as a cosponsor) was of Holocaust-related songs in German, Yiddish, Polish, and other European languages.

Our collaboration with Saint Michael's College is close and fruitful. Frank Nicosia, professor of history at Saint Michael's and coeditor of *The Columbia Guide to the Holocaust,* is an active member of our board of advisers. He not only provides excellent advice but also collaborates in other ways, organizing our Miller Symposia, for example, with Jonathan Huener. The first such symposium was in 2000 and titled "Medicine and Medical Ethics in Nazi Germany." The lectures given on that occasion are available in a book of the same title (Nicosia and Huener). The symposia are offered every two years. The 2002 topic was "Business and Industry under the

Nazi Regime." The proceedings have also been published. The 2004 Miller Symposium was "The Arts in Nazi Germany."

After the first summer seminar for teachers, we found that we needed a textbook suitable for teachers who had never had a course on the Holocaust themselves but who were now trying to fill this gap in their education. We were looking for not only a textbook with history but also one that suggested teaching strategies and ways of approaching the topic; unable to find one, we decided to produce our own textbook, using the resources of the course. The book we produced, *The Holocaust: Introductory Essays* (Scrase and Mieder), is divided into three sections; the first covers the history, the second deals with cultural approaches to the Holocaust, and the third covers the lessons and legacy of the Holocaust. Although we intended the book only for use in the summer seminar, we have found it very useful in our undergraduate classes as well. In the meantime, it is also being used in high schools and in other colleges, some as far away as New Mexico, Utah, and Tennessee.

The summer seminar taught us each succeeding year that our group of survivors, liberators, and rescuers was dwindling. We therefore put together a volume, *The Holocaust: Personal Accounts* (Scrase and Mieder), that contains the experiences of these witnesses. We use this book in our regular classes too, and some local schools are also using it. In addition we have published a slim volume of some thirty-seven pages: *Holocaust Poems, 1965–1975*, which contains fourteen poems and four drawings. The author-artist is Joseph Hahn, a German-speaking artist and poet from Czechoslovakia who emigrated in 1939 and who now lives in retirement in Middlebury, Vermont. The poems are in German with English translations on the facing page. Other publication ventures over the past decade are occasional papers (usually the annual Hilberg Lecture) and a Festschrift for Hilberg on the occasion of his seventy-fifth birthday (Mieder and Scrase). A second Festschrift honors our own (as we like to think) "righteous gentile," Marion Pritchard, a remarkable Dutch-born rescuer. This Festschrift, appropriately enough, is on rescuers.

One other publishing venture, which satisfies our mission to reach both students and the general public, is our center's bulletin, which appears twice a year and contains a broad mix of information. In the

Bulletin for the Center of Holocaust Studies, readers find notice of forthcoming events, reports of past events that they might not have been able to attend, short articles, poems, translations, book reviews, and general information about the center. Writers and reviewers are scholars from home and abroad as well as students. The bulletin is sent out to a mailing list of over one thousand that includes friends of the center, alumni, donors, and scholars.

Outreach to the local schools remains an important component of our program. Our faculty members regularly visit local schools at the request of teachers who have, often, attended our summer seminar. We also have a registry (all too brief) of survivors who are willing and, despite advancing age, still able to visit schools. On occasion we have invited a survivor from out of state to speak on campus to 150 or so students bused in from their schools.

The above indicates what we have done over the years and what we continue to do, but we remain flexible. Our basic philosophy is to use what is available to us and to satisfy our varied constituents.

Note

1. For a detailed description of my basic course on the Holocaust through literature and film, see Lauckner and Jokiniemi 3–16.

Works Cited

Hahn, Joseph. *Holocaust Poems, 1965–1975.* Trans. David Scrase. Burlington: Center for Holocaust Studies Occasional Paper 3. U of Vermont, 1998.

Huener, Jonathan. *Auschwitz, Poland, and the Politics of Commemoration, 1945–1979.* Athens: Ohio UP, 2003.

Lauckner, Nancy A., and Miriam Jokiniemi, eds. *Shedding Light on the Darkness: A Guide to Teaching the Holocaust.* New York: Berghahn, 2000.

Mieder, Wolfgang, and David Scrase, eds. *Reflections on the Holocaust: Festschrift for Raul Hilberg on his Seventy-Fifth Birthday.* Burlington: Center for Holocaust Studies, U of Vermont, 2001.

Nicosia, Francis R., and Jonathan Huener, eds. *Medicine and Medical Ethics in Nazi Germany: Origins, Practices, Legacies.* New York: Berghahn, 2002.

Scrase, David, and Wolfgang Mieder, eds. *The Holocaust: Introductory Essays.* Burlington: Center for Holocaust Studies, U of Vermont, 1996.

———. *The Holocaust: Personal Accounts.* Burlington: Center for Holocaust Studies, U of Vermont, 2001.

Joshua L. Charlson

Teaching the Holocaust in a Jewish American Literature Course

Does the Holocaust have a place in the Jewish American literature classroom? If so, how large a space should it occupy and how might one go about defining its role? These questions seem important to me for a number of reasons. More English departments are likely to include a Jewish American literature course in their undergraduate curriculum than one specifically devoted to representations of the Holocaust; therefore, such a course may offer one of the few opportunities for students to encounter literature of the Shoah. Yet many teachers of Jewish American literature may be uneasy about this topic, approaching it only peripherally, either because they believe they lack expertise in the subject or because they question the relevance of the Holocaust in an American context. Moreover, many academics still harbor a bias against American representations of the Holocaust, assuming that they are invariably distorted or trivialized.[1]

I suggest, however, that it is crucial to devote a substantial section of a Jewish American literature course to the Holocaust. The event is a central factor in the construction of postwar Jewish identity, many aspects of which arise in an American context. Moreover, American artists have produced in recent decades a significant body of works involving the Holocaust, giving teachers an ample supply of worthwhile texts from which to choose. Finally, it is the very distance of most Americans from the atrocities of the Holocaust that, in my view, grants many of these works their aesthetic and intellectual interest, to the degree that the gaps of time, geography, and experience become the very subject addressed. I find that the most useful texts for teaching in a Jewish American context are those that self-consciously frame the events of the Holocaust in relation to later acts of memory, testimony, and narrative in an explicitly American setting. In what follows, I first sketch out what I take to be the major pragmatic and pedagogical issues a teacher must consider when designing a unit on the Holocaust for a Jewish American literature class; then I put forth some possibilities for how to construct such a unit, drawing on my experience teaching Jewish American literature in the English department of a private research university.

To begin with a practical question any teacher must consider when constructing a syllabus: Where should one place a unit on the Holocaust in the course schedule? As schematic as this problem seems, the placement of the unit inevitably conveys a message to students regarding the relative importance accorded to the material and thus influences their frame of perception. Placing the unit last might unwittingly assign undue weight to the Holocaust. Yet a chronological solution often proves messy, for while the historical event itself is limited to the early 1940s, important American literary responses appear across the subsequent decades. For a topically or thematically arranged course, the teacher must consider how the subject of the Holocaust will speak to the surrounding units. In my own classes, I have placed the unit on the Holocaust about two-thirds through the course. The earlier units are concerned with narratives of immigrant experience and the processes of acculturation and suburbanization at work in American Jewish culture of the 1940s and 1950s. Subsequent units address the diverse contemporary constructions of the American Jew, focusing on topics such as

Diaspora experience, conceptions of Israel, multiculturalism, and the return to ritual. Situating the study of Holocaust literature at this transitional point allows me to emphasize the ways that later cultural and historical effects may be viewed as reactions (both latent and overt) to the Shoah.

A second practical concern is how to introduce historical background on the Holocaust and integrate the historical in a literary context. This question could apply, of course, to any literature course dealing with earlier historical periods or events, but the Holocaust seems to demand a more intense historical accounting, given the limited knowledge with which most students enter the course and the enormity of the history on which the imaginative works are based. This demand creates a bind for the conscientious teacher: on the one hand, factual knowledge of the Holocaust is indispensable; on the other hand, the time constraints of a literature classroom inevitably shortchange the opportunities for historical contextualization. Nevertheless, there are some strategies a teacher can pursue to effect a compromise. I try to merge historical and literary questions by beginning the unit with a discussion of the various names by which the destruction of European Jewry has been called — *Holocaust*, *Shoah* (Hebrew), *churbn* (Yiddish), *Nazi genocide*, and others — and the etymological and sociological reverberations of these labels.[2] Opening the unit in this way helps convey to students that linguistic coding and interpretation are, at some level, unavoidable when we discuss the Holocaust. From here, I can move the discussion toward the problematics of any sort of representation of a historical event and the particular challenges posed by the Holocaust to historical and aesthetic representation. An accessible critical reading, such as an excerpt from James Young's *Writing and Rewriting the Holocaust* or Irving Howe's "Writing and the Holocaust," can help further illuminate the theoretical dimensions of Holocaust representation. Finally, although my classes are primarily discussion-based, I find it necessary to do some lecturing on the historical background of the Holocaust. I limit lectures to a general introduction to the political background, the experience of Jewish victims in the ghettos and camps, and American responses to the events in Europe. This overview should be supplemented with a good general history book on the Holocaust that can be placed on reserve at the library.[3] In addition, I distribute annotated handouts that correlate to the individual readings and that provide definitions and descriptions of specific terms, places, and events that may appear in a given text.

Most teachers will want to spend class time concentrating on the literary works. I favor texts that self-consciously raise the question of America's relation to the Holocaust through framing or other metanarrative devices. Among the questions such texts might enable teachers to put before students are the following: What are the relevant cultural lenses through which Americans have come to view the Holocaust? To what extent can one say that the Holocaust has become Americanized during its contact with our culture? What forms of transmission (of memory, of history, of trauma) seem particularly suited to America? To what degree does identification with the Holocaust shape other manifestations of Jewish American identity in the late twentieth and early twenty-first centuries?

My syllabus typically focuses on the work of three authors: poetry by Jacob Glatstein; the novella *The Shawl* by Cynthia Ozick; and the hybrid-genre, two-volume work *Maus* by Art Spiegelman. In addition to raising in powerful ways the above questions, these texts have the practical benefit of being brief and accessible enough to fit comfortably into a two-and-a-half- to three-week sequence in the course schedule. I begin with the Yiddish-language American poet Glatstein, in part because he has a wide body of available poems on the Holocaust and because his work aptly embodies the central dilemma of Americans who write about the Shoah. Like many writers of the Yiddish Diaspora, Glatstein witnessed the unfolding persecution of the Jews of Europe from afar with a mixture of guilt and terror, bearing the painful knowledge that his own fate was separated from that of the victims by only the smallest of margins. Glatstein's 1938 poem "Good Night, World" evokes both anger and guilt in a caustic, ironic stream of language. The poem opens:

Good night, wide world,
big, stinking world.
Not you, but I slam the gate.

With my flaming, yellow patch,
with my proud gait,
At my own command—
I return to the ghetto.
(*American Yiddish Poetry* 305)

Students tend to be drawn to Glatstein's fiery expressiveness and inventive word combinations ("Flabby democracy," "Jesus-marxe" [305, 306]), but their attention should be directed to the central conceit of the poem: that the speaker is rejecting the modern world and choosing to return to the Jewish ghetto: "I grant you, world, / all my liberators," the speaker proclaims (306), and students should be asked to consider why. Why does antisemitic violence spur Glatstein to want to return to "the quiet ghetto-light" (306)? To what extent does guilt or nostalgia drive the poem, to what extent an authentic need to connect with a community from which Glatstein has been separated?

"Good Night, World" can be usefully paired with "I'll Find My Self-Belief" (1953) to chart shifts in Glatstein's attitudes and poetic approach in the aftermath of the Holocaust. The latter poem also builds a nostalgic remembrance of the Jewish world of Glatstein's past, but it ends by turning on itself and tearing down the edifice it has constructed:

And I'll buckle myself up with my last days
and, for spite, count them in you, my frozen past
who mocked me,
who invented my living, garrulous
Jewish world.
You silenced it
and in Maidanek woods
finished it off with a few shots. (Glatstein 103)

Students should be encouraged to examine not only how the poem contends with the violent loss of a culture to which the author was closely attached but also the deep suspicion of history and memory evidenced in his attack on his "frozen past." The poet at once reaches for and resists the past, because he finds that it is also a trap, binding him to memories and events that threaten his sense of self.

Alerting students to the ways in which the past can possess the present helps set the stage for Ozick and Spiegelman, whose writings confront these same problems on an expanded scale. Both writers use narrative devices that frame the brutal experience of the Holocaust with narratives of postwar experience in America that inevitably mourn, testify, retell, and otherwise reflect on the losses of the past. With each text I therefore find that the formal elements make a compelling starting place for discussion.

Ozick's *The Shawl* pairs two stories: the brief story "The Shawl" presents a direct (if highly stylized) depiction of violence in a death camp, and the longer "Rosa" follows the postwar life in America of the woman whose child was murdered in the first story. I often ask students how their reading experience would differ had they read only one of the stories (which was how readers originally encountered the stories in the *New Yorker*, since they were published three years apart). This line of questioning can help move students past the frustration they often feel with the dense language and overwhelmingly painful subject matter of "The Shawl" and toward a consideration of the work as a meditation on the obstacles to Rosa Lublin's transcending trauma and remaking her life in the aftermath of the Shoah. Although each story is powerful in its own right, students recognize that neither fully accounts for the truth of Rosa. I encourage them to consider how the stories represent the difficulties in adapting to life in America, in both the character of Rosa and the depiction of American culture. Rosa demonstrates a common trait of survivors of trauma by collapsing past and present, viewing the denizens of modern-day Miami through the lens of her own tragedy and in language encoded with Holocaust imagery: "They were all scarecrows, blown about under the murdering sunball with empty rib cages" (16). Equally important, though, is her lack of a sympathetic audience in America, her inability to find anyone who can act as a secondary witness to her testimony. This point is frequently difficult for students to grasp, but I have found that by emphasizing the way that motifs of voice and muteness carry over from the first story to the second, I can help them understand that Rosa's silence—

her loss of voice and intense need to give expression to her pain — is critical to unlocking the novella's many levels of meaning.

Although *The Shawl* is brief at only seventy pages, students tend to find Ozick's language challenging; they usually describe Spiegelman's *Maus* as far more accessible. I try to incorporate their reactions into our discussions as we move from Ozick to Spiegelman. Is accessibility necessarily a good thing when it comes to representations of the Holocaust? Does the difficulty of the material demand a more difficult style, or do the needs of an American audience call for a more accessible aesthetic? These questions lead us to examine the formal aspects of *Maus*, whose hybridity I locate in both the development of postmodernism in America and the use of comics, an inherently American form of art. The framing technique is even more pronounced in Spiegelman, but the focus shifts from the experience of the survivor to the transmission of trauma and memory for children of survivors and other secondary witnesses. Put another way, Spiegelman's work pointedly asks how it is possible for those who were not there to make sense of the Holocaust and whether they even have the right to attempt narrative reconstruction of the past. Some of *Maus*'s most powerful moments, those to which my discussions with students gravitate, occur when Spiegelman self-consciously illuminates his struggles as an artist and a son of a Holocaust survivor: the insertion into *Maus* of *Prisoner on the Hell Planet*, an early Spiegelman comic about his mother's suicide; the opening section of "Auschwitz (Time Flies)" in *Maus II* (*And Here My Troubles Began*), in which Spiegelman depicts himself at his drawing table, literally and metaphorically atop a pile of Jew-mouse bodies; the scene in which Art attempts to find the proper visual metaphor for depicting his wife, a Frenchwoman who has converted to Judaism. I also press students to consider the ways in which *Maus* opens up broad issues of Jewish American literature, such as the notion that Jewish identity is not fixed (brilliantly embodied in the masks worn by Spiegelman and a few other characters in the present-tense sections of the text), the troubled relationships of sons with mothers and fathers, and the public and private roles of the Jewish artist. These aspects of Spiegelman's profound work help students read *Maus* not only as a work of Holocaust literature but also as a text that, like the Holocaust itself, is intimately bound up in the way American Jews have imagined their relation to both their religion and their nation.

The texts I recommend here should be taken as suggestive only. Many others could substitute equally well, from Irving Feldman's poem "The Pripet Marshes"—in which the speaker projects himself back to the Holocaust in an act of failed rescue—to Thane Rosenbaum's intensive meditations on the experience of children of survivors in *Elijah Visible* or *Second Hand Smoke*. What is essential is that the texts chosen inspire reflection on the fate of the Holocaust in America. American authors cannot replicate the achievement of a Primo Levi and provide firsthand testimony; what they can accomplish, however, is to cast light on the role of the Holocaust in the formation of contemporary Jewish American identities.

Notes

1. See Rosenfeld for an influential statement of this position. Recently, critics have taken a more open-minded, culturally oriented approach to American writing of the Holocaust. The collection of essays edited by Flanzbaum, *The Americanziation of the Holocaust*, addresses a range of genres—from literature to television to film—and represents varied theoretical approaches. Mintz's synthetic study of the subject emphasizes popular reception of Holocaust texts.
2. Young presents a cogent analysis of the various names of the Holocaust (83–99).
3. Bauer and Hilberg are both good options, of the many available, in the general-textbook category. Novick's *The Holocaust in American Life* presents a thorough, if at times tendentious, account of the Holocaust's gradual emergence as a cultural and political force in American Jewish life in the postwar decades.

Works Cited

American Yiddish Poetry. Ed. Barbara Harshav and Benjamin Harshav. Berkeley: U of California P, 1986.

The Americanization of the Holocaust. Ed. Hilene Flanzbaum. Baltimore: Johns Hopkins UP, 1999.

Bauer, Yehuda. *History of the Holocaust.* New York: Watts, 1982.

Feldman, Irving. *"The Pripet Marshes" and Other Poems.* New York: Viking, 1965.

Glatstein, Jacob. *Selected Poems of Jacob Glatstein*. Trans. Ruth Whitman. New York: October, 1972.

Hilberg, Raul. *The Destruction of the European Jews*. New York: Holmes, 1985.

Howe, Irving. "Writing and the Holocaust." *New Republic* 27 Oct. 1986: 27–36.

Mintz, Alan. *Popular Culture and the Shaping of Holocaust Memory in America*. Seattle: U of Washington P, 2001.

Novick, Peter. *The Holocaust in American Life*. New York: Houghton, 1999.

Ozick, Cynthia. *The Shawl*. New York: Knopf, 1990.

Rosenbaum, Thane. *Elijah Visible*. New York: St. Martin's, 1996.

———. *Second Hand Smoke*. New York: St. Martin's, 1999.

Rosenfeld, Alvin. "The Americanization of the Holocaust." *Commentary* 99.6 (1995): 35–40.

Spiegelman, Art. *And Here My Troubles Began*. New York: Pantheon, 1991. Vol. 2 of *Maus: A Survivor's Tale*.

———. *My Father Bleeds History*. New York: Pantheon, 1986. Vol. 1 of *Maus: A Survivor's Tale*.

Young, James E. *Writing and Rewriting the Holocaust: Narrative and the Consequences of Interpretation*. Bloomington: Indiana UP, 1988.

Michael Rothberg

Pedagogy and the Politics of Memory: "The Countermonument Project"

The Politics of Memory

From debates about secretive Swiss banking practices during the Nazi era to the moving spectacle of South Africa's Truth and Reconciliation Commission, the last decade has witnessed the growth in significance of a politics of memory that is global in scope and implication and yet intensely local in its stakes. In *The Guilt of Nations*, a study of the recent proliferation of claims to restitution made by the victims of historical wrongs, historian Elazar Barkan charts the emergence in the 1990s of this "new international emphasis on morality [that] has been characterized not only by accusing other countries of human rights abuses but also by self-examination." What Barkan terms the "national self-reflexivity" (xvii) in contemporary grappling with crimes against humanity constitutes a phenomenon whose effects need to be taken into account in debates about international politics; in theories of history and memory; and even, I suggest here, in thinking about the teaching of the Holocaust. Indeed, the recent global trend toward the establishment of truth commissions and the granting of restitution for historical crimes signals that political, intellectual, and pedagogical concerns are inseparable in coming to terms with traumatic histories.

Barkan's study of the struggle for reparations after crimes against humanity confirms an argument that scholars of Holocaust literature have been making for some time: memory matters; it has material and political effects. And if memory matters, then representation matters as well, since memory arrives belatedly and is thus shaped by the form and context in which it is articulated. Recognition of the importance of memory and representation should not render literary scholars complacent in their understanding of the historical and political significance of their work. Ultimately, what matters is not memory and representation alone but the consequences of their articulation and interpretation. As James Young argues:

> We should also ask to what ends we remember. That is, how do we respond to the current moment in light of our remembered past? This is to recognize that the shape of memory cannot be divorced from the actions taken in its behalf, and that memory without consequences contains the seeds of its own destruction. (15)

Young's challenge helpfully underlines the difference between an often psychologically necessary act of memorialization or mourning and a more self-conscious politics of memory, a memory that guides action.

Among the actions that we as scholars take on behalf of memory are those that define our practice in the classroom. Once we have recognized the significance of memory and representation for historical understanding and political praxis, we have also markedly increased the stakes of pedagogy. Although I always seek to encourage students to link literary aesthetics with history and politics, I can't deny that teaching the Holocaust often seems, rightly or wrongly, to add burdens of responsibility beyond those in, say, a survey of twentieth-century American literature. And yet, what precisely do we want our students to take away from a course on the Nazi genocide? This is not an easy question. While there are, without doubt, multiple ways of answering, my own tendency is to attempt to provoke a kind of self-reflexivity analogous to that which Barkan describes as lying behind the most powerful examples of contemporary human-rights discourse. Encouraging self-reflexivity in the context of the classroom means encouraging awareness of one's simultaneous implication in and distance from the events under consideration. When I teach the Holocaust, I do not want my students to believe that they can easily put themselves in the position of victims (or perpetrators, for that matter), nor do I want them to look on the events of genocide as so distanced from their lives that the events become "merely" historical. The attempt to produce this charged middle ground of self-aware engagement has inspired the course project that I focus on here.

For students to recognize the stakes of memory in the classroom demands that they become active participants in the construction of knowledge in ways that are in tension with everyday pedagogical expectations. This recognition also necessitates moving beyond—without abandoning—the traditional explications de texte and analytic essays that ordinarily define assignments in literature courses. In this essay, I discuss an assignment from my Literature of the Holocaust class in order to reflect on pedagogical strategies for engaging with the Holocaust in a moment when history and memory seem to matter more than ever. Inspired by the work of contemporary artists who have challenged traditional forms of memorialization in the wake of the Nazi genocide and other histories of extreme violence, "The Countermonument Project" is an assignment that demands creative thinking as well as critical acumen: students are asked to combine analytic writing with the design of their own Holocaust countermonument. This assignment challenges them to confront both practical and theoretical problems of memorialization—problems that are relevant to the Holocaust in particular and to questions of historical representation more broadly.

The Countermonument

Focusing in the classroom on problems of memorialization has proved to be a provocative way to raise fundamental questions about the nature of the Nazi genocide and the response to it by those who did not experience it. Which groups should be included in the narrative of the Holocaust? Only Jews or also Roma and the handicapped? Can bystanders or perpetrators be memorialized? What events or sites are most crucial to defining the genocide? What meanings (if any) can be taken away from the Holocaust's dark events? Can those events be represented figurally or only abstractly and indirectly? In seeking to raise these kinds of general issues in a hands-on way, I focus on the genre of the countermonument. A countermonument is a self-reflexive aesthetic form that both draws on elements of traditional monuments and seeks to subvert traditional forms by frustrating viewers' expectations about what constitutes a monument. While traditional monuments are supposed to be stable, timeless, "monumental," and aesthetically pleasing, countermonuments are often dynamic, temporary, fleeting, and deliberately unaesthetic. Since countermonuments comment on their own monumental status and on the process of memorialization itself, they already raise many of the essential questions I address in the classroom.

While the countermonument aesthetic has been elaborated most fully in the context of German memorials, a similar tendency can be found in the United States.[1] The countermonument addresses both general problems with monumental form and the specific problem of how to come to terms with the crimes that have been committed by the nation sponsoring the monument—especially when those crimes were committed before the artist and audience could have been legally or morally responsible. Just how difficult this latter task is can be seen in the paucity of monuments in the United States addressing the founding crimes of the Americas—genocide of the indigenous population and slavery. Countermonument artists recognize the ways that traditional monuments have served to glorify the nation-state and to justify sacrifice and violence in the name of patriotism. They thus seek to create self-questioning forms that are both aesthetically and ideologically challenging. Countermonuments square the need to remember with the incongruous need for independent critical activity by transferring the burden of memory from the monument to the audience.

To bring out the ambivalences of memorialization in a United States context, I often refer to the controversy surrounding Maya Lin's design for the Vietnam Veterans Memorial in Washington, DC. Lin's proposal provoked hostility before it was built because its dark, sunken form refused to glorify the war it was meant to memorialize or to "raise up" the dead in the name of a just patriotic cause. Paradoxically, however, once the memorial was constructed, the very abstract minimalism of its form made it one of Washington's most beloved monuments. The untraditional openness of its response to the war has made it a perfect analogue and site for an ongoing, unfinished, and multilayered mourning process; the possibilities it creates for interaction — seeing one's reflection in the monument, making a rubbing of a name — foster individual memorial activity. As Marita Sturken has argued in her useful study of the politics of American memories of Vietnam and AIDS, Lin's memorial has evoked such powerful responses because of the ways that it refuses the "closure" offered by most war memorials, a closure that "can by its very nature serve to sanctify future wars by offering a complete narrative with cause and effect intact" (51). In its self-reflexive rejection of the national-patriotic function of the war monument, Lin's Vietnam Veterans Memorial exemplifies the critical countermonument aesthetic.[2]

In taking the idea of the countermonument into the American classroom, I ask students to focus on the problems of memorializing the Holocaust in a United States context.[3] What is and ought to be the relation of a generation of multicultural American and international students born in the 1980s to the events and aftermath of the Nazi genocide? The forms of self-reflexivity that make sense for young Germans are not the same as those that are relevant to most students studying in the United States. Ideally, an American Holocaust countermonument would take into account the links that bind as well as the distances that separate Americans from the events. While German artists feel called on to resist reproducing Fascist aesthetics or, in other instances, to make the relative post-Holocaust absence of European Jewish culture into a felt or present absence, American students face other issues. If, as Gertrud Koch cogently remarks in a critique of *Schindler's List*, "[t]he 'ethics' of Holocaust aesthetics is to insist that all kinds of human scars and injuries be included, and not only those whose healing can be monumentalized" (405–06), then an ethics of Holocaust aesthetics will find quite a bit of resistance in an American context, which insists that all wounds must be healed!

Some of the most pressing questions that I address in the context of translating goals of the German countermonument tradition into an American setting are how to evoke the genocide's relation to modernity and technology in a society dedicated to progress; how to understand the persistent wounds suffered by Holocaust survivors in a land founded on optimism, healing, and moving on; how to avoid sensationalizing suffering in the face of a culture industry of unparalleled scope and power; and how to balance the specificity of the Holocaust with a recognition of other traumatic histories. Although it is too early to tell whether the September 11 attacks on New York and Washington will fundamentally transform American discourses of trauma, memory, and mourning, it seems certain that the questions I raise here with respect to Holocaust memorialization will become more charged and relevant in the months and years to come. As debates about what to do with the site of the former World Trade Center towers have already suggested, a new American countermonument movement may arise in the aftermath of the attacks. "The Countermonument Project" provides one avenue of access to addressing this emergent politics of memory.

The Assignment

Let me now give concrete information about my assignment and its place in my class. I introduce the project midway through the semester, when we have already covered historical context (through the reading of primary texts, such as the Nuremberg Laws of 1935 and Himmler's Posen speech, and historical works, such as Browning's *Ordinary Men*), diaries of the pre-Holocaust and Holocaust periods (such as selections from Klemperer's *I Will Bear Witness* and ghetto diaries), the poetry of Dan Pagis and Abraham Sutzkever, and some camp testimonies (Wiesel's *Night* followed by Glazar's

Trap with the Green Fence and Delbo's *Auschwitz and After*).[4] This background gives the students a sense of both the historical context and the types of problems of representation that emerge in the wake of the Holocaust. At this point, I assign them two chapters from Young's *The Texture of Memory* and occasionally supplement Young with other important works on problems of memorialization, such as Edward Linenthal's *Preserving Memory*, Timothy Ryback's essay "Evidence of Evil," and Sturken's *Tangled Memories*. After spending a class period or two discussing these texts, I distribute the assignment. Over the course of the second half of the semester, students develop their own design for a countermonument and write a paper that discusses the readings on memorialization, describes (and sometimes portrays) their monument, and analyzes their own design. I often invite students to present their designs to the class.

Here is a recent version of the assignment, as specifically created for a spring 2000 Holocaust literature class at the University of Miami:

Countermonument Project

A wealthy, anonymous donor has offered a substantial prize in a contest for the design of a Holocaust counter-monument to be located in Miami or on the University of Miami campus. The donor is looking for a monument that will be both a memorial to the events of the Nazi genocide and a lesson for present and future generations. Taking the examples of countermonuments described by Young as inspiration, design a Holocaust countermonument to be placed on campus or in the Miami area. The final version is due on the last day of class, at which time you will present it to your classmates. The project should consist of a minimum of four pages of writing and optional visual aids. The class as a whole will serve as a jury and will vote on which are the best designs. The designer of the winning monument will receive two bonus points on her or his final grade.

1. First, drawing on course readings, discuss some of the problems specific to memorializing the Holocaust. What factors make the preservation of the memory of the Holocaust difficult? What aspects of traditional memorials are problematic for remembering the Holocaust? How are counter-

monuments designed to respond to the problems of traditional monuments? What specific problems might accompany the design of a Holocaust memorial in Miami or on the University of Miami campus?

2. After having considered those questions of memorialization and memory, describe the countermonument you propose to build for the contest. Describe precisely where you would locate it, what it would look like and be made of, and how it would be created and maintained. You might want to use illustrations, sketches, or maps in order to orient the reader. Your design should be realistic and buildable. It should also be based on a decision about whom you want to memorialize (which group or groups of victims, perpetrators, or bystanders) and what you want the message and effect of your design to be.

3. Once you have described your monument, you must justify it and analyze it (as Young and Sturken do). Why did you choose the location or context you did? What is the significance of its design? What are the materials used? What are your plans for its future? How do you expect people to interact with the monument? How does your countermonument challenge viewers and preconceived ideas about memory, monuments, and the Holocaust? How does it memorialize the victims and warn those who see it?

Your grade for this assignment will be based on the originality and appropriateness of your design, your engagement with our analytic readings on monuments, your integration of ideas and issues raised in the other readings we have done this semester, and evidence that you have put thought and effort into this project. I will not judge you on your artistic abilities!

I offer this assignment with the hope that it will prove adaptable to different pedagogical needs and contexts. To be truthful, I must admit that as with all assignments the results are not uniformly satisfying. It is sometimes difficult to get students to move in an aesthetically and intellectually aware manner from a familiar monumental design to a countermonument that addresses problems of representation. Similarly, sentimentality and sensationalism are not uncommon. And, as one might expect, there is always a marked divide in the effort and thought that different students put into the assignment.

Nevertheless, I feel confident in claiming that students will find this one of the most challenging and provocative assignments they confront in a literature class. It will also add a hands-on depth and complexity to their response to an event that puts forth so many obstacles to comprehension.

I begin this essay by stating that I often have the sense that there is more at stake in teaching the Holocaust to undergraduates than there is in most other literature classes. Students often share this sense and bring to their participation in the class a greater degree of seriousness and dedication than one ordinarily sees. "The Countermonument Project," which students frequently tell me is one of the most difficult but ultimately satisfying assignments they have encountered, can serve as a means to tap into this engagement in order to foster a self-reflexive understanding of how history, memory, and representation matter. An incident that happened to me illustrates how real a rhetorical act of witnessing can be.[5] One day on my way to the office, I was riding the university shuttle that connects the parking garage at the edge of campus to the building that houses the English department. A student who had been in my Holocaust literature class the year before sat down next to me and, after the usual pleasantries, asked, "So have they built that monument?" "Which monument do you mean?" I asked in response. "The one from the contest," she replied. I realized that she had taken my imaginary premise to the assignment literally and had assumed that the winner of the class countermonument-design contest would really have his or her monument built on campus (not a bad idea, I might add!). My student's misunderstanding was slightly disconcerting and suggests the care that needs to be taken to ensure that creative assignments don't ignore the line between the imaginary and the real. But I also found in her earnestness about the assignment a confirmation of my sense that teaching the Holocaust can produce a thoughtfulness that extends beyond the classroom.

The key question remains, however—what kind of thoughtfulness do we want to encourage? For my part, I hope that my students will understand that it is not only the Holocaust that ought to command the kind of intense belief and respect that this anecdote illustrates. Ultimately, American literature classes, and many others, ought to lead to a similar self-reflexivity about the stakes of cultural production.[6] For, as Walter Benjamin warned, "There is no document of civilization that is not at the same time a document of barbarism" (256).

Notes

1. The genre and significance of the countermonument have come to be known in Holocaust studies primarily through the important work on memorialization by Young; see his essay in this volume as well as *The Texture of Memory* (esp. 27–48). Young's discussion of the origins of the countermonument aesthetic reveals that a generation of young artists in 1980s Germany anticipated and had already given form to the kind of "national self-reflexivity" that Barkan finds in the international political realm starting only in the 1990s.

2. This is not to say that Lin's memorial is without problems (what memorial could be?). Particularly troubling is its silence about the millions of Vietnamese dead. Unlike German memory, which has in recent years been deeply if not always successfully engaged with the Nazis' Jewish victims, the scope of American critical memory does not extend this far.

3. One condition shared by contemporary German artists and American students, which I always emphasize in the classroom, is being born in the aftermath of world-historical events. While I extend the term *postmemory* somewhat beyond the boundaries of its initial formulation, I find Hirsch's concept of postmemory crucial in defining this shared generational space (see *Family Frames*).

4. For the Nuremberg Laws of 1935 and Himmler's speech, see Dawidowicz (45–49, 130–40). The poetry of Pagis and Sutzkever is collected in Langer.

5. For an extended discussion of the possibilities and perils of rhetorical acts of witnessing, see my analysis of the United States Holocaust Memorial Museum (*Traumatic Realism* 247–63).

6. Because of the importance of sharing the insights developed here about the politics of memory, I was pleased when a colleague adapted my countermonument project for use as an in-class assignment for a course on nineteenth-century American literature. After my colleague explained what was behind the concept of the countermonument, he asked students to work in small groups to design countermonuments appropriate to the memorialization of Native American peoples and cultures. It is equally clear to me that the concept of the countermonument would lend itself to a critical engagement with the legacies of slavery in the United States.

Works Cited

Barkan, Elazar. *The Guilt of Nations: Restitution and Negotiating Historical Injustices.* Baltimore: Johns Hopkins UP, 2000.

Benjamin, Walter. "Theses on the Philosophy of History." *Illuminations.* Trans. Harry Zohn. New York: Schocken, 1968. 253–64.

Browning, Christopher. *Ordinary Men: Reserve Battalion 101 and the Final Solution in Poland.* New York: Harper, 1992.

Dawidowicz, Lucy. *A Holocaust Reader.* West Orange: Behrman, 1976.

Delbo, Charlotte. *Auschwitz and After.* Trans. Rosette Lamont. New Haven: Yale UP, 1995.

Glazar, Richard. *Trap with a Green Fence: Survival in Treblinka.* Trans. Roslyn Theobold. Evanston: Northwestern UP, 1995.

Hirsch, Marianne. *Family Frames: Photograph, Narrative, and Postmemory.* Cambridge: Harvard UP, 1997.

Klemperer, Victor. *I Will Bear Witness: A Diary of the Nazi Years, 1933–1941.* Trans. Martin Chalmers. New York: Random, 1998.

Koch, Gertrud. "'Against All Odds' or the Will to Survive: Moral Conclusions from Narrative Closure." *History and Memory* 9 (1997): 393–408.

Langer, Lawrence, ed. *Art from the Ashes: A Holocaust Anthology.* New York: Oxford UP, 1995.

Linenthal, Edward T. *Preserving Memory: The Struggle to Create America's Holocaust Museum.* New York: Penguin, 1995.

Rothberg, Michael. *Traumatic Realism: The Demands of Holocaust Representation.* Minneapolis: U of Minnesota P, 2000.

Ryback, Timothy. "Evidence of Evil." *New Yorker* 15 Nov. 1993: 68–81.

Sturken, Marita. *Tangled Memories: The Vietnam War, the AIDS Epidemic, and the Politics of Remembering.* Berkeley: U of California P, 1997.

Wiesel, Elie. *The Night Trilogy.* Trans. Stella Rodway. New York: Farrar, 1987.

Young, James. *The Texture of Memory: Holocaust Memorials and Meaning.* New Haven: Yale UP, 1993.

Sondra Perl

Writing the Holocaust: The Transformative Power of Response Journals

> The image of the Holocaust is *with us* — a memory which haunts, a sounding board for all subsequent evil — in the back of the mind . . . for all of us now living: we, the inheritors.

I begin my course on the Holocaust with the above quote from Terrence Des Pres (viii). I want to be clear from the start that while the subject matter of the course is the past, my emphasis will be on the present: on inviting students to explore their responses to the material they will be reading. I call the course The Holocaust: Yesterday's History, Today's Response.

Like others writing in this volume, I am interested in the issue of representation and the question of what it means to teach the Holocaust, but I come at this inquiry from a slightly different angle, as a scholar in composition and rhetoric. A writing teacher, I believe that students confronting this history must write, must attempt to make sense of their responses, and must find a way to articulate the precarious emotional and intellectual journey they are undertaking.

I do not want to overlook or, even worse, ignore the opportunity to help students engage fundamental, human questions, questions that bedevil the world, questions that haunt. And while I imagine that such questions are often raised in courses on the Holocaust, asking students to write about them and making student responses an important text in the class help students come to terms with this complicated legacy.

Writing, then, is vital to my course; the response journal central, not peripheral. From the first class meeting, students know that each week they will be expected to write at home about the readings, then to bring their journals to class and to read aloud from them, either to the entire class or a small group. They know that individual journal entries will not be graded, that I will collect journals at least twice, and that I will quote from their journals in developing course materials. I also tell them that the more thoughtful and thorough their journals are, the higher their grades will likely be.[1]

I focus here on journal writing, on what happens when I invite my students to bring the questions raised by a study of the Holocaust into the present moment. I show what happens as students voice concerns, shock, doubt, even agony; as they write about their struggles with the material and with themselves; and as, in most instances, they begin not only to react to the material but also to speak back to it. I describe, as it unfolded, my 1998 Holocaust course at Lehman College, the only four-year college of the City University of New York located in the Bronx.[2]

I offer this course under the auspices of either the Lehman Scholars Program or the Adult Degree Program. Since the course lies outside the purview of any one department, I can design it in any way I like: I choose to focus on history, testimony, and theology. I want my students to understand the social and economic conditions that prepared the way for the Third Reich; enter intimately and imaginatively into the experiences of those who were the victims; and grapple with questions of national character, evil, and forgiveness. I have, admittedly, an ambitious agenda. But I am convinced that a course on the Holocaust is an appropriate place for such grappling and that response journals, if written without fear of censure, provide students with a place to engage in honest and probing inquiry.

I begin the course with a letter to my students, deliberately bringing my written voice into the room, marking myself as a writer among them. In it, I discuss the readings; the course requirements, which include an independent project and the weekly response journal; the films we will view; and plans for meeting a Holocaust survivor.[3] But equally important, I also frame our inquiry in personal terms. I write, in part:

> What we are about to begin is not easy. The Holocaust forces us to be witnesses to atrocity. It forces us to look at the evil that can be perpetrated by human beings against other human beings. It forces us to look at genocide — the planned destruction of an entire race — the systematic torture, humiliation, and eventual murder of millions of innocent people.
>
> Why should we do this? This is the first question you need to answer for yourself. Why did you elect to take this course? What brought you here?
>
> Second, what do you already know? How much have you studied? Read? Seen? What comes to mind when you think of the Holocaust: Hitler? Concentration camps? *Schindler's List*? Take some time to write about the images in your head.
>
> Third, think about the others in your life. Hitler managed to convince an entire population that some of those who lived among them warranted extermination. While our own prejudices may not be so extreme, think about which groups you and members of your family or ethnic group sometimes joke about or consider inferior.
>
> Please write about these questions in your journal. Let your mind wander freely over these questions and any others that come to you in the next week.

From day 1 of my course, I use writing to invite writing. And I look to begin where my students are: with why they came, what they know, and the questions they bring. From several decades of teaching at Lehman, I know that those who register will reflect the rich diversity of New York City. Sitting in my classroom will be recent immigrants from Europe, the Caribbean, China, Korea, Ghana, Pakistan. African Americans born in New York and in the South. Hispanics from Puerto Rico, the Dominican Republic, or the five boroughs — streetwise Bronx kids, churchgoing grandmothers, single parents, a few Jews, maybe a Muslim. Many will work, most full-time and attend school part-time; most will not know much about the Holocaust. No one will want to write.

But during the second week of the term, as students read aloud from their journals, we all learn about the range of their interests and the issues that drew them to the course. Some admit that they are here by default: this is the only course that fit their schedules. Others reveal a secret interest in Hitler. Still others are embarrassed to admit how much they don't know:

> I must confess that I know very little about the Holocaust. Like many people, I paid no attention to any information on the plight of the Jews. I did not see it as part of my past or as part of my history. Why bother to take notice?

> I am wondering if I am unique or if I represent the majority of people in my age group (32). I really know nothing about the past, maybe bits and pieces. When I was growing up, my teachers taught me about World Wars I and II, . . . the first settlers in America . . . the president in the 1920s. Why do I not remember this now? Why don't I care?

> Growing up I always heard antisemitic slogans and stereotypical phrases about Jews: "Have a Jew for a lawyer — you'll win." "Have a Jew doctor — you'll receive the best health care." "Jewish men make the best providers." "If you want smart advice, ask a Jew." "Jews are cheap, stingy, tight with a dime." Myths . . . but powerful just the same.

In response to the question about the others in their lives, my students define themselves, describe their histories, frame their own cultural contexts:

> The "others" in my life are the Yoruba and Hausa people of Nigeria. I'm Ibo. During the Biafran war of 1967–70, the Ibos felt the Yorubas betrayed them, thus leading to the Ibos'

defeat. The lack of trust among all three tribes is the foot-stool of all the political problems in Nigeria.

The "others" in my life are the Europeans which later changed to white people. It's no secret the injustice they did to us during the slave trade and the colonial era. They came and exploited us. They took our men, women, gold, bronze, artifacts, and mineral resources—and our petro-leum, which they are still taking even today.

Growing up in a traditional Puerto Rican household, I was a witness to prejudice. My parents often spoke of the *blan-cos* or white people with some slight hatred. It was because of the *blancos* that we Puerto Rican and blacks were held back. The *blancos* thought we were stupid. They thought all we did was use drugs and live off of welfare.

As I thought about what "other" meant, I realized that there are so many "others" in my life. As a Hispanic, I some-times see white people as the "other" or sometimes black people. As a Puerto Rican, I see Dominicans and Mexicans as the "other." As a math major, I see English majors as the "other." As a Roman Catholic, I see Jews as the "other." It scares me.

By the third or fourth week of the term, the journals become a place for students to record their reactions to texts. Sitting in a circle, journals open, they become accustomed to my beginning class by asking for volunteers to read aloud responses to the reading as-signed for the week. After reading Elie Wiesel's *Night*, we might hear, for example:

Hardly any Jews believed they were about to be destroyed. I certainly would not believe anyone who told me that people were destroying black people. I would be wary, but I would have cast them aside just like the Jews did to Moshe.

I am honestly having a hard time talking about how I feel— something I usually never have a problem with. I want to detach myself from myself to lessen the impact. . . . A few days ago, I had a nightmare full of visions I'd imagined as I was reading *Night*.

Now any time I see smoke coming from a boiler on top of a building in the city, it reminds me of those who were cremated.

After hearing any one of these responses, students tend to nod and realize that they too have had similar reactions, similar thoughts. They begin to find common ground, to speak and write more freely. They learn, by listening to others, that it is useful to pay attention to what they are experiencing as they are reading, that they can describe what they are noticing not only about the texts but also about their own reactions:

Before class, I was drinking milk and reading Primo Levi's *Survival in Auschwitz*. I was OK until I got to the section where Levi was describing again, in intricate detail, the substance and manner of eating in Buna. Suddenly my stomach contracted severely, my throat became closed, and my milk sour-tasting. I could not finish it.

In "The Farewell" [Charlotte] Delbo speaks of the howling of the women. I could hear the voices clearly. It is an eerie sound, not quite human, but it reaches you in the deepest part of your soul, a sound you will never forget. I am more aware of sounds and smells in Delbo's book. It's as if Delbo has the gift of words to make you see so clearly what she saw and felt.

Listening to one student respond poetically enables others to follow suit.

"You cannot understand, you who never listened to the heartbeat of one about to die" (Delbo 127). I feel that by reading this entry I have heard the sound of the heartbeat of a person about to die.

Occasionally, a student will stand back and reflect on several readings at once:

When I think of the Holocaust, I think primarily of Germans and Poles. . . . But Levi is Italian, Wiesel is Hungarian, Delbo is French. I'm beginning to detect a trend here. These readings add identity to the victims. It actually makes me ask a simple question: What were these people like?

How did they live their lives? Who was rich, who was poor? Who did what for a living? Who liked to do what? I think it's important to ask these questions because these were real people. Every single man, woman, and child was different. It wouldn't be right always to lump the victims together using the term *6 million*.

Each one of my students' responses gives me, if I choose, an opportunity to address issues of language, representation, identification, denial, silence. But I find, more often than not, that as they pursue the implications of what they are writing, the students themselves have made the points I want to make.

In class, we watch newsreels of Hitler addressing the cheering crowds in Berlin and Vienna. We construct a time line of world events from 1900 to 1945. We discuss the power of propaganda and, using posters and children's illustrated books from the 1930s, analyze how the Nazis constructed images of the Jews as sinister and salacious specimens, who were fearful and frightening as the plague and resembled vermin in need of being exterminated. But whatever else we do, we begin and conclude each class with writing.

Frequently, and predictably, my students struggle. As the images and the information start to overwhelm them, I ask them to pause, write more, and mark the difficulty without trying to resolve it. Some students write their way to understanding; some don't. But always, their writing and their perceptions anchor us in the present:

> Rage, disbelief, shock; these words mean nothing. I feel a sense of helplessness. Did I do the right thing in taking this class? I thought I'd be able to handle it but now I'm not so sure. Exhausted emotionally, I lean back in my chair and pray for an end to human suffering.

> The *Einsatzgruppen*. Reading about them [in Berenbam] is one of the times I cannot comprehend or stomach the reality of such atrocity, let alone do it any justice with my words. The fact that there were volunteers for this baffles and disgusts me.

> Why would the gay community today use the inverted pink triangle as a symbol when it was given to them to wear in

the camps? It seems rather odd and even twisted to use a symbol the Nazis had given you in the camps to represent who one is. I never understood this. Now I am even more confused.

It was not until I took this course that I became confused over this subject. The more facts you know, the more confusing Hitler and the Holocaust become. The more you know, the more questions you have.

About six weeks into the term, as I read of my students' dismay, my own becomes more visible to me. What makes me think I can teach this? I wonder. I've never *not* trusted myself in a classroom, but with this subject matter, nothing seems to fit. Then, I tell myself to do what I tell my students to do: to write. And soon I realize that my writing, too, is a part of our classroom text; my doubts, a part of our inquiry. The result is another letter, one I read to my students. It reads, in part:

Dear Students of the Holocaust,
I no longer know why I am teaching this course. What made me think the Holocaust is something one can teach? Most courses have a point. But what is my point here? . . . I think about Violet's comment last week about how upset she has become—how changed by this inquiry—and yet how disturbed she remains. I remember how many of you nodded your heads in agreement. And so I start to wonder: How do we enter this history? What impact are the stories we are reading having on us? Why are we doing this? . . .
The Holocaust in its enormity defies understanding.
It's not that we can't look at Germany in the 1920s, after World War I, and work out the steps Hitler used to come to power. It's not that we can't imagine the way antisemitism was used to turn Jews into objects of derision and hate. It's not that we can't look at the complicity of the church and the rest of the world.
It's that in the face of atrocity—in coming face-to-face with individual agony and suffering, in reading the testimony of survivors—there is nothing to say. Only silence seems to be a fitting response—and that too may be inadequate.
How do we take on this inquiry? Why do we take it on? . . .
I bring these questions to you because if I am sensing them,

I imagine some of you may be too. I bring them because it means we are at a crossroads—one of those moments in a class when we can begin to discern the shape of what's to come. One in which we are being forced to confront more than we might have imagined. . . . Somehow, I trust this process. I trust that our inquiry will take us somewhere— that in our confusion and despair, we will find our way. And we will find our way not by turning away from our responses but by turning toward them—toward the questions we find ourselves asking and toward the responses that begin to be evoked—as we read, write, and listen to one another. . . . What I ask of you . . . is to give voice to your own experience of the material . . . and to continue to ask, What is this inquiry for me? . . . Each voice in the group contributes a different piece—a different perspective—a different place to stand. Alone we may not find a path. But as a community of inquirers, we can likely create one together.

Although I certainly didn't plan it, my own despair seems to bring comfort to students. They are relieved to see that I too tremble when faced with the enormity of what we are studying. Their writing, though, remains at the center of the course.

In the middle of the semester, I collect their journals, take them home, read through them, choose an excerpt from each one, and create a handout that I then photocopy and give to the class. My interest in doing so is to bring each student's voice into the room, to give the students a shared sense of the struggle that is going on, to highlight important differences in perceptions, to raise questions about the texts, and in some sense to take our collective pulse.

The handout I create—using their words but not their names— runs to six single-spaced pages. Before I distribute it, I explain that everyone's voice is included. Then I hand it out and wait, quietly, as they read the words of their classmates (what follows are just a few excerpts from only two sections):

Doubts and Fears

At times, when faced with the horrors of the Holocaust, I have felt awful. The images have haunted me at night and even come into my consciousness when I have passed an old

Jewish man on the street. But facing this issue head on and not shutting it out has helped me through this. I always look forward to Tuesday nights and leave class feeling unburdened as I listen to others and have my say.

At the beginning of the course, I only had a vague knowledge of the Holocaust. Whenever the Holocaust came up in conversation, I would mutter an emotionless statement such as, "That's really messed up, what happened to all those Jews." I didn't know anything about ghettos, killing squads, or treacherous train rides. At this point, midway through the semester, the reality of what happened has begun to sink in. By now I have read the unimaginable and the unthinkable.

I see in my journal how I refer to the facts and figures—enough already. I know the victims, the perpetrators, the methods, the atrocities, the reasoning, etc. But I still don't understand WHY? I have decided that I am grateful to have this question.

I used to argue good historical reasons why Hitler wanted to exterminate the Jews. But now in my heart I realize there never was and never will be a good reason. . . . I have learned to look at the Holocaust with as much misunderstanding as knowledge and I am glad of this.

Religious Belief, the Church, and the Question of Revenge

From biblical times, the Jews were the Chosen people of God. If that was/is true, where was He when all this was happening?

Why is it whenever cruelty or savagery are carried out, God becomes responsible? Why do we blame him for the actions of animalistic men?

The Church—by her silence and dubious excuses—becomes jointly guilty for the world's outbursts of hatred.

Goldhagen writes: "In the face of the persecution and annihilation of the Jews, the churches . . . exhibited an apparent, striking impassiveness" (*Hitler's Willing Executioners* 437). How can anyone stand by and watch an entire group of people be murdered? Doesn't anyone in this world have a conscience? This reading was difficult. I am glad you warned us beforehand. I could not believe what I was reading. . . . These [ordinary German soldiers] were calculating, cold-blooded murderers.

Being able to kill another human being? I know I could if my loved ones were threatened. I am a mother — that says it all. Yet to kill another because he is different is a sin. To degrade is also an atrocity. What gives anyone the right to judge? These are the questions I grapple with as I read. . . . I know it is important to know the nitty-gritty of such inhumanity. That is why I read with tears in my eyes.

While students are reading these excerpts, I am struck by the quiet in the room. There is almost no fidgeting, not even side comments. Instead, there is the concentrated silence that comes when students are thoughtfully engaged. Only now these students are not confronting the horrors of the Holocaust on their own; they are entering one another's frames of reference, becoming implicated in one another's reactions and responses. When they finish reading, they look at each other differently. To me, it looks like respect, even awe. At this point, I ask them to take out a piece of paper and to write a response to an excerpt that touches them. I then collect these and the following week deliver them to the authors.

In a classroom tale, it's tempting to conclude by recounting how students and teacher arrive at a place of understanding. It's tempting to write about the ways inquiry leads to insight. But teaching the Holocaust is, in my experience, never so straightforward or simple. By its very nature, it can lead to no such glorious ending. Instead, at the end of the term, when I invite my students to reflect in writing on the class and on what they have learned, I see once again that there are no satisfactory answers to the questions we have explored. In the place of resolution, however, my students discover their own hard-won struggle, documented in their journals. This writing, I suggest, has helped them engage in personal inquiry, in an extended form of soul-searching. They have, each in his or her own way, grappled with blindness, silence, and atrocity; with the roots of evil; and with the power of inherited hatred and deepened their

sense of the human predicament. Some students write what this inquiry has led them to see; some claim an important insight; most
leave the semester with more questions:

> Why hasn't the world learned yet? The Holocaust is again
> happening on a lesser scale in so many areas of the world—
> Bosnia, Rwanda. Why won't we, the so-called civilized
> people, realize it is once again happening? . . . Where are
> man and God in the face of man's inhumanity?

> As for the question, "Where was God?," I have found an
> answer in another question, "Where was man?"

> If I had been born a young German during World War II
> and had seen Hitler's propaganda, I don't know how I
> would have reacted. Terror and fear make a person and ulti-
> mately a nation desperate. . . . You do anything to stay safe
> and alive; you do anything to protect your family and those
> you love. . . . To be honest, I probably would have done
> anything too.

> As I pass from narrative to narrative, instead of panic and
> terror, admiration has begun to emerge. . . . In the midst of
> such devastation, under such humiliation, the human being
> refuses to crumble completely.

> Sometimes space and time appear to be illusions. I am alive
> right now but the Nazi dilemma haunts me. . . . The vic-
> tims of the Holocaust are dead; the survivors are old. One
> day, there will be the "last survivor of the death camps."
> Does this mean the subject becomes a closed book? I don't
> think so. They will live on in us if we are strong enough to
> carry their burdens . . .

> It's not a question of why the German people hated the
> Jews—it should be, "Why do we as a people hate what is
> alien to us?"

> A deep conviction has begun to emerge in my conscious-
> ness: as emotional and painful as the class is, it has a rightful
> place in the Lehman College curriculum. . . . Sometimes
> one must cause pain to cure pain. We are looking at some-
> thing ugly, painful, even shameful. But we don't make it less

real by not looking at it. For me, looking into the belly of the beast, and a beast it was, has been a sobering experience — one that will follow me and assist me whenever I have the human urge to class together any group of people based only on the actions of a few.

Steeping themselves in atrocity, allowing the stories and then the questions to awaken or deepen their sensibilities, my students first confront their ignorance and blindness; then, in examining the horror, they often discover the depth of their compassion. As I wrote earlier, I imagine that similar perceptions surface in many courses on the Holocaust. I am convinced, however, that writing about these perceptions enables students to capture them, reflect on them, and then take them one step further. For something else happens when students write and then explore their responses. They are no longer passive recipients of images that sicken them or of stories they cannot abide; they are no longer victims of the history, nor do they remain bystanders. Through writing all term, students actively construct what this history means to them and how they will carry its message forward. Writing not only gives them some measure of control over the material, it also helps them construct in their own voices how they choose to relate to it. In essence, writing about the Holocaust enables them to write the Holocaust for themselves.

At the end of the term, many agree with one student who wrote, "This course has been a cleansing, a catharsis. Who *selected* us to be here?" I know his choice of the word *selected* was deliberate, harkening back to discussions we had of the camps and the selections on the ramps. There were no tattoos in our classroom, nor were the stakes so high as to reflect life-and-death decisions; nonetheless, this young man felt as if he and his classmates had been marked. His sense of being selected was not, I think, a function of the material we were reading; it speaks, rather, to what happens when students write about this material, for in the writing they become agents in the making of their own meaning. Holocaust history, once so foreign and removed, comes alive in their own words. Writing their way into its rich legacy, they take on its call.

Notes

1. Journal writing composes one-third of students' grades; similarly reading from journals, writing in them, and discussing student responses normally take up about a third to a half of each class session. Brief lectures, films, a visit from a survivor, and presentations on independent projects take up the rest of our time. Semester grades are based on overall performance, which is judged on attendance, participation in group work, and the quality of independent projects. Since the journals are personal, I neither correct them nor mark down for surface errors. I read primarily for engagement. A thoughtful journal can boost a grade; a cursory one can have the opposite effect.

2. I have taught this course several times but am using representative student samples from only one semester. Students were informed that I would likely quote from their written work in faculty workshops or articles. All gave me permission to use their work with or without names.

3. I divide the course into three main areas. Under history, we read Michael Berenbaum (*The World Must Know*), who introduces a broad range of issues and events to readers who have limited background knowledge. This reading is supplemented by newsreel footage on the rise of Nazism and illustrations of propaganda posters and children's books. Testimonies we read include Livia Bitton-Jackson's *I Have Lived a Thousand Years*, Delbo's *Auschwitz and After*, Primo Levi's *Survival in Auschwitz*, and Wiesel's *Night*. Richard Rashke's *Escape from Sobibor*, 1995), based on interviews, provides a compelling description of organized resistance. Third, we look at the question of forgiveness raised in Simon Wiesenthal's *The Sunflower*, supplemented with excerpts from Tzvetan Todorov's *Facing the Extreme*, Wiesel's memoir, *All Rivers Run to the Sea*, and Goldhagen's *Hitler's Willing Executioners*.

Work Cited

Des Pres, Terrence. Introduction. *Treblinka*. By Jean-François Steiner. New York: Meridian, 1994. vii–xviii.

Marianne Hirsch and Irene Kacandes

Afterword

Toward the conclusion of the video testimony of the Holocaust survivor Rabbi Baruch G., he returns to his experiences of liberation
and subsequent time spent in a displaced-persons camp. When asked
by his interviewer how he felt there, he responds:

> So, feelings was just existing. If you would talk to me — just
> talk to me, I would start crying. Why? Because as I — I said
> to myself, is it true that you're talking to me? Why should
> you talk to me? It's probably not true. There was all confu-
> sion around that whole thing of existence. Obviously, at
> least to my way of thinking, they [the Nazis] got us to — at
> least they got me to think of myself so little, that nobody
> should talk to me. What this does, it takes years, and again,
> here if I may interject a religious thought, is the idea that
> it's the potential of the human being, he can't pull himself
> up even with his own bootstraps. (qtd. in Kacandes 204)

The camps had dehumanized Baruch G. to the point where he
did not consider himself worthy of being a conversation partner, of
even being addressed for the briefest moment. To contemplate the
processes that took a human being to this kind of self-view can be one
goal of our pedagogical efforts. To help our students realize with

Baruch G. that the potential of human beings can't be achieved alone can be another. The project of teaching Holocaust representation, in whatever context and through whatever genre, ultimately comes down to this—the voice of the victim or survivor and our attempt to respond to its call. Without exception, the essays in this volume have contemplated the pedagogical challenges posed by this "you." One need only look at the table of contents to see how often the second-person pronoun and other terms associated with it appear. When the student is cast as a listener and when students and teachers share that role, the classroom acquires a unique dynamic, the course a unique mission. For this reason, courses on the Holocaust are often more difficult to end, and to grade, than other courses. Is it appropriate to have an exam? a group discussion? individual oral presentations or written assignments? Having learned that closure can be as false as the artificial fairy-tale ending of Spiegelman's *Maus*, students nevertheless must emerge from the class with a sense of closure, however tenuous.

The same need is true for this book. Although we have been able to broach many more topics than any single course can address, much remains unexplored. New pedagogical materials and new relevant methodologies are still appearing, challenging us to reframe our perspectives. Thus the two of us do not agree with Eric Weitz's assessment when he argues in this volume that no new, paradigm-shifting work is likely to come out of the study of the Holocaust alone. The work on comparative genocide that he presents in itself offers a shift in paradigms and a new direction for the study and teaching of the Holocaust.

Another such shift might occur as a result of the recent controversy in France (initially between Claude Lanzmann and Jean-Luc Godard) about the evidentiary status of the four clandestine images showing the burning of corpses by the *Sonderkommando* in Auschwitz. Godard, Georges Didi-Huberman, and others argue that these images challenge the trope of unrepresentability that has dominated Holocaust studies since Lanzmann's *Shoah* and is articulated in this volume by Bathrick. (See Didi-Huberman for a detailed discussion of the images and their implications.)

What is more, documents are still being discovered, little-known work is still being translated, survivors and their children and grand-children are still writing and publishing texts that pose new conceptual and pedagogical challenges. In 1944, for example, the Polish *Son-derkommando* prisoner Salmen Gradowski wrote a remarkable manuscript in Auschwitz-Birkenau. He entitled it "In the Heart of Hell," and, before his execution, he buried it in a sealed canteen near one of the crematoriums in which he had been forced to work. Discovered shortly after the war, Gradowski's remarkably poetic account of the functioning of the death machine and the systematic destruction of his people and his culture was not published in the original Yiddish until 1977, and then only in a limited printing of three hundred copies. While sections were translated into English and published in different anthologies (this translation is cited in Stark's essay in this volume), the entire manuscript is presently available only in French and in Italian. "Dear finder, search everywhere, every inch of soil. Tens of documents are buried under it, mine and those of other persons, which will shed light on everything that happened here," Gradowski writes (Letter 74).[1] Clearly, we have not yet searched every inch of soil. Much remains to be discovered, translated, published, read, and written.

At the same time, new technologies and the possibilities they have opened up for distribution of these materials pose new ethical questions and call for greater vigilance and thoughtfulness. In the 1990s, Holocaust scholars, many themselves survivors or children of survivors, worried that the easy reproducibility of photography, video, and cinema and the endless repetition of certain scenes and images from the Holocaust in the media would produce compassion fatigue and even resistance in viewers of younger generations. With greater temporal distance from the event, they envisioned the possibility of diminishing concern for historical accuracy or truth. Now, at the beginning of a new century, we are conscious that as the World Wide Web creates even greater access to primary materials, including the faces and voices of survivors giving testimony, it creates more and more opportunities for distortion and appropriation.

This danger is especially present in view of the historical moment during which we are confronting these questions: Will the disappearance of survivors and eyewitnesses from among our midst not also introduce a paradigm shift in our conceptual approaches and capabilities? Perhaps our notions of immediacy and authenticity, of empathy and identification will have to be further qualified and redefined with greater historical distance from the events of World War II. The canon of key texts of the past may well have to make room for works that speak more directly to members of the third or fourth generation, generations for whom the Holocaust will coexist with other genocides in their histories and their lifetimes.

It will be up to our students to sort out these and no doubt other as yet unknown questions about the Holocaust and its legacies. Our courses can at best provide some of the tools they will need if they wish to act as responsible witnesses to the present moment in which they live and to the past they have inherited. Perhaps, then, the most important goal we teachers can achieve is to model how we talk to Baruch G. and other Holocaust victims, survivors, bystanders, and perpetrators, by combining analysis and emotional engagement.

At the end of our own courses, we often find ourselves asking, along with Geoffrey Hartman in his essay in this volume, a question that is fundamental to this pedagogical enterprise: "How do we transmit so hurtful an image of our species without killing hope and breeding indifference?" This book cannot provide an answer. Only in the very human context of classroom interaction can we hope to avoid either false redemption or unending despair.

Note

1. For Gradowski's entire manuscript, see his *Au cœur de l'enfer*.

Works Cited

Baruch G. Edited testimony. A–50. Fortunoff Video Archive for Holocaust Testimonies. Yale U Lib., New Haven, CT.

Didi-Huberman, Georges. *Images malgré tout* [Images after All]. Paris: Seuil, 2003.

Gradowski, Salmen. *Au cœur de l'enfer: Document écrit d'un Sonderkommando d'Auschwitz—1944.* Ed. Philippe Mesnard and Carlo Saletti. Paris: Kimé, 2001.

———. Letter. *Amidst a Nightmare of Crime: Manuscripts of the Sonderkommando.* Ed. Jadwiga Bezwinska and Danuta Czech. New York: Fertig, 1992. 74–77.

Kacandes, Irene, "'You Who Live Safe in Your Warm Houses': Your Role in the Production of Holocaust Testimony." *Insiders and Outsiders: Jewish and Gentile Culture in Germany and Austria.* Ed. Dagmar C. G. Lorenz and Gabriela Weinberger. Detroit: Wayne State UP, 1994. 189–213.

Notes on Contributors

Ulrich Baer, associate professor of German and comparative literature at New York University, is the author of *Remnants of Song: Trauma and the Experience of Modernity in Charles Baudelaire and Paul Celan* (2000) and *Spectral Evidence: The Photography of Trauma* (2002), editor of *"Niemand zeugt für den Zeugen": Erinnerungskultur und historische Verantwortung nach der Shoah* (2002) and *110 Stories: New York Writes after September 11* (2002), and editor and translator of *The Poet's Guide to Life: The Wisdom of Rilke* (2005).

David Bathrick is Jacob Gould Schurman Professor of Theatre, Film, and Dance and German Studies and a member of the Jewish Studies Program at Cornell University. His publications include *The Dialectic and the Early Brecht* (1976); *Modernity and the Text* (1989; coedited with Andreas Huyssen); *The Powers of Speech: The Politics of Culture in the GDR* (1995), and numerous articles on the theory and history of twentieth-century European culture. He is a cofounder and coeditor of *New German Critique*. He is currently finishing a book on film and the Holocaust.

Doris L. Bergen, associate professor of history at the University of Notre Dame, is the author of *Twisted Cross: The German Christian Movement in the Third Reich* (1996) and *War and Genocide: A Concise History of the Holocaust* (2003) and editor of *The Sword of the Lord: Military Chaplains from the First to the Twenty-First Century* (2004). Her research and teaching concern religion, ethnicity, and gender in Europe during the Nazi era. She is completing a manuscript on German military chaplains in the Third Reich.

Pascale Bos, assistant professor of Netherlandic and Germanic studies at the University of Texas, Austin, and affiliated at the university with comparative literature, Jewish studies, and women's studies, has published several articles on German Jewish and Dutch Jewish literature and women and the Holocaust. Her book *German-Jewish Literature in the Wake of the Holocaust: Grete Weil, Ruth Klüger, and the Politics of Address* is forthcoming.

Bella Brodzki, professor of literature at Sarah Lawrence College, is the editor of *Life/Lines: Theorizing Women's Autobiography* (with Celeste Schenck) and the author of essays on twentieth-century literature, feminist theory, postcolonial literature, testimonial and Holocaust narratives, and translation. She is currently working on two book projects: "'Can These Bones Live?' Translation, Survival, and Cultural Memory" and "The Munich Years: Holocaust Survivors in German Universities, 1945–1955" (with Jeremy Varon).

Joshua L. Charlson is lecturer in the Department of English at Northwestern University. Author of several articles on Holocaust literature and Jewish American literature, he is completing a manuscript on American representations of the Holocaust and launching a study of the figure of the absent child in literature of the Holocaust and in contemporary American film and fiction.

Jonathan Druker is assistant professor of Italian at Illinois State University, where he also teaches Holocaust literature and film. He has published articles on Primo Levi in *Shofar: An Interdisciplinary Journal of Jewish Studies, Italian Culture: The Journal of the American Association of Italian Studies,* and *Clio: An Interdisciplinary Journal of Literature, History, and the Philosophy of History.* He is working on a book that applies postmodern interpretations of the Holocaust to Levi's texts.

Sidra DeKoven Ezrahi, professor of comparative Jewish literature at the Hebrew University of Jerusalem, is a member of the editorial boards of *History and Memory* and *Tikkun* and academic adviser to Words and Images, a video archive of Jewish writers worldwide. Her publications include *By Words Alone: The Holocaust in Literature* (1980), *Booking Passage: Exile and Homecoming in the Modern Jewish Imagination* (2000), and "Representing Auschwitz" (1996–97). She is currently completing a manuscript on mimicking the sacred.

Sander Gilman is distinguished professor of liberal arts and sciences and of medicine at the University of Illinois, Chicago, and director of the Jewish studies program there. Among his many books are *Jewish Self-Hatred: Anti-Semitism and the Language of the Jews* (1986), *Jewish Frontiers: Essays on Bodies, Histories, and Identities* (2003), and *Jurek Becker: A Life in Five Worlds* (2003). He is the editor, with Lilian Friedberg, of *A Jew in the New Germany: Selected Writings of Henryk Broder* (2004).

Judith Greenberg teaches at the Gallatin School at New York University. She is the editor of *Trauma at Home: After 9/11* (2003) and author of "Paths of Resistance: French Women Working from the Inside" in *Experience and Expression: Women and the Holocaust* (ed. Baer and Goldenberg), "The Echo of Trauma and the Trauma of Echo" in *American Imago* (1998), and articles on Virginia Woolf and trauma.

Susan Gubar is distinguished professor of English at Indiana University, Bloomington. She has coauthored and coedited a number of books with Sandra M. Gilbert, including *The Madwoman in the Attic*, the three-volume *No Man's Land*, and the *Norton Anthology of Literature by Women*. Her most recently published books are *Critical Condition: Feminism at the Turn of the Century*, *Racechanges: White Skin, Black Face in American Culture*, and *Poetry after Auschwitz: Remembering What One Never Knew* (2003).

Geoffrey Hartman is Sterling Professor of English and Comparative Literature, emeritus, and senior research scholar at Yale University. At Yale he cofounded the Fortunoff Archive for Holocaust Video Testimony. He is the editor of *Bitburg in Moral and Political Perspective* (1986) and *Holocaust Remembrance: The Shapes of Memory* (1994) and author of *The Longest Shadow: In the Aftermath of the Holocaust* (1996), *The Fateful Question of Culture* (1997), and *Scars of the Spirit: The Struggle against Inauthenticity* (2002).

Susannah Heschel is Eli Black Associate Professor of Jewish Studies at Dartmouth College and chair of the Jewish studies program there. She is the author of *Abraham Geiger and the Jewish Jesus* (1998), editor of *On Being a Jewish Feminist* (1983), and coeditor (with David Biale and Michael Galchinsky) of *Insider/Outside: Multiculturalism and American Jews* (1998) and (with Robert P. Ericksen) of *Betrayal: German Churches and the Holocaust* (1999). She is currently completing a manuscript on theology in Nazi Germany, "When Jesus Was an Aryan."

Renée A. Hill is associate professor of philosophy and codirector of the Institute for the Study of Race Relations at Virginia State University. Among her publications are "Seeing Clearly without Being Blinded: Obstacles to Black Self-Examination" (2003) and "Compensatory Justice: Over Time and Between Groups" (2002). She is working on a paper about cruel and unusual punishment.

Marianne Hirsch is professor of English and comparative literature at Columbia University and the editor of *PMLA*. She is the author of *Family Frames: Photography, Narrative, and Postmemory* (1997) and articles on Holocaust memory, visuality, and gender. She edited or coedited *The Familial Gaze* (1999); *Time and the Literary* (2002); and *Gender and Cultural Memory*, a special issue of *Signs* (2002). She is currently writing a book with Leo Spitzer, "Ghosts of Home: Czernowitz and the Holocaust."

Marcia D. Horn is professor of English at Ferrum College, where she coordinates an interdisciplinary Holocaust course. Her article "*King Lear* and the Holocaust" appeared in *Shakespeare and the Classroom* (1997). She has been a summer fellow at the United States Holocaust Memorial Museum's Center for Advanced Holocaust Studies.

Sara R. Horowitz, associate professor of humanities and associate director of the Centre for Jewish Studies at York University, Keele, is the author of *Voicing the Void: Muteness and Memory in Holocaust Fiction* (1997) and numerous articles on gender, memory, and the Holocaust in journals such as *Dimensions* and *Prooftexts.* Her current book project is entitled "Gender, Genocide, and Jewish Memory."

Amy Hungerford, associate professor of English at Yale University, is the author of *The Holocaust of Texts: Genocide, Literature, and Personification* (2003). She teaches and writes on twentieth-century American fiction, poetry, criticism, and theory; genocide and literature; and religion and literature. Her current book projects are "Cambridge Introduction to the American Novel since 1945" and "Postmodern Supernaturalism: Belief and Meaninglessness in Late-Twentieth-Century American Literature."

Irene Kacandes, associate professor of German studies and comparative literature at Dartmouth College, is the author of *Talk Fiction: Literature and the Talk Explosion* (2001). She coedited (with Scott Denham and Jonathan Petropoulos) *A User's Guide to German Cultural Studies* (1997). She has taught and published on Holocaust video testimony, trauma theory, neo-Nazism, German and European processing of the Nazi past, narrative theory, and feminist linguistic theory. Her current research project concerns children of Holocaust survivors.

Adrienne Kertzer, professor of English at the University of Calgary, is the author of *My Mother's Voice: Children, Literature, and the Holocaust* (2002) and of articles on children's Holocaust fiction, theater, and second-generation memory. Her current projects include the place of trauma in children's war fiction, fairy tales and Holocaust representation, and comedy and trauma.

Michael G. Levine, visiting associate professor of comparative literature at Cornell University, is the author of *Writing through Repression: Literature, Censorship, Psychoanalysis* (1994) and of several articles on Art Spiegelman's *Maus*. *The Belated Witness: Literature, Testimony, and the Question of Holocaust Survival* is forthcoming. His new project concerns the changing structure of the literary, philosophical, and operatic work in nineteenth-century German culture.

Orly Lubin is chair of the Department of Poetics and Comparative Literature and of the Women Studies Forum of the National Council of Jewish Women at Tel Aviv University. She is the author of *Women Reading Women* (2003; in Hebrew) and of articles on feminist theories, cinema, literature, drama, visual culture, autobiography and testimony, and Israeli women artists.

Nancy K. Miller is distinguished professor of English and comparative literature at the Graduate Center, City University of New York. Her most recent books are *But Enough about Me: Why We Read Other People's Lives* and *Bequest and Betrayal: Memoirs of a Parent's Death*. She is coeditor, with Jason Tougaw, of *Extremities: Trauma, Testimony, and Community*.

Adam Zachary Newton, Jane and Rowland Blumberg Centennial Professor in English, member of the Committee on Comparative Literature and of the Center for Middle Eastern Studies, and director of Jewish studies at the University of Texas, Austin, is the author of *Narrative Ethics* (1995), *Facing Black and Jew: Literature as Public Space* *in Twentieth-Century America* (1999), *The Fence and the Neighbor: Emmanuel Levinas, Yeshayahu Leibowitz, and Israel among the Nations* (2001), and *The Elsewhere: On Belonging at a Near Distance* (2004).

Ranen Omer-Sherman, assistant professor of English and Jewish studies at the University of Miami, is the author of *Diaspora and Zionism in the Jewish-American Imagination* (2002). His essays have appeared in journals such as *College Literature, Texas Studies in Literature and Language, Religion and Literature, MELUS, Shofar,* and *Modernism/ Modernity.* His book *Jewish Literature and the Desert* will appear in 2005.

Sondra Perl is professor of English at the Graduate Center, City University of New York. She sees the classroom as a site of inquiry. Her work in Holocaust studies began in 1996, when she traveled to Austria to teach writing and literature to teachers whose parents had been Nazis. "On Austrian Soil: Teaching Those I Was Taught to Hate," a memoir describing her journey, is forthcoming.

Christian Rogowski, professor of German at Amherst College, is the author of two books on Robert Musil and articles on Musil, Hugo von Hofmannsthal, Bertolt Brecht and Kurt Weill, Ingeborg Bachmann, Wim Wenders, Thomas Brasch, Heiner Müller, the Medea myth, German studies in the United States, colonial propaganda in Weimar Germany, and Siegfried Kracauer and Weimar popular cinema. He is currently working on racial discourse in Weimar Germany.

Alan Rosen is a research fellow at the Center for Advanced Judaic Studies at the University of Pennsylvania (2004–05) and Solson Research Fellow at the United States Holocaust Memorial Museum's Center for Advanced Holocaust Studies (2005). He is the author of books and articles on Holocaust literature, including *Sounds of Defiance: The Holocaust, Multilingualism, and the Problem of English.* He is working on a book, "The Evidence of Trauma: David Boder and Writing the History of Holocaust Testimony."

Michael Rothberg, associate professor of English and comparative literature and director of the Unit for Criticism and Interpretive Theory at the University of Illinois, Urbana, is the author of *Traumatic Realism: The Demands of Holocaust Representation* (2000) and coeditor of *The Holocaust: Theoretical Readings* (2003). His recent essays have appeared in *The Yale Journal of Criticism, History and Memory, African American Review, Symploke,* and *PMLA.* His current book project is "Decolonizing the Holocaust: Multidirectional Memory and the Legacies of Violence."

David Scrase is professor of German and director of Holocaust studies at the University of Vermont. He has published on modern German literature and the Holocaust. Most recently he edited, with Wolfgang Mieder, *Making a Difference: Rescue and Assistance during the Holocaust: Essays in Honor of Marion Pritchard.*

Efraim Sicher, associate professor of comparative and English literature at Ben-Gurion University of the Negev, is editor of *Breaking Crystal: Writing and Memory after Auschwitz* (1998) and *The Holocaust Novelists* (2004; volume 299 of the Dictionary of Literary Biography) and the author of *Beyond Marginality: Anglo-Jewish Literature after the Holocaust* (1985) and *Rereading the City / Rereading Dickens* (2002), as well as essays on Dickens, George Eliot, and Holocaust memory. His new book on the Holocaust novel is forthcoming.

Leo Spitzer, Kathe Tappe Vernon Professor of History at Dartmouth College, is the author of *Hotel Bolivia: The Culture of Memory in a Refuge from Nazism* (1998), *Lives In Between: Assimilation and Marginality in Austria, Brazil, and West Africa* (1990), and *The Creoles of Sierra Leone: Responses to Colonialism* (1974) and coeditor of *Acts of Memory: Cultural Recall in the Present* (1999). He is currently cowriting a book with Marianne Hirsch entitled "Ghosts of Home: Czernowitz and the Holocaust."

Jared Stark, assistant professor of literature at Eckerd College, is the author of *No Common Place: The Holocaust Testimony of Alina Bacall-Zwirn* (with Alina Bacall-Zwirn) (1999) and essays on Holocaust memory and representation in the *Yale Journal of Criticism* and *History and Memory.* His current book project explores the interpretation of suicide in modern aesthetics, historiography, and politics.

Susan Rubin Suleiman, C. Douglas Dillon Professor of the Civilization of France and professor of comparative literature at Harvard University, is the author of *Authoritarian Fictions: The Ideological Novel as a Literary Genre* (1983), *Subversive Intent: Gender, Politics, and the Avant-Garde* (1990), *Risking Who One Is: Encounters with Contemporary Art and Literature* (1994), and *Budapest Diary: In Search of the Motherbook* (1996). Among her edited and coedited volumes are *Exile and Creativity* (1998) and *Contemporary Jewish Writing in Hungary: An Anthology* (2003).

Gary Weissman, visiting assistant professor at the University of Cincinnati, is the author of *Fantasies of Witnessing: Postwar Efforts to Experience the Holocaust* (2004) and several essays in *Holocaust Literature: An Encyclopedia of Writers and Their Work,* edited by S. Lillian

Kremer (2003). He is currently working on a book-length photo-essay entitled "Injuries of Time."

Eric D. Weitz, professor of history, Arsham and Charlotte Ohanessian Chair in the College of Liberal Arts, and director of the Center for German and European Studies at the University of Minnesota, Twin Cities, is the author of *Creating German Communism, 1890–1990: From Popular Protests to Socialist State* (1997) and *A Century of Genocide: Utopias of Race and Nation* (2003) and two coedited volumes, *Between Reform and Revolution: Studies in German Socialism and Communism from 1840 to 1990* (1998) and *Fascism and Neofascism: Critical Writings on the Radical Right in Europe* (2004).

James E. Young, professor and chair of the Department of Judaic and Near Eastern Studies at University of Massachusetts, Amherst, is the author of *Writing and Rewriting the Holocaust* (1988), *The Texture of Memory* (1993), and *At Memory's Edge* (2000) and editor of *The Art of Memory* (1994). He is editor in chief of "The Posen Library of Jewish Culture and Civilization: An Anthology of Primary Sources, Texts, and Documents in Ten Volumes" (2005–09).

Froma Zeitlin, professor of classics and comparative literature and director of the Program in Judaic Studies at Princeton University, is the author of "The Vicarious Witness: Belated Memory and Authorial Presence in Recent Holocaust Literature" (1998) and "New Soundings in Holocaust Literature" (2003).

Index

Abse, Dannie, 171
Abzug, Robert H., 216n12
Aciman, André, 427
Adair, Gilbert, 384n3
Adelson, Alan, 195, 213, 253
Adorno, Theodor W., 24, 37, 165–67,
    172, 175–76, 176n1, 220, 265,
    294, 296, 299n6, 316, 321,
    345–46, 347n3, 361, 423, 426
Agamben, Giorgio, 8, 226, 291, 340,
    347n1
Akhmatova, Anna H., 146
Aleichem, Sholem, 151
Allport, Gordon, 10
Alter, Robert, 429n3
Améry, Jean, 200–01, 291, 316
Amichai, Yehudah, 304
Amis, Martin, 174, 186, 187
Anderson, Benedict, 141
Antschel, Paul, 315. *See also* Celan, Paul
Appelfeld, Aharon, 43, 54, 60, 62, 180,

189n5, 250, 303, 304, 305, 373,
    425
Arendt, Hannah, 73, 141, 187, 289–90
Ashcroft, Bill, 157
Auden, W. H., 165
Augustine, Saint, 92
Avisar, Ilan, 221–22

Baal-Makhshoves, 157
Bacall-Zwirn, Alina, 202, 397, 398
Bach, Johann Sebastian, 318
Baer, Ulrich, 16, 29, 305, 405
Bailey, Richard, 157
Bakhtin, M. M., 425
Bandura, Albert, 9
Bankier, David, 105
Barbie, Klaus, 216n11
Barkan, Elazar, 466–67, 468, 475n1
Barnouw, Dagmar, 290, 298n1, 354
Bar-On, Dan, 263